The Responsive Public Library

Sources for Library Materials in FY10
Albany County Public Library

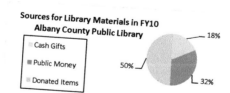

THE RESPONSIVE PUBLIC LIBRARY

How to Develop and Market a Winning Collection

Second Edition

SHARON L. BAKER
and
KAREN L. WALLACE

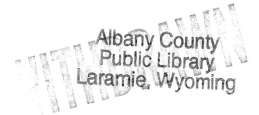
2002
Libraries Unlimited
A Division of Greenwood Publishing Group, Inc.
Englewood, Colorado

For Margaret Nyholm,
who I very much wish was here to read this.
—KLW

Libraries Unlimited
A Division of Greenwood Publishing Group, Inc.
P.O. Box 6633
Englewood, CO 80155-6633
1-800-237-6124
www.lu.com

Library of Congress Cataloging-in-Publication Data

Baker, Sharon L.
  The responsive public library : how to develop and market a winning collection /
Sharon L. Baker and Karen L. Wallace.-- 2nd ed.
    p. cm.
  Rev. ed. of: The responsive public library collection. 1993.
  Includes bibliographical references and index.
  ISBN 1-56308-648-4
    1. Libraries and community--United States. 2. Public libraries--United
States--Marketing. 3. Public libraries--Collection development--United States. I.
Wallace, Karen L. II. Baker, Sharon L. Responsive public library collection. III. Title.

Z716.4 .B25 2002
027.473'068'8--dc21
                                                                    2001038272

CONTENTS

LIST OF FIGURES AND TABLES

FIGURE

TABLE

PREFACE

The first edition of *The Responsive Public Library Collection*, published in 1993, grew out of the recognition that few published works discussed in detail how marketing principles could be modified, then applied, to collection development in public libraries.

This new edition updates and expands the original, referencing new studies (published since 1992), encompassing more of the literature from other countries, and discussing certain topics not directly addressed in the first edition, such as relationship marketing concepts, outreach services, and the interaction between employee satisfaction and customer satisfaction. The book also incorporates changes that have occurred in the world at large and the library world since the early 1990s. Notably, it reflects the impact of the Internet, explaining how libraries can use this tool to develop and market their collections and offering many examples from individual institutions' Web sites.

This work attempts to provide a broad, introductory overview of issues affecting the marketing of library collections. In it we ask questions that we hope you will consider, state a number of guiding principles for designing collections to which public library patrons can respond, and cite both research and examples of current practice to document the points made.

We recommend that you consult the original sources for detailed discussions of topics of particular interest. In the pages that follow, we often only share a few refrains from others' findings or experiences, but through the collection at your institution, electronic sources, and interlibrary loan, a symphony awaits you.

Sharon (Shay) L. Baker
CEO
DesignLynx
5076 Grasshopper Lane
Westerville, Ohio 43081
Designworks_2000@yahoo.com
(614) 882-6541

Karen Wallace
Circulation/Reference Librarian
Drake University Law Library
2507 University Avenue
Des Moines, Iowa
Karen.Wallace@drake.edu
(515) 271-2989

ACKNOWLEDGMENTS

For reading Chapter 7 as published in the first edition and making suggestions, thanks to William Sannwald, Assistant to the City Manager and Manager of Library Design and Development in San Diego.

For providing collections and other resources and support, thanks to the Park Ridge Public Library, especially Vivian Mortensen, Tony Letrich, and Bill McCully (now of the Prospect Heights Public Library); the Des Plaines Public Library, especially Sandra Norlin, Martha Sloan, and Paul Audino; the Drake University Law Library, especially John Edwards, Sue Lerdal, Shawn Madsen, and Sherry VonBehren; the Arlington Heights Memorial Library; the Skokie Public Library; the Dominican University Library; the University of Iowa Libraries; and the State Library of Iowa.

For listening, thanks to Kris Andrews, Lise Prusko, Jenna Slawski, Lynn Zmija, Julie Thomas, Becky Lutkenhaus, and David Hanson.

And for reading the manuscript, encouraging perseverance, not complaining about the piles of paper everywhere, and giving backrubs, Marc Wallace.

— KLW

Special thanks go to the University Libraries, the School of Library and Information Science, and the Center for Advanced Studies at the University of Iowa, for providing collections, space, equipment, and other support for this work.

Additional thanks go to the following individuals for their intellectual and/or emotional support: Padmini Srinivasan, David Eichmann, and Carl Orgren at the University of Iowa; staff at the North Liberty, Coralville, and Iowa City Public Libraries; Ken Shearer, Duncan Smith, Mary Kay Chelton, Catherine Ross, and others researching related topics who have willingly discussed ideas over time; and the numerous students and public librarians who have contributed directly and indirectly to my thinking over the years.

— SLB

OVERTURE

"Whatever is worth doing at all is worth doing well"—4th Earl of Chesterfield (Jones 1997).

Across the country and around the world, those working on behalf of public libraries strive to serve patron needs, keep performance high, and meet standards of public accountability. They continue to do this while the volume of materials published, library expenditures, and competition from other information sources continue to rise (e.g., Coffman 2000) but their resources remain exhaustible.

In the last 25 years, people have continued to augment their use of print with nonprint materials: high-speed access to Internet resources, DVDs, audiobooks, e-books, compact discs, CD-ROMs, and the like. The usefulness of these latter formats is beyond question. A beginning sculptor may find Arlene Siegel's intimate video *Sculpture Classroom* (West Chester, PA: VideoCine Services, 1990) as inspiring as John Plowman's book *Encyclopedia of Sculpting Techniques* (Philadelphia: Running Press, 1995) or any of many Web sites devoted to the topic.

In their search for fulfillment, some community residents will ask public librarians to help meet their wide-ranging needs. In a two-month period, members of just one family may seek consumer opinion Internet sites, travel guides for France, a *Mona Lisa* print, animated children's videos, the book *The Hobbit*, recent satellite pictures of earthquake damage, and a CD-ROM study guide for a college entrance exam. Add the desires of all other families in the library's service area, and the extent of the challenge comes into sharp focus.

Numerous studies (e.g., D'Elia and Rodger 1996; Cullen and Calvert 1996, 1993) reinforce what those working in the field know. Patrons want current materials of reasonable quality covering a broad range of genres and subjects; suitable for varied literacy, age, and sophistication levels; and readily available for checkout in diverse formats. In addition, patrons want

- helpful, friendly, knowledgeable staff;
- strong, readily available reference services and materials;
- access to computers and the Internet and training in their effective use;
- rational, quickly comprehensible shelving arrangements and catalog access;
- helpful signs to guide users to relevant collections;
- convenient hours;
- safe locations easily accessible from home, work, and public transit;
- remote access to library resources;
- adequate, reasonably priced (preferably free) parking;
- ample, comfortable seating;
- wired study areas where patrons can use their own laptops; and
- quiet, well-designed spaces conducive to examining the collection.

As we all know, even affluent libraries are not fully meeting these needs. Consider the following:

- When seven different constituency groups ranked factors they considered important to library effectiveness, patrons' choices correlated most closely with, in descending order, funding officials, board members, local opinion leaders, Friends of the Library, *library managers*, and *library staff*! (Childers and Van House 1989).

- When different constituency groups ranked both perceived importance of and actual library performance on more than 50 effectiveness measures, only one indicator, helpfulness and courtesy of staff, appeared high on both the performance and wish lists of librarians, local government officials, and users (Calvert and Cullen 1994).

- Numerous studies (both regional and of individual institutions) show fair-sized pockets of individuals and groups who have library-related needs yet do not routinely use public libraries. For example, Vaughan, Tague-Sutcliffe, and Tripp (1996) found that the local public library came after *all* of the following information sources used by business people: customers; suppliers; friends, associates, and relatives; newspapers, magazines, and trade publications; consultants, lawyers, and accountants; trade associations and business clubs; and banks and other financial agencies. It was mentioned more than only three other sources: government publications and statistics, small business centers, and the Internet.

- In the 1980s, even large public libraries in the United States and elsewhere were providing "half-right" collection development efforts, filling only 50 to 65 percent of patron requests for specific items on the same day (e.g., Gajerski 1989; Kuraim 1983). Certainly this rate has improved. Title fill rates reported in *Public Library Data Service Statistical Report 1998* ranged from 46 to 96 percent, with averages in the upper 60s or lower 70s for libraries serving populations between 25,000 and 499,000 people (Public Library Association 1998). Nevertheless, our aim must be to improve these and related rates to the 90 percent effectiveness levels recommended by Baker and Lancaster (1991).

What choices do patrons have when a library does not meet their needs?

- They can remain loyal to the institution, using it without directly expressing their dissatisfaction, and accepting the inherent limitations of existing service;
- They can voice their concerns (e.g., by calmly sharing them with a staff member, angrily demanding to see the director, or writing a letter to the library board or the local newspaper) to see if they can obtain a remedy for the situation;
- They can neglect the problem, only indirectly expressing displeasure (e.g., rolling their eyes in disgust, sighing in frustration, or avoiding staff members with whom they are displeased); or
- They can exit, either giving up on meeting library-related needs or seeking to fulfill these elsewhere.[1]

To improve service and satisfy users over the long term, library staff can encourage patrons to quietly voice any dissatisfaction they feel, a topic discussed in greater detail in Chapter 7. Today unhappy patrons may choose from a large number of alternative information outlets, including friends, brick-and-mortar bookstores, Internet sites developed by subject experts, online retail outlets, compact disc clubs, and electronic database providers. Those who have sufficient resources and knowledge to use such services may readily obtain the desired information or materials. But what happens to those who do not?

MARKETING: A BRIEF RATIONALE

Integrating marketing principles with our accumulated practices and knowledge can help keep collections as easily accessible, current, and enriching as possible and promote community awareness of these resources. In essence, marketing library collections involves using strategic planning techniques to both anticipate and respond to the short- and long-term collection-related needs and desires of the individuals and groups whom the library serves.

Many librarians have flirted with the four main focuses of marketing—product development, pricing, place or location considerations, and promotion—for centuries. For example, a number of public libraries in ancient Greece and Rome were located in gathering places such as baths and forums; others used tract writing and philanthropic activity to promote precursors of English public libraries. In 1910, John Cotton Dana even used a billboard to advertise a public library's services. Patron-centered services began to develop more fully and spread widely in the nineteenth and twentieth centuries as the entry-level educational requirements for the field increased and flirtation gave way to professional ideals. Today, libraries are increasingly

- playing a more integral role in many societies worldwide (Kies 1987);
- trying innovative techniques to attract patrons;
- studied in an in-depth fashion; and
- explored in a growing disciplinary (and multidisciplinary) literature (virtual and otherwise) that considers both practice and theory, hits and misses.

Particularly in the 1980s and 1990s, discussions of marketing techniques have become increasingly substantive. Popular, how-to, and review pieces are now regularly supplemented by articles, journal issues, and a few dozen full-length books that employ increasingly sophisticated methodologies. We have Koontz's (1997) research on site selection for public libraries, Majid's (1996) discussion of promotional techniques for CD-ROM services in Malaysian libraries, and Alire and Archibeque's (1998) strategies for marketing library materials and services to Latino communities, to name a few.

Moreover, major organizations such as the International Federation of Library Associations and, in the United States, the Public Library Association, encourage the use of marketing techniques to ensure the design and low-cost distribution and promotion of both basic and sophisticated library collections.

Overcoming Potential Barriers to Marketing

Although it would be possible to falsely equate marketing with extremes of entrepreneurial behavior, such as greed, superficiality of purpose, spin, and hard-sell techniques, numerous constraints (from the characters of the people working in public libraries to the public scrutiny that our policies and performance receive) discourage such behavior.[2] Furthermore, librarians may adopt beneficial *intrapreneurial* business strategies, retaining the entrepreneur's innovation and problem-solving abilities without simultaneously reflecting a profit motive that might be detrimental to the public interest.

As for the initial uneasiness that continued references to "competition" in the marketing literature can cause, we find it reassuring to consider that talented *competition* (a word with the same root as *competence*) encourages us to continually develop our own expertise while promoting commendable public library characteristics, including

- retrospective collections, local history materials, and other unique holdings;
- the capacity to perform author, subject, title, and keyword searches to retrieve relevant materials; and
- an ability to meet patron demands at a monetary cost few profit-oriented institutions can match.

Finally, we suggest a need to recognize the reasonableness of the request, one made to any professional, to invest significant amounts of time and money in comprehending the complexity of the situation (in this case, community needs) and developing relevant and vital service responses. Successfully enacting these practices will not necessarily create an unreachable level of demand as long as staff simultaneously try to boost productivity in other fashions (e.g., gaining efficiency through automation) to keep service quality (and employee morale) high. For example, allowing patrons to reserve materials online will multiply the number of reserve requests, yet the reduction of staff time spent filing these helps offset the increased workload of filling them.

Strong marketing efforts will use the library's budget in a manner that seeks to achieve all four of the following:

Efficiency (doing things right)

Effectiveness (doing the right things)

Cost-effectiveness (using great service techniques at reasonable costs)

Cost-benefit (indicating clearly the value gained from the long-term cost of service)

The Benefits of Marketing

Mounting evidence documents that adopting thoughtful, cohesive marketing plans can help staff provide collections and services that satisfy patron and library objectives at reasonable costs while attracting public support for future endeavors. Consider these examples of successful marketing plans used by libraries:

- When the East Los Angeles branch revised its internal sign system, enhanced its Spanish-language materials collection, installed special shelving for bestsellers, creatively displayed Spanish and children's materials, and used bilingual advertising in community newspapers, the number of registered borrowers tripled, and walk-in count, in-house use, and circulation significantly increased ("Marketing" 1991). These results helped set the stage for use of marketing techniques throughout the County of Los Angeles Public Library system.

- In 1986, the Pine Mountain (Georgia) Regional Library provided a minimum level of service and had short supplies of funding and staff. Staff intensely focused their efforts on providing popular and educational materials to fulfill community needs, with children's needs paramount; carried out the marketing activities specified, including significant redistribution of monies to support these goals; and evaluated the success of these efforts. Increased levels of responsiveness to community members, effectiveness in decision making, and communication with community residents and funding officials helped librarians earn, in a time of local fiscal stability, a 91 percent funding increase for the system over a three-year period (Hopper 1991).

- In the early 1990s, aided by state funds, the Linda Vista branch of the San Diego Public Library hired bilingual library assistants, formed regular and strong coalitions with leaders among three groups of immigrants (Vietnamese, Laotians, and the Hmong), and significantly redirected collection development and programming patterns to attract these patrons. Circulation in this library rose from 129,000 in 1989 to 216,000 in 1993. Again, the city recognized the program's value, picking up the tab once state funding ended (Hoffert 1994).

Such successes contribute to a swelling recognition that effective marketing efforts are neither executed in isolation nor relegated to a single department. Well-conducted marketing efforts set the tempo for all, helping to ensure that library operations remain in sync with community needs and that concern for service permeates the facility.

Marketing provides a means by which libraries can deploy resources to their maximum effect. Intuitively or otherwise, knowing the basics of marketing can help us develop innovative applications to keep service quality high. For example, we could facilitate patron access to materials by employing technological developments, such as amazon.com-like search capacities that link patrons seeking particular items with similar titles other (anonymous!) patrons have borrowed.[3] This online technique, commonly used by amazon.com and other online bookstores, can combine circulation, selective keyword, and subject heading information (the online bookstore method often only considers purchase statistics) to increase the likelihood that suggested titles will be of interest to the patron.

Furthermore, thoughtful marketing encourages us to explore ways to cooperate with others who share similar objectives. Fortunately, many potential partnerships exist, including

- Friends of the Library and other volunteers already giving time or financial support to the library;

- patrons whose feedback provides invaluable assistance in creating collections that entice, intrigue, teach, and even inspire and whose testimonials can effectively promote use;

- the individuals and organizations who create or produce the items in our collections;

- key politicians, such as Nashville mayor Phil Bredesen and former Illinois governor Jim Edgar, who have worked for years to provide reasonable levels of funding for libraries under their jurisdictions (St. Lifer 1998a, 1998b);

- funding agencies that continue to provide support;

- those in other libraries who work across geographic boundaries to make assembled print and virtual resources widely available, including the 17-member Collaborative Digital Reference Service, an international network providing round-the-clock reference service, routing questions based on member libraries' holdings and time of day ("Reference" 2000);

- subject specialists willing to give their expertise to evaluate existing collections and recommend titles for purchase;

- other collectors who allow access to their resources through Web links, special loans, and the like;

- teachers, parents, satisfied patrons, and others who recommend the use of our collections;

- philanthropists, among them the more than 10,000 individuals and organizations who gave gifts totaling more than $1 million as part of the Seattle Public Library's a grassroots funding campaign (Collings 1998) and the numerous others who contributed millions to help libraries in Central America connect to the Internet (Makris 1998);

- foundations supporting a single or numerous libraries, like the Libri Foundation (PO Box 10246, Eugene, OR 97440), which collects and distributes children's titles to institutions with limited resources, and the Bill and Melinda Gates Foundation (http://www.gatesfoundation.org); and

- all others willing to work with libraries to provide better services the world over.

CONCLUSION

Effective library board members, employees, volunteers, and Friends—working in locales as diverse as the United States, Sweden, Zambia, and India—consciously seek to expand their repertoires of skills and knowledge to build vital collections (e.g., West 1997). To this end, library planners will ideally consider

- the requirements of those whom the library serves (discussed in Chapter 2);

- methods of integrating marketing techniques with the strategic planning process (discussed in Chapter 3);

- ways to build varied, rich collections that meet diverse needs without devastating the budget (discussed in Chapters 4, 8, and 9);

- techniques for keeping the monetary and psychological costs of accessing and using collections low (primarily discussed in Chapter 5);

- cost-effective methods of distributing these materials (primarily discussed in Chapter 6);

- potent promotional techniques (discussed in Chapters 7 and 10); and

- ways to ensure that marketing concepts and practices go beyond the boardroom to permeate the organization as a whole (discussed in Chapter 11).

We present here marketing-related research results and numerous examples of successful practices in hopes of making this work engaging and useful. We also implore anyone interested in research to note the gaps in the profession's current knowledge (partially indicated by old or no citations) and conduct further experiments and studies to fill these deficits—sharing results through journals like *Public Libraries* and the *Unabashed Librarian* and electronic mailing lists with searchable archives such as Publib. Further, we encourage those intrigued by a particular discussion to consult the original publications or institutions we cite.

In writing this book, we have tried to address the disparity between large and small and affluent and non-affluent libraries by proposing techniques befitting a range of circumstances. We ask you to help make this a relevant text by lending your imagination to it and adapting suggested strategies to suit the particulars of your situation.

NOTES

1.   Malafi (1991) investigates these choices, albeit in a non-library-specific context.

2.   For more on this subject, see St. Clair (1996).

3.   David Eichmann, a faculty member at the University of Iowa with a background in software engineering, is intrigued by the idea of working with public libraries on such a project. Dr. Eichmann may be reached at david-eichmann@uiowa.edu.

REFERENCES

Alire, Camila, and Orlando Archibeque. 1998. *Serving Latino Communities: A How-to-Do-It Manual for Librarians*. New York: Neal-Schuman.

Baker, Sharon L., and F. Wilfrid Lancaster. 1991. *Measurement and Evaluation of Library Services*. Arlington, VA: Information Resources Press.

Calvert, Philip J., and Rowena J. Cullen. 1994. "Further Dimensions of Public Library Effectiveness II: The Second Stage of the New Zealand Study." *Library and Information Science Research* 16, no. 2 (Spring): 87–104.

Childers, Thomas, and Nancy A. Van House. 1989. *The Public Library Effectiveness Study: Final Report*. Philadelphia: Drexel University, College of Information Studies.

Coffman, Steve. 2000. " 'And Now, a Word from Our Sponsors . . .': Alternative Funding for Libraries." *Searcher* 8, no. 1 (January): 51–57.

Collings, Terry A. 1998. "Books, Bytes, and Believers: Seattle's Grassroots Fundraising Campaign." *American Libraries* 29, no. 9 (September): 40–42.

Cullen, Rowena, and Philip J. Calvert. 1993. "Further Dimensions of Public Library Effectiveness: Report on a Parallel New Zealand Study." *Library and Information Science Research* 15, no. 2 (Spring): 143-64.

———. 1996. "New Zealand University Libraries Effectiveness Project: Dimension and Concepts of Organizational Effectiveness." *Library and Information Science Research* 18, no. 2 (Spring): 99–119.

D'Elia, George, and Eleanor Jo Rodger. 1996. "Customer Satisfaction with Public Libraries." *Public Libraries* 35, no. 5 (September/October): 292–97.

Gajerski, B. 1989. "Edmonton Public Library: 1989 User Survey." Edmonton, Alberta: Edmonton Public Library. ERIC ED327184.

Hoffert, Barbara. 1994. "Dragon Dancers and Eastern Westerns: Serving the Asian American Community." *Library Journal* 119, no. 12 (July): 42–45.

Hopper, Lyn. 1991. "Planning Pays for the Small, the Poor, and the Busy: An Exhortation and a Bibliography." *Public Libraries* 30, no. 1 (January-February): 21–24.

Jones, Alison, ed. 1997. *Chambers Dictionary of Quotations*. New York: Chambers.

Kies, Cosette N. 1987. *Marketing and Public Relations for Libraries*. Metuchen, NJ: Scarecrow Press.

Koontz, Christine M. 1997. *Library Facility Siting and Location Handbook*. Westport, CT: Greenwood Press, 1997.

Kuraim, Faraj Mohamed. 1983. "The Principal Factors Causing Reader Frustration in a Public Library." Ph.D. diss., Case Western Reserve University.

Majid, Shaheen. 1996. "Usage and Promotion of CD-ROM Services in Malaysian Academic Libraries." *Computers in Libraries* 16, no. 9 (October): 51–54.

Makris, Joanna. 1998. "The Ultimate Startup." *Data Communications* 27, no. 15 (October 21): 75–76.

Malafi, Teresa N. 1991. "Exit, Voice, Loyalty, & Neglect: A New Approach to Consumer Dissatisfaction." In *Proceedings of the Society for Consumer Psychology* from the 1990 Annual Convention of the American Psychological Association, Division 23—Consumer Psychology, Boston, MA, August 10–13, eds. Curtis P. Haugvedt and David W. Schumann, 87–94. Washington, DC: American Psychological Association, Society for Consumer Psychology.

"Marketing: It Works!" 1991. *Library Administrator's Digest* 26, no. 8 (October): 58.

Public Library Association. 1998. *Public Library Data Service Statistical Report 1998*. Chicago: Public Library Association.

"Reference 24/7: Libraries Test Collaborative Digital Reference Service." 2000. *The Library of Congress Information Bulletin*, [Online] (October). Available: http://www.loc.gov/loc /lcib/0010/ref.html [Accessed September 26, 2001].

St. Clair, Guy. 1996. *Entrepreneurial Librarianship: The Key to Effective Information Services Management*. London: Bowker-Saur.

St. Lifer, Evan. 1998a. "Edgar Ups Budgets for Libraries/Schools." *Library Journal* 123, no. 5 (March 15): 18.

———. 1998b. "LJ's Second Annual Politician of the Year 1998: Phil Bredesen." *Library Journal* 123, no. 19 (November 15): 26–28.

Vaughan, Liwen Qui, Jean Tague-Sutcliffe, and Pat Tripp. 1996. "The Value of the Library to Small Businesses." *RQ* 36, no. 2 (Winter): 262–69.

West, W. J. 1997. "Starved of Books." *The Times Literary Supplement*, no. 4909 (May 2): 15.

KNOW YOUR MARKET

"Knowledge speaks, but wisdom listens"—
Jimi Hendrix (Robins 1994–2001).

A key irony of our profession is that those in the field must simultaneously recognize, promote, and believe deeply in the many benefits of public libraries, while acknowledging that a significant number of individuals do not use or want to use these institutions. One person may think of libraries as cold, gloomy places staffed by intimidating, rule-bound shushers. Another may have failed to find interesting materials on past visits. A third may not like to use computers or the assortment of audiovisual materials libraries carry. Yet another might have such heavy responsibilities that he or she cannot indulge in a natural love of reading. Understanding the general characteristics and motivations of those who use the library regularly, occasionally, or rarely can help us try to meet those user needs that fall inside the library's purview. This chapter examines frequency of and motivation for use as well as techniques to encourage it.

FREQUENCY OF USE: CORE MARKETS, FRINGE MARKETS, AND HARD-CORE NONUSERS

In the United States, public library use has significantly expanded since 1948, when the Public Library Inquiry documented that only 19 percent of adults had used library services during the previous year (Scheppke 1994). In 2000, Rodger et al. documented a 66.4 percent rate of use at least once during the previous year among adults in the continental United States, and in the 1990s, Gallup discovered nationwide use rates of 66 percent ("Gallup Poll" 1998) and 67 percent

(Mazmanian 1996) among adults. Brick et al. (1992) noted a 63 percent rate, and the National Center for Education Statistics (Collins and Chandler 1997) found a rate of 65 percent, with ranges of 51 to 76 percent among the 50 states. Library practices and population characteristics in the highest five states—Alaska (76 percent), Washington and Utah (75 percent), and Wyoming and Maryland (73 percent)—merit further exploration to determine what factors keep these use levels significantly above the norm,[1] as do practices in the lowest use states.

Yet despite the increase in the last half of the twentieth century in the number of adults who use libraries, a large portion of library visits were made by a small percentage of users. Two relatively recent studies tested the applicability of Pareto's Law, or the 80-20 rule (a majority of use comes from a minority of patrons), to library circulation. Although the 80-20 ratio did not precisely hold, a relatively small number of borrowers did account for a disproportionately large percentage of circulation. A nationwide investigation in Great Britain found that "around 30 percent of borrowers [check out] over 80 percent of books" (*Heavy Book Borrowers* 1996, 3). In the United States, Clark (1998) found 35 percent of all borrowers at the Ocean County (New Jersey) Library responsible for 78 percent of all book circulation.

These heavy users—our core market—visit the library regularly and use the collection intensely. Others may fall into the library's fringe market or be hard-core nonusers. Fringe market members, although interested in public library offerings, often, or even always, prefer to obtain these from other sources. The primary reasons they may develop this preference include a lack of specific knowledge about what public libraries offer and the perception of use as too costly, in terms of time, money, or convenience (e.g., D'Elia 1980). In contrast, hard-core nonusers state that they have little or no interest in the kind of goods libraries offer; on the few occasions when they do want these, they often choose alternative sources or end up doing without the materials entirely; frequently, they do not know where to get them or find it difficult to bear the costs of obtaining them.[2]

CHARACTERISTICS OF LIBRARY USERS

What differentiates members of the core and fringe markets from those who do not use the library at all? Over the years, researchers have conducted literally hundreds of local, statewide, regional, and national inquiries, which have yielded a web of data about those inclined to use libraries. For example, the *1996 National Household Education Survey* documented that households with children under age 18 were significantly more likely to have at least one member who had used the library within the past month or year than households without minors, and that Asian and Pacific Islanders were most likely to use the library and Hispanics least (Lynch 1997). A study of 34 Connecticut communities supported the finding that those with children under 18 were more likely to use the library but identified no significant racial or ethnic differences between users and nonusers (Welch and Donohue 1994). Rodger et al. (2000) also found that library use was not significantly related to race. Such research reinforces that demographic elements alone may not accurately predict library use.

Studies have more consistently indicated that library users often possess

- a general desire to explore the world around them;
- the desire to do this via books and other media; and
- a familiarity with and knowledge of libraries and their organizational schemes.

A General Desire to Explore the World around Them

Some individuals (e.g., out of habit or fear) repeat the same or similar experiences for long periods, despite the availability of time and other resources necessary to investigate new ideas and endeavors. Library users less frequently fall into this group than nonusers. For example, when Madden (1979a, 1979b) reviewed a national marketing study to obtain pictures of the lifestyles of users and nonusers, he concluded that regular library users actively sought new experiences and consistently worked on bootstrapping activities to improve themselves, their family, careers, hobbies, and the like. In contrast, a majority of nonusers disliked change, were highly conservative, watched many hours of television each week, had few activities outside the home, and were significantly less educated than users.

Although studies have repeatedly shown that those who enjoy school and continually gain formal education are very heavy users of all types of libraries (e.g., Wittig 1991; Willits and Willits 1991; Lange 1987/1988),[3] other library users may choose to learn through less formal channels, which corresponds with Pratt's (1998) finding that the percentage of college-educated members of a community correlates only slightly with per capita circulation.

Other studies support Madden's conclusions, at least in part. For example, Zweizig (1973) found that the extent to which a person was dogmatic correlated negatively with library use, whereas level of community involvement and desire to scrutinize and influence the world through book reading, newspaper use, and education correlated positively. Becker and Connor (1982) documented that those who read more than 10 books per year demonstrate an achievement orientation and value imagination. Rodger et al. (2000) found that as a whole, library users had attained significantly higher educational levels than nonusers; 75 percent of Internet users also used the library. Other studies that have substantiated Madden's claims include Willits and Willits (1991), "NEA Study" (1989), Zill and Winglee (1989), Lange (1987/1988), Bolton (1982), and Lucas (1982).

A Desire to Explore the World Via
Books and Other Media

Nature and nurture both affect future library use. Whether due to personal desires, the influence of parents, teachers, or significant others, or both, some people regularly read books, e-books, and magazines; use computers; listen to CDs; watch DVDs and videos; and enjoy other media that libraries carry. Studies have demonstrated that children who read vociferously come from families that encourage reading (Palsdottir 1998; Louizides 1993; NFO Research 1990), and children whose parents read to them make greater use of the library (Lamme and Olmsted 1977). Reading in childhood helps foster a preference for lifelong reading (Matheny and Lockledge 1986; Duncan and Goggin 1982; Ribovich and Erickson 1980).

But people living in impoverished neighborhoods may not have easy, abundant access to books or other media. For example, Smith, Constantino, and Krashen (1997) found that the mean number of books in the home was 199.2 in Beverly Hills, 2.67 in Compton, and 0.4 in Watts; moreover, the poorer neighborhoods had fewer books in the classroom and in school and public libraries, as well as fewer bookstores in their locale. By the very nature of their circulating collections, public libraries can increase access to media in the homes of those who do not currently live in print-rich environments, as well as those who do. Ramos and Krashen (1998) found that taking inner-city second- and third-graders to the public library on a monthly basis to check out interesting books greatly increased the children's desire to read. Chapters 6 and 10 describe further techniques to facilitate access to books and help foster a love of reading and media use.

Individual methods of acquiring knowledge may also influence enjoyment of library use. Cognitive psychologists have noted 21 variables in the way people learn, often condensed into four main learning styles. Visual learners prefer obtaining information through words and pictures. Auditory learners absorb information best through listening. Kinesthetic learners maximize a learning experience when they involve their entire bodies in it. Tactual learners prefer using their hands in a learning experience (Filipczak 1995). Most people exhibit a preference for one or two of these styles, although they may also move among all four, depending in part on the nature of the subject to be explored.

In the past, public library collections emphasized books, magazines, and other print materials best suited to visual learning. Fortunately, they now include an increasing number of materials that benefit all four learning preferences. For example, computers with Internet access; interactive databases, games, and other software; kits; puzzles; and toys may appeal to tactual and kinesthetic learners,[4] whereas the library's audiobooks (both tapes and CDs) may attract auditory learners and those with learning disabilities (Gorman 1997b). The Meriden (Connecticut) Public Library thoughtfully responded to learning style differences when it created a Learning Diversity Resource Center, which offers materials about learning disabilities as well as a significant collection of auditory, visual, and multimedia materials especially suitable for those with learning disabilities (Gorman 1997a).

Although research shows that library users enjoy using various forms of media (e.g., Gallup 1978), to date none has comprehensively explored which of the learning styles (and the 21 elements that they comprise) correlate strongly with library use, research we encourage as lying well within the purview of the field.

Familiarity with and Knowledge of Libraries in General

Most adult library users acquired the habit of use in childhood, at least in part because of family or school environment (Razzano 1985; Welch and Donohue 1994). For example, Powell, Taylor, and McMillen (1984) found that steady library patrons usually had access to and began using public or school libraries during their childhood years and visited the library with a parent 10 or more times per year as a child. In addition, Lange (1987/1988) found that adults who had frequent, positive library experiences as children used the public library more often than adults who rarely used the library as children. In other words, familiarity with library services breeds use.

Familiarity reduces the fear and anxiety that many patrons feel when entering a library (e.g., Mellon 1988, 1986),[5] anxiety that can persist until continued, successful exposure to either libraries in general or to specific libraries helps decrease it. Patrons also frequently experience frustration related to the overwhelming size of the collection and complexity of the catalogs, indexes, and other finding mechanisms (Ross 1991; Baker 1986; Totterdell and Bird 1976). When patrons persist and have success in spite of their apprehension and frustrations, they actually create a positive, self-reinforcing cycle, becoming more familiar with the library's collection and retrieval mechanisms, sharpening their skills, finding desired information, and feeling greater satisfaction, which in turn helps keep use high.[6]

Finally, as patron knowledge of libraries increases, their awareness of the full benefits of use also rises. Thus, patrons who use a service new to them (whether interlibrary loan, reserves, or Internet searching) and find that the service meets their needs over time will likely continue using it.

MOTIVATION AND INCENTIVES TO USE THE LIBRARY

Although these three broad characteristics that probable patrons share provide a starting point for understanding who uses the public library, they must be supplemented by a comprehension of internal motivation. As Marchant notes, "Lack of use occurs when motivation is absent or when a patron's motivation is weaker than inhibitors that discourage use" (1994, 2). In a first step toward testing this theory, Marchant surveyed Provo, Utah, community residents and found a significant correlation between four broad life motivators—home and family, vocational growth, religion, and politics—and the specific uses patrons made of the library.

We condense Marchant's theory and add one clause: Library use occurs when motivation *plus incentives* outweigh inhibitors (costs). In this model librarians

can affect many *external* incentives and inhibitors. In essence, patrons are motivated to use the library by their perception of the benefit(s) that use will provide.
For example, patrons may choose to use the library because they believe such use
will help them

- gain knowledge;

- earn a good grade;

- meet others who value education, creativity, and the like;

- improve the quality of their lives;

- appear intelligent; or even

- get a date with that cute reference librarian!

Unpublished qualitative research (Baker 1998) corroborates the idea that
patrons have deeply personal and varied motives for using the public library either
regularly or on any given occasion. (See figure 2.1, pages 17–18.)[7] Motivation may
change depending on the specific ways in which a patron uses the library. For
example, Wojciehowski (1996) considers one particular kind of use—reading fiction—and proposes several motivators: philosophical (reflective); aesthetic; educational; affectional (emotional); recreational; substitutive (escapist), which may
include retrogressional (deriving comfort from re-reading familiar texts), prestige,
or sheer escape; veristic (informational); and cognitive (enriching consciousness),
which accompanies most of the other motivators.

How does this theory fit with the previously described characteristics of
public library users? The first two broad characteristics—an enjoyment of exploring
the world around them and a desire to use the materials libraries can offer—provide two strong motivations to use the library. The third characteristic—a familiarity with libraries—also serves as an incentive for use; patrons knowledgeable
about libraries will likely feel comfortable in them and comprehend their policies,
procedures, and benefits, which in turn reduces the costs of use.

Incentives can also be external. For example, librarians may encourage
patrons to borrow CD-ROMs by doubling that collection's budget and increasing
the loan period. Assuming they can meet demand, librarians will want to encourage or create as many incentives for use as possible while abating inhibitors that
can dampen use.[8] Childers and Van House (1989) reinforced much previous research with their findings that patrons feel that effective libraries reduce costs of
use, in terms of time and aggravation. As noted in Chapter 1, patrons want libraries
to provide easily accessible locations, adequate free parking, convenient hours of
operation, guidance in using the facilities, quick service, and ready availability of a
wide range of materials and services.

Patron Motivations to Use the Library

♥ When our son developed leukemia, we scoured the collection of our small town library, identified other titles . . . then borrowed a dozen more works through interlibrary loan. We identified a specialist with a new experimental treatment. Richard is alive today, 20 years later.

♥ In the last year, I've used the library to get information on a zoning change proposed in my neighborhood and on writing résumés when I needed to change jobs.

♥ I switched to using the public library when they closed the browsing room at the college where I work. Have you ever tried to browse for fiction within the Library of Congress classification scheme?

♥ I come here for income tax information every year; I also use the magazines; I'd rather spend any spare money I earn directly on my family.

♥ Materials go out of print so fast I often use public libraries when I'm doing research, for the fifth graders I teach or my own use.

♥ I've loved to read ever since I was a kid. . . . Now that I'm retired, I check out books for my grandchildren and read cartons of mysteries.

FIGURE 2.1. Patron Motivations to Use the Library. Derived from Baker (1998).

(Fig. 2.1 continues on page 18.)

FIG. 2.1—*Continued*

- ♥ I wanted to be a nurse when I was 10, so I read all the Sue Barton, Nurse novels I could find and biographies of Clara Barton and others at the public library. I discovered, in a novel called *Princess Sophia,* that men nibbled on women's breasts, and began exploring all the stacks. . . . Whenever I move to a new town, I get a public library card within the first few days, even though I also use other libraries and the Net.

- ♥ My brother got me interested. He would bring home books that explained why people did what they did. I want to understand what is happening around me.

- ♥ I believe in recycling, so I often read books that I'm unfamiliar with at the library before I buy them. . . . I heard Michael Oondaatje at a poetry reading last year, so I checked out several titles of his, including *The English Patient.*

- ♥ My four-year-old likes Sesame Street videos and Walt Disney, my husband is exploring international folk music, and I want literature on audiobooks for my evening run.

- ♥ I didn't use the local library much until my daughter was born; I started reading a week's worth of the *Wall Street Journal* when Katie was old enough to bring to story hour on Saturdays.

The degree to which a patron can obtain, when needed, desired materials—whether a public Internet station or the latest bestseller—often affects collection use. Although no public library can purchase everything available, it is possible for selectors to aggravate the situation by subconsciously purchasing materials they will enjoy to the detriment of those with different tastes. For example, a sculptor may avoid a public library art book collection that focuses far more heavily on the crafts than the fine arts. Subconscious preference may also limit the availability of materials that appeal to those of various genders, ages, ethnic and cultural backgrounds, religions, political persuasions, and learning styles.

Although actual evidence is scanty, it does lend support to the idea of such subconscious bias. Consider, for example, that Australian investigators found males significantly more likely to have read hobby or teach-yourself books in the week prior to the study and females more likely to have read craft books and romances (Delin, Delin, and Cram 1995). And U.S. book purchasing data collected by Gallup (1999) indicates that although males and females bought approximately the same number of nonfiction books in 1998, women were nearly two times as likely to buy a cookbook, whereas men were over twice as likely to buy history titles. Hole (1990) has argued that public libraries (heavily staffed by women) emphasize "female-oriented" materials such as romance novels and cookbooks. This holds true even when items on the subject are fairly technical or specialized, like a book on cooking with flowers. Many public libraries still fail to provide enough "male-oriented" books, like hard-core adventure fiction, technical books on electrical repair, or detailed works about the hard sciences. Becoming aware of these subconscious preferences and consciously working to eradicate them can result in collections truly designed for the communities we serve.

We also want to avoid committing different service errors that inhibit patron use. For example, librarians may not

- order and process new items quickly,
- provide enough duplicate copies of popular classic and current works so that at least one copy is always available for checkout or at least available within a reasonable period, or
- ensure that returned items are reshelved quickly.

Although librarians can manage many inhibitors, others may be more difficult to influence. For example, in an open-ended question on the *Park Ridge Library Community Survey 1995*, 43 percent of all respondents volunteered that they would be more likely to visit the library if they had "more personal time" (Northern Illinois University 1995). A survey of adults throughout the continental United States found that 55.6 percent of nonusers chose, "don't have the time to go to the library," the most frequently selected of 17 suggested reasons for nonuse (Rodger et al. 2000). Moreover, Ballard's (1986) review shows that factors completely or partially outside the library's control, such as lack of free time or interest in library resources, consistently account for a large portion of nonuse.

Contrast the potential customer who cannot use the library because it is only open during hours he or she works (external inhibitor) with the extremely busy person who would have great difficulty finding time to use the library even if it were open 24 hours a day, every day (internal inhibitor). In the first case, the library can remove or reduce the external inhibitor by extending opening hours or providing anytime Internet access to an online catalog and a mechanism for after-hours pickup of the holds placed through it. (See Chapter 5 for a discussion of this.) In the second case, although library staff will not be able to eliminate the inhibitor, they may be able to slightly decrease it, for example by promoting the collection of audiobooks that can be enjoyed while simultaneously engaging in other tasks.

When motivation and incentives are strong enough, patrons may be willing to overcome inhibitors to use the library. Conversely, patrons who lack motivation to use the library (e.g., hard-core nonusers) do not use it in the short term, no matter how convenient we make it. For example, 43 percent of the residents served by the Enoch Pratt (Baltimore, Maryland) Free Library acknowledged that nothing the library could do would persuade them to use it; 20 percent of those responding to the *Park Ridge Library Community Survey 1995* offered a similar comment (Northern Illinois University 1995). There has been little longitudinal study of what happens to these attitudes over long periods of time, a topic ripe for research.

It's the Match That Counts

Savvy librarians recognize that although they can affect many incentives and inhibitors, these factors are highly personal, even unique, to a given patron. For one individual, the library's extensive DVD and video feature film collections might be a significant incentive to visit the library. The same superior collection has little or no appeal to a non-movie buff.

Patrons will also idiosyncratically weigh disparate factors relevant to library use. Consider, for example, the avid reader who obtains materials from the library because he cannot afford to buy everything he wants. On a particular day, this man visits the library looking for two books. Although he finds the first on the shelf, he learns he will have to wait about two months to obtain the other through the reserve system. He complains about the wait but continues to use the library; he cannot meet his voluminous need for materials elsewhere. In contrast, someone who reads fewer titles every year or has more disposable income may simply buy the second book.

Economic reasons inspired the first patron's loyalty, a motivation that may be particularly widespread; consider Roy's (1984) study showing a high correlation between heavy reading (10 or more books per year) and library use. Van House (1983) has suggested that those most likely to use the library belong to the middle class; those who are poor or rich face high costs for such use. Individuals in the first group may lack a family tradition of library use and a strong educational background and find the typical library frustrating and inconvenient to use. This may encourage them to obtain information and materials through other sources, such as friends, or even do without them entirely. In contrast, the affluent may purchase the information and materials they need through online or brick-and-mortar bookstores, fee-based information services, or consultants who will quickly provide the materials, often packaged in a convenient, personalized way. Book sale data for the United States support this contention, showing that those with incomes of $75,000 a year or more are the heaviest book buyers (Book Industry Study Group 1999) and at least 42 percent of all book buyers earn $50,000 a year or more (Gallup 1999). Middle-class patrons often have a solid education and enough experience with libraries to lessen the psychological costs of using them, yet may be financially unable to purchase large quantities of information, print items and media, and other desired library products.

Patron perceptions (well-founded or not) also play a critical role in the decision to use the library. For example, 15 years ago, a county library in southeastern Ohio exhibited the work of six folk artists during a summer festival. Although all the art drew a number of onlookers, the tattoo expert's original works attracted a large number of leather-jacketed motorcyclists sporting their own inked designs. When the library's assistant director chatted with more than a dozen of these men and women, she uniformly heard that although they routinely brought their children to the library, during the year in which the new building's doors had been open few had been in themselves. Until they saw the notice of the tattoo display, they felt the library would have little to meet their interests—an uninvestigated belief independent of the actual state of the collection.

Figure 2.2, pages 22–23, exemplifies how different patrons may weigh motivation, incentives, and inhibitors as they decide whether to use the library.

Embrace Serenity

As Van House notes in her classic article on the costs of public library use, "The library makes itself available and attractive, but in the end the individual decides whether or not to use it" (1983, 365). Those planning library services may do well to consider the beginning of Reinhold Niebuhr's serenity prayer: "God grant me the serenity to accept the things I cannot change, courage to change the things I can, and wisdom to know the difference" ("Grant" 2001). Libraries that cannot serve every member of their service population effectively may maximize limited resources by concentrating major efforts on the core market while simultaneously using a limited number of well-considered, targeted efforts to reach individuals who currently lack motivation to use the library, an attitude subject to change over time. Librarians can reinforce, directly and indirectly, the benefits of use (a concept developed further in Chapters 7 and 10) to nonusers with the following caveats in mind:

- These benefits must have meaning for an individual before they will significantly influence library use.

- Efforts to convert these hard-core nonusers to patrons will be more costly than serving those already inclined to use the library.

Case One. Motivation: Lucy loves to read romances. With her limited budget, she cannot afford to buy them all. She lives about 10 miles from the library.

Incentives: The library owns many romances, shelved in a separate collection in a prominent location. Librarians are knowledgeable about the romance collection and willing to help patrons find a suitable book.

Inhibitors: Parking facilities are insufficient. The library duplicates few romances, so Lucy often has to wait to get the book she wants.

Result: Lucy circles the parking lot, using the library after finding a space. Although she may have to wait for specific titles desired, the librarians often suggest available titles she will enjoy. For Lucy, waiting for parking spaces and books is a smaller price to pay than the monetary cost of buying all the titles she wants.

Case Two. Motivation: Fred enjoys a wide range of DVDs. He spends many hours traveling on business and likes to watch DVDs on his laptop during flights.

Incentives: The library owns a wide variety of DVDs. Even though the collection is very popular, Fred can normally find something intriguing on the shelf.

Inhibitors: DVDs check out for one week, are not renewable, and have an overdue fine of 50 cents a day.

Result: Many of Fred's business trips exceed one week; because he cannot keep DVDs this long without incurring fines, he uses the collection only for shorter trips, a fraction of the use he would make were he able to check out DVDs longer. (A longer loan period or renewals might also adversely affect his chances of finding titles he wants on the shelf.)

Case Three. Motivation: Trent needs library resources to complete a school paper. He wants to get a good grade and does not have access to other resources that would provide the necessary information.

Incentives: The library offers access to the indexes, online databases, Internet sites, books, and journals that Trent needs.

Inhibitors: In the past, some of the librarians have not adequately helped Trent. (He feels they disapprove of teens.)

Result: Despite these inhibitors, Trent feels that the library is his only viable option. Although he gets the information he needs, he feels so uncomfortable in the library that he is not likely to return if he can avoid it.

FIGURE 2.2. Examples of Factors Influencing a Patron's Decision to Use the Library.

Case Four. (Potential) Motivation: Tina loves rock music. She can only afford to buy a fraction of the CDs she wants.

(Potential) Incentives: The library owns many relevant rock CDs. (The new music selector keeps up-to-date on what is popular and routinely purchases items on the top of the Billboard charts.) There is no charge to check out CDs.

Inhibitors: Tina is unaware of the library's outstanding CD collection, although she vaguely remembers seeing a large number of Lawrence Welk records several years ago when she was looking for the water fountain.

Result: Tina does not use the library. Although the CD collection would delight her, she does not know it exists.

Case Five. Motivation: None. Working two jobs to try to make ends meet, Susann doesn't have time to use the library. Moreover, she has never really used the library and has little desire to start. She enjoys tennis in her limited free time.

Incentives: Although the library has a fantastic, well-promoted collection, ample parking, extensive hours, and a friendly, knowledgeable staff, at the present time Susann has no interest in what the library has to offer.

Inhibitors: Even if the library was open 24 hours a day, seven days a week, Susann currently feels she does not have enough personal time to use library materials.

Result: Susann does not use the library. The library does not want to ignore her, especially given the underlying problem, a situation that information in the library may help her address (e.g., via materials on thrift, financial planning, career development, and time management). Although staff will concentrate resources on meeting user needs, they will continue efforts to publicize materials in the collection that Susann and others struggling to make ends meet could find useful.

Notes: In several of these cases, use results even though the library is performing suboptimally. Clearly, use in and of itself is not a complete measure of success. The knowledge of the librarians serving Lucy helped meet her needs, but they may also wish to seek solutions to the parking problem. And the librarians serving Fred may wish to find ways to supplement collection funds to purchase sufficient DVDs to allow renewals or extend the loan period. As an increasing number of resources become available in patrons' homes, libraries may lose former users like Trent, who feel the library is their only option in spite of poor service.

Moreover, librarians will want to concentrate on factors over which they have some control, as opposed to those like a person's lack of free time. For example, on the Park Ridge survey, roughly 22 percent of patrons suggested a change the library could make, ranging from allowing coffee in the building to improving the collection (Northern Illinois University 1995). Rodger et al. (2000) found that 17 percent of nonusers nationwide perceive library hours as inconvenient, 15.6 percent feel the collection does not meet their needs, 10.6 percent believe the library does not have enough parking, and 5.6 percent consider library service to be poor. And Upper Goulburn (Victoria, Australia) Regional Library Service managers concluded, after analyzing the results of a user survey, that the 55 to 78 percent of current nonusers who were also "potential" users could best be reached by better promotion and more technology-based services (Flowers 1995).

Libraries can change incentives and inhibitors through permanent measures, such as building current, relevant, attractive collections that include the full range of desired formats or providing Internet access to the collection and superior bookmobile service to neighborhoods far from the library. They can also encourage reading and other media use by presenting booktalks, promoting segments of the collection on their Web site, or judiciously distributing used works to those who cannot otherwise afford them. For example, materials remaining after a Friends' sale (such as last year's bestsellers) could be distributed at no cost by churches and other organizations in areas with high poverty rates. Special promotions can also bolster use. For example, when the Ela Area (Lake Zurich, Illinois) Public Library District sent a game piece, redeemable at the reference desk for a prize, to every home within its district, reference questions increased 26 percent over the same period during the previous year (Collins, Blake, and Rose 1999).

Key Into the Community

A central contention of this book is that librarians who intensely study the populations they serve, focusing on comprehending residents' motivations for library use as well as incentives or inhibitors to use, can better design collections and services that successfully meet residents' needs. Such responsive collections and services, when well promoted, will in turn increase library use.

Although informal observations about who uses the library may be part of a user analysis study, hard data can help to avoid mistaken beliefs and check the validity of staff assumptions. For example, in one British study librarians asked to characterize their typical users described people very similar to themselves (Vincent 1999). When staff at the Indianapolis-Marion County (Indiana) Public Library began keeping track of who actually entered the library, they found that, "The group we thought was typical (Anglo women at or approaching retirement age) made up a small percentage of our users. However, the group that we thought it would take a massive free stereo giveaway program to lure through our doors, the young adults, were our largest group of users. It didn't take us long to realize that the mature women were the patrons who talked to us the most and for whom no doubt we were selecting" (Gibson 1998, 37).

To gather more reliable information about their service populations, librarians can employ a variety of techniques, including

- examining data collected by other agencies, such as local school districts and governmental planning units;

- surveying randomly selected, individual community members over the telephone, via mail, or face-to-face;

- employing a research firm, purchasing data, or using a geographic information system;

- questioning community leaders and members of various community groups and agencies; and

- paying close attention to local concerns, issues, and happenings by reading, listening to, and watching local media; attending meetings of local governmental bodies and other select groups; participating in local organizations, and/or attending area events.[9]

Some libraries have developed elaborate methods of researching their communities. For example, the King County (Washington) Library System studies four libraries' service areas each year. In their in-depth process a nine-member team of employees with expertise in different areas gathers community information from a variety of primary and secondary sources (Thorsen 1998). We applaud such efforts and encourage their widespread adoption in public libraries worldwide.

CONCLUSION

The increasing rates of library use in the United States undoubtedly result from a combination of factors. These include some that libraries cannot control, such as changes in leisure time and higher average levels of educational attainment among adults, as well as others that libraries can direct, notably becoming increasingly customer centered. Librarians who know their patrons well and think first of service as they make decisions and proceed with their daily work will be vastly better prepared to navigate the challenges of an increasingly competitive environment than those whose focus lies elsewhere.

NOTES

1. Worldwide reported rates of usage range widely. For example, 61 percent of United Kingdom residents use libraries of some type (Sumsion 1996), whereas only 25 percent of residents of the Flanders region of Belgium use the public library (Hoflack 1999), and 16 percent of Japanese residents have registered with their public library (Endo 1992).

2. D'Elia (1980) was one of the first to apply the term "hard-core nonusers" in a public library setting.

3. See also Ballard (1986) for a review of studies connecting educational attainment and the use of books and libraries.

4. Faulkner (1998) elaborates on other benefits of including toys in children's collections, and Poller (1988) explores (and supports) the value of public libraries offering both videogames and machines on which to play them.

5. Wurman's (1989) *Information Anxiety* provides an excellent guide for exploring the psychological context of this problem. Those who wish to delve further into the topic may also find Onwuegbuzie and Jiao's (1998) investigation of the relationship between learning style and library anxiety of interest.

6. This finding parallels one that shows that the more familiar the average reference librarian is with the resources in the collection, the more accurate he or she will be in answering reference questions. See, for example, Halldorsson and Murfin (1977).

7. Librarians may also remember the American Library Association's multiyear National Library Week theme, "Libraries Change Lives," from the early to mid-1990s. During the campaign, librarians collected over 40,000 letters from library users that illuminated their range of motivations to use the library and the benefits they received from that use (Sliz 1996). For selected letters or excerpts from them, see Sliz (1996), Wallace (1994), "Indiana" (1994), and "Actors" (1993).

8. Van House (1983) and D'Elia (1980) note some of these inhibitors.

9. For further discussion of how to gather and analyze community data, see Consulting Librarians Group (2001), Coursen (1996), Kim and Little (1987), Zweizig (1992), Alire and Archibeque (1998), Rossman (1997), Evans (1992), Cassell and Futas (1991), Kaufman and English (1979), and, especially for librarians in Colorado and those just beginning the *Planning for Results* PLA planning process, "Community" (2001) and Logan (2000).

REFERENCES

"Actors, Writers, Sports Stars Agree: Libraries Do Change Lives." 1993. *American Libraries* 24, no 4 (April): 304–6.

Alire, Camila, and Orlando Archibeque. 1998. *Serving Latino Communities: A How-to-Do-It Manual for Librarians*. New York: Neal-Schuman.

Baker, Sharon L. 1986. "Overload, Browsers, and Selection." *Library and Information Science Research* 8, no. 4 (October-December): 315–29.

——— . 1998. "Why We Read What We Do!" Unpublished qualitative research, University of Iowa, School of Library and Information Science.

Ballard, Thomas H. 1986. *The Failure of Resource Sharing in Public Libraries and Alternative Strategies for Service*. Chicago: American Library Association.

Becker, Boris W., and Patrick E. Connor. 1982. "The Influence of Personal Values on Book Reading Behavior." *Journal of Library Administration* 3, no. 1 (Spring): 13–23.

Bolton, W. Theodore. 1982. "Life Style Research." *Library Journal* 107, no. 10 (May 15): 963–68.

Book Industry Study Group, Inc. [1999]. "New Consumer Research Study on Book Purchasing Shows Overall Consumer Demand for Adult Books Declined in '98 Despite Robust Economy: Internet Arrives Capturing 2% of All Books Bought by Consumers in 1998." [Homepage of Book Industry Study Group, Inc.], [Online]. Formerly available: http://www.bookwire.com/bisg/pressrelease98.html [Accessed July 2, 1999].

Brick, J. M., et al. 1992. *National Household Education Survey Adult and Course Data Files User's Manual*. Washington, DC: U.S. Department of Education, National Center for Education Statistics. ERIC ED347178. NCES Publication No. 92-019.

Cassell, Kay Ann, and Elizabeth Futas. 1991. *Developing Public Library Collections, Policies, and Procedures: A How-to-Do-It Manual for Small and Medium Sized Public Libraries*. New York: Neal-Schuman.

Childers, Thomas, and Nancy A. Van House. 1989. *The Public Library Effectiveness Study: Final Report*. Philadelphia: Drexel University.

Clark, Philip M. 1998. "Patterns of Consistent, Persistent Borrowing Behavior by High-Intensity Users of a Public Library." *Public Libraries* 37, no. 5 (September/October): 298–306.

Collins, Liza L., with Sandra Blake and Dianne Rose. 1999. *"Fall Into Books": A Reading Promotion and Community Relations Campaign*. Lake Zurich, IL: Ela Area Public Library.

Collins, Mary, and Kathryn Chandler. 1997. "Use of Public Library Services by Households in the United States: 1996." *Statistics in Brief* (March): 1–11. ERIC ED406985.

"Community Analysis Resources on the WWW." 2001. [Homepage of Library Research Service], [Online]. Available: http://www.lrs.org/html/topics&tools/community _analysis_web.html [Accessed September 26, 2001].

Consulting Librarians Group in cooperation with MGT of America, Inc. for the Library of Virginia. [2001]. *Community Analysis Methods and Evaluative Options: The CAMEO Handbook*. [Homepage of the Library of Virginia], [Online]. Available: http://www .lva.lib.va.us/ldnd/cameo/toc.htm (and linked pages) [Accessed September 26, 2001].

Coursen, Derek. 1996. "Community Analysis Data Resources." *The Unabashed Librarian*, no. 99: 11–12.

D'Elia, George. 1980. "The Development and Testing of a Conceptual Model of Public Library User Behavior." *Library Quarterly* 50, no. 4 (October): 410–30.

Delin, Catherine R., Peter S. Delin, and Laura Cram. 1995. "Patterns and Preferences in Recreational Reading." *Australian Library Journal* 44, no. 3 (August): 119–31.

Duncan, Patricia W., and William F. Goggin. 1982. "A Profile of the Lifetime Reader: Implications for Instruction and Resource Utilization." Paper presented at the 26th College Reading Association Annual Conference, Philadelphia, October 28. ERIC ED223994.

Endo, H. 1992. "The Number of Registered Borrowers in Public Libraries." *Toshokan Zasshi* 86, no. 11 (November): 797.

Evans, G. Edward. 1992. "Needs Analysis and Collection Development Policies for Culturally Diverse Populations." *Collection Building* 11, no. 4: 16–27.

Faulkner, M. 1998. "Toy Libraries within Existing Library Services." *Play Matters* 17 (Spring): 7.

Filipczak, Bob. 1995. "Different Strokes: Learning Styles in the Classroom." *Training* 32, no. 3 (March): 43–48.

Flowers, Louise. 1995. "Non-users of the Upper Goulburn Library Service." *Australian Library Journal* 44, no. 2 (May): 67–85.

Gallup Organization. 1978. *Book Reading and Library Use: A Study of Habits and Perceptions.* Princeton, NJ: Gallup Organization.

———. 1999. *American Booksellers Yearly Report on Book Buying 1998.* Princeton, NJ: Gallup Organization.

"Gallup Poll Shows 66% of Adults are Library Users." 1998. *American Libraries* 29, no. 7 (August): 6.

Gibson, Catherine. 1998. " 'But We've Always Done It This Way!': Centralized Selection Five Years Later." In *Public Library Collection Development in the Information Age,* ed. Annabel K. Stephens, 33–40. New York: Haworth Press.

Gorman, Audrey J. 1997a. "The 15% Solution: Libraries and Learning Disabilities." *American Libraries* 28, no. 1 (January): 52–54.

———. 1997b. "The 15% Solution: Kids with LD Can't Wait." *American Libraries* 28, no. 6 (June/July): 97–98.

"Grant Me the Serenity . . . The Serenity Prayer." [2001]. [Homepage of Open Mind], [Online]. Available: http://www.open-mind.org/Serenity.htm [Accessed September 26, 2001].

Halldorsson, Egill A., and Marjorie E. Murfin. 1977. "The Performance of Professionals and Nonprofessionals in the Reference Interview." *College and Research Libraries* 38, no. 5 (September): 385–95.

Heavy Book Borrowers: A Report of the Leisure Habits of Key Library Users. 1996. London: Book Marketing Limited.

Hoflack, M. 1999. "De openbare bibliotheek: kosteloos? [Public libraries—priceless?]" *Bibliotheek en Archiefgids* 75, no. 5: 191–94.

Hole, Carol. 1990. "Click! The Feminization of the Public Library." *American Libraries* 21, no. 11 (December): 1076–79.

"Indiana Libraries Change Lives." 1994. *Indiana Libraries* 13, no. 1: 1–45.

Kaufman, Roger, and Fenwick English. 1979. *Needs Assessment.* Englewood Cliffs, NJ: Educational Technology Publications.

Kim, Choong Han, and Robert David Little. 1987. *Public Library Users and Uses: A Market Research Handbook.* Metuchen, NJ: Scarecrow Press.

Lamme, Linda, and Pat Olmsted. 1977. "Family Reading Habits and Children's Progress in Reading." Paper presented at the Annual Meeting of the International Reading Association, Miami Beach, Florida, May 2–6. ERIC ED138963.

Lange, Janet M. 1987/1988. "Public Library Users, Nonusers, and Type of Library Use." *Public Library Quarterly* 8, nos. 1/2: 49–67.

Logan, Rochelle. 2000. "Ready, Set, Plan! Community Analysis Help Online." *Public Libraries* 39, no. 4 (July/August): 220–23.

Louizides, Susan M. 1993. "The Effect of Reading Aloud on a Child's Reading for Pleasure after Entering School." Master's research paper, Kean College of New Jersey. ERIC ED355482.

Lucas, Linda. 1982. "Reading Interests, Life Interests, and Life-style." *Public Library Quarterly* 3, no. 4 (Winter): 11–18.

Lynch, Mary Jo. 1997. "Using Public Libraries: What Makes a Difference?" *American Libraries* 28, no. 10 (November): 64, 66.

Madden, Michael. 1979a. "Library User/Nonuser Lifestyles." *American Libraries* 10, no. 2 (February): 78–81.

———. 1979b. "Lifestyles of Library Users and Nonusers." *Occasional Paper* no. 137 of the University of Illinois Graduate School of Library Science.

Marchant, Maurice P. 1994. *Why Adults Use the Public Library: A Research Perspective.* Englewood, CO: Libraries Unlimited.

Matheny, Constance, and Ann Lockledge. 1986. "Finding the Road to Lifelong Reading." Paper presented at the Annual Meeting of the Southwest Regional Conference of the International Reading Association, January 30–February 1. ERIC ED266444.

Mazmanian, Adam. 1996. "Library Use Up, Says Magazine Poll." *Library Journal* 121, no. 2 (February 1): 18–19.

Mellon, Constance A. 1986. "Library Anxiety: A Grounded Theory and Its Development." *College and Research Libraries* 47, no. 2 (March): 160–65.

———. 1988. "Attitudes: The Forgotten Dimension in Library Instruction." *Library Journal* 113, no. 14 (September 1): 137–39.

"NEA Study Finds 56% of Americans Claim to Read Some Literature." 1989. *Publishers Weekly* 236, no. 8 (August 25): 9–10.

NFO Research, Inc. 1990. *Final Report: Reading Rainbow Study.* Technical Report. Battle Creek, MI: Kellogg Foundation. ERIC ED331027.

Northern Illinois University's Public Opinion Laboratory. 1995. *Park Ridge Public Library: Report from Community Survey.* DeKalb: Northern Illinois University's Public Opinion Laboratory.

Onwuegbuzie, Anthony J., and Qun G. Jiao. 1998. "The Relationship Between Library Anxiety and Learning Styles among Graduate Students: Implications for Library Instruction." *Library and Information Science Research* 20, no. 3: 235–49.

Palsdottir, A. 1998. "Vidhorf og lestur [Reading in Icelandic Families]." *Bokasafnid* 22 (April): 15–20.

Poller, Anna C. 1988. "Videogames as Public Library Material—A Theoretical Evaluation." *South African Journal of Library and Information Science* 56, no. 1: 38–43.

Powell, Ronald R., Margaret A. T. Taylor, and David L. McMillen. 1984. "Childhood Socialization: Its Effects on Adult Library Use and Adult Reading." *Library Quarterly* 54, no. 3 (July): 245–64.

Pratt, Allan D. 1998. "Questionable Assumptions." *Public Libraries* 37, no. 1 (January/February): 52–56.

Ramos, Francisco, and Stephen Krashen. 1998. "The Impact of One Trip to the Public Library: Making Books Available May be the Best Incentive for Reading." *Reading Teacher* 51, no. 7 (April): 614–15.

Razzano, Barbara Will. 1985. "Creating the Library Habit." *Library Journal* 110, no. 3 (February 15): 111–14.

"Results of Pratt Market Study Show Nonusers Not Willing to Try." 1987. *Library Journal* 112, no. 13 (August): 18.

Ribovich, Jerilyn K., and Lawrence Erickson. 1980. "A Study of Lifelong Reading with Implications for Instructional Programs." *Journal of Reading* 24, no. 1 (October): 20–26.

Robins, Gabriel. 1994–2001. "Good Quotations by Famous People." [Homepage of Gabriel Robins] [Online]. (Updated August 13, 2001). Available http://www.cs.virginia .edu/_robins/quotes.html [Accessed September 26, 2001].

Rodger, Eleanor Jo, et al. 2000. The Impacts of the Internet on Public Library Use: An Analysis of the Current Consumer Market for Library and Internet Services. [Homepage of the Urban Libraries Council], [Online]. (October). Available: http://www.urbanlibraries.org/pdfs/finalulc.pdf [Accessed September 26, 2001].

Ross, Catherine Sheldrick. 1991. "Readers' Advisory Services: New Directions." RQ 30, no. 4 (Summer): 503–18.

Rossman, Marlene L. 1997. *Multicultural Marketing*. New York: American Management Association.

Roy, Loriene. 1984. "Sources of Books for Adults in Eight Illinois Communities." *Illinois Library Statistical Report* 15 (November): 1–24.

Scheppke, Jim. 1994. "Who's Using the Public Library?" *Library Journal* 119, no. 17 (October 15): 35–37.

Sliz, Tari Marshall. 1996. "How Do Libraries Change Lives? Let Us Count the Ways!" *American Libraries* 27, no. 1 (January): 87–88, 90.

Smith, Courtney, Rebecca Constantino, and Stephen D. Krashen. 1997. "Differences in Print Environment for Children in Beverly Hills, Compton and Watts." *Emergency Librarian* 24, no. 4 (March/April): 8–9.

Sumsion, J. 1996. "Staying in the Top Flight." *Bookseller* no. 4745 (November 29): 20–22, 24, 26.

Thorsen, Jeanne. 1998. "Community Studies: Raising the Roof and Other Recommendations." In *Public Library Collection Development in the Information Age*, ed. Annabel K. Stephens, 5–13. New York: Haworth Press.

Totterdell, Barry, and Jean Bird. 1976. *The Effective Library: Report of the Hillingdon Project on Public Library Effectiveness*. London: Library Association.

Van House, Nancy A. 1983. "A Time Allocation Theory of Public Library Use." *Library and Information Science Research* 5, no. 4 (Winter): 365–84.

Vincent, John C. 1999. "Are Your Users Just Like You?" *Public Library Journal* 14, no. 4 (Winter): 93, 95.

Wallace, Linda. 1994. "Libraries and Kids: Telling the Story." *The Bottom Line* 7, no. 3–4 (Winter/Spring): 55–62.

Welch, Alicia J., and Christine N. Donohue. 1994. "Awareness, Use, and Satisfaction with Public Libraries: A Summary of Connecticut Community Surveys." *Public Libraries* 33, no. 3 (May-June): 149–52.

Willits, Harold W., and Fern K. Willits.1991. "Rural Reading Behavior and Library Usage: Findings from a Pennsylvania Survey." *Rural Libraries* 11, no. 1: 25–37.

Wittig, Glenn R. 1991. "Some Characteristics of Mississippi Adult Library Users." *Public Libraries* 30, no. 1 (January/February): 25–32.

Wojciechowski, Jacek. 1996. "Belles-Lettres in the Library." *Public Libraries* 35, no. 2 (March/April): 121–23.

Wurman, Richard Saul. 1989. *Information Anxiety*. New York: Doubleday.

Zill, Nicholas, and Marianee Winglee. 1989. "Literature Reading in the United States: Data from National Surveys and Their Policy Implications." *Book Research Quarterly* 5, no. 1 (Spring): 24–58.

Zweizig, Douglas. 1973. "Predicting Amount of Library Use: An Empirical Study of the Role of the Public Library in the Life of the Adult Public." Ph.D. diss., Syracuse University.

———. 1992. "Community Analysis." In *Keeping the Book$: Public Library Financial Practices*, eds. Jane B. Robbins and Douglas L. Zweizig for the Urban Libraries Council, 225–38. Fort Atkinson, WI: Highsmith.

CREATING
YOUR MASTER PLAN

> "If a man knows not what harbor he seeks, any wind is the right wind"— Seneca ("Quoteland" 1997–2001).

We are heartened by the fact that of the 116 public libraries responding to an American Library Association (ALA) survey, 79 percent had long-range "strategic plans" ("ALA PR/Communication" 1999; "1998 ALA/PR" 1999). We suspect that the major elements influencing this widespread adoption parallel those Pungitore (1993) found during a qualitative study of nine small public library systems:

Exposure to knowledge about planning and its benefits (either via workshops or other libraries that have successfully used formal planning processes)[1]

The philosophy or inclination of the library director

A local funding agency or state library requirement for planning. For example, most state library agencies in the United States encourage public libraries to use either the process recommended by the Public Library Association or a general strategic planning process (Smith 1994)

A problematic situation at the local level, such as a sharp plunge in revenues

The perceived flexibility of the planning process under consideration

The same ALA study showed that only 28.4 percent of these public libraries developed "marketing" plans, valuable for their identification of

- target markets the library will serve;
- collections and services on which marketing efforts will focus;
- specific marketing tasks and responsibilities;
- deadlines for accomplishing these;
- resources allocated for each; and
- techniques to measure the marketing tasks' effectiveness.[2]

Figure 3.1, pages 35-38, presents an excerpt from one such plan, created by the Durham County (North Carolina) Library in 1999.

This smaller percentage of "marketing plans" may well indicate that a number of librarians are trying what we recommend here: avoiding unnecessary duplication and optimizing resources, particularly precious staff hours, by integrating their marketing and strategic plans. Such integration can result in fine-level clarification of mission and goals, united efforts to determine user needs, and the considered establishment of quality programs to meet these. Integration also helps promote high levels of institutional self-awareness, effective communication, and honing of everyday operations (Sutton 1993). This synchronicity allows such plans to be fine tuned as often as annually, thus encouraging flexibility in meeting changing needs. Moreover, strategic planning and management (SPM) plans combine philosophy with carefully designed concrete actions, which may help overcome one criticism of "strategic planning" processes, that they emphasize theoretical process at the expense of product (see, e.g., Ammons 1995).

This chapter provides an SPM model that combines and builds upon elements that Weingand (1999) and the Public Library Association (PLA) (Nelson 2001) advocate. Rather than delving into aspects of the planning process thoroughly covered by these publications, we encourage librarians to refer to them directly to gain a deep comprehension of the process. The Weingand title, *Marketing/Planning Library and Information Services*, is particularly useful in exploring theoretical aspects and basic concepts, whereas the PLA's *The New Planning for Results* (Nelson 2001) provides guidance on organizing and carrying out the endeavor. It may also be helpful to consult Hayes and Walter (1996), who provide a broad conceptual framework and suggestions for assessing the library's strategic position within the community.

We assume here that libraries share similarities that allow them to use a broadly modeled framework for planning. However, they also have unique characteristics and conditions—linked to the individuals and communities served; the library's current resources, culture, and market position; the staff and board members at each institution; local politics; and so forth—that will unfold along with the planning process.

MARKET SUMMARY:

The Durham County Public Library provides library services to Durham City and County. The estimated population of Durham is 211,708, with a projected population for 2010 of 245,256. Services are available to all of the people of the community, a population which is characterized by wide diversity in age, ethnicity, education, and economic status.

Changes in the market affecting library services include population increases, especially in outlying areas; growth in the number of children attending charter schools and home schools; increasing numbers of retirees; and a growing Hispanic population.

PRODUCT DEFINITION (Mission Statement):

The Durham County Library is dedicated above all to a standard of excellence in offering books, information and other traditional and innovative library services to the residents of Durham County through its network of libraries that are conveniently located and easy to use. The library will provide residents with highly professional and cost-effective service that will help its users continue learning, enjoy reading, and enhance the quality of their lives.

COMPETITION

The major competitors for the library's market are local bookstores and Internet services. Nonprofits and other county agencies serve as competitors in regards to funding and in some services, particularly those related to information and referral.

POSITIONING

A clear goal for positioning the library in the forefront of the community is to strengthen its position as a key component of education. It is imperative that the community also has a clear understanding of the library's role as provider of information. The fact that the library is the only institution in Durham to provide free access to materials and information for all individuals must be continually reiterated. As the library positions itself in the forefront of the community, it will continue to provide a regular program of activities and services, offered collaboratively with other agencies which promotes reading and literacy. The library's public image will hinge on our ability to reinforce its unique and essential services to all members of the community.

FIGURE 3.1. A Selection from the Durham County (North Carolina) Library's Marketing Plan. Reprinted, in modified form, with permission from the Durham County Library.

(Fig. 3.1 continues on page 36.)

FIG. 3.1—*Continued*

MARKETING GOALS

<u>Service Excellence:</u> The Library is recognized by the Durham community as an institution which values service excellence, innovation, and resourcefulness and is responsive to the needs of a diverse population.

<u>Technology:</u> The Library is recognized as a community center for public Internet access and as the community institution with primary responsibility for collecting, linking, organizing, and distributing local information on-line.

<u>Public Presence:</u> The Durham community views the Library as an exciting and essential resource for information and life-long learning.

<u>Staff:</u> Library staff are recognized as leaders in education and information, guiding the community with their ever-expanding knowledge, skills, and commitment to excellence.

<u>Facilities:</u> Durham citizens fully utilize the library facilities serving their neighborhoods and view these facilities as essential centers of neighborhood activity and gateways to the world of information.

<u>Funding and Governmental Relationships:</u> Public officials and private individuals understand the value of the Library as a key component of the educational and informational infrastructure of the community and support the Library with public appropriations and private donations sufficient to sustain the Library's continued growth.

Outcome: The public will know of the location and services of the library service outlet closest to their home and place of work.

Strategies

Utilize media resources to promote library services.

New borrowers will be provided with information on library services and facilities.

Evaluation: Increase in borrowers, door count, and circulation. Community surveys demonstrate increased awareness.

FY00

Action Goal: Promote existing facilities and services while highlighting the needs for library facility improvement.

Objective: Increased awareness of patrons for library services is demonstrated in usage.

Objective: Media resources highlight need for facility improvement on a regular basis.

Objective: The Public supports library facility improvement through letters to the editor and County Commissioners.

Action Steps:

➢ Highlight special collections in branch libraries
    ongoing

➢ Target mailings to populations in library service areas
    ongoing

➢ Develop summary of library facility needs
    April 99

➢ Newspaper story highlighting library facility needs
    May 99

➢ Promotional materials at each location focusing on improvements
    May 99

➢ CIP summary plan available for distribution
    May–June 99

➢ Open houses at branches - North Durham anniversary celebration
    July 99

Outcome: Durham's citizens communicate regularly and positively to funding officials regarding the value of library services

Strategies:

Actively involve library staff in encouraging patrons to express appreciation for library services to County Commissioners

Utilize patron suggestions, collected systemwide, to identify patrons willing to write letters of support

Evaluation methods: Track amount of publicity; track feedback from County Commissioners; Level of Commissioner support of library programs and budget

FY00

Action Goal: Develop a systematic and ongoing program encouraging individuals to contact funding officials in support of library services and development

Objectives: At least 2 patrons each month agree to contact funding officials to solicit their support of library services and the (CIP).

(Fig. 3.1 continues on page 38.)

FIG. 3.1—*Continued*

Action Steps:

➢Update contact sheet for funding officials - research use of e-mail for contacting Commissioners
    April 99

➢Update mailing list for state legislators
    April 99

➢Keep library's home page updated and publicize library's Web site address. Compile information packets for community
    ongoing

➢Work with library staff to identify community supporters
    ongoing

➢Work with Development Officer to hold small gatherings for community champions
    April–Aug. 99

➢Hold community meetings at each library to educate supporters
    April–August 99

➢Publicize in at least two library newsletters during the fiscal year requests for community support
    ongoing

➢Speak to a minimum of 4 community groups and encourage their support through phone calls and letters
    ongoing

➢Attend Library Legislative Day in Raleigh; encourage attendance by Board and Friends members.
    May

➢Encourage Board and Friends members to write Legislators regarding the library's legislative program, provide sample letters
    May–July

Evaluation methods: Response from funding officials in regards to library funding, track number of hits on the Web site

The SPM process has three major phases:

Setting the stage—choosing the players, instruments, and performance date

The composition itself—developing themes and supporting goals, objectives, and strategies

Performance and review—implementation and evaluation

SETTING THE STAGE: PARTICIPANTS, RESOURCES, AND DEADLINES

Initially, board members, administrators, and other library leaders need to select planning committee members, allocate resources, and establish major deadlines for the process. A carefully chosen committee will include members with varied traits, backgrounds, talents, and viewpoints without becoming too large to operate effectively.

Figure 3.2, page 40, shows our recommendations for characteristics of the SMP chair and members.

In addition, we suggest that committee members have varied personal and personality styles, such as innovators, detail-oriented people, those with highly developed emotional quotients, and judicious skeptics. Presumably the library will draw a fair proportion of committee members from individuals active in local political or civic affairs, business or educational endeavors, and religious and social groups, as well as individuals working or volunteering in a variety of settings. We also encourage committee members to solicit and judiciously consider input from other constituency groups not directly represented, including those in the hard sciences, a contingency frequently left out of library work groups. Figure 3.3, pages 41–42, lists stakeholder groups common to public libraries and the communities they serve.

Up-to-Date Knowledge Of:	The Ability and Willingness to:
The individual residents and constituency groups of a community.	Consider the needs of the many and few and establish numerous strong, cooperative relationships for the benefit of the library.
The talents and skills of staff, board members, volunteers, Friends, and other library advocates, as well as other resources and capabilities of this institution and libraries in general.	Actively commit a significant amount of time, energy, and other resources to the planning process and delegate duties judiciously among committee members and staff.
Principles of library and information science and other disciplines dedicated to collecting, organizing, and retrieving ideas and information.	Collect, screen for accuracy, organize, and analyze information for decision-making purposes.
Principles of leadership and of verbal and nonverbal communication.	Listen and communicate clearly, paying attention to the social aspects of these transactions.
Principles of innovation and intrapreneurial behavior.	Act for the benefit of all by innovating or recognizing the innovations of others.
Both the generalities and fine points of local, state, national, and international legal mandates and of professional codes of ethics that the library must meet.	Make fine distinctions where these laws and codes differ (e.g., a public library may be located in a state outlawing consensual sex between adults of the same gender, yet include in its collection works that present a variety of views on homosexuality).

FIGURE 3.2. Desired Characteristics of SPM Members.

Those who fund libraries, including

- local governing bodies (from which most public libraries in the United States receive their major support) and the taxpayers who make this support possible;
- regional or federal agencies that contribute directly to library support;
- corporations, foundations, and granting agencies that provide money or other contributions to support special programs and services; and
- individuals who give donations of all sizes to the library.

Service recipients, current and future, including

- individual residents of the community;
- various target market groups;
- those who pay non-resident fees for service;
- those who participate in reciprocal borrowing programs between libraries;
- those who benefit from service provided via e-mail, telephone, or interlibrary loan; and
- future generations.

Watchdog groups, including

- funding agency representatives,
- political party representatives,
- members of the media,
- advocacy groups, and
- representatives of employee unions.

Those who work in or on behalf of the library, including

- administrators,
- employees,
- trustees,
- volunteers, and
- members of Friends groups.

FIGURE 3.3. The Constituency Groups of Public Libraries.

(Fig. 3.3 continues on page 42.)

FIG. 3.3—*Continued*

> **Those who consistently refer individuals to the library, including**
>
> - librarians and other employees of academic, corporate, public, school, special, and virtual libraries;
> - teachers;
> - parents, friends, and acquaintances of potential patrons;
> - employers; and
> - representatives of social service and other governmental agencies.
>
> **Designers, vendors, and creators of**
>
> - computer equipment,
> - software,
> - office supplies,
> - furniture, and
> - books and other materials libraries collect.

To ease fears related to change, encourage flexibility and creativity, help SPM members comprehend complex implementation issues, and bolster staff support, we suggest that the committee include numerous staff members from various departments—both professional and paraprofessional, full-time and part-time.

Choosing the right members for the committee provides a firm foundation for the work to follow. For additional suggestions about how to enhance group performance, see Weingand (1999), Shapiro (1996), Schlegel (1993), and Waddell (1990).

As a second step, library leaders must determine what resources they will provide the committee. At a minimum, the SPM efforts will require clerical and photocopying support and meeting space. We also recommend that the library provide access to computers, e-mail, and Internet connections when possible and designate at least one member of the reference staff to support committee research needs.

Finally, the managers must set overall deadlines for developing the groundwork, implementation plans, and evaluation efforts. Presumably the initial composition process will be fairly in-depth and flow quickly without unreasonably taxing those donating their time. The PLA suggests committing four to five months to developing the plan, enough time to create something valuable but a short enough period to reserve energy for actually implementing the plan (Nelson 2001).

DEVELOPING THEMES

As Chapter 2 notes, effective library decision-makers make choices about library services and collections based on an understanding of community needs and desires.[3] Therefore, the SPM committee can begin by considering personal impressions of the community as well as relevant hard data gathered via the analysis techniques discussed in Chapter 2. Vision exercises that require thinking about both the current and exemplary states of the community and means of getting there can reveal possibilities and build enthusiasm for the work ahead. Such exercises must consider a number of different factors potentially affecting library operations, including legal and humanitarian mandates and a variety of both external and internal environmental forces.

Legal and Humanitarian Mandates

The committee will, of course, work within the constraints of legal and humanitarian mandates, including local, regional, and national legislation (from that which created the library to national and international copyright provisions), union or vendor contracts, various codes of ethics, and so forth. Early identification of these will increase the likelihood of meeting them.

To decrease the cost of assembling relevant data, we suggest that librarians work with advisory agencies, including state or regional libraries and library associations, to gather directives applicable to many libraries into a single, easily accessible source. For example, the *Bowker Annual* lists pertinent legislation in a friendly format, as does, on a regional basis, the Illinois State Library's publication *Illinois Libraries*.

External Environmental Forces

Major external environmental forces and trends (often overlapping) may have an impact at a local, regional, national, or international level and include political, economic, competitive or collaborative, social/cultural, and technological/scientific factors.

Political

The beliefs of elected officials and the sentiments of the voting public can greatly affect both library budgets and autonomy of efforts, including recruiting staff, building collections, and designing services. Libraries can influence this force. For example, the record of the Public Library Directors Association in North Carolina indicates that combined lobbying forums can help keep legislator recognition of and funding for library services high. Such forums also help keep library boards and staffs aware of legislative and public expectations for institutional accountability.

Economic

The strength of the economy often influences library funding. It may also affect library use, influencing the amount of leisure time available to individuals, the amount of money they have to spend on purchasing rather than borrowing materials, and their desire to seek additional education. Economic forces will also affect the amount of pay and benefits that libraries must offer to attract and keep high-quality workers.

Competitive or Collaborative

Other entities may compete or collaborate with the library, including

- both virtual and brick-and-mortar stores offering books, DVDs, videos, e-books, software, serials, CDs, and other media (Consider, for example, that online used bookstores such as www.half.com often offer last year's bestsellers for a cost of as little as 75 cents per book, plus shipping charges.);
- other libraries, of all types and sizes and in all geographic regions;
- Internet service providers that allow individuals to access a range of resources (including those on the library's Web site) from home or work;
- institutions and individuals who compile, organize, and distribute information on the Internet;
- both for-profit and nonprofit institutions that offer computer access and training;
- individual and organizational collectors of print and audiovisual materials willing to lend these (e.g., teachers, hobbyists, churches);
- those that serve the same target markets as libraries, like the Campfire Girls, the Lions Club, the United Way, and the local garden club; and
- other individuals, businesses, associations, agencies, organizations, and clubs that may be willing to donate time, money, or expertise to help provide top-quality library services.

Planners who are aware of these entities and individuals can seek ways to work with them.

Social/Cultural

The social and cultural activities and values in a community affect expectations of what the library can offer and its manner of presentation. In addition, broad trends, such as globalization, increased casualness, civil rights movements, and changes in career patterns, also affect both possibilities and expectations for library collections and services.

Technological/Scientific

The continued fast pace of technological and scientific change presents a challenge for libraries. Committee members will want to explore how the library and others in the community currently use technology and the library's physical and financial ability to support new technologies, including providing the necessary training for staff members and patrons. The committee will also need to address legal issues related to technology, including privacy and copyright.[4] Keeping up with scientific advances will also help minimize such problems as the purchase of collection-related materials based on inaccurate scientific principles.

Internal Environmental Forces

Among the elements that SPM members must consider within the internal environment are library staff members, other resources, current performance, and organizational structure and culture.

People

In many ways, libraries can only perform as well as the individuals who work for them. SPM committee members will need to identify the talents, backgrounds, and attitudes of library employees, board members, and volunteers as well as the work they do. And because even skilled, efficient individuals can only do so much, the committee will also need to know the numbers of people in each group and how many hours per week they can dedicate to the library. Finally, the committee must consider by what means they can encourage continuing development of these individuals, such as sponsoring in-house continuing education programs.

Other Resources

In particular, we recommend that committee members be given useful specifics related to the state of regular and supplemental funds, collections, connections, technologies, and facilities.

Performance

Among the past and possible performance measures that will be useful are

- the statistical data the library collects on circulation, in-house use, visits to the library's Web pages, program attendance, and so forth;
- comparable objective measures of performance from top-quality libraries with similar resource levels;
- professional standards for outstanding service as outlined in documents issued by regional, national, and international library organizations; and

- qualitative measures of patron satisfaction, presumably collected via surveys or comment boxes.

Organizational Structure and Culture

Providing an organizational chart that outlines key departmental functions and sharing information about the library's culture (for example, through discussions with staff members at varying levels of the organization or an anonymous survey of all employees and volunteers) can help committee members better comprehend the work environment. For the SPM process to succeed, committee members must address such factors as the degree of teamwork, the influence of key employees in the library (regardless of their position), the amount of freedom and decision-making ability employees have, and their feelings about change.

The culture is also potentially influenced by the service orientation a library has exhibited in the past, which can guide decision making and influence the manner in which staff interact with patrons. Possible orientations include sales, production, product, shallow marketing, or societal-marketing.

Production (Service) Orientations:
The "Minute Waltz" in 53 Seconds!

An organization with a production orientation strives to improve the efficiency of producing or distributing its goods or services (Kotler and Armstrong 1999). A pure production orientation could err by valuing efficiency more than customer convenience or satisfaction. For example, checking e-mail reference questions only once each day is efficient but gives short shrift to those who contact the library via computer as opposed to in person or on the phone. Hyman (1999) suggests that libraries frequently enact such policies because of a perception that relatively new services and formats are "extras" that don't merit the same type of commitment, support, and promotion, that more established services do.

Sales (Service) Orientations: We Don't Have Any Metallica CDs,
But Surely You'd Like This Streisand!

An organization with a predominant sales orientation defines its major task as stimulating the interest of potential consumers in the organization's existing offerings (Kotler 1982). The belief that customers who do not demand the organization's products simply lack awareness could prompt the organization to focus on this rather than considering whether the product doesn't meet the customer's needs in some significant way.

Certainly, promotion can increase use of library collections, as Chapters 7 and 10 discuss. Indeed, good publicity presents "the case for the merits of a cause or an institution so cogently, so winningly, so irresistibly, that the hearts and minds of men will be captured" (Rice 1972, 3–4). But promotional campaigns that entice patrons to try poorly designed services or collections, or ones poorly matched to patron needs, may leave patrons dissatisfied enough so that they question the library's credibility and distrust future messages (Corrick 1983).

A Product Orientation: High Quality or Else!

A strict product orientation stresses generating or distributing products the organization deems beneficial (Kotler 1982). The focus on "quality" products, as determined by standards other than how well they suit "the customer's purpose" (Van Loo 1984), echoes throughout public library history. For example, a librarian writing in 1903 advocated attempting to improve patrons' reading tastes by removing all poor-quality materials from the collection, substituting high-quality ones, and habituating readers to using the latter by emphasizing typographic attractiveness and prominent display of titles (Bloom 1976).

A product orientation in collection development supports purchasing only items of high quality, what Merritt (1979) has dubbed the "give-them-what-they-should-have" theory of book selection. Advocates claim that focusing entirely on quality book selection helps the library accomplish its educational mission in at least three ways (Berry 1990; Bob 1982; Dessauer 1980; Kister 1971). First, the library provides works of permanent value, thus introducing patrons to the delights of superior literature and the intricacies of a variety of nonfiction topics. Second, the library provides quality materials for a wide range of people, encouraging the development of diverse points of view and a public commitment to intellectual freedom, a basic tenet of the democratic ideal. Finally, the library serves as a depository of civilization that will preserve knowledge for the future. These arguments have appeal as long as librarians do not embrace an overly paternalistic selection philosophy.

A Shallow Marketing Orientation: The Tyranny of the Majority

Although a shallow marketing orientation also has an established place in library history, it is predicated on the belief that all selections must be based on customer preferences, a theory described in some detail by McColvin (1925). Charles Cutter, in an address to the Western Massachusetts Library Club in 1901, thoughtfully posed the query "Should libraries buy only the best books or the best books that people will read?" His response? "Of course, we are to buy the best books. . . . But equally, of course, this means the best books for the particular library in question, and that is the same as the best books that its people will use; for an unused book is not even good . . . the best books to satisfy the just demands of our clients for amusement and knowledge and mental stimulus and spiritual inspiration. The library should be a practical thing to be used, not an ideal to be admired" (1901, 101).

Proponents of the demand or "give-them-what-they-want" theory of collection development advance two other major reasons for following it. First, as a tax-supported institution, the public library should have something for everyone (e.g., Merritt 1964). Second, libraries that emphasize user demand will meet patron needs and wants more successfully and gain higher overall use and a broader-based clientele, an argument that has some hard data to support it (e.g., Sullivan 2000).

Critics accuse libraries with predominantly demand-driven collection development practices of becoming today's "elitist authoritarians" who serve only middle-class popular fiction readers (Spiegler 1980), surrender responsibility for book selection to the publisher's publicity experts who create demand (Bob 1982), equate circulation counts with the library's goals (Dessauer 1980), and reduce collection quality and depth (Akey 1990).

A Societal-Marketing Orientation: A Rich Medley

A societal-marketing orientation combines the positive aspects of the first four orientations. This approach requires that librarians identify the needs and wants of their customers and satisfy these, maintaining or enhancing the well-being of both patron and society (Kotler and Armstrong 1999). To balance the immediate demands of their users with the long-term needs of society, librarians employ professional expertise, drawing on their comprehension of community needs and potential ways to meet these, rather than merely providing specific items requested by members of the general public (Cramer 2000). As Wilson (2000) notes, "To be successful, we need to be essential to people and stay ahead of client expectations. Library managers need to show vision and leadership on behalf of their clients, rather than simply respond to client feedback"

Both individual librarians and organizations have repeatedly discussed the library's responsibility toward society as a whole. For example, the Public Library Association has avowed,

> Free access to ideas and information, a prerequisite to the existence of a responsible citizenship, is as fundamental to America as are the principles of freedom and equality and individual rights. This access is also fundamental to our social, political and cultural systems, . . . Access to information and the recorded wisdom and experience of others has long been held a requirement for achieving personal equality, and for improving the quality of life and thought in the daily activities and relationships of individuals. (1982, 1)

Indeed, municipalities, counties, and regions fund public libraries with this goal in mind. We recommend a focus on the societal-marketing approach throughout this book.

Focus: Service Responses and Mission Statement

To avoid the temptation to try to be all things to all people, we recommend that the SPM committee follow the recommendations made by the Public Library Association (Nelson 2001), identifying several service responses to emphasize to meet distinct community needs. Figure 3.4 lists the specific service responses outlined in *The New Planning for Results*.

Basic Literacy
   (may include other daily living skills in addition to reading)

Business and Career Information

Commons (providing shared, public spaces)

Community Referral

Consumer Information

Cultural Awareness
   (may include the predominant and minority cultures)

Current Topics and Titles

Formal Learning Support

General Information

Government Information

Information Literacy

Lifelong Learning

Local History and Genealogy

FIGURE 3.4. List of Service Responses Described in the Public Library Association Planning Process, *The New Planning for Results* (Nelson 2001).

Such a focus will be useful at this stage of the process in which the SPM committee either reviews or re-creates a library mission statement that focuses on central, enduring, and distinctive aspects of service and expresses the beliefs, values, and culture of the organization and the needs the library exists to meet. Among the numerous sources that discuss composing a mission statement, we recommend Abrahams (1995), Nelson (2001), and Weingand (1999).

THE COMPOSITION ITSELF: IDENTIFICATION OF GOALS, OBJECTIVES, AND STRATEGIES

The selected service responses will suggest a very broad market the library will pursue; for example, the formal learning support response seeks to assist enrolled students. Goal development carries this one step further, requiring thinking about specific segments of the population to be served. The committee writes goals, keeping in mind the environmental forces identified previously, then submits these, in due course, to the staff for review and the board for approval. Building on the work of Bunge (1984), figure 3.5, page 50, briefly defines a goal and presents two sample goals for a business and career information response.

Goals: Clear, general statements of what the library intends to accomplish.

Sample Collection-Related Goals for a Business and Career Information Service Response:

> To build an outstanding management collection to help develop the supervisory skills and ideas of local business people.

> To cultivate a multimedia collection capable of meeting the needs of a diverse group of job seekers.

FIGURE 3.5. Goals—Definition and Examples.

Market Segmentation

Market segmentation is the further subdivision of an audience into smaller target markets, or groups that share common characteristics (e.g., motivations and needs) affecting the ways that they will use library products and services. Thus, kindergartners and high school music students could be two target markets that a library with a formal learning support response wants to serve.

Market segmentation offers many benefits. Libraries can more cost-effectively design services and collections for smaller numbers of user groups that share common characteristics than for thousands of unique individuals. Segmentation also encourages analysis of target markets in some depth. The resultant understanding of patron requirements can help librarians build collections better able to meet user needs, raising service quality. Segmenting the market can also provide insight into the benefits that various target markets receive from using the library and help identify clear channels for dissemination of information to the desired audiences.

To help predict use of their resources by the target market, libraries may define various market segments by

- listing characteristics of community residents that might affect use;
- determining the size and composition of groups that possess those characteristics; then
- noting the collection-related needs of each group, as well as the benefits it might receive from using the library's collection.

Although markets can be segmented using any characteristic that identifies or defines actual or potential customers, four broad groups of factors clearly are associated with use of a library's collection.

- *Demographic characteristics* include such qualities as age, sex, income level, ethnic background, occupation, and educational level.

- *Geographic characteristics,* such as the ability to travel (by foot or vehicle) to a library facility, the distance that must be traveled, and the residential or nonresidential status of the potential patron, may also influence a person's library use.

- *Behavioral characteristics* describe the extent and type of a patron's past use of the library in general or of specific collections and services within it. For example, Massey (1976) uses five different market groupings: those who 1) use the library for help completing a specific project; 2) routinely need specific information or materials; 3) want new materials to feed personal fantasies; 4) infrequently use the library, have little knowledge of services, and often feel intimidated by staff; and 5) seek social contact.

- *Psychographic characteristics* relate to socioeconomic class, lifestyle, personality, interests, and opinions. Libraries may find it particularly useful to segment their markets by family and life cycle characteristics. Consider, for example, the different collection-related needs of single-parent families with small children, dual-parent families with teenagers, and elderly couples with grown children.

After listing relevant characteristics of potential target markets, the library must determine the size and composition of each group. Professionals can readily do this using census records, user studies, and other data the library gathered during the community analysis stage of the planning process.

At this point, the SPM committee must decide how many market segments can be feasibly served. Four major factors will influence this decision. First, the *diversity* of the target markets influences the degree to which the marketing strategy can be focused. A model target market contains persons with common interests, preferences, and needs that the library can fill. For example, it will be easier to devise effective marketing strategies to reach high school English teachers than to devise one for persons with last names ending in "man."

The *size* of the target market is the second factor. A library will not find it fiscally feasible to devise separate marketing strategies for groups of 10 recent Polish immigrants, 15 Chinese students, 20 Central American exiles, and so forth. It could, however, combine target groups too small to serve economically by identifying common characteristics or interests. Thus, it could develop a marketing program to reach 500 newly arrived foreign-born residents, who share needs for information about English as a second-language, local laws and customs, and procedures for becoming a citizen.

Librarians will also need to consider the *viability* of reaching the target market. At least two major factors affect viability: the extent and type of resources available for this effort and the willingness of the target market to be served by the library. When a library cannot directly devote resources to a selected target market, it may consider reaching members through a secondary market, which includes individuals who can "help get the word out to others and perhaps provide support for new programs and services" (Kies 1987, 47). Public libraries in Maryland took this approach, publicizing health information resources to school nurses, health clinics, and other individuals and agencies that served members of their primary target market (Paznekas and Stephan 1995).

Finally, librarians will want to consider the possible *humanitarian and/or public relations advantages* of choosing one target market over another. For example, a library may decide to serve target markets that would otherwise have little access to library services, such as residents of area nursing homes or homeless shelters for people of all ages. It could also decide to emphasize service to the city council to help keep lines of communication with this vital funding body open. Using technology to help identify and define market segments within its community, the Lakewood (Ohio) Public Library has very successfully used this process, greatly increasing its number of Generation X patrons (St. Lifer 2001).

Development and Implementation of Action Strategies

Staff members will assume primary responsibility for developing objectives (measurable targets of action to be attained within a given time frame) and strategies (specific actions designed to achieve an objective) to support the approved goals, although some SPM committee members may continue to serve in an ad hoc oversight role.

Planners must be particularly aware of staff roles and attitudes at this stage, when fears, anxieties, resource concerns, and other barriers to change can readily influence the harmony or discord of the composition. Relevant research suggests that plans are highly likely to succeed when

- individuals assume personal responsibility for collecting and summarizing information and knowledge about a specific area (Stewart and Stasser 1995);

- administrators concentrate on keeping communication flowing and obtaining key resources (Rodriguez and Hickson 1995); and

- technical staff are involved in day-to-day implementation issues (Rodriquez and Hickson 1995; Sutton 1993).[5]

The Marketing Mix: A Four-Part Harmony

In developing objectives and strategies, staff will need to consider the "Four Ps," a quartet of elements that potentially influence use of and satisfaction with the collection: product, price, place, and promotion. A cohesive composition stressing superior service judiciously mixes all of these:

- Product questions focus on the collection itself and the use of the same.

- Price questions focus on the individual monetary, convenience, and psychological costs of use.

- Place considerations may be both external (e.g., geographic location of branch libraries and electronic access) and internal (e.g., the layout of collections and placement of special displays).

- Promotion questions address the extent and accuracy of patron awareness of collection resources and the effectiveness of various promotional techniques.

With a goal of building an outstanding management collection to allow local business people to improve their supervisory skills, librarians might consider the following questions. What (not just money!) keeps our management collection from being great? What elements are absent (e.g., access to an extensive, full-text online business index; management topics on audiobook) or overly prevalent (e.g., works that focus on a single solution to a complex problem)? How would changing the product itself affect use? What subject experts outside the library (e.g., a consultant who specializes in training and development activities for business people) might work with staff to identify potential holes in the collection and/or directions for proceeding? How much cooperation exists between those who select books, magazines, and computer and audiovisual resources for this collection? What changes can we make in selection and other policies to keep use high? How much do members of the target market know about the types of materials in this collection? What media and techniques could we use to increase awareness levels? Which other target groups and individuals use the collection, and which don't? What elements beyond the library's control (e.g., the availability of a collection at the business itself) have a significant impact on use? Would changing the distribution of the collection help (e.g., rotating standard management titles between branches, ensuring remote access to relevant online resources, or offering a drive-through window to pick up reserved items)? An implementation plan based on these questions might include the objectives and strategies shown in figure 3.6, pages 54–55.

(Text continues on page 56.)

Goal: To build an outstanding management collection to help develop the supervisory skills and ideas of local business people.

- *Objective:* By January 1 of the next year raise an additional $2,500 to allow access to an online management index.

  ✓ *Strategies:*

    Work with local realtors, the Chamber of Commerce, and a service club to raise $1,500 additional for management resources this fiscal year.

    Ask the Friends to donate $250 toward database fees.

    Solicit additional corporate donations of $750.

- *Objective:* Spend at least 90 percent of the current year's budget for circulating management materials on current best-selling works, award-winning titles, and other high-quality books, audiobooks, e-books, and videos. With the remainder, purchase replacement titles for damaged or lost works of continuing interest.

  ✓ *Strategies:*

    Check relevant sources, such as lists from library jobbers and amazon.com, to determine which management titles are in high demand.

    Solicit ideas for recommendations from members of area businesses and business organizations or associations.

    On a monthly basis, review lists of award winners and order those titles not already in the collection that will meet the needs of local users. Use precompiled lists of award winners, such as those featured on www.bn.com (the Barnes and Noble Web site), to help keep current.

    Regularly check standard library reviewing tools for relevant titles. Supplement this by scanning periodicals like *Business Week* to identify other relevant titles.

- *Objective:* Conduct annual evaluations of the management collection to ensure breadth and depth of coverage, currency, use, and user satisfaction.

  ✓ *Strategies:*

    Keep track of the percentage of new titles added in the management collection.

    Keep track of three measures of use for management materials: circulation, stock turnover rate, and relative use.

    Obtain a list of all management titles that have not circulated during the past year. Consider each for discard, retaining works that are still current, of high quality, in reasonable condition, or expected to have some continuing use over time.

FIGURE 3.6. Bringing Goals, Objectives, and Strategies Together: Sample Implementation Plan.

- *Objective:* Within the next year, expand the selector's knowledge of management works, ensuring that she can name at least 10 significant titles or authors in each of three subsections of the collection, briefly describing what makes them important.

  ✓ *Strategies:*

  Meet with at least two business leaders and business teachers to discuss what they seek in an outstanding management collection. Obtain a commitment from at least one individual to provide advice on the management collection for next year.

  Visit large bookstores at least three times to keep track of current best-selling and high-quality works and continued classics.

  Attend at least one workshop or seminar discussing management resources.

  Prepare bookmark noting outstanding management Web sites (to serve the dual purpose of increasing the selector's knowledge and assisting patrons).

- *Objective:* Increase the business community's awareness of this collection by 10 percent over the next one and one-half years.

  ✓ *Strategies:*

  Next month, and then again in 17 months, survey awareness levels of two target groups: Chamber of Commerce members and students in the nearby university's master of business administration program.

  Write a short column promoting services for the Chamber newsletter each month.

  Send e-mail messages to local business people, students, and organizations to inform them of additions to the management collection.

  Prepare targeted, annotated bibliographies of useful sources semiannually, distributing them via Chamber meetings, business teachers, and the library's Web site.

  Replace existing (tiny) signs promoting business materials with large, well-designed signs.

  Feature provocative management titles in a prime display near the circulation desk during the months of October and June.

  Promote Internet access to the library's catalog and the drive-through window service to potential users.

PERFORMANCE AND REVIEW: IMPLEMENTATION AND EVALUATION

As works in progress, library services and collections benefit from internal and external evaluation. When creating measurable objectives, library staff will have already determined some of the standards by which they will judge the success of a particular effort. Evaluation during the planning stages and soon after implementation may include, at a minimum,

- the use of Gantt charts, which identify the parties responsible for completing specific actions and the associated deadlines;

- close tracking of funds to ensure the adequacy of the budget allocated to specific tasks;

- the qualitative review by peers and library managers of initial efforts in an area;

- soliciting input from potential users, other community members, or members of the SPM committee with insight and expertise relevant to particular strategies; and

- checking early measures of use (e.g., circulation) or satisfaction (e.g., patron comments) to gauge how effective the change seems to be.

Such formative evaluation can allow library staff to adjust their work as necessary over time.

Staff also should conduct periodic evaluations of programs in place. In the chapters that follow, we discuss evaluation of each aspect of the marketing mix in context. We also recommend examining the findings from *The Public Library Effectiveness Study* (Childers and Van House 1989) and the New Zealand studies that build on these (Calvert and Cullen 1994; Cullen and Calvert 1993) as well as techniques described in *The TELL IT! Manual* (Zweizig et al. 1996); all discuss a broad spectrum of measures useful for reviewing both the managerial and service effectiveness of public libraries.

CONCLUSION

Interwoven strategic and marketing plans can help ensure relevance, value, and cost-effectiveness throughout the gamut of library operations, many of which lie significantly beyond the scope of this specialized title. The rest of this book focuses on how the four Ps (product, price, place, and promotion) of the marketing mix can inform the creation of goals, objectives, and strategies related to developing and marketing the collection.

NOTES

1. Wood (1988) gives an excellent overview of the principles of strategic planning.

2. For detailed advice on formally writing a marketing plan, see McDonald and Keegan (1997); Kassel (1999); Gumbs (1999); Gumpert (1996); State Library (1993), Dalmon (1992); and Wood (1988).

3. In one study on decision making, McClure and Samuels (1985) found that librarians often fail to read research findings even when a topic has been well studied; instead they rely on personal opinion as a major source of evidence to use when making decisions.

4. Bertot and McClure (1997) note a number of policy issues affecting public libraries in the context of a national networked environment, including universal service, subsidization of public library connection costs, free access to government information, and strategies to handle the endless need for upgrades.

5. See Chapter 11 for more information on managing resistance to change.

REFERENCES

Abrahams, Jeffrey. 1995. *The Mission Statement Book: 301 Corporate Mission Statements from America's Top Companies*. Berkeley, CA: Ten Speed Press.

Akey, Stephen M. 1990. "McLibraries." *The New Republic* 202, no. 9 (February 26): 12–13.

"ALA PR/Communication Survey Results Are In." 1999. *Marketing Library Services* 13, no. 6 (September): 8.

Ammons, David N. 1995. "Overcoming the Inadequacies of Performance Measurement in Local Government: The Case of Libraries and Leisure Services." *Public Administration Review* 55, no. 1 (January/February): 37–47.

Berry, John. 1990. "Leaning Toward 'Quality'." *Library Journal* 115, no. 11 (June 15): 76. (Originally published in *Library Journal* 104, no. 17 (October 1, 1979): 2013.)

Bertot, John Carlo, and Charles R. McClure. 1997. *Policy Issues and Strategies Affecting Public Libraries in the National Networked Environment: Moving Beyond Connectivity*. Washington, DC: National Commission on Libraries and Information Science. ERIC ED417719.

Bloom, Herbert. 1976. "Adult Services: 'The Book That Leads You On.' " *Library Trends* 25, no. 1 (July): 379–98.

Bob, Murray. 1982. "The Case for Quality Book Selection." *Library Journal* 107, no. 16 (September 15): 1707–10.

Bunge, Charles A. 1984. "Planning, Goals, and Objectives for the Reference Department. *RQ* 23, no. 3 (Spring): 306–15.

Calvert, Philip J., and Rowena J. Cullen. 1994. "Further Dimensions of Public Library Effectiveness II: The Second Stage of the New Zealand Study. *Library and Information Science Research* 16, no. 2 (Spring): 87–104.

Childers, Thomas, and Nancy A. Van House. 1989. *The Public Library Effectiveness Study: Final Report*. Philadelphia: Drexel University, College of Information Studies.

Corrick, Annabelle. 1983. "Marketing as Applied Through Publishing: Converting Theory to Practice." *College and Research Libraries* 44, no. 1 (January): 38–45.

Cramer, Dina. 2000. "How Are We Treating Our Customers?" *Public Libraries* 39, no. 2 (March/April): 67–68.

Cullen, Rowena, and Philip J. Calvert. 1993. "Further Dimensions of Public Library Effectiveness: Report on a Parallel New Zealand Study." *Library and Information Science Research* 15, no. 2 (Spring): 143–64.

Cutter, Charles A. 1901. "Should Libraries Buy Only the Best Books or the Best Books That People Will Read?" *Library Journal* 26, no. 2 (February): 70–72.

Dalmon, Diane. 1992. "Planning for Progress." *ASLIB Information* 20, no. 1 (January): 24–26.

Dessauer, John P. 1980. "Are Libraries Failing Their Patrons?" *Publishers Weekly* 217, no. 2 (January 18): 67–68.

Durham County Library Marketing Plan. 1999. Durham, NC: Durham County Library.

Gumbs, Barbara. 1999. "How to Develop a Marketing Plan." In *Marketing Information Products and Services: A Primer for Librarians and Information Professionals*, ed. Abhinandan K. Jain et al., 49–107. New Delhi: Tata McGraw-Hill.

Gumpert, David E. 1996. *How to **Really** Create a Successful Marketing Plan*. 3d ed. Boston: Inc.

Hayes, Robert M., and Virginia A. Walter. 1996. *Strategic Management for Public Libraries: A Handbook*. Westport, CT: Greenwood Publishing.

Hyman, Karen. 1999. "Customer Service and the 'Rule of 1965'." *American Libraries* 30, no. 9 (October): 54, 56–58.

Kassel, Amelia. 1999. "How to Write a Marketing Plan." *Marketing Library Services* [Online] 13, no. 5 (June). Available: www.infotoday.com/mls/jun99/how-to.htm. [Accessed September 26, 2001].

Kies, Cosette N. 1987. *Marketing and Public Relations for Libraries*. Metuchen, NJ: Scarecrow Press.

Kister, Kenneth. 1971. "Let's Add Diversity." *Library Journal* 96, no. 16 (September 15): 2745.

Kotler, Philip. 1982. *Marketing for Non-Profit Organizations*. 2d ed. New York: Prentice-Hall.

Kotler, Philip, and Gary Armstrong. 1999. *Principles of Marketing*. 8th ed. Upper Saddle River, NJ: Prentice-Hall.

Massey, Morris. 1976. "Market Analysis and Audience Research for Libraries." *Library Trends* 24, no. 3 (January): 473–91.

McClure, Charles R., and Alan R. Samuels. 1985. "Factors Affecting the Use of Information for Academic Library Decision Making." *College and Research Libraries* 46, no. 6 (November): 483–98.

McClure, Charles R., et al. 1987. *Planning and Role Setting for Public Libraries: A Manual of Options and Procedures*. Chicago: American Library Association.

McColvin, Lionel Roy. 1925. *The Theory of Book Selection for Public Libraries*. London: Grafton and Company.

McDonald, Malcolm H. B., and Warren J. Keegan. 1997. *Marketing Plans That Work: Targeting Growth and Profitability*. Boston: Butterworth-Heinemann.

Merritt, Leroy Charles. 1964. "Editorial." *ALA Newsletter on Intellectual Freedom* 13, no. 5 (September): 71–72.

———. 1979. "Book Selection and Intellectual Freedom." In *Background Readings in Building Library Collections*, 2d ed., ed. Phyllis Van Orden and Edith B. Phillips, 19–28. Metuchen, NJ: Scarecrow Press.

"1998 ALA PR/Communications Survey Results." 1999. [Homepage of American Library Association], [Online]. Available: http://www.ala.org/pio/archives/pr%20survey/totalresults.html [Accessed September 26, 2001].

Nelson, Sandra, for the Public Library Association. 2001. *The New Planning for Results: A Streamlined Approach*. Chicago: American Library Association.

Paznekas, Susan J., and Sandra S. Stephan. 1995. "Making Libraries Essential the HIP Way." *Public Libraries* 34, no. 6 (November/December): 352–55.

Public Library Association. 1982. *The Public Library: Democracy's Resource. A Statement of Principles*. Chicago: American Library Association.

Pungitore, Verna L. 1993. "Planning in Small Libraries: A Field Study." *Public Libraries* 32, no. 6 (November/December): 331–36.

"Quoteland." 1997–2001. [Homepage of Quoteland], [Online]. Available: http://www.quoteland.com [Accessed September 26, 2001].

Rice, Betty. 1972. *Public Relations for Public Libraries*. New York: H. W. Wilson.

Rodriguez, Suzana Braga, and David Hickson. 1995. "Success in Decision Making: Different Organizations, Differing Reasons for Success." *Journal of Management Studies* 32, no. 5: 665–78.

Schlegel, John F. 1993. "The Committee Chair's Role." *Association Management* 45, no. 1 (January): 59–61.

Shapiro, Samuel B. 1996. "Why Committees Work: Collective Wisdom That Can't Be Beat." *Association Management*. 48, no. 1 (January): 54–56.

Smith, Nancy Milnor. 1994. "State Agency Use of Planning and Role Setting for Public Libraries and Output Measures for Public Libraries." *Public Libraries* 33, no. 4 (July/August): 193–97.

Spiegler, Jerry. 1980. "BCPL: Road to Extinction." *Library Journal* 105, no. 1 (January 1): 2.

St. Lifer, Evan. 2001. "Tapping into the Zen of Marketing." *Library Journal* 126, no. 8 (May 1): 44–46.

State Library of Ohio and H. Baird Tenney, et al. 1993. *Marketing & Libraries Do Mix: A Handbook for Libraries & Information Centers*. Columbus: State Library of Ohio.

Stewart, Dennis D., and Garold Stasser. 1995. "Expert Role Assignment and Information Sampling During Collective Recall and Decision Making." *Journal of Personality and Social Psychology* 69, no. 4: 619–28.

Sullivan, Michael. 2000. "Giving Them What They Want in Small Public Libraries." *Public Libraries* 39, no. 3 (May/June): 148–55.

Sutton, Brett. 1993. "Long-Range Planning in Public Libraries: Staff Perspectives." *Library and Information Science Research* 15, no. 4 (Fall): 299–323.

Van House, Nancy A., et al. 1987. *Output Measures for Public Libraries.* 2d ed. Chicago: American Library Association.

Van Loo, John. 1984. "Marketing the Library Service: Lessons from the Commercial Sector." *Health Libraries Review* 1, no. 1 (March): 36–47.

Waddell, Fred. 1990. "Effective Brainstorming." *Manage* 41, no. 4 (March): 4–6.

Weingand, Darlene E. 1999. *Marketing/Planning Library and Information Services.* 2d ed. Englewood, CO: Libraries Unlimited.

Wilson, Marion. 2000. "Understanding the Needs of Tomorrow's Library User: Rethinking Library Services for the New Age." *Australasian Public Libraries and Information Services* (Expanded Academic ASAP) [Online] 13, no. 2 (June). Available (via subscription): http://infotrac.galegroup.com/menu [Accessed August 4, 2001].

Wood, Elizabeth J. 1988. *Strategic Marketing for Libraries: A Handbook.* Westport, CT: Greenwood Press.

Zweizig, Douglas, et al. 1996. *The TELL IT! Manual: The Complete Program for Evaluating Library Performance.* Chicago: American Library Association.

COLLECTION CHOICES

"Men have not all the same tastes and likes. . . . Their tastes vary, and they call for widely different things"—Horace (Stevenson 1967).

The degree of patron satisfaction with collection contents provides one key measure of a library's responsiveness. It also greatly affects levels of library use. When a collection contains dated or otherwise inadequate materials or lacks desired items, community residents may turn to other sources to obtain the information and stories they need. Developing winning collections requires librarians to make wise choices about purchasing, maintaining, and weeding materials.

Answers to at least three important questions influence the ongoing evaluation of collections to ensure that they meet user needs over time:

- What elements influence user selections?

- What mix of products (that is, items in the collection) best meets user needs?

- How will the life cycles of particular products affect overall demand?

WHAT ELEMENTS INFLUENCE
USER SELECTIONS?

Understanding the distinction between a core and a tangible product illuminates one important aspect of how patrons select materials. A core product reflects the end result the user actually desires, such as entertainment, scientific knowledge, spiritual satisfaction, or other—frequently intangible—outcomes. We can fill these requirements directly by leading book discussions, telling stories, and offering similar programming or indirectly, by providing DVDs, CDs, computer databases, and other tangible products that patrons use to fulfill their needs.

The tangible products that public libraries offer need not be limited to print, audiovisual, and computer resources. For example,

- the Berkeley (California) Public Library features a tool collection ("Tool" 2001);

- the Ridgefield (Connecticut) Library offers portable cassette players (Rindfleisch 1999);

- the Des Plaines (Illinois) Public Library lends closed-caption decoders ("Loan Periods" 2000–2001);

- the Brooklyn Branch of the Cuyahoga (Ohio) County Public Library allows borrowing of more than 400 toys ("Toy" 2001);

- several libraries in the Suffolk (Bellport, New York) Cooperative Library System make specially adapted toys available for children with disabilities (Klauber 1998);

- the Queens Borough (New York) Public Library works with the Bell Atlantic phone company to lend TTYs (text telephones) ("Queens" 2000);

- the Public Library of Nashville and Davidson County (Tennessee) has engraving pens available for circulation (Parker 1999); and

- six Northeastern Connecticut public libraries check out Quinebaug-Shetucket Heritage Corridor nature trail daypacks that include binoculars, hiking and biking trail maps, a disposable camera, and other supplies to facilitate responsible enjoyment of the great outdoors ("Daypacks" 1997).

To determine what tangible products to procure, librarians must be knowledgeable about patrons' needs and tastes and those product elements that strongly influence use, including subject, genre, format, excellence, style and appeal, reading level, currency, language, packaging, and awareness of the author or title of a work.[1]

Subject

Subject matter constitutes a major factor in many patrons' selections. For example, studies have found that 61 percent of adults purchased nonfiction books based primarily on their subjects (NPD Group 1996), that subject matter most influenced teenagers' book selections (Samuels 1989), and that 63 percent of audiobook listeners chose titles based on subject matter ("New APA" 2001).

Media distributors periodically release statistics that illuminate the very broad subjects that interest patrons. For example, each edition of *The Bowker Annual: Library and Book Trade Almanac* carries information about the number of works published in different subject areas (which roughly reflect what publishers think will sell) for four different formats: hardcover books, mass market paperbacks, trade publications, and CD-ROMs. Table 4.1 presents select findings of a recent *Consumer Research Study on Book Purchasing* (Book Industry Study Group 2000).

TABLE 4.1. U.S. Nonfiction Bookstore Sales, 1998–1999.*

Nonfiction Category	Percent of Total Adult Sales**
Cooking/Crafts	10
Religion	9.3
General Nonfiction	7.8
Psychology/Recovery	5.2
Technical/Science/Education	5.8
Art/Literature/Poetry	3.3
Reference	2.2
Travel/Regional	1.4

*Table compiled from figures reported in *The 1999 Consumer Research Study on Book Purchasing* (Book Industry Study Group 2000).

**Figures do not add up to 100 percent because sales of fiction (53.3 percent) and all other sales (1.7 percent) were included in the data reported.

Although reports derived from sales figures or publication output can be useful, bear in mind that people do not necessarily want to borrow the same things they will buy. For example, a British study found that the two highest selling categories of nonfiction—gardening and cooking books—reside far down the list of subjects most frequently borrowed from local public libraries (Smith 1999); clearly, people want to own works they will be referring to repeatedly.

Studies of what circulates well at a particular library or set of libraries have value for others. Initial evidence suggests that relatively consistent levels of interest in these broad subjects exist from place to place, at least within culturally similar geographic areas. Ottensmann, Gnat, and Gleeson's (1995) analysis of circulation patterns (using broad, Dewey divisions) at 21 branches of the Indianapolis-Marion County (Indiana) Public Library, located in socioeconomically diverse neighborhoods, revealed fairly similar circulation patterns of subjects in different branches, even when *total* circulation at these branches varied widely.[2] When Davis and Altman (1997) examined circulation data (broken down by Dewey 100 levels) from 11 Midwestern and Southwestern libraries serving populations with different demographic and lifestyle characteristics, they too found very similar broad circulation patterns at these libraries. The concept of "everyman and everywoman" needs—those related either to universal human requirements or culturally related demands placed on us (e.g., the obligation to pay income tax)—explains these findings.

The make-up of an individual community will influence circulation patterns for smaller, precisely defined subject areas. We can reasonably hypothesize that a library on the North Carolina coast would face higher demand for works on boating than one located in Washington's Yakima desert, and that a library located in Green Bay, Wisconsin, would have a stronger demand for titles about ice fishing than one in Dallas. Moreover, local characteristics finely affect the popularity of specific topics within a broad subject area. Thus, we can expect more people in Minneapolis to desire books on the Minnesota Twins than on the Oakland As.

What evidence supports this claim? Angel (1998) notes that although titles of widespread attraction, such as those by fiction superstar John Grisham, sell well throughout the country, regional appeal also affects sales. For example, Nicholas Evans's *The Horse Whisperer*, which features a horse trainer on a ranch, sold particularly heavily in North Dakota, and *Into the Wild*, Jon Krakauer's story of a man lost in the Alaskan wilderness, sold especially well in that state. Such findings support librarians' continuing efforts to create and promote special collections of local interest materials.

Specific events may also galvanize interest in related subjects. For example, the Detroit Public Library's National Automotive History Collection experienced a 50 percent increase in customers during 1996, the centennial of the U.S. auto industry (Gay 1996). A library can even help community efforts to heal after a tragedy, as did the Wilmette (Illinois) Public Library District when it created a bibliography of books and videos on tolerance and diversity and co-sponsored race-relations workshops after two racially motivated murders occurred in the city ("Reflecting" 1999).

A few demographic factors, including age, gender, and community size, correlate with broadly defined subject interests.[3] For example, Scales (1996) found that older adults read more religious materials than younger adults. Delin, Delin, and Cram (1995) found that older readers enjoy a greater variety of books than their younger counterparts; males were more likely than females to have recently read hobby and self-instructional books, and females were more likely to have recently read craft books and romances. When Willits and Willits (1991) surveyed a broad base of rural and urban library users on their reading preferences, they found rural patrons far more likely to want works on gardening, crafts, and religion than urban dwellers. In contrast, urban users read significantly more classic works of fiction and nonfiction. Similarly, when Lucas (1982) polled public library patrons in six Illinois communities, she discovered that subject interests varied according to community size. For example, residents of larger communities expressed more interest in science and business materials, whereas residents of smaller communities had more interest in religion and hobbies, games, and sports. Such results suggest a need to pay attention to these and comparable findings when designing our own studies, as well as to continue to support, conduct, and publish data on patron preferences.

This area begs for further studies addressing causality, whether these are sophisticated quantitative studies (e.g., D'Elia 1980) or rich qualitative analyses of library use (e.g., Ross 1991), in addition to comprehensive and finely delineated literature reviews. Such work could, for example, explore such questions as: At what level of subject specificity do unique local characteristics affect circulation? Researchers could also explore psychographic attributes that significantly influence use or patron preferences.

Several clearer subject-oriented patterns of library use recur. First, the general subject interests of patrons often correspond to the patterns of punctuated equilibrium, a concept familiar to evolutionary biologists. Whereas given subject areas will experience long, stable periods of use, others will experience rapid advances or declines in use, related to environmental change. Thus, we see continuing long-term interest in topics such as raising children, patterns of little or no use in subjects that were once used (e.g., shorthand), and intense use of subjects that did not even exist a decade ago, such as Photoshop software guides. Individual titles also exhibit similar patterns of use (Ettelt 1986, 1987). In other words, we must make selections that jointly consider past use and current environmental changes (or relative lack thereof).

Although analyses of electronic resources (e.g., which Internet sites patrons access most frequently), circulation data, and in-house use records can all reveal subject interests, we encourage you to creatively seek out related data that can potentially inform selection. For example, you could compare local results with the 25 most frequently accessed sites on a national basis, available at the Nielsen //NetRatings site ("Hot" 1999–2001), or with portraits of U.S. citizens' broad Internet activities, derived from Pew Internet and American Life Project Surveys ("Internet" 2001).

Another recurring pattern is that nonfiction works on subjects that many people must deal with in their everyday lives will usually receive heavy use. Consider, for example, the immense popularity of many how-to resources. Patrons consult Web sites, books, videos, and other materials that help them prepare income tax returns, prepare winning résumés, fix their cars, or remodel their kitchens much more extensively than works that discuss the third Crusade, Brazilian flora, or Tang burial horses. Any analysis of nonfiction items that appears on bestseller lists in the United States will verify that works of popular psychology, health and fitness, cooking, and those regarding current people and events featured in the daily news appear repeatedly.

Finally, well-conceived nonfiction that provides a broad overview of a subject area will often attract a broad audience initially. If, for example, a librarian buys two recent cookbooks of equivalent excellence (in terms of recipes, writing, photography, etc.), he or she can logically expect the one that covers appetizers, soups, main courses, and desserts to receive more use over time than the one that focuses solely on soups. A key question for the librarian will then be, "When is an overview needed (e.g., when the title does not significantly duplicate other works) and when will a narrower focus be relevant?" A library located near a school of art and design may reasonably collect the best titles on sculpting, even when they have a slightly narrower focus (e.g., on sculpting human figures in clay), knowing that they will receive significant use.

These patterns appear among non-book materials as well. For example, when staff at the Metropolitan (Oklahoma City) Library System monitored use of magazines at 11 branches, they found the three most popular were works of general interest: *People, Time,* and *Newsweek.* Other heavily used magazines presented general approaches to topics of widespread interest, such as *Better Homes and Gardens, Popular Mechanics,* and *Scientific American.* Technical and special interest magazines figured prominently among the significant number of magazines that received no use (Little 1990).

Genre

A work's genre also influences many patrons' choices. For example, Steptowe (1987) indicated that 81 percent of patrons search for novels of a particular genre, and Yu and O'Brien (1999) found that category and author searching are the two main methods by which patrons locate fiction.

Circulation data reinforce patron selection by genre. For example, when staff at the Cliffdale branch library of the Cumberland County (North Carolina) Public Library and Information Center categorized and separately shelved fiction by a mix of genre and subject (e.g., shelving mysteries and true crime titles together), circulation increased by 36 percent. When two other libraries in the same system added genre spine labels but left the books intershelved in one alphabetical system, circulation increased by 10 percent (Cannell and McCluskey 1996).

Separately cataloging and/or labeling genre fiction can help staff explore the relative popularity of different genres. For example, staff at the Rochester Hills (Michigan) Public Library found that among books, mysteries had the highest turnover rate (13.3 times per year),[4] followed by general fiction (9.25 times), romances (8.64 times), and science fiction/fantasy (5.89 times) (Hage 1997).[5] Similar studies could be done for audiobooks, videos, and other formats.

Turnover rate and other circulation-based measures require further investigation because they may reflect collection caliber as well as (or instead of) demand. In other words, although a low turnover rate for a particular genre may suggest that not many patrons care for that genre, it could also signify an inadequate or out-dated collection, one that genre fans bypass.

Again, purchasing statistics offer librarians one way to check the validity of circulation figures—bearing in mind that patrons may not buy exactly the same types of materials they borrow—by suggesting the relative popularity of different genres of works. For example, figures gathered by the Recording Industry Association of America show that rock music accounted for the most sales of recorded music in 1999 (25.2 percent), and new age music accounted for the least (.03 percent) ("Sales" 2001). A library that has a new age turnover rate five times as high as the rock rate will want to consider whether this has occurred as a result of unique community characteristics or collection imbalances.

To better understand genre literature and its readers' needs, librarians may form genre study groups[6] as well as examine relevant published research. For example, *Genreflecting* (Herald 2000) both explores the general appeal of genre fiction and separately considers eight different genres and their sub-genres (see also *Teen Genreflecting* [Herald 1997] and *Junior Genreflecting* [Volz, Welborn, and Scheer 2000]). Several other series titles cover a single genre (Fonseca and Pulliam 1999; Herald 1999; Pearl, Knappe, and Higashi 1999; Ramsdell 1999), as do a variety of other works, such as *Anatomy of Wonder* (Barron 1995), which includes bibliographic essays on different periods of science fiction writing and science fiction from many countries.

A few, significant, published works provide an in-depth analysis of the appeal of different genres or the readers most likely to prefer them. *Reading the Romance: Women, Patriarchy, and Popular Literature* (Radway 1991) is one of the best-known examples. *The Reader's Advisory Guide to Genre Fiction* (Saricks 2001), a newer title written from a librarian's view, provides an overview of the most popular genres and sub-genres; discusses characteristics, appeal, and reference sources; identifies key authors to read to understand the genre better; and offers tips on working with readers.

Information obtained from fans, publishers, or authors of a particular genre also offers insight. We can examine fanzines like *Armchair Detective* or *Romantic Times*[7] and explore Internet sites such as "Readers' Resources" (1996–2001), "Overbooked" (2001) and "Genrefluent" (Herald 2001), that note significant key authors writing in a genre, sub-genres and their characteristics, reader preferences, publishing trends, and so forth.

Anyone with an e-mail account may also join an electronic discussion group, or mailing list, that focuses on a particular genre and includes candid discussions of reader likes and dislikes. This option allows those who have not read much in a particular genre to "lurk" on the list, reading others' comments without contributing themselves, and (at least initially) educating themselves in the comfort of anonymity. Many lists maintain searchable archives, helpful for those looking for information on a specific topic. Well-established genre mailing lists include DOROTHY_L for mystery readers, RRA_L (Romance Readers Anonymous), and SF-LOVERS for science fiction readers.[8] We can also add our names to conventional mailing lists of genre-related organizations. For example, the Romance Writers of America, Inc., offers a Library Affiliates Program that produces a free newsletter and has sponsored at least one very inexpensive conference for librarians (Linz 1999).[9]

Those seeking another approach to understanding genre trends may want to read the essays at the beginning of each section of the *What-Do-I-Read-Next?* series (Barron et al. annual) or check *Publishers Weekly*, in print or on the Internet, for its "Category Closeups" feature (2001), which examines publishing and purchasing trends within a specific genre or subject area. Whatever mechanism is chosen, we encourage in-depth study of the appeal of genre fiction to help build awareness of fiction trends, especially over the long term, and encourage effective, efficient collection development practices. (See Chapter 10 for a related discussion of readers' advisory issues and resources.)

Format

Whether because of personal preference or other reasons (e.g., an assignment requires consulting an Internet source), format can be a deciding factor in patron selection. Purchases of audiovisual materials and computerized resources continue to increase, along with demand and circulation (Speer 1995; Oder 1998).

In part, libraries are accommodating requests for more recent innovations, such as DVDs, CD books, and e-books, by reducing or eliminating technologically dated formats such as music cassettes and print indexes (Hoffert 2001). In 2001 the Kalamazoo (Michigan) Public Library began lending digital audiobooks and players, becoming the first U.S. public library to do so ("Digital Audiobooks" 2001). The Algonquin Area (Illinois) Public Library District blazed a trail as one of the first libraries to circulate Rocket e-book readers, each of which can store up to 100 average-length novels at a time, and the Public Library of Charlotte and Mecklenburg (North Carolina) County tested demand for e-books through a six-month trial collection of 1,500 titles available to patrons from library or offsite Internet connections ("Briefly" 1999; "netLibrary" 2000). This trend will likely continue. In a survey of 100 public libraries diverse in geography and size, *Library Journal* found that almost one-third have e-book collections, and close to another third plan to start one in the next year (Hoffert 2001).

New formats may also attract new patrons. For example, Robinson (1987) noted that many former nonusers began using the library to obtain videos and became more familiar with and began to use other collections as well. Libraries that offer facilities for playing videogames (Poller 1988) or accessing the Internet (Gordon, Gordon, and Moore 2001) have documented a similar phenomenon.

A growing number of studies have attempted to describe the audience for a particular format, a trend we heartily applaud.[10] When Aron (1992) randomly surveyed Books-on-Tape subscribers, 47 percent of whom say they also borrow audiobooks from the public library, she found that they often read print books and periodicals, too. Overwhelmingly, users selected audiobooks rather than print materials to be able to absorb books while engaging in other activities, especially driving. A recent Audio Publishers Association survey confirms this finding, although it also shows an increase in the number of people choosing audiobooks primarily for the pleasure of listening ("New APA" 2001).[11]

This makes commuters, vacationers, truckers, and others who spend considerable time on the road one prime audience for audiobook promotional efforts. Companies like Book-N-Along, Books in Motion, and Rezound, which have successfully pursued the trucker market, have learned that at truck stops, unlike general bookstores, business and self-help titles don't do well. Instead, westerns, action-adventure, science fiction, mystery, and true crime stories dominate (Rosenblum 1996).

Listeners also frequently choose audiobooks they would not have time to read or would not select in print, which may, in part, explain the popularity of the classics on cassette (Aron 1992; Kaye and Baxter 1994). The APA survey indicates that unabridged fiction sells about twice as well as abridged versions. Articles in the library press suggest that both abridged and unabridged audiobooks enjoy a loyal following (e.g., Sager 1996; Kaye and Baxter 1994; Annichiarico 1991). The latter finding merits further exploration to determine the extent to which patrons choose the versions they do simply because they have no other options.

Libraries can investigate their own patrons' preferences for a certain format by surveying them, as did the Plano (Texas) Public Library System, which included its homepage as one distribution point for an audiobook listener survey ("Audio" 2001).

In addition to promoting a format to a particular audience, it is also possible to reach a target market by selecting formats that will appeal to it. For example, the Poplar Creek (Streamwood) and Bartlett public library districts in Illinois worked together to obtain a Library Services and Construction Act (LSCA) grant to purchase collections of large-print books, audiobooks, and videos for senior citizens who might have difficulty reading standard-sized print (Kiefer 1987). Other options include purchasing paperbacks and graphic novels to attract young adults, as well as online databases licensed for remote use and CD-ROMs (preferably in both Windows and Macintosh versions) to attract home computer owners.

Quality or Excellence

Quality, a third characteristic of a tangible product, can be defined in many ways. Consider, for example, Mann's (1971) proposition that quality fiction challenges the reader's attitudes and beliefs, whereas recreational fiction reinforces them. A more common understanding equates an item's quality with the degree of aesthetic or artistic excellence it possesses. Librarians who believe in quality selection advocate purchasing titles that are thoughtful or insightful, cover significant subjects, present facts accurately and comprehensively, are written clearly, or possess literary merit (e.g., Gorman and Howes 1989).

The awards that an item earns or receives a nomination for provide one indicator of its excellence. Librarians can help patrons quickly identify these titles by including award information in their catalog records, creating bibliographies or displays of award winners, or labeling these items. For example, the Downers Grove (Illinois) Public Library stamps "Award Winner" on the pockets of such books and then notes which award(s) it won (Saricks 1998). Affixing spine stickers on winning titles can also help patrons identify them. Numerous sources provide lists of literary award winners, including The AwardWeb (Mann 2001), *Literary Laurels: A Reader's Guide to Award-Winning Fiction* and *Literary Laurels: A Reader's Guide to Award-Winning Children's Books* (Carlson, Creighton, and Cunningham 1995; 1996), the Web sites of booksellers like Barnes & Noble (1997–2001), and many general almanacs. Similar sources exist for award-winning media.

The extent to which patrons consider an item's excellence when making selections is unknown. The phrase "quality-versus-demand," a reference to a selection debate familiar to librarians both in the United States and abroad (e.g., Johnson 1999; Brewis, Gericke, and Kruger 1996),[12] may suggest that items in heavy demand are not of high quality, and vice versa. However, consider that a National Book Award winner, *Cold Mountain* by Charles Frazier, earned the number one spot on the bestseller list longer than any other title in 1997. In fact, Susan Baker (1995) notes that almost 16 percent of the annual top ten U.S. fiction bestsellers from 1965 to 1990 earned literary awards. As Shay has noted elsewhere, excellence and demand represent two intersecting, multidimensional continuums measuring different aspects of the same work (Sharon Baker 1996).

At least three attempts have been made to determine the relative use of high-quality and lesser-quality items. Two studies revealed that titles circulate in proportion to their presence in the collection. That is, when quality titles (defined by the number of positive reviews received) represent 20 percent of the collection, they will account for 20 percent of circulation (Goldhor 1959, 1981a, 1981b). The third study revealed that a significant number of patrons do demand high-quality works. Employing a definition of quality that included critical acclaim and stood in opposition to materials intended primarily for entertainment, librarians at the Espoo City (Finland) Library conducted a survey to ascertain which patrons use the high-quality materials in their collection and how much use these items receive. They found that almost half of all users borrow high-quality items at one point or another, and one-fifth check out only such items. High-quality borrowers were most likely to be between 30 and 60 years of age and equally likely to be men as women (Pohjanvalta 1993).

A second definition of quality focuses on the identifying characteristics or aspects of a work and suggests that quality indicates, at least in part, the suitability of match for the patron, reflecting highly personal and situational factors. Consider the following definitions of a quality title provided by students in an introductory collection development class:

- "One that answers the questions that I have."
- "A book that has lots of facts and figures."
- "A work of pure imagination. I hate being interrupted by facts."
- "A book that makes me laugh."
- "Something that has an intricate plot."
- "One, like something by Barbara Pym, that has little plot but fascinating characters."

- "A fast-paced title with lots of action."
- "A work that makes me think."
- "A fast read when I'm tired."
- "A book that reveals that the author has values similar to mine."

These student definitions reflect the fact that for many a quality book offers a reasonable fit by meeting their specific needs at a given time.

Several authors have addressed this issue. For example, Genco (1988) has argued that children have a number of psychological needs that can be met by mass market books, which often offer less-complicated views of the world. These include the need for security, the need to belong, the need to love and be loved, the need to achieve, and the need for change, as well as the need for aesthetic satisfaction.

People's reading preferences also reflect fluctuating needs. As Ross and Chelton (2001) note, patrons' moods (what they feel like reading at a given time) greatly influence their selections, especially of fiction. In a series of in-depth interviews to determine how people choose books, Ross (1991) found that the amount of stimulation that readers desired at any given moment significantly influenced their selections. Generally, in calm times, readers frequently reached for something different: works that were intellectually challenging, explored new topics, or illuminated familiar subjects. In contrast, during hectic periods, people limited their outside activities to those that were more familiar and often read works about well-known subjects, read genre titles that followed predictable formulas, or re-read books by their favorite authors. This relates to what Wojciechowski (1996) calls the retrogressional function of literature, which suggests that people may repeatedly read favorite categories of books or titles to limit surprise and enjoy the comfort of the familiar.

These studies and others have found that people often use libraries to find books and other forms of media that can help them satisfy numerous desires—for entertainment and escape as well as for information and enlightenment.[13] Guided by a societal-marketing orientation, librarians can attempt to build diverse collections capable of meeting a broad spectrum of individual needs to fit patrons' particular requirements for "quality" works at any given time.

Style and Appeal

As defined in the *Dictionary of Publishing*, style refers to "the distinctive tone, rhythms, and mode of expression that characterize the work of a particular writer, making it stand out from all other such work; [it is] agonized over by many writers, sought after by many editors, and always a matter of individual assessment" (Brownstone and Franck 1982, 265). Even when they cannot identify the author, most readers can easily discern Ernest Hemingway's spare writing from Charlotte Brontë's melodramatic, flowery prose. Similarly, rock-n-roll listeners can readily distinguish Dylan from the Dead and viewers Spike Lee's films from those of Steven Spielberg.

Style often varies by type of work. For example, a self-help book and a textbook will have very different flavors, even when they cover the same topic. Likewise, the style of an article in *JAMA* (*The Journal of the American Medical Association*) reporting the results of new medical research will differ markedly from a *USA Today* item on the same research.

Clearly different styles or aspects of the same style appeal to different people. For example, among the definitions of a quality title presented in the previous section, one student values a book with "an intricate plot" whereas another desires a title "that has little plot but fascinating characters." In addition to depth of characterization and plotting, other stylistic elements that may be important to a patron include reading level (which will be considered separately in the following section); rhythm; use of imagery, dialogue, dialect, obscenity, and profanity; tone; sense of humor; experimental or conventional writing techniques; and pacing.

At times, patrons may seek the same stylistic traits in a work while differing about which titles satisfy this desire. For example, take the real case of two patrons, both of whom seem to value realistic characterization, evaluating the works of Jeffery Archer. One says, "I don't like him. His heroes and heroines are always perfect. I wonder where on earth are the ordinary men and women." The other reader states, "I think I have read every one of his books. I like his writing. His characters are always real" (Yu and O'Brien 1999, 40).

Spiller's (1980) study of fiction browsers also supports the view of style assessment as highly individualistic. He found that readers wanted to locate books with "a good plot," "interesting characters," and "a style that did not grate," but the definitions of these characteristics varied greatly from patron to patron. Patrons tried to increase the likelihood that they would find what they wanted stylistically by reading the summary or reviews on the book jacket (88 percent) or examining the text itself (33 percent). Ross (1999) has also found stylistic elements an important factor in book selection.

In recent years, librarians, scholars of popular culture, teachers, and psychologists have begun exploring the reasons why people choose certain styles of reading. For example, Baker (1994) proposes that studying personality and cognitive styles can help readers' advisors suggest books for their patrons. A very literal mystery reader may prefer the work of Ed McBain, who writes in highly concrete and visual terms. Someone else may value works that use metaphor, such as can be found in G. K. Chesterton's Father Brown series.

Delin, Delin, and Cram (1995) have also explored the link between personality and reading preference, comparing results on established psychological tests with recreational reading choices. They found a few significant patterns, including the fact that those who read history or politics tend to be more extroverted and have a wider social network than those who do not read these subjects. Because only a few other authors have explored underlying reasons why patrons prefer works of a certain style, the findings in this area remain tentative.[14] One conclusion remains certain: Patrons heavily consider style when selecting materials.

Reading, Listening, and Other Levels of Sophistication

For certain groups of patrons—notably children, newly literate adults (who have relatively low reading skills but often higher sophistication levels) and those just learning the language used in an item—reading level may be one of the more significant factors considered when choosing print materials. Separately shelving collections of children's easy readers, adult new readers, and English-as-a-Second-Language items; subtly labeling these to make them easier to locate; and ensuring that staff have the other knowledge and skills necessary to assist potential users of these materials all contribute to strong service.

A relatively recent study underscores the need to educate staff about both user groups and collection products. Hypothesizing that adult new readers who ask for help finding suitable materials and do not receive it may not summon the courage to ask again, Scates (1999) spoke to the reference librarians on duty (rather than the literacy specialists) at five different libraries to learn about their adult literacy collections. Only one of the librarians knew about these materials, although every library offered such titles, most shelved with the juvenile collections![15]

Reading and sophistication levels also influence the selections of other patrons. Notably, works (of any format) with involved sentence structures or patterns (Faulkner, anyone?), complicated vocabularies, complex ideas, or highly technical data will likely appeal to a smaller audience than more accessible works that contain simpler writing or dialogue, mix text with colorful graphics or photos, or cover fewer ideas at one time.

A number of studies illustrate this concept. In one, psychologist Nell (1988) asked 129 university students to read 30 abstracts (with no designations as to author or title) and choose those with which they would be most and least likely to relax. Forty-four librarians placed the same abstracts in order by their expected use. Both students and librarians ranked works in a consistent order, with easy-to-read works of best-selling and genre fiction first, more complicated narratives in the middle, and hard-to-read expository works of nonfiction last. In a similar vein, Spiller (1980) found that patrons borrowed recreational (genre) fiction three times as often as serious fiction (works complicated in ideas, vocabulary, or tone) in five British public libraries.

Of course, this does not imply that sophisticated works will never receive strong use. Consider the case of Michael Ondaatje's *The English Patient* (1992). In this 1993 Booker Prize winner, Ondaatje employs an elevated vocabulary, presents multiple, slow-moving plot lines with many flashbacks, depicts unpleasant events, delves into the thoughts of his characters, and avoids a tidy, "happily-ever-after" ending, making the novel, which became an international bestseller, a potentially challenging read ("The English Patient" 1997).

Currency

Overall, newer materials receive significantly more use than older ones. For example, Ettelt (1987) found that new books displayed at one community college library circulated three to six times as often as older titles. Further, he discovered that when taken off display, circulation of new books decreased but still remained higher than that of older books. This fact helps explain why many online catalogs either display search results by date of publication (preferably most recent first) or at least offer patrons the option of sorting results in this manner.

Patrons want and need new materials, especially in subject areas with recent innovations, continual changes (e.g., computer technology, politics, or current events), or high obsolescence rates (e.g., medical research findings). A number of authors have provocatively argued that it is better for a library to have no holdings in critical subjects, such as law and medicine, than to have only out-of-date (expired) materials (e.g., Jenkins 1994).

Owning older materials can enhance other areas of the collection, adding depth. For example, fiction readers who have only recently discovered an author often want to read that writer's earlier works. Other older works likely to be in demand include classic titles in all formats, books made into feature films, and items that receive numerous word-of-mouth recommendations, from *Monty Python and the Holy Grail* to *The Rocky Horror Picture Show*, many of which may be considered cult classics.

Language

Research has also documented that materials written in the primary language(s) spoken in the library's geographic area circulate significantly more than materials written in other languages (e.g., Britten and Webster 1992). Although U.S. public librarians who serve predominantly English-speaking clientele typically have a rather small audience for secondary languages and purchase few foreign-language materials, those working in geographic areas with high concentrations of immigrants may buy substantial collections of non-English-language works. For example, the Los Angeles Public Library offers substantial collections of books, magazines, newspapers, audiobooks, videos, computer programs, and travel posters in 28 languages ("The International Languages" 2001).

Libraries may also offer related services to make collections more accessible. For example, librarians at the Queens Borough (New York) Public Library provide multilingual access to the online catalog and Internet resources (Strong 2000). The San Jose (California) Public Library's Biblioteca Latinoamericana branch features a large Spanish-language collection of print and nonprint materials, as well as bilingual staff and story hours, and a Spanish book club (Grand 2000). More than a decade ago, the Denver Public Library expanded its collection of Vietnamese materials and conducted workshops to train staff members to help Denver's growing Vietnamese community make full use of the library's collections and services ("Denver" 1988).

Foreign language selectors also benefit from understanding the culture of the target groups. One library learned this lesson the hard way when they discovered why their Vietnamese titles rarely circulated; the mostly pro-communist books, many purchased at a single bookstore, affronted the library's patrons (Hoffert 1994). In addition, many immigrants come from countries without strong traditions of free public libraries, necessitating the provision of basic information about how the library works (e.g., residents do not need to purchase cards). We suggest that foreign-language materials will circulate best when placed in obvious locations with clear, multilingual signage and when librarians are highly responsive to these patrons' needs.

Packaging

Media distributors know that exciting packaging can make the difference between mediocre and good sales of the product; well-designed covers help entice potential customers to pick up the work. For example, when Vintage redesigned its classic fiction covers, items with the newer, brighter, more sophisticated covers outsold the same books with the old covers by as much as a three-to-one ratio, although the old and new titles were displayed side-by-side and the new ones cost significantly more (Youman 1989).

Results like these help explain why publishers constantly try to come up with new ways to enhance the packages in which their products are sold, including the use of gimmicks and special effects. For example, Dell included holograms on Star Wars series book covers to increase their visibility and give them "galactic pizazz" (Stevenson 1997, 141). Distributors of children's and young adult titles are using more vibrant cover images to grab the attention of a generation of kids raised on computers and MTV (Stevenson 1997) and attempting to distinguish their titles from the crowded field of series paperback covers by offering completely redesigned formats. Scholastic designed its successful *Dear America* series of historical fiction journals as hardcover diaries, complete with fabric ribbons to use as bookmarks (Lodge 1998).

Based on observation and discussion with kids, youth librarians have long known that cover designs greatly influence children's and young adults' selections. Books for these age groups languish on the shelves when they bear poorly designed, dated, or overly gender-specific covers (Sullivan 1998; Caywood 1993; Feldman 1991). Indeed, a few savvy librarians have influenced circulation of great books with unappealing covers by replacing them with new ones, created by students (e.g., Darch 1998; "New Life" 1995).

Research indicates that both the cover art and use of teasers or summary information influence adult patrons' selections. Goodall (1989) documented that cover design entices patrons to pick up a book, but the summary text most significantly affects their decision to borrow it. Summary information influences patrons' selections of other formats as well. For example, Hall (1992) found that almost 74 percent of patrons selecting videos at the Grandview Heights (Columbus, Ohio) Public Library considered the plot information on the container, 68.3 percent the film's cast, and 19.7 percent the director-producer.

We recommend that librarians take advantage of publishers' and distributors' extensive efforts to stimulate demand through design by using original packaging and covering as little information as possible with labels and stickers, given other library needs (e.g., placement demands of self-checkout machines). Librarians may want to repackage a product when the original package is damaged, when they need to control a product for security reasons, or when they need more durable packaging. However, even in these cases, it is to the library's advantage to use as much of the original packaging as possible. Thus, although a video may need to be placed in a hard-sided box to prolong its life, the box will preferably be made of clear plastic and contain the video box's original cover.

Awareness of the Author and/or Title

Like brand-name recognition, the patron's awareness of a particular work often affects whether he or she will choose it. For example, 46 percent of fiction readers leaving Kent, England libraries had made selections based on author (Jennings and Sear 1986). Spiller (1980) discovered that 54 percent of fiction readers either actively sought works by a particular author or, while browsing, recognized an author they had heard of and were interested in reading; he also found that many of those "just browsing" either couldn't remember the names of authors or were unaware of what had been published.

Yu and O'Brien (1999) have classed adult fiction readers into three significant groups. Author-bound readers loyally peruse all works by a limited number of authors and do not easily accept replacement authors. Author-oriented readers prefer certain authors yet will select other writers' works when they cannot obtain their first choices. Members of the third group, author-free readers, pay little attention to the writer's name and often seek unfamiliar titles to try. (We suspect these overlap significantly with Ross's readers experiencing calm states of life.)

Other studies have shown that most media users will willingly try works by new authors at least occasionally. For example, the Gallup Organization (1985) found that six in ten book buyers will purchase books written by an unfamiliar author. Those most likely to try new authors include heavy book buyers and the college educated. Despite this willingness, many readers often do not try a title by a new writer unless they know the merits of the actual work. Thus, first-time authors famous for other reasons—like wrestler Chyna, National Public Radio's Cokie Roberts, and comedian Drew Carey—often enjoy significant demand. Similarly, many artists' CDs will circulate more when they begin getting video or radio airplay.

A patron may be more familiar with a title than with the author, particularly with videos. Hall (1992) found that 85 percent of patrons selecting videos at one public library were looking for a particular title. This can also happen with books, as it did with Joe Klein's anonymously published novel *Primary Colors* and J. K. Rowling's phenomenally successful Harry Potter series, which received a great deal of media attention, including one *Time* magazine cover featuring Harry ("The Magic of Harry Potter" 1999). In other cases, patrons may be more familiar with a brand name than with a particular author. For example, public library patrons may request Silhouette Special Edition romances or Masterpiece Theatre videos.

The degree and type of publicity that an item receives directly affects the likelihood that a patron will hear about and want to borrow an item. Works likely be in high demand among library patrons include those prominently featured in newspaper, magazine, and Internet reviews; advertisements; television and radio talk show spots; bookstore signings; and other media.

Several sources, including trade magazines and select Internet sites, detail publishers' publicity budgets, print runs, and planned author tours for a title; note whether the Book-of-the-Month or other special interest club will feature the item; or indicate whether the title will be promoted via a television show or feature film. Specific sources for this type of information include

- the publisher's advertisements, the "Forecasts" and "Rights" columns, and the seasonal announcements in *Publishers Weekly*;

- notations of planned author tours, large promotional budgets, and purchased movie rights at the end of the reviews in *Publishers Weekly* and *Kirkus Reviews*;

- the "PrePub" Alert section of *Library Journal*;

- the *Get Ready Sheet*, a bimonthly newsletter that lists titles receiving national promotion via author interviews, television programming, or movie tie-ins;[16] and

- the Web site of the American Booksellers Association that contains the "Media Guide" (2001) noting titles currently being featured on the radio, television, and in print.

Although publishers and distributors formally sponsor most promotional efforts, serendipity also plays a role in generating demand. One well-known example occurred well over a decade ago, when an unknown author named Tom Clancy published an obscure technological thriller called *The Hunt for Red October* through the Naval Institute. Then President Ronald Reagan, who received a copy of the book from a friend, mentioned the work in a news conference. A national magazine and other media picked up the story and featured Clancy's book in some depth. Within one month, Clancy became a best-selling author, a status he retains today.

Other publishers and authors have received tremendous exposure when Oprah Winfrey has selected their books as featured titles on her popular television talk show. When Winfrey announced her first selection, Jacquelyn Mitchard's *The Deep End of the Ocean*, demand for the title overwhelmed many libraries and bookstores; the book went on to become a blockbuster bestseller (Starks 1997).[17] Several seasons later, the "Oprah effect" continued to work its magic. Elizabeth Berg's *Open House*, Oprah's first selection for the 2000–2001 season, suddenly moved from "selling well" to the single best-selling title on amazon.com (Maryles 2000).

The power that promotion in the media exerts on the demand for a particular item helps explain why older titles do not receive as much use as newer ones. In the past, a number of researchers have shown that works in the social sciences and sciences circulate less as they grow older (e.g., Van Styvendaele 1981). A portion of this disuse certainly relates to the growing obsolescence of factual information these books contain. However, the circulation of many works in the humanities, which often contain less fact-based information, and the circulation of fiction titles may also decline fairly quickly, generally within three to five years after their publication and purchase (e.g., Hardesty 1981). This decline, at least in part, stems from the fact that publicity for these titles decreases significantly during that time.

Effective media publicity can greatly increase demand for older titles. For example, after Winfrey chose Toni Morrison's *Song of Solomon*, published in 1977, book orders for a single month were 10 times what they had been running for an entire year (Nguyen 1996). Winfrey's recommendation provided a bigger sales boost for Morrison than did her 1993 Nobel Prize for Literature. In response to the ongoing demand, staff at the Park Ridge (Illinois) Public Library label these works (in all formats) with "OPRAH'S BOOK CLUB" stickers. Staff also shelve the hardcover and paperback titles together on a special "Oprah" shelf and have added the category "Oprah books" as a choice in their automatic reserve request program (Mortensen 1999).

Although another type of promotion, word-of-mouth referral, shows more limited effects in the short run, it may significantly affect long-term demand as individuals promote titles among friends, family members, and colleagues. Word-of-mouth helped Richard Bolles's career guide *What Color Is Your Parachute?* and Steven Covey's *7 Habits of Highly Effective People* stay on trade bestseller lists for years. Classic titles, from Charles Darwin's *Voyage of the Beagle* to J. R. R. Tolkien's *Lord of the Rings* trilogy, also remain popular, in part because of such referrals.

Use of items promoted within the library—through booklists, displays, prominent positioning, and the like—also tends to be higher. For example, studies have revealed higher use among materials displayed near the library's door, near the circulation desk, or on eye-level shelves (Baker 1986; and classic studies by Shaw 1938 and Carnovsky 1933). Findings such as these are discussed in significantly more detail in Chapter 10.

Other Factors

Many other factors can influence book choice, often to a lesser degree. For example, Spiller (1980) found that less than 1 percent of 500 fiction readers in five British public libraries were influenced by size of print, design of typeface, page length (a factor that may be more significant for certain groups,, as evidenced by resources like Bodart's [2000] *The World's Best Thin Books: What to Read When Your Book Report Is Due Tomorrow*), sex of the author (many men did not want to read works penned by women), and number of date due stamps in the book. In addition, Ross (1999) has found that setting and ending (whether happy or sad, surprise or anticipated, pat or unresolved) influence readers' choices.

WHAT MIX OF PRODUCTS (ITEMS IN THE COLLECTION) WILL BEST MEET USER NEEDS?

To maximize use and user satisfaction, librarians must make informed decisions about the product items, lines, and mixes of their various collections. A product item is an individual work within the collection, such as a Tony Hillerman paperback, a *Wizard of Oz* video, or the NoveList online database. Product lines (groups of items closely related to each other) may include, for example, all works in a particular format, on a particular subject, of a particular genre, with the same title (regardless of format), or by the same author. Product mixes, the entire set of product lines and items a library offers, often vary (presumably for valid reasons) between branches of the same system.

Public librarians trying to develop a responsive collection will periodically review their product mix, evaluating the usefulness of all product items and lines. They can do this by

- identifying products heavily used by patrons;

- identifying products not used; and

- identifying products desired by patrons or potential patrons but not in the collection.

Each of these approaches is discussed briefly in the following sections and in more detail in Chapter 8.

Identifying Products Heavily Used by Patrons

Whenever doing so will not significantly impair collection depth over time, we suggest increasing access to product items in such high demand that patrons have trouble obtaining them, whether stations to access online resources, best-selling titles, or frequently requested classics. We also recommend identifying and expanding popular product lines so that sufficient quantities exist to meet the needs of regular users.

Identifying Products Not Used by Patrons

Discontinuing infrequently used product lines and weeding items that have lost their relevance and have little likelihood of getting it back (e.g., a 1962 book on space exploration) can free resources to expand product items and lines that users want. However, like other agencies operating under a societal-marketing orientation, libraries may keep other little-used products with a long-term cultural or historical value. For example, public librarians in Omaha may choose to keep fiction titles written by Nebraska natives, even if they have not circulated well, making a renewed commitment to promoting these works on a continuous basis.

Identifying Products Desired by Patrons
or Potential Patrons But Not in the Collection

Satisfaction with, and possibly overall use of, the collection can clearly increase when librarians add materials patrons want. For example, when Dorrell (1980) introduced comic books to a junior high school library, user satisfaction rose, circulation of other materials increased by 30 percent, and the number of students visiting the library jumped an astonishing 82 percent.

HOW DOES THE LIFE CYCLE OF
A PARTICULAR PRODUCT AFFECT THE LEVEL
OF DEMAND FOR IT?

Most stores carry a few staple product items or lines that continue to sell well over a long period of time. In a public library, staples include classics or works on ever-popular topics like making persuasive speeches. However, the majority of products in a library have a finite life span, passing through several distinct life cycle stages before suffering an eventual decline in demand.

Slow acceptance and limited use of a product characterize the introductory stage, one in which consumers study its advantages and disadvantages. This helps explain the number of patrons who seek the works of familiar, beloved authors before browsing among the works of others (Spiller 1980). Demand may also rise slowly in the introductory stage because of delays in distribution or consumer reluctance to buy new products until technical problems in production have been resolved. For example, a number of consumers waited to buy a video player (and hence to borrow library videos) until manufacturers chose VHS over BETA as the industry standard. Although a small contingent open to sampling new items keeps demand for the product afloat during this stage, librarians can also take steps to build product awareness—for example, by displaying new works.

Once word about product excellence begins to spread rapidly, the product enters its growth stage. For very popular works, like titles written by Mary Higgins Clark, the introductory and growth stages may occur almost simultaneously; libraries may have a substantial waiting list for such works before receiving them, or, in some cases, even before their release.

Techniques for meeting the quickly increasing demand of the growth stage include offering the product in various formats; rapidly distributing these to as many library locations as possible; reducing loan periods; and, to meet the needs of browsers as well as those who file reserves, purchasing or leasing additional copies. For example, the Skokie (Illinois) Public Library offers a special "Most Wanted" collection that duplicates the most popular new titles in its regular book collection but are only available for checkout to local cardholders, have a shorter loan period and higher fines, and cannot be reserved ("Loan Policies" 2001; Nordmeyer 1999). These restrictions help stretch a limited budget, providing a cost-efficient method for increasing the availability of items in heavy demand without hampering collection diversity.

In the maturity stage, when many consumers have already used the product, demand will wane. Promoting worthy (e.g., still current) mature items can help ensure a sufficient, revitalized demand to warrant keeping them on the shelf. When the Davidson County (North Carolina) Public Library System promoted older books whose use had waned via booklists distributed to patrons, circulation of these works increased by 220 percent (Parrish 1986). Librarians can also keep demand from declining by reducing the cost of the item. For example, libraries with video collections might follow the lead of retail video stores, allowing longer loans for older titles.

The decline stage reflects a strong decrease in demand. This may parallel technological innovations; for example, as the price of players continues to come down, DVDs will eventually significantly undercut demand for videos. A decline may also mirror changes in style or tastes, as with older books on interior decoration or shifts in cultural or social values, such as a children's series introducing different careers that only shows female nurses and male doctors. Whatever the reason, product items and lines that have become unacceptable to users are prime candidates for quick elimination from the collection.

The demand for certain formats, subject areas, genres, and well-known authors (e.g., John Irving) will likely remain in the growth or maturity stage for a number of years and thus will continue to meet user needs. Other product lines have somewhat shorter life cycles as newer, more convenient, or more fashionable lines replace them.

Not all products follow the standard life cycle described in this chapter. Mature products can gain new life via promotion, as all of Robert Parker's Spenser titles did when a television series based on the character aired. In other cases, products alternate between periods of relatively high and low use. Seasonal works are an obvious example, from stories about Christmas, Hanukkah, and Kwanzaa to works on air conditioning repair, snowmobiling, and camping. Cyclical patterns of use also commonly occur among works necessary for school assignments.

Products with faddish, or very rapid, life cycles, attract quick and vigorous, but brief, market attention. Consider, for example, books on current events of intense public interest, like the spate of O. J. Simpson tell-alls and analyses published around the time of his trial. Although such books circulate very heavily at first, demand drastically drops as public attention moves on to more recent events. To meet immediate patron demand for faddish books, we recommend purchasing multiple copies in low-cost formats whenever feasible and/or obtaining them on a lease-purchase plan from vendors like McNaughton and Baker and Taylor, adopting short loan periods, and weeding heavily once demand wanes.

CONCLUSION

The product decisions librarians make affect the extent of patron satisfaction and use as well as communitywide support in both the short and long terms. Studying community tastes and becoming familiar with the specific considerations likely to influence an individual's material selections can help us provide stellar collections to offer patrons true satisfaction.

NOTES

1. The information presented in the following sections is based on research findings. Katz (1990) also provides a non-research-oriented, humorous slant on the issue.

2. This finding may support the idea that libraries are more successful at attracting certain types of users than others and/or that those who work at particular branches may be doing more things right to attract and keep patrons.

3. Community size was not a variable in the Ottensmann, Gnat, and Gleeson (1995) study, which considered branches of a single urban library.

4. Chapter 8 includes a more detailed discussion of calculating turnover rates.

5. Biographies had a turnover rate of 4.9 (Hage 1997). For an explanation of how turnover rate is calculated, see Chapter 8.

6. For advice on forming and conducting a genre study group, see Balcom (1997).

7. For subscription information, see *Ulrich's* (2000).

8. To subscribe to one of these lists, send a message that says subscribe *listname yourfirstname yourlastname* to the following addresses: for DOROTHY_L and RRA-L mail to listscrv@listscrv.kcnt.edu. For SF-LOVERS mail to sf-lovers-request@rutvml.rutgers.edu. Leave the message content line blank. To find other genre mailing lists, consult the section entitled "Finding a List to Join" in Chapter 5 of *The Book Lover's Guide to the Internet* (Morris 1998) or through Internet sources such as "Fiction Mailing Lists" (Johnson 2000).

9. The Romance Writers of America can be reached at 3707 F.M. 1960 West, Ste. 555, Houston, TX, 77068; 281-440-6885; info@rwanational.com; www.rwanational.com (Sheets 2000).

10. See, for example, "The Whole World" (1994) for videos and Bell (1980) for large print.

11. Aron (1992) noted that 80 percent of respondents listened to audiobooks in the car and 7 percent while exercising. The APA survey found that 44.5 percent listen in the car, 37.4 percent at home, 7.6 percent while exercising, 4 percent at school or daycare, 3.8 percent at work, 1.3 percent on a plane, and 1.3 percent on mass transit.

12. Burris (1995) also provides an in-depth look at arguments on both sides of the issue. And Radway (1988) describes the debate that goes on within and among the editors responsible for choosing the titles that the Book-of-the-Month Club features.

13. A number of other works have addressed reading from this psychological perspective. Intriguing examples are Gold (1990), Sabine and Sabine (1983), and Holland (1975).

14. Roberts (1990), Saricks and Brown (1997), and Cawelti (1976) present fascinating discussions of stylistic concerns.

15. See "1999 Top Titles" (1999) for the most recent published adult new reader suggestions from the Public Library Association's Adult Lifelong Learning Services cluster.

16. For subscription information, see *Ulrich's* (1998).

17. For example, at the time that Winfrey announced her reading club and its first selection, the Arlington Heights (Illinois) Memorial Library owned seven copies of *Deep End of the Ocean*. By the end of the day they had 49 holds on the title. See Starks (1997).

REFERENCES

Angel, Karen. 1998. "Handselling at Opposite Ends of the U.S." *Publishers Weekly* 245, no. 28 (July 13): 17.

Annichiarico, Mark. 1991. "Spoken Word Audio: The Fastest-Growing Library Collection." *Library Journal* 116, no. 9 (May 15): 36–39.

Aron, Helen. 1992. "Bookworms Become Tapeworms: A Profile of Listeners to Books on Audiocassette." *Journal of Reading* 36, no. 3 (November): 208–12.

"Audio Book Survey." 2001. [Homepage of the Plano Public Library System], [Online]. (Last updated March 7). Formerly available: http://www.planolibrary.org/audioform .htm [Accessed March 14, 2001].

Baker, Sharon L. 1986. "The Display Phenomenon: An Exploration into Factors Causing the Increased Circulation of Displayed Books." *Library Quarterly* 56, no. 3 (July): 237–57.

———. 1994. "What Patrons Read and Why: The Link Between Personality and Reading." In *Research Issues in Public Librarianship: Trends for the Future*, ed. Joy M. Greiner, 131–47. Westport, CT: Greenwood Press.

———. 1996. "A Decade's Worth of Research on Browsing Fiction Collections." In *Guiding the Reader to the Next Book*, ed. Kenneth Shearer, 127–47. New York: Neal-Schuman.

Baker, Susan E. 1995. " 'Trash 'em or Treasure 'em?': A Study of Demand for and Characteristics of the Annual Top Ten Fiction Bestsellers, 1965–1990." Master's research paper, University of North Carolina at Chapel Hill.

Balcom, Ted. 1997. "First, You Read." In *Serving Readers*, ed. Ted Balcom, for the Illinois Library Association, 1–8. Fort Atkinson, WI: Highsmith Press.

"Barnes&Noble.com Awards." 1997–2001. [Homepage of Barnes&Noble], [Online]. Available: http://www.barnesandnoble.com/awards/awards.asp? [Accessed September 27, 2001].

Barron, Neil, ed. 1995. *Anatomy of Wonder*. 4th ed. New Providence, NJ: Bowker.

Barron, Neil, et al., ed. annual. *What Do I Read Next?* Detroit: Gale.

Bell, Lorna J. 1980. *The Large Print Book and Its User*. London: Library Association.

Bodart, Joni Richards. 2000. *The World's Best Thin Books: What to Read When Your Book Report Is Due Tomorrow*. Lanham, MD: Scarecrow Press.

Book Industry Study Group, Inc. 2000. "New Study Shows Consumer Adult Book Purchases Rose 3% in 1999; Reversing 1998 Decline. Internet Captures 5.4% of All Books Bought by Consumers in 1999, Nearly Tripling in Volume from 1998." [Homepage of Book Industry Study Group, Inc.], [Online]. (Released June 2). Available: http://www.bisg.org/pressrelease_june2_2000.html]. [Accessed September 27, 2001].

Brewis, W. L. E., E. M. Gericke, and J. A. Kruger. 1996. "The Policy of Public Libraries Regarding the Provision of Fiction for Adult Readers." *Mousaion* 14, no. 2: 16–31.

"Briefly Noted." 1999. *Library Hotline* 28, no. 40 (October 11): 3.

Britten, William A., and Judith D. Webster. 1992. "Comparing Characteristics of Highly Circulated Titles for Demand-Driven Collection Development." *College and Research Libraries* 53, no. 3 (May): 239–48.

Brownstone, David M., and Irene M. Franck. 1982. *The Dictionary of Publishing*. New York: Van Nostrand Reinhold.

Burris, Amy E. 1995. "A Comparison of the Attitudes of Public Librarians and Public Library Patrons Toward the 'Quality' Versus 'Demand' Debate in Collection Development." Master's research paper, University of North Carolina at Chapel Hill.

Cannell, Jeffrey, and Eileen McCluskey. 1996. "Genrefication: Fiction Classification and Increased Circulation." In *Guiding the Reader to the Next Book*, ed. Kenneth D. Shearer, 159–65. New York: Neal-Schuman.

Carlson, Laura, Sean Creighton, and Sheila Cunningham, eds. 1995. *Literary Laurels: A Reader's Guide to Award-Winning Fiction*. New York: Hillyard Industries.

———. 1996. *Literary Laurels: A Reader's Guide to Award-Winning Children's Books*. New York: Hillyard Industries.

Carnovsky, Leon. 1933. "The Dormitory Library: An Experiment in Stimulating Reading." *Library Quarterly* 3, no. 1 (January): 37–65.

"Category Closeups." 2001. [Homepage of Publishers Weekly], [Online]. Available: http://www.publishersweekly.reviewnews.com [Accessed September 27, 2001].

Cawelti, John G. 1976. *Adventure, Mystery, and Romance: Formula Stories as Art and Popular Culture*. Chicago: University of Chicago Press.

Caywood, Carolyn. 1993. "Judge a Book by Its Cover." *School Library Journal* 39, no. 8 (August): 58.

Darch, Darlene. 1998. "Redis'COVER' a Reading Treasure." *School Librarian's Workshop* 18, no. 7 (March): 14.

Davis, Hazel M., and Ellen Altman. 1997. "The Relationship Between Community Lifestyles and Circulation Patterns in Public Libraries." *Public Libraries* 36, no. 1 (January/February): 40–45.

"Daypacks to Go." 1997. *Public Libraries* 36, no. 5 (September/October): 274.

D'Elia, George. 1980. "The Development and Testing of a Conceptual of Public Library User Behavior." *Library Quarterly* 50, no. 4 (October): 410–30.

Delin, Catherine R., Peter S. Delin, and Laura Cram. 1995. "Patterns and Preferences in Recreational Reading." *Australian Library Journal* 44, no. 3 (August): 119–31.

"Denver P(ublic) L(ibrary) Reaches Out to Vietnamese Community." 1988. *Library Journal* 113, no. 20 (December): 29.

"Digital Audiobooks Now Being Loaned." 2001. *Library Journal* 126, no. 6 (April 1): 22.

Dorrell, Larry Dean. 1980. "Comic Books and Circulation in a Public Junior High School Library." Ph.D. diss., University of Missouri-Columbia.

" 'The English Patient' Author Gives Reading at LaSells." 1997. *Oregon State University Daily Barometer Online* [Online] (April 21). Formerly available: http://www.orst.edu /Dept/Barometer/1997/spring/week4/1mon/97042N_theenglishpat.html [Accessed July 3, 1999].

Ettelt, Harold. 1986. "What Our Book Use Study Shows Us." Hudson, NY: Columbia-Greene Community College. ERIC ED274376.

―――. 1987. "New Books, and Those Previously Used, Lead the Band, by a Lot." Hudson, NY: Columbia-Greene Community College. ERIC ED286526.

Feldman, Beth. 1991. "Covers That Catch the Eye: A Look at How Book Jackets Influence Prospective Young Readers." *Publishers Weekly* 238, no. 48 (November 1): 46–48.

Fonseca, Anthony J., and June Michele Pulliam. 1999. *Hooked on Horror.* Englewood, CO: Libraries Unlimited.

Gallup Organization. 1985. *The Gallup 1985 Annual Report on Book Buying.* Princeton, NJ: Gallup Organization.

Gay, Cheri. 1996. "Detroit Mounts Show Worth Honking About." *American Libraries* 27, no. 11 (December): 48–51.

Genco, Barbara A. 1988. "Mass Market Books: Their Place in the Library." *School Library Journal* 35, no. 4 (December): 40–41.

Gold, Joseph. 1990. *Read for Your Life: Literature as a Life Support System.* Markham, ONT: Fitzhenry and Whiteside.

Goldhor, Herbert. 1959. "Are the Best Books Most Read?" *Library Quarterly* 29, no. 4 (October): 251–55.

―――. 1981a. "Evaluation of a Sample of Adult Books in the Kingston and St. Andrew Parish Library of Jamaica." Urbana: University of Illinois, Graduate School of Library Science. ERIC ED201334.

―――. 1981b. "A Report on an Application of the Inductive Method of Evaluation of Public Library Books." *Libri* 31, no. 2 (August): 121–29.

Goodall, Deborah. 1989. "Browsing in Public Libraries." *Occasional Paper* no. 1 of Loughborough (England) University of Technology, Department of Library and Information Studies, Library and Information Statistics Unit.

Gordon, Margaret, Andrew Gordon, and Elizabeth Moore. 2001. "New Computers Bring New Patrons." *Library Journal* 126, no. 3 (February 15): 134–38.

Gorman, G. E., and B. R. Howes. 1989. *Collection Development for Libraries.* New York: Bowker-Saur.

"Grand Opening of Biblioteca Latinoamericana in San Jose." 2000. *Public Libraries* 39, no. 3 (May/June): 136.

Hage, Christine Lind. 1997. "The Fact Is That Fiction Dominates." *Public Libraries* 36, no. 3 (May/June): 153–54.

Hall, Audrey L. 1992. "A Study of Information Used by Public Library Patrons to Select Videocassettes." Master's research paper, Kent State University. ERIC ED356803.

Hardesty, Larry. 1981. "Uses of Library Materials at a Small Liberal Arts College." *Library Research* 3, no. 3 (Fall): 261–82.

Herald, Diana Tixier. [2001]. "Genrefluent." [Homepage of Genrefluent], [Online]. (Updated September 26). Available: http://www.genrefluent.com/ [Accessed September 27, 2001].

———. 1997. *Teen Genreflecting*. Englewood, CO: Libraries Unlimited.

———. 1999. *Fluent in Fantasy*. Englewood, CO: Libraries Unlimited.

———. 2000. *Genreflecting: A Guide to Reading Interests in Genre Fiction*. 5th ed. Englewood, CO: Libraries Unlimited.

Hoffert, Barbara. 1994. "Dragon Dancers & Eastern Westerns: Serving the Asian American Community." *Library Journal* 119, no. 12 (July): 42–45.

———. 2001. "Book Report 2001: The Budget Shifts." *Library Journal* 126, no. 3 (February 15): 130–32.

Holland, Norman N. 1975. *5 Readers Reading*. New Haven, CT: Yale University Press.

"Hot off the Net." 2001. [Homepage of Nielsen//NetRatings], [Online]. Available: http://www.nielsen-netratings.com/ [Accessed September 28, 2001].

"The International Languages Department." [2001]. [Homepage of Los Angeles Public Library], [Online]. Available: http://www.lapl.org/central/international.html [Accessed September 27, 2001].

"Internet Activities." [2001]. [Homepage of Pew Internet & American Life Project], [Online]. Available: http://pewinternet.org/reports/index.asp [Accessed September 27, 2001].

Jenkins, Joyce. 1994. "No Health Information Whatsoever Better Than Wrong Information." *PNLA Quarterly* 58 (Winter): 21.

Jennings, Barbara, and Lyn Sear. 1986. "How Readers Select Fiction—A Survey in Kent." *Public Library Journal* 1, no. 4: 43–47.

Johnson, Peggy. 1999. "Dollars and Sense in Collection Development: Theories of Selection: Evolving Perspectives." *Technicalities* 19, no. 3 (March): 11–13.

Johnson, Roberta S. 2000. "Fiction Mailing Lists." [Homepage of Fictional.org], [Online]. (Updated April). Available: http://www.fictional.org/ralists.html#Listsearch [Accessed September 27, 2001].

Katz, Bill. 1990. "Perspective: The Allure of the New Books Section." *Collection Building* 10, nos. 3–4: 58–60.

Kaye, Sheldon, and Beth Baxter. 1994. "Breaking the Sound Barrier: Starting and Maintaining an Audiobook Collection." *Library Journal* 119, no. 9 (May 15): 34–36.

Kiefer, Marjorie. 1987. "Cooperative Outreach Services for Seniors." *Illinois Libraries* 69, no. 10 (December): 716–19.

Klauber, Julie. 1998. "Living Well with a Disability: How Libraries Can Help." *American Libraries* 29, no. 10 (November): 52–55.

Linz, Cathie, ed. 1999. "RWA's New Affiliate Program." *Checking Out Romance: The Romance Writers of America Library Affiliates Program Newsletter* 1, no. 1 (Winter): 2.

Little, Paul. 1990. "Collection Development for Bookmobiles." In *The Book Stops Here: New Directions in Bookmobile Services*, ed. Catherine Suyak Alloway, 59–70. Metuchen, NJ: Scarecrow Press.

"Loan Periods." 2000–2001. [Homepage of the Des Plaines Public Library], [Online]. Available: http://www.desplaines.lib.il.us/library/GeneralInfo.html#loanpolicies [Accessed September 27, 2001].

"Loan Policies at Skokie Public Library." 2001. [Homepage of Skokie Public Library], [Online]. (Updated July 24). Available: http://www.skokie.lib.il.us/about/loan.html [Accessed September 27, 2001].

Lodge, Sally. 1998. "Breaking Out of Format Formulas." *Publishers Weekly* 245, no. 45 (November 9): 31–33.

Lucas, Linda. 1982. "Reading Interests, Life Interests, and Life-style." *Public Library Quarterly* 3, no. 4 (Winter): 11–18.

"The Magic of Harry Potter." 1999. *Time* 154, no. 12 (September 20): cover.

Manley, Will. 1990. "Facing the Public." *Wilson Library Bulletin* 64, no. 10 (June): 89–90.

Mann, Laurie D. T. [2001]. [Homepage of AwardWeb: Collections of Literary Award Information], [Online]. Available: http:/dpsinfo.com/awardweb [Accessed September 27, 2001].

Mann, Peter H. 1971. *Books: Buyers and Borrowers*. London: Deutsch.

Maryles, Daisy. 2000. "Behind the Bestsellers: Oprah's 'Open'-ing." *Publishers Weekly* 247, no. 35: 21.

"Media Guide." 2001. [Homepage of the American Booksellers Association], [Online]. Available: http://www.bookweb.org/news/1273.html [Accessed September 27, 2001].

Morris, Evan. 1998. *The Book Lover's Guide to the Internet*. Rev. ed. New York: Fawcett Columbine.

Mortensen, Vivian. 1999. (Head of Reader Services, Park Ridge [Illinois] Public Library). Conversation with Karen Wallace, July 3.

Nell, Victor. 1988. *Lost in a Book: The Psychology of Reading for Pleasure*. New Haven, CT: Yale University Press.

"netLibrary eBooks Available to Public Library Patrons." 2000. *Public Libraries* 39, no. 4 (July/August): 193.

"New APA Statistics Show Audio Market Growing: Market Penetration Up 75%." [2001]. [Homepage of the Audio Publishers Association], [Online]. Formerly available: http://www.audiopub.org/99stats.html [Accessed April 9, 2001]. (See http://www.audiopub.org/apafaqs.html#stats for a related item.)

"New Life for Old Books." 1995. *American Libraries* 26, no. 7 (July/August): 636.

Nguyen, Lan N. 1996. "Touched by an Oprah." *People Weekly* 46, no. 23 (December 2): 36.

"1999 Top Titles for Adult New Readers." 1999. *Public Libraries* 38, no. 5 (September/October): 320–21.

Nordmeyer, Ricki. 1999. (Head of Readers' Services, Skokie [Illinois] Public Library). "Re: Most Wanted Collection." E-mail to Karen Wallace, July 9.

NPD Group and Carol Meyer. 1996. *The 1996 Consumer Research Study on Book Purchasing.* Tarrytown, NY: Book Industry Study Group.

Oder, Norman. 1998. "AV Rising: Demand, Budgets, and Circulation Are All Up." *Library Journal* 123, no. 19 (November 15): 30–33.

Ondaatje, Michael. 1992. *The English Patient.* New York: Knopf.

Ottensmann, John R., Raymond E. Gnat, and Michael E. Gleeson. 1995. "Similarities in Circulation Patterns Among Public Library Branches Serving Diverse Populations." *Library Quarterly* 65, no. 1 (January): 89–118.

"Overbooked Table of Contents." [2001]. [Homepage of Overbooked], [Online]. Available: http://www.overbooked.org/ [Accessed September 27, 2001].

Parker, Laurie. 1999. "Re: Media Request for Info." [Online posting to prtalk@ala.org]. (August 24).

Parrish, Nancy B. 1986. "The Effect of a Booklist on the Circulation of Fiction Books Which Have Not Been Borrowed from a Public Library in Four Years or Longer." Master's research paper, University of North Carolina at Greensboro. ERIC ED282564.

Pearl, Nancy, with assistance from Martha Knappe and Chris Higashi. 1999. *Now Read This: A Guide to Mainstream Fiction, 1978–1998.* Englewood, CO: Libraries Unlimited.

Pohjanvalta, Terhikki. 1993. "Surveying the Use of Quality in Espoo City Library." *Scandinavian Public Library Quarterly* 26, no. 4: 24–27.

Poller, Anna C. 1988. "Videogames as Public Library Material—A Theoretical Evaluation." *South African Journal of Library and Information Science* 56, no. 1: 38–43.

"Queens Library Lends TTY Units." 2000. *The Unabashed Librarian* no. 114: 10.

Radway, Janice A. 1991. *Reading the Romance: Women, Patriarchy, and Popular Literature.* Rev. ed. Chapel Hill, NC: University of North Carolina Press.

———. 1988. "The Book-of-the-Month Club and the General Reader: On the Uses of 'Serious' Fiction." *Critical Inquiry* 14, no. 3 (Spring): 516–38.

Ramsdell, Kristin. 1999. *Romance Fiction.* Englewood, CO: Libraries Unlimited.

"Readers' Resources." 1996–2001. [Homepage of BookBrowser], [Online]. Available: http://www.bookbrowser.com/Resources/Index.html [Accessed September 27, 2001].

"Reflecting Local, Nat'l Events, Wilmette PL Promote Unity." 1999. *Library Hotline* 28, no. 38 (September 27): 3–4.

Rindfleisch, Mary. 1999. "Re: Media Request for Info" [Online posting to prtalk@ala.org]. (August 24).

Roberts, Thomas J. 1990. *An Aesthetics of Junk Fiction.* Athens: University of Georgia Press.

Robinson, Charles W. 1987. "Fees for Videocassettes—An Opportunity for Service and Growth." *Public Libraries* 26, no. 3 (Fall): Fast Forward insert.

Rosenblum, Trudi M. 1996. "Truck Stops: A Growing Market for Audio." *Publishers Weekly* 243, no. 41 (October 7): 28, 30.

Ross, Catherine Sheldrick. 1991. "Readers' Advisory Services: New Directions." *RQ* 30, no. 4 (Summer): 503–18.

Ross, Catherine Sheldrick, and Mary K. Chelton. 2001. "Reader's Advisory: Matching Mood and Material." *Library Journal* 126, no. 2 (February 1): 52–55.

———. 1999. "A Model of the Process of Choosing a Book for Pleasure." Presentation in Growing Readers' Advisory Services seminar at American Public Library Association Spring Symposium, Chicago, March 25–27.

Sabine, Gordon, and Patricia Sabine. 1983. *Books That Made the Difference.* Hamden, CT: Library Professional Publications.

Sager, Don. 1996. "Not So Quiet a Revolution: Audiobooks in Public Libraries." *Public Libraries* 35, no. 2 (March/April): 113.

"Sales of Recorded Music and Music Videos, by Genre and Format, 1995–99." 2001. In *The World Almanac and Book of Facts 2001*, ed. William A. McGeveran, Jr., 312. Mahwah, NJ: World Almanac Books.

Samuels, Barbara G. 1989. "Young Adult Choices: Why Do Students 'Really Like' Particular Books?" *Journal of Reading* 32, no. 8 (May): 714–19.

Saricks, Joyce G. 1998. "Providing the Fiction Your Patrons Want: Managing Fiction in a Medium-Sized Public Library." In *Fiction Acquisition/Fiction Management: Education and Training*, ed., Georgine N. Olson, 11–28. New York: Haworth Press.

———. 2001. *The Reader's Advisory Guide to Genre Fiction.* Chicago: American Library Association.

Saricks, Joyce G., and Nancy Brown. 1997. *Readers' Advisory Service in the Public Library.* 2d ed. Chicago: American Library Association.

Scales, Alice M. 1996. "Examining What Older Adults Read and Watch on TV." *Educational Gerontology* 22, no. 3 (April/May): 215–27.

Scates, Denni Kay. 1999. "How Do Adult New Readers Locate High-Interest, Easy-to-Read Books?" *Public Libraries* 38, no. 5 (September/October): 294–98.

Shaw, Ralph R. 1938. "The Influence of Sloping Shelves on Book Circulation." *Library Quarterly* 8, no. 4 (October): 480–90.

Sheets Tara E., ed. 2000. *Encyclopedia of Associations.* 36th ed. Vol. 1. Detroit: Gale.

Smith, Ian M. 1999. "What Do They Read?" *Public Library Journal* 14, no. 1 (Spring): 5–10.

Speer, Tibbett L. 1995. "Libraries from A to Z." *American Demographics* 17, no. 9 (September): 48–55.

Spiller, David. 1980. "The Provision of Fiction for Public Libraries." *Journal of Librarianship* 12, no. 4 (October): 238–65.

Starks, Carolyn. 1997. "Libraries Scramble after Oprah Picks Book: When Talk Show Host Speaks, Readers Listen." *Chicago Tribune* (May 1): sec. Metro Du Page 1, 5.

Steptowe, C. G. 1987. "A Case Study of Fiction Provision in a Public Library." Master's research paper, Loughborough University.

Stevenson, Burton, ed. 1967. *The Home Book of Quotations*. 10th ed. New York: Dodd, Mead.

Stevenson, Nanette. 1997. "Hipper, Brighter and Bolder: Publishers Struggle to Make Book Jackets Stand Out on Ever More Crowded Shelves." *Publishers Weekly* 244, no. 7 (February 17): 139–41.

Strong, Gary E. 2000. "LinQing the World to Queens—and Queens to the World." *American Libraries* 31, no. 9 (October): 44–46.

Sullivan, Edward T. 1998. "Judging Books by Their Covers: A Cover Art Experiment." *Voice of Youth Advocates* 21, no. 3 (August): 180–82.

"Tool Lending Library." 2001. [Homepage of the Berkeley Public Library], [Online]. (Updated September 11). Available: http://www.infopeople.org/bpl/tool/index.html [Accessed September 26, 2001].

"Toy Library at the Brooklyn Branch" [2001]. [Homepage of Cuyahoga County Public Library], [Online]. Available: http://clio1.cuyahoga.lib.oh.us/home/event.html [Accessed September 27, 2001].

Ulrich's International Periodicals Directory 2001. 2000. 39th ed. New Providence, NJ: Bowker.

Van Styvendaele, B. J. H. 1981. "University Scientists as Seekers of Information: Sources of References to Books and Their First Use Versus Date of Publication." *Journal of Librarianship* 13, no. 2 (April): 83–92.

Volz, Bridget Dealy, Lynda Blackburn Welborn, and Cheryl Perkins Scheer. 2000. *Junior Genreflecting: A Guide to Good Reads and Series Fiction for Children*. Englewood, CO: Libraries Unlimited.

"The Whole World Is Watching." 1994. *Video Software Magazine* (January): 20–41.

Willits, Harold W., and Fern K. Willits. 1991. "Rural Reading Behavior and Library Usage: Findings from a Pennsylvania Survey." *Rural Libraries* 11, no. 1: 25–37.

Wojciechowski, Jacek. 1996. "Belles-Lettres in the Library." *Public Libraries* 35, no. 2 (March/April): 121–23.

Youman, Nancy. 1989. "Marketing Solutions: Vintage's Novel Approach to Repackaging Classics." *Adweek's Marketing Week* 30, no. 39 (September 25): 20–21.

Yu, Liangzhi, and Ann O'Brien. 1999. "A Practical Typology of Adult Fiction Borrowers Based on Their Reading Habits." *Journal of Information Science* 25, no. 1 (January): 35–49.

COST OF COLLECTIONS AND USE

"What? All this for a song!"—
William Cecil, Lord Burleigh (*Oxford Dictionary* 1980, 112).

During the twentieth century many individuals expressed principles recognizing the economics of library use. These include Ranganathan (1957)—"save the time of the reader"—and Mooers (1960)—"an information retrieval system will tend not to be used when it is more painful and troublesome for a customer to have information than for him not to have it." Such statements clearly recognize that people consider both costs and benefits when choosing where they will obtain materials to read, listen to, and view. Although some will seek these items from the library, others will use bookstores, the Internet, friends' collections, and other non-library venues or decide they can do without them.

The cost-benefit model of library use suggests that cost elements influence both patrons' initial decisions to visit (in real or virtual form) the library and later decisions to use particular collections or materials offered there. The costs of using the library and its collections include

- traveling to a physical library or accessing a virtual one;
- obtaining a borrower's card;
- locating desired items;
- queuing up to obtain answers to questions and/or check out items;
- renting items for which the library charges fees;

- paying fines for overdue books, damaged items, and lost works;
- reserving, and later collecting, titles in use by another patron or otherwise not immediately available;
- requesting interlibrary loans; and
- returning borrowed items.

Although concrete costs, such as the daily overdue book fine, may be uniform, perception of these costs varies, based on factors such as an individual's ability to use libraries, discretionary time and income, stress levels, and degree of need for an item. For example, a graduate student who must take the bus to the nearest small public library branch may forego obtaining materials there, preferring both the convenience of use and the breadth of selection at the university library. A retiree may deem insignificant the costs of driving to that same branch, borrowing three-fourths of the materials he needs from that collection, and requesting the rest through intra- or interlibrary loan. A busy executive may consider the same costs so high that she purchases what she wants to read online and requests next-day delivery to her office.

To encourage use by individuals, who weigh their private out-of-pocket, convenience, and psychological costs and benefits when deciding whether to use the library (Van House 1983a, 1983b), librarians will adopt and refine techniques to keep combined costs as low and combined benefits as high as possible for community residents.

WHAT PRICE OBJECTIVES CAN A LIBRARY ADOPT?

Public librarians can choose variations on four basic pricing objectives—maximizing use, limiting use, recovering costs, and maximizing profits—based on criteria such as library mission and service responses, the cost of providing certain forms of materials, and the existence of one or more special situations. We suggest that maximizing profits will apply primarily to the investment of library funds and Friends of the Library activities, so we discuss here the other three, directly related to responsive collections, in the following sections.

Maximizing Use

Attempts to maximize collection use stem from the belief that both individual patrons and society at large receive benefits from high use. Presumably individuals gain pleasure, information, and knowledge when they obtain and use library materials. Society in turn benefits from having content, well-informed, knowledgeable members. In addition, shared collections contribute to significant environmental savings—of trees, recycling costs, and the like. The library can attempt to maximize use by reducing waiting time for desired materials, limiting the out-of-pocket costs patrons pay, and otherwise keeping costs low as well as publicizing benefits of library service.

Limiting Use

A scarcity of desired materials commonly causes libraries to attempt to moderate use. One Saskatchewan library with a small and popular audiobook collection set a three-title per patron borrowing limit on these works. Overnight, complaints about title accessibility dropped by half and the likelihood of finding a particular work rose from 25 to 55 percent. Librarians spent the next six months raising funds that tripled the size of the collection.[1]

A desire to keep access relatively high without limiting collection diversity may also prompt attempts to discourage use. With an extremely limited collection budget, one Illinois library decided to shorten loan periods for highly popular comic strip anthologies so that it would be able to purchase other art books with allocated funds.

Other major attempts to moderate use relate to ethical and legal considerations. Complex problems, such as protecting minors from exposure to Internet pornography, result in the potential clash of one good, children's physical and emotional safety, with another, individual rights to access information. Our solutions will continue to be controversial unless and until perfectly calibrated responses replace imperfect ones such as filters, parental permission forms, and privacy screens.

Recovering Costs

In a competitive economy, a library may not be able to provide both a broad and deep collection with the money given to it by its funding body. We encourage libraries to seek additional funding from other sources as a long-term solution (see Chapter 9); they may also consider stretching tight budgets, recovering part or all of the costs of providing value-added collections by charging fees, another controversial practice discussed in more detail in this chapter.

Most value-added services supplement rather than replace regular access.[2] For example, the Indian Prairie (Darien, Illinois) Public Library District offers a rental collection of popular titles that duplicate items in the regular collection (Freeland 1997).

SETTING PRICES

We advocate that librarians avoid setting prices based on tradition (the "but-we've-always-charged-five-cents-for-overdue-materials" approach) and instead use cost-oriented or demand-oriented pricing.

Cost-oriented pricing occurs when library staff set the product's cost to correspond with the actual monetary cost that the library incurs to provide that product. A national study (now more than 15 years old) examining this practice among medium-sized public libraries confirmed that this method was most commonly used to determine the fee to be charged (Phelan 1985). A more recent but still dated examination of public libraries in London supports the popularity of this approach; 60 percent of the surveyed libraries determine prices by setting income targets (Tilson 1995). Suppose, for example, that a library has a rental collection of popular fiction. The average book in the collection costs $36.00 to purchase and process and circulates 18 times. If staff charged patrons $2.00 for each circulation, the library would break even in terms of cost. Staff could funnel the fees earned back into the rental collection and have a self-supporting collection. The library could partially subsidize the cost by charging patrons only $1.00 for each circulation. The Tauranga (New Zealand) District Libraries have built self-supporting high demand collections of fiction, nonfiction, large print, music, magazines, and bestsellers, following a very detailed version of this approach. They determined that 56 percent of revenues collected must cover overhead; the remaining 44 percent can purchase additional materials (Peacocke and Nees 2000).

Demand-oriented pricing occurs when library staff members estimate how much value patrons see in a particular product and then price it accordingly, bearing in mind the fact that patrons may continue to use popular items even when the cost rises slightly. Numerous public libraries base their overdue fines on the availability of and demand for certain types of items. For example, the Urbana (Illinois) Free Library charges overdue fees for adult materials ranging from 10 cents per day for books to 25 cents for compact discs to 50 cents for videos ("Borrower Information" 2000).

One form of demand-oriented pricing discriminates (in the positive sense of the word) on a customer basis, for example, by offering library volunteers a grace period before they incur fines. Libraries may offer concessions depending on a patron's age; the Westerville (Ohio) Public Library waives fines for patrons at least 60 years of age ("Circulation" 2000), and numerous libraries either waive children's fines or keep them very low. A library might also decrease fines for individuals whose annual income falls below a certain dollar amount. The application for new and renewed cards could solicit this information, clearing identifying this as an optional question the answer to which, while potentially reducing fee and fine assessments, will not be shared with others. The circulation system can then be programmed to take this into account when assigning charges.

The second form of demand-oriented pricing discriminates on a product basis. For example, the library may set a higher cost (e.g., a shortened loan period) for new books or a popular product line such as CDs than it does for older titles or less popular formats. The Lewistown (Montana) Public Library does this indirectly by assessing fines based on the checkout length of a particular item, which varies inversely with the popularity. Lewistown charges 5 cents per day for materials with a 30-day loan and 25 cents per day for 14-day loans ("Policies" 2001).

Another alternative to pricing by tradition, *competition-oriented pricing*, occurs when library staff set prices in relationship to what local competitors charge. For example, before imposing fees for video rental, staff may call local video outlets to determine charges for tape rentals, the length of time tapes can be rented out, and the fee for returning late tapes. Staff can then set prices that match or undercut those of the video outlets. (We suggest that librarians de-emphasize this approach to avoid incurring charges of unfair competition from a government entity.)

PRICE INCREASES AND REDUCTIONS

Staff may reasonably consider raising the price when facing significantly increased levels of demand for or costs of providing a particular collection. For example, when a teacher requires 150 students to prepare reports on a specific state, the public library may either limit the number of works that each student may borrow or place books about that state on reserve.

In the same vein, staff members can cut costs when the price of doing business declines or they wish to stimulate demand. For example, one Midwestern library noticed that circulation of the rental collection housed at its mall branch fell significantly when a bookstore moved in two doors away. When the branch quit charging fees for popular materials, use rose again, exceeding its previous level.

We encourage librarians to estimate the effects of a price change on use when considering one. Staff can survey patron attitudes toward the proposal, asking a relevant version of one of the following questions:

- If the library increases the price of (a particular product) to XXX, would you still use it?

- To what extent would you be more likely to use (a particular product) if we reduced its cost from XXX to XXX?

For example, when the West Lothian (Scotland) Public Library Services was considering expanding CD availability by eliminating its collection of music on tape and reducing the CD loan period from three weeks to one, it first surveyed audio users. Overwhelming support existed for the first proposal and strong aversion to the second (Kerr 1999).

Staff may also be able to anticipate customer reactions to a proposed price change either by relying on general knowledge of patrons or by reviewing past use data to determine the effects of earlier price adjustments. When one city manager in the southeastern United States pressured his local library to double existing fees for using certain materials in the collection, the library director provided statistics to the manager and the city council. These data, which showed that past small fee increases had had little effect on usage, but significant increases caused circulation to fall, helped the director persuade city officials to raise user fees by only 30 percent.

Public libraries can also gauge customer reactions by actually changing the price of a product on a trial basis and examining the results. The Hawaii State Public Library System tried this approach when it first offered its "Hot Picks" seven-day bestseller loan program as a six-month pilot project ("Best Sellers" 1999).

OUT-OF-POCKET COSTS

Getting There

Public libraries also expect most patrons to bear the monetary costs (as well as the non-monetary ones discussed elsewhere in this chapter) of traveling to and from the library, both initially and to return materials. Potential techniques for reducing these costs for some patrons include offering

- low-priced metered or free parking spaces on the street adjacent to the library;
- large lots next to the library that allow patrons to park free;
- drive-up windows and materials drops so patrons can obtain pre-reserved materials and return items quickly and without having to find parking;
- reimbursement for transit fares for indigent patrons and children who use the library; such policies may be funded by the governing body, local charitable associations, or the Friends;
- services at satellite locations, through personal delivery, or on board mobile facilities; and
- full-text databases available via a dial-in or Internet connection to eliminate the need to come to the physical facility for some materials. Librarians can require patrons to type in their library card and personal identification numbers to ensure that only community residents use these services, a common part of the vendor licensing agreement.

Chapter 6 more fully discusses methods of making library resources easily accessible.

Fees and Fines

To a large extent, the financial capacity of our funding bodies depends on the amount of taxes the public can bear and the competition for funding among programs. In recent years, librarians have dealt with financial constraints by increasing their internal efficiency and cost-effectiveness, lobbying for a substantial share of public funds; and increasing the amount of money obtained from less traditional revenue sources. (See Chapter 9 for a fuller discussion.) Libraries have spent time and effort pursuing corporate donations, foundation grants, endowment funds, and other voluntary income, but they have also charged fees for some services for years (e.g., Walker 1989; Phelan 1985).

As rising costs and demand continue to confront (and sometimes confound) libraries, many have argued that libraries will increasingly have to charge fees to provide a reasonable level of service (e.g., Anderson 1999; Coffman 1995). More than 15 years ago the National Commission on Libraries and Information Science (1985) summarized arguments on both sides of the issue, presented in figures 5.1 and 5.2, pages 97–98. The dispute continues to rage around the globe (e.g., Kishimoto 2000; Jaeger 1999).

- Library services are a public good.
- The American tradition of free library services is damaged by charging fees.
- Fees are illegal.
- Fees are discriminatory.
- Fees represent a form of double taxation.
- Libraries will place emphasis on revenue-generating services.
- Fees will have the long-term effect of reducing public support for libraries.
- Fees might not be used to support library services.
- The social benefits of library services are difficult to measure; therefore, a fee cannot be efficiently assigned.
- It is difficult to define special services and basic services and to distinguish between them.
- Private and public sector markets are separate and should remain separate.
- The cost of administering and collecting fees outweighs the financial benefits of fees.
- Most users have little need for fee-based online services.
- If the service cannot be provided without a fee, the service should not be provided.
- Improvements within library management and delivery of services would diminish the need for fees.
- There is considerable staff resistance to fees.
- Charging for a service subjects libraries to liability risks.

FIGURE 5.1. **Arguments Against Charging Fees in Public Libraries.**
Reprinted from National Commission on Libraries and Information Science (1985, 4).

- Charging fees increases recognition of the value and importance of library services.
- Fees encourage efficient use of public resources.
- Fees promote service levels based on need and demand.
- Fees encourage management improvements.
- Fees limit waste and over-consumption.
- Fees enhance investment in ongoing maintenance and repair of public facilities.
- Fees encourage a better understanding of the financial limitations of the local government.
- Premium service should be provided only to those willing to pay a premium.
- The tradition of charging for services is part of American culture.
- Fees control growth of and lower demand for services.
- Escalating service costs make user fees a necessity.
- Most library users can afford to pay a fee.
- Without fees, public and academic libraries could not serve the larger community or nonresidents.
- Fees cover only a small portion of the total cost of service provision.
- Fees for most services are simple and inexpensive to collect.
- Local policy may require libraries to charge for services.

FIGURE 5.2. Arguments in Favor of Charging Fees in Public Libraries.
Reprinted from National Commission on Libraries and Information Science (1985, 5).

Kinnucan, Ferguson, and Estabrook (1998) note that the public often finds fees less suspect than librarians do. In a 1991 U.S. survey, 44.1 percent of respondents supported user fees as a solution to a public library fiscal crisis, 47.2 percent favored raising taxes, and only 8.7 percent wanted services cut. The same research found that the more people use the library, the more they favor raising taxes and the less they favor cutting services or imposing user fees.

How do individual libraries resolve this matter? Library staff, with the trustees' support, most often determine the need for fees and the amount to charge, although funding officials, state or federal policy makers who place legal limits on fees, and patrons may influence these decisions (Phelan 1985).

Common charges include fees for obtaining a nonresident borrower's card, for borrowing certain types of materials, and for making reserve or interlibrary loan requests, as well as fines for overdue, lost, or damaged materials.

Nonresident Fees

Many libraries charge those who do not live in a community (and therefore do not pay income, sales, or other taxes used to fund libraries) for some services. The question then becomes "How much?" We advocate that libraries set a fee roughly equivalent to what the average community resident would pay by following one of three standard practices for nonresidents who plan to use library services for a full year:

- Charge the amount patrons would pay if their current residences were in the library service area. For example, the Glen Ellyn (Illinois) Public Library multiplies the assessed valuation of property owned by the nonresident by the millage rate charged for local library services; for renters, the library calculates that 20 percent of their rent goes toward taxes (Lansdale 1999).

- Charge the average annual library taxes per household. For example, at the beginning of its fiscal year, the Orion Township (Lake Orion, Michigan) Public Library obtains the number of households that actually pay taxes in the community, divides the total tax revenue by this figure, then rounds the result to the nearest dollar to obtain a family nonresident fee (Lansdale 1999).

- Charge each individual an amount equivalent to the per capita costs of running the library, as does the Escanaba (Michigan) Public Library (Lansdale 1999). The library can divide the total library budget by this figure, then round the result to the nearest dollar to obtain a reasonable nonresident fee.

Some potential users will balk at paying full nonresident fees, particularly if they only want to use the public library on a short-term basis. Issuing temporary, pro-rated borrowers' cards, for periods ranging from one week to a year, provides a partial solution, reducing the nonresident's cost without "cheating" the residents of the area the library serves.

Another common practice involves reciprocal-borrowing agreements, wherein neighboring libraries (or even libraries throughout an entire state) honor each other's cards, a particularly welcome practice in an era in which many catalogs (individual library or union) are readily available via the Internet. Such an arrangement works best when participating libraries offer different hours, convenient locations, or something else that attracts residents from other communities, including one or more stellar collections (e.g., by genre, subject area, or format). Indeed, Kies (1993) and Welch and Donohue (1994) both found perceived collection quality the most popular rationale for using a library other than the "home" one. To ease the strain of disproportionately high use sometimes experienced under reciprocal borrowing, the net-lending library may charge the home library a per transaction fee, part of the St. Louis (Missouri) Public Library and St. Louis County Library reciprocal borrowing agreement (Holt 1999). Alternately, the state may offer reimbursement, as occurs in the State Library of Iowa's Open Access reciprocal borrowing program, which over 600 public libraries have joined ("Open Access" 2001).

Some libraries also waive nonresident fees for certain classes of patrons. For example, nonresidents who own property or a business within city limits, certified teachers in the local school district, and library volunteers who contribute 10 or more hours per month do not have to pay the standard nonresident card fee at the Richland (Washington) Public Library (Lansdale 1999).

Fees to Rent Items or Obtain Information

The concept of "rental" collections is not new. As Giacoma (1989) notes, studies conducted in the 1920s, 1940s, and 1950s found that almost half the public libraries surveyed provided duplicate copies of best-selling titles for a small rental fee. One 1977 survey of 716 U.S. public libraries found that 10 percent charged for renting art prints, 13 percent for renting books, and 20 percent for renting films (Lynch 1978). At the end of the 1980s, a survey of 619 U.S. public libraries of all sizes found that 29 percent of the libraries surveyed charged fees for borrowing videos, 23 percent for borrowing films, and 5 percent for borrowing art (Lynch 1988). Although the literature does not provide a recent statistical picture, a significant minority of public libraries continues to charge fees.

A number of large public libraries also design and promote fee-based services on a grand scale. For example, in 1991 the County of Los Angeles Public Library received a large entrepreneurial loan to launch Audio Express, a fee-based cassette-by-mail service (described more fully in Chapter 6) designed to meet the needs of the large number of Los Angeles residents with long commutes to work ("Upfront News" 1991). And in 1989 staff at the County of Los Angeles Public Library's Norwalk Regional Library established FYI, a full-cost recovery service designed to meet the collection-related needs of individuals who want accurate, up-to-date information to aid with their work but who lack the personal time to get it. For example, it provides research for a cost of $80.00 per hour ($120.00 per hour for rush requests) with additional charges for other direct expenses incurred for searching databases, photocopying, delivery (via fax, courier, or U.S. mail), and so forth ("Los Angeles" 1989; "Business" 1998). The Hawaii State Public Library

System offers a similar service, charging $60.00 per hour plus fees for custom research service (Schindler 2001).

Instituting fees may allow libraries to provide new services or collections without cutting current, vital ones. However, charging fees for certain items—frequently audiovisual and best-selling materials—may be indicative of subconscious elitist biases (e.g., Smith 1993). We suggest that public librarians closely examine their own motivations and biases when deciding whether and for which services they will charge fees.[3]

Reserve and Interlibrary Loan Fees

Several older studies (there's a dearth of new ones) show that approximately 10 percent of public libraries charge for interlibrary loan services (Strong 1984; Lynch 1978). Such charges were instituted to discourage patrons from filing large numbers of these requests, which can be expensive to fill and take items out of circulation while they sit on a hold shelf awaiting pickup. These fees may also help recover costs of providing the service, such as notifying a patron when a requested work becomes available or paying lending library charges.[4]

A few studies document that most patrons do not or cannot bear the full costs of interlibrary loan and other document delivery services. Library staff at the University of Oklahoma assessed this by explaining to those with real interlibrary loan requests that the service could involve fees and asking patrons to indicate the maximum amount they would pay. Researchers found that 44.3 percent (of 648 respondents) were willing to pay less than 99 cents, 17.1 percent up to $4.99, 21.3 percent up to $9.99, and a mere 16.7 percent more than $10.00. The actual cost of the service exceeded the latter figure 48.1 percent of the time (Murphy and Lin 1996). Kingma (1998) found that on average university library patrons were willing to pay $2.55 for one-hour delivery of an interlibrary loan item and $1.61 for one-day delivery. Similarly, the Houston Public Library found few patrons willing to purchase full-text articles for more than $4.00 (the cost averaged $8.00 to $9.00); a significant number of users will even change their research topic if doing so enables them to use free, rather than fee, full-text databases (Rollins 1996).

Fines for Lost or Damaged Items or Late Returns

Most libraries currently charge borrowers for damaged or lost works. Fines vary greatly for damaged items, in correspondence with the item cost and extent of the damage. Libraries commonly charge the entire (original or replacement) cost of lost items and may assess an additional fee to cover the cost of reordering and reprocessing the replacement works. Policies flexible enough to allow staff to reduce or even waive fines in the face of extenuating circumstances can help the library retain the patron's business and goodwill.

Many libraries also assess overdue fines in the hopes that they will deter patrons from returning materials late. Some evidence suggests that fines do in fact encourage patrons to return materials more quickly (Shontz 1999); however, the revenue raised by overdue fines may not always cover the cost of processing overdue notices. Moreover, Shontz (1999) found that factors outside the library's control—particularly individual conscientiousness and when the user no longer needs an item—also significantly affect when borrowers return materials.

This explains why some libraries have eliminated fines entirely. The year after the Somerville (New Jersey) Free Public Library (SFPL) did this, it experienced significant increases in the number of registered resident borrowers (+11 percent), the number of registered nonresident borrowers (+17.5 percent), and overall circulation (+19 percent) (Adams 1991). Findings like these suggest that the costs of charging overdue fines may outweigh their benefits in many instances.

Of course, libraries take steps to see that eliminating overdue fines does not significantly reduce the total number of items returned to the library. For example, when the number of overdue works rose in response to its new no-fine policy, SFPL suspended patrons' borrowing privileges until they returned overdue materials. This action caused the number of overdue works to decline to normal levels.

Some libraries more aggressively encourage patrons to return long-overdue items or pay for them, sending bills to a collection agency, as does the Seattle Public Library ("Materials" 2001), or issuing a municipal ticket, as does the Mobile (Alabama) Public Library ("Overdues" 2001). The Ames (Iowa) Public Library has even published the names of patrons owing more than $25.00 in fines (almost 600 of them!) in the local newspaper, a move that elicited patron outrage—not at the library but at the delinquent patrons (Hoffman 1996).

Libraries have also tried the softer approach of sponsoring a forgiveness day or week during which patrons can return late materials without paying fines. The Free Library of Philadelphia did this on a rather large scale in 1984. Stories in area newspapers alerted patrons to the event, with intriguing leads like the following: "Somewhere in every house lurks an overdue library book; it's probably lying where no one will ever have to see it, alone and in the dark" (Milner 1984, 629). During the well-publicized, week-long event, an estimated 35,000 patrons returned almost 160,000 overdue items valued at $1.5 million in what the library's public relations director called a "citywide absolution of guilt." The Broward County (Florida) Library offered a similar amnesty week in 1996 that brought 27,295 items back to the library, over 1,000 more than a year overdue (Adams 1996), and the Martinsburg-Berkeley County (West Virginia) Public Library waives fines for all materials but videos every Friday ("About" 2000). Other libraries, including the Oak Creek (Wisconsin) Public Library, the Lyons (New York) Public Library, the Missoula (Montana) Public Library, the Ottawa (Kansas) Library, and the Hobbs (New Mexico) Public Library, have combined overdue amnesty periods with charitable giving, offering food-for-fines days ("Food" 1999).

To regain both long overdue materials and lapsed borrowers without forfeiting fine revenue, the Multnomah County (Oregon) Public Library and Starbucks Coffee offered a free latte to select patrons for settling their overdue balances. Starbucks paid to create and mail 65,000 postcards explaining the offer to patrons blocked from checking out materials due to excessive overdue fines. The "Better Latte than Never" promotion yielded $35,000 in fines (MacLeod 1998).

CONVENIENCE COSTS

Although monetary expenses may be the most obvious costs associated with borrowing materials from the public library, other equally important costs exist. As economist Adam Smith observed centuries ago, "The real price of everything, what everything really costs to the man who wants to acquire it, is the toil and trouble of acquiring it" (1937, 30).

As Van House (1983a) has noted, both the library and the user influence the amount of time required to locate a desired item. A patron can reduce the time it takes to use the library by such actions as learning how to use the library effectively, checking the online catalog to see if materials are available, and asking staff for assistance. Librarians can also save patrons' time and trouble by providing bibliographic instruction programs, offering to help patrons rather than waiting to be asked for assistance, preparing pathfinders and bibliographies, and pursuing other approaches to make the library easy to use.

By offering their services in multiple, convenient locations (a topic more fully discussed in Chapter 6), libraries can also save patrons significant amounts of time. Hours of service constitute another important time factor affecting patrons' abilities to use the collection.[5] In addition to establishing a schedule with extended hours, including evenings and weekends, libraries can employ "time-bending" techniques through such actions as offering off-site access to the catalog, full-text databases, and digitized collections 24 hours a day, 365 days a year. The Warren-Newport (Illinois) Public Library District also offers after-hours materials pickup; staff place requested items in a locker accessible from the outside of the building, give patrons the locker number, and program the patron's card number as the access code ("Library Goes" 1998; Jacobsen 1998).

Obtaining a Borrower's Card

For residents of the public library's service area, time and aggravation are the primary costs associated with obtaining a borrower's card. Libraries can help keep these costs low by ensuring that patrons do not have to stand in line too long to get a card or stand in the wrong line due to inadequate signage.

Libraries can also simplify regulations for obtaining a borrower's card. One in-depth survey found circulation policies in public libraries excessively complex (Intner 1987). Optimally, application forms will only require patrons to provide necessary information. (Although this book suggests in several places that soliciting nonessential data on registration forms can give libraries an opportunity to learn more about their patrons and better serve them, such questions must clearly be labeled as voluntary.) Because only residents pay (directly or indirectly) the taxes that fund the library, staff will usually have to verify that those applying for cards reside in the area served. Staff also should confirm the patron's contact information, which may include address, phone number, or e-mail address, in case they later have to contact the patron about missing or overdue items. However, taking verification to an extreme will discourage use and help perpetuate the tiresome stereotype of librarians as curmudgeonly individuals who want to keep library materials on the shelves rather than in the hands of the borrowers. Consider the Delray Beach (Florida) Public Library, which used to require that applicants show three forms of identification to get a card. It now asks, but does not require, patrons to show one ID and gives out multilingual welcome brochures and card applications at community events. The changes have helped more than double new card registrations ("Barriers" 1998).

Locating and Gathering Desired Items

Time and aggravation are also the primary costs of locating materials. It takes time to check the catalog to see whether the library owns desired items and has them available for checkout, then find them on the shelves. During the process, the user may experience various frustrations.

Catalog use is a good example. Patrons may bypass the catalog because they prefer to seek help directly from library staff or they already know where to find desired materials. However, some patrons bypass the catalog because they find it confusing. For example, 29 percent of patrons surveyed by the Edmonton (Alberta) Public Library reported finding the catalog so difficult to understand that they use it "only as a last resort" (Gajerski 1989). Librarians can reduce patron costs by offering sufficient numbers of intuitive, easy-to-use catalog stations near the library's entrance and scattered throughout the public service areas. They can also post clear directions for catalog use near each terminal, provide both individual and class training for users, and approach patrons at catalog stations, volunteering assistance—an offer that 44 percent of patrons accepted in one study (Joe 1999).

The patron also normally bears the cost associated with finding an item on the shelf. Although this cost is relatively small for skilled library users (Eaton 1991), it may loom large for the novice. For example, Mellon found that 80 percent of the freshmen in a large academic library had some form of library anxiety, as this typical response illustrates: "I . . . was lost in the library for a very long time. It was like a big maze" (1986, 162).

Librarians can reduce the cost of physically finding items in several ways. First, they can work to eliminate unnecessary complexity in collection arrangement.[6] Shay once visited a public library in the southeastern United States with a general fiction collection (adult hardback titles) located in several different areas and the nonfiction shelved on three different floors in an order that did not precede logically from the 000s through the 999s of the Dewey Decimal System. Redesigning the floor plan and shifting items into a more logical order would have alleviated patron confusion.[7]

Second, libraries can create maps that indicate the locations of various parts of the collection and post these near the main entrance, the catalog terminals, the elevator and stairs, and other prominent places and also make paper copies available for patrons to pick up. Maps are especially effective in large buildings or in buildings where more than one floor houses the collection.

Designing useful sign systems to guide patrons to the collections they seek offers a third way to reduce patron costs. Effective signs use colors and lettering that can be easily read, have non-glare surfaces, and are large enough to be seen easily. Wording and positioning must also be carefully considered. (Chapter 6 provides more detail on effective signage.)

Fourth, staff can show patrons the location of desired items. Because patrons may be reluctant to ask for help, this cost reduction works best when staff approach patrons who look lost or confused and offer assistance. Staff members at the Orange County (Florida) Library System actively greet patrons at the door, directing novice users to relevant departments and services (Miller 1996). It also helps when staff at service desks smile, make eye contact, and are scheduled in sufficient numbers to prevent long lines, which discourage patrons from asking questions.

Finally, staff can offer short tours to show new borrowers the library's collections. Although most libraries cannot afford to give tours to single patrons, they can arrange tours on a monthly basis, publicizing them, for example, to new borrowers (e.g., by giving them a program flier and by sending a reminder postcard closer to the tour date). Libraries can also use self-guided audio tours, which require a significant initial investment to produce but can substantially save staff time over the long run (Curry 1997).

The patron's cost of actually locating items on specific shelves can also be decreased. First, the library can ensure that materials are shelved in their correct locations by carefully training new shelvers, working to reduce shelving errors when these occur, and reading shelves frequently to correct mis-shelvings.[8] To increase the regularity with which shelf reading occurs, some libraries recruit volunteers to adopt a section of shelves and at frequent intervals shelf read, straighten, and check for damaged items in each area. For example, at the Wilbraham (Massachusetts) Public Library, members of the Junior Friends of the Library do this (Chadbourne 1990), and at the Park Ridge (Illinois) Public Library, Adopt-a-Shelf volunteers, including individuals, club members, and parent-child teams, sign up for this task.

Second, the staff can reshelve materials quickly, preferably within one working day, and can locate reshelving stacks on the public floor or place carts of materials, already sorted and awaiting reshelving, near the relevant stack sections, so that diligent patrons can also search there. Third, librarians can try to make call numbers easy to understand. For example, they can use the word "oversized" rather than "folio" or post simple signs explaining terminology at intervals around the stacks and at catalog terminals.

Once patrons find items they want, they have to collect them. The weight and bulk of library materials can make it difficult to carry very many at a time. A considerable number of libraries, including the Hussey-Mayfield (Zionsville, Indiana) Memorial Public Library and the Emporia (Kansas) Public Library, ease this cost by providing bags or baskets, often purchased by Friends groups, for in-library use ("The Hussey-Mayfield" 2000; "Friends" 2000). The Hastings (Nebraska) Public Library allows patrons to use these bags or baskets for browsing and then check them out to more easily carry materials home ("News" 1997). These aids will be most helpful to patrons when placed at locations throughout the stacks so they are available when needed (Underhill 1999). Staff can also offer baskets to patrons they see toting a stack of items or volunteer to bring the items to the circulation desk for the patron to collect when ready to check out.

Libraries can further reduce the total costs of locating and gathering materials—from determining availability to finding the item on the shelf—by allowing patrons to phone, fax, or e-mail requests to staff, who then either file a reserve request for the patron or have the item waiting for pickup. Offering remote access to a catalog that indicates shelf status can also save significant amounts of time and trouble. Those that include information for branches throughout a system, or even neighboring libraries, can particularly benefit the patron who needs an item quickly and will travel to obtain a work known to be on the shelf or held for him or her. Libraries without access to this information can inform patrons (e.g., through signs posted near the catalog) that reference staff can call to check on the immediate availability of titles housed in other branches or libraries. A number of libraries even take this service a step further, allowing patrons to pick up reserves at a drive-through window, an option that has proved as popular as a McDonald's drive-through at lunchtime at the Kearney Branch of Springfield-Greene County (Missouri) Library District ("New" 2000).

Standing in Line to Check Out Items

In repeated studies in the retail environment, Underhill (1999) has found that waiting time is the single most important influence on a patron's perception of the quality of service received. Patrons who had to wait "too long" are more likely to feel they received poor, even incompetent, service. In most libraries the time spent waiting for service, or queue time, depends largely on the level of staffing offered. Optimally, libraries will schedule more circulation staff on the desk during the busiest periods of use, including relevant evening and weekend hours and possibly weekday lunch hours. Libraries can also supplement circulation clerks with backup workers who can perform other duties (e.g., filing and shelving), until a "checker to the front" call draws them to help reduce the line at the desk. Scheduling break times dependent on lines (e.g., a long line at 10:00 A.M. would delay—but not eliminate—that break time until the line becomes reasonable) can also reduce waiting time and prevent the exasperation patrons feel when an already long line essentially becomes longer as checkout stations close.

In addition, the cost of waiting in line will not be equal for all patrons; the cost "is always discriminatory, because the same amount of time has different values to different people, depending on the opportunity cost of their time" (Van House 1983a, 56). Moreover, research shows that people's perceptions of the amount of time that has passed while waiting greatly increases, and can as much as double, once actual wait time surpasses 90 seconds; for unaccompanied people queue time can seem to pass particularly slowly (Underhill 1999).

Obviously, decreasing waiting time is the best means of addressing this problem. However, libraries can also take other steps to make waiting time more palatable. Underhill's (1999) years of research suggest the following strategies:

- Have employees acknowledge patrons waiting in line, because studies show that time seems to pass more quickly after an employee-initiated interaction.

- When possible, give patrons an idea how long the wait will be, which relieves "time anxiety."

- Have patrons wait in clear lines rather than "massing" at the counter.

- Offer a diversion. For example, the Iowa City (Iowa) Public Library locates display shelving near the checkout line, and at the Park Ridge (Illinois) Public Library waiting patrons can watch a monitor tuned to a cable channel that broadcasts library programming announcements. Signage can also ease queue time as well as effectively get a message out to patrons.

Libraries can also reduce queue time by offering patrons self-service options. One study found that over half of self-checkout users believed it to be faster than staff-provided checkout (Carey and McKechnie 1998). Many libraries throughout the world report high levels of patron satisfaction with self-checkout and cite these additional advantages: heightened patron privacy, independence, and control; decreased staff injuries; and increased staff time available to assist patrons with other more challenging tasks (Kobayashi 2000; Jakobsen 1996). At the Richmond (British Columbia, Canada) Public Library, self- or "Express" checkout accounts for 85 to 90 percent of total circulation (McNeely 2000). Self-checkout stations will receive the most use when positioned in the patron's line of vision as he or she approaches the full-service circulation counter (Underhill 1999) and when staff members encourage patrons to try the self-checkout machine (Carey and McKechnie 1998).

In addition, librarians will want to try to reduce waiting time when responding to patron messages, whether received via phone or e-mail. Lay's (1999) study of e-mail reference at Ohio public libraries reveals that 44.1 percent of libraries respond to questions within a day, and 32.2 percent respond within two days. This surpasses the response time of many Fortune 500 companies, which took as long as 25 days, 1 hour, and 25 minutes (or never responded at all) to answer an e-mail in a recent study. However, at the other end of the spectrum, United Parcel Service responded in an impressive 5 minutes and Home Depot in 34 minutes ("Rainier" 2000). Such quick turnaround times may not be an unreasonable goal for libraries as e-mail becomes a more prevalent communication medium. Libraries with ample staff computers might achieve this by establishing a separate library e-mail account and staying logged on to it at the reference desk, using the option many e-mail programs offer of making a sound when new mail has been received.

Returning Borrowed Items to the Library

Patrons face two primary costs associated with returning borrowed items to the library. First, they must revisit the library to drop off materials. A library will optimally absorb part of the cost of return travel by allowing patrons to return materials to any library outlet, not just the location where the patron initially borrowed a work.[9]

Libraries can also reduce patron travel costs by locating return drops for books and other items outside each library building, allowing patrons to return items after hours. In addition, some libraries place materials drops at other community locations; for example, the Davenport (Iowa) Public Library has installed book returns at area grocery stores ("Book" 2001). Libraries that do not permit items other than books to be placed in the book drop to prevent damage to these may also provide a well-marked drop to hold other, more fragile materials, such as CDs.

Patrons face a second cost when they must return items before they have finished using them. Libraries can reduce this cost by establishing longer borrowing periods for patrons when the level of demand makes it possible. This allows patrons to use and return items more or less at leisure and reduces the possibility of accruing overdue fines. In fact, one study of 760 public libraries shows that libraries with longer loan periods (21 to 28 days) have annual circulation rates and per capita circulation rates significantly higher than those of libraries with loan periods of only 14 days (Nelson and Goldhor 1987).[10]

Librarians need to remember that if loan periods for high-demand items are too long, patrons will be less likely to find these materials on the shelves. The Queens Borough (New York) Public Library discovered this when they lengthened the loan period for new fiction and popular nonfiction from 7 to 21 days. When hundreds of patrons complained that this policy change made these items almost impossible to obtain, staff returned the loan period to its original level (Sivulich 1989).

Allowing patrons to renew items can also reduce costs. Renewals via telephone or Web-accessible catalog can be especially beneficial because they save patrons the cost of travel time. Moreover, Internet or automated phone renewals also save staff time.

Libraries with short (and therefore potentially inconvenient) loan periods may particularly wish to consider allowing renewals. In fact, Goldhor (1990) found that libraries with two-week loan periods had a renewal rate three times higher than libraries with four-week loan periods.

Filing Reserve Requests

Today, most public libraries allow patrons to reserve materials, sparing them the aggravation of continually checking the shelves for hot titles that other patrons may already have checked out. However, patrons bear a number of costs when they file reserve requests. In addition to possible monetary charges, discussed previously in this chapter, patrons must take time to complete and turn in the reserve card. Libraries can help by making these cards readily available to users and ensuring that users do not have to stand in long lines to turn them in. For example, libraries may install boxes in which reserve cards can be dropped. They can also allow patrons to place their own holds with the automated catalog when possible, even when accessed over the Internet, a convenience that helped the Fairfax County (Virginia) Public Library break its previous circulation record ("Library Credits" 1999). And some libraries, including the Davenport (Iowa) Public Library and the Springfield-Greene County (Missouri) Library District, offer automatic reserve programs in which the library automatically places holds for a patron on new works by designated authors (Sarff 1998; "Bestsellers Club" 1997).

Patrons also face a second, often significant, cost: the delay in receiving the requested item. Although delay time merely reflects the inability of libraries with finite funds to have readily available all the information that anyone might need and enough copies of heavily used materials to meet peak demands, many patrons may be unwilling to wait long for desired items. This is particularly true when with a phone call or a few clicks of a mouse the item can be quickly delivered to their home or office (for a fee).

Librarians can take various steps to reduce delay time, such as purchasing multiple copies of high-demand items; reducing the length of the loan period for popular authors, titles, or subject areas; and leasing supplemental collections of popular works. (Chapter 9 discusses these techniques in more detail.)

Occasionally, patrons will file so many reserve requests that a library cannot fill them all in a reasonable amount of time. Some libraries faced with this problem have decided to disallow reserves for some type of materials, such as fiction video-tapes. (Libraries also often make this decision for materials with short loan periods that may be tied up "awaiting pickup" longer than they would be checked out.) However, such decisions can raise patron costs of using the collection, imposing the burden of repeatedly checking the shelves for desired materials.

Returning to the library to pick up the desired item is a final cost of filing a reserve. Although we know of no published study exploring the relationship between the time taken to fill a reserve request and the percentage of requests that patrons never pick up (often because they have either obtained the works else-where or no longer need them), we believe the two correlate positively. In other words, libraries can decrease the percentage of never collected holds by decreasing the time it takes to fill reserve requests.

No one is currently studying, in an in-depth fashion, the length of time it takes public libraries to fill reserves. However, we take heart from the fact that fairly recent data suggest that medium-sized libraries are more quickly filling requests for materials that were checked out when the patron sought them, were located at another branch, or were located at another library system. In 1991 less than half of surveyed libraries were able to fill such requests within a week's time, and a quarter had not been filled one month after the requests were filed (Public Library Association 1991). In 1998 slightly more than half of medium-sized librar-ies filled these requests within a week, and about 85 percent filled them within a month (Public Library Association 1998). Clearly, libraries that continue this course by reducing reserve-fill time demonstrate a strong service ethic.

Many patrons will judge the cost of filing a reserve request (in terms of fees, initial filing time, delay time, and return travel time) as too high unless strongly motivated to obtain a particular work. For example, 31 percent of patrons at the Edmonton (Alberta) Public Library preferred to "settle for something else instead" rather than file reserve requests, and 40 percent more (presumably regular users) said they would rather check the shelves on the next visit than file reserve requests (Gajerski 1989). Ross's qualitative research (Ross and Chelton 2001; Ross 1999) has shown that patrons become more willing to file reserves when they anticipate deriving a high degree of satisfaction from a particular title, a finding that supports the "motivation plus incentives must be greater than inhibitors" model of library use presented in Chapter 2.

Note that patrons will often file reserves for items they deem "necessary," but not for "nice to have, rather than necessary" materials. For example, when Spiller (1980) surveyed 500 readers in five British public libraries, 63 percent said that they hardly ever filed fiction reserve requests because they did not find it worthwhile to do so; these same readers were much more likely to file reserve requests for specific nonfiction titles.

Obtaining Desired Materials from Another Branch

If a desired item is located at a branch other than the patron's customary one, travel and time costs may also arise. At least two factors influence whether a patron will be willing to travel to a different branch to obtain a desired item. One is the "necessity" of obtaining the work. Although a patron may be willing to bear a higher cost for a work he or she considers essential to his or her information needs, the patron will be less likely to bear travel costs for a "tangential" title. A second factor is the patron's perception of how convenient it will be to reach the branch. For example, a patron might find it inconvenient to travel 15 miles to another branch until he or she realizes the proximity of that branch to his or her office. A patron who has to rely on the city's transit system may be less likely to travel to another branch than a patron who has a car. The library can absorb some of these costs by delivering requested materials to the branch of the patron's choice within a reasonable period, optimally a few days.

Libraries can also consider mailing requested items to patrons. Because of its expense, libraries generally reserve this option for patrons who cannot bear any costs of travel. For example, the Akron-Summit (Ohio) County Public Library serves homebound patrons using a van that contains a small collection of materials. When patrons request titles not in the van collection, staff will mail them the next day, rather than requiring the patrons to wait two weeks for the next visit (Berry 1990).

Filing Interlibrary Loan Requests

Only a small number of patrons take advantage of interlibrary loan (ILL) services in medium-sized and large libraries. In fact, on average, items borrowed from other libraries via ILL account for less than 2 percent of public libraries' total circulation (Chute and Kroe 2001).

Three major factors account for this low level of use. As noted previously, the fees charged for these services may discourage use. Second, many patrons are not aware of ILL services, because few public libraries regularly and systematically promote these. Moreover, some librarians may actively discourage patrons from filing ILL requests, possibly to avoid the work associated with filling them. For example, Hébert found that 10.8 percent of ILL requests at the 38 largest public libraries in Canada were refused (some, presumably, for valid reasons); one patron was even told there was "no such thing" as ILL (1994, 11). Publicity can significantly increase use, as demonstrated when 10 Illinois public libraries conducted vigorous ILL campaigns that increased use of the service by an average of 38 percent during the four-month period of heavy promotion (Goldhor 1988).

But the most significant cost is delay time: the days that elapse between completing an ILL request form, having the item retrieved and sent to the branch of choice, waiting to be notified that the item is available for pickup, and returning to the library to collect it. In Hébert's study (1994), only about half of all requests were filled, turnaround time averaged 38 days, and patrons felt they received poorer service than expected.

Libraries can increase ILL requests and patron satisfaction by lowering these costs. In the 1980s, the University of Illinois at Urbana-Champaign library system reduced these substantially. If a searcher failed to find an item in the library's online catalog, he or she received an on-screen message asking if he or she would like to search the holdings of other libraries in the state of Illinois for the work. If the user replied "yes," the computer searched the other catalogs and checked on the immediate availability of the title. If available, the work was sent to the user's campus mailing address. This easy-to-use system had no fee associated with it and delivered materials quickly (generally within a week of the request). In a two-year period, the library increased the percentage of circulation that came from items requested via ILL from 3 to 8 percent (Potter 1986).[11]

More recently, the Southern Illinois University, Carbondale Morris Library has successfully implemented a similar system, increasing ILL requests by 111 percent over the previous year, cutting average turnaround time by 60 percent, and raising customer satisfaction (Preece and Kilpatrick 1998). The Public Library of Cincinnati and Hamilton County (Ohio) has experienced similar success with its patron-initiated ILL program, which attracted 174 percent more requests in its first six months than during the same period the previous year. Moreover, staff members feel their workload has not increased beyond available means due to the time saved through patrons entering their own information (Fender 1995). And Colorado State University Libraries designed a system that combines patron-initiated, electronically submitted loans; a streamlined process for filing requests working with six partner libraries; and delivery straight to the user to achieve an impressive average turnaround time of 1.27 days at an average cost of less than $5.00. This compares to the 15.6 days and $28.00 average for members of the Association of Research Libraries (Wessling and Delaney 2000).

PSYCHOLOGICAL COSTS

As mentioned previously, a significant number of individuals become frustrated or anxious when using a library. Those likely to experience especially high levels of aggravation, apprehension, or cognitive confusion include

- recent immigrants who may not understand library terminology or be familiar with the American philosophy of free and open public libraries, as well as American classification systems and subject headings, and might feel afraid (or embarrassed) to ask for help (Liu 1995; Keller 1996), and others with limited language or literacy skills;

- individuals experiencing mobility impairment, low-vision, or other long-term or temporary medical conditions;

- those new to a particular library; and

- people unable to concentrate completely because of the presence of children who need to be watched, personal worries, or mental dysfunctions.

Libraries can reduce the psychological costs of use (and meet ADA requirements) by presenting a welcoming environment through both physical layout and a helpful, friendly staff, as well as creating materials or programs to assist these patron groups. For example, staff members working for the New Americans Program at the Queens Borough (New York) Public Library offer in-service training on cultural diversity issues to other staff members. They have also produced a booklet in 12 languages that includes basic words and expressions to use at the reference and circulation desks and bilingual bookmarks that staff and patrons can use together to understand each other (Gitner 1999). We recommend that libraries

- increase staff awareness of physiological, psychiatric, and psychological conditions that may adversely affect library use. For example, one major section of a day-long continuing education workshop could note basic symptoms of Alzheimer's disease, anxiety disorder, agoraphobia, attention deficit disorder, dyslexia, severe depression, paranoia, and other conditions that may deter or inhibit information handling and library use. Another might deal with specific costs that area immigrants may face, and another could involve role playing to increase awareness of psychological costs—for example, asking staff to navigate the library while wearing goggles that simulate macular degeneration.

- both adhere to guidelines expressed in the Americans with Disabilities Act and other codes that help make buildings accessible and provide home delivery of materials and other alternative means of access for those who cannot come to the facility.

- undertake consistent, strong efforts to publicize materials or programs to meet the needs of individuals learning to read and/or speak the principal language(s) of the region.

- investigate other ways to reduce psychological costs. For example, libraries can offer volunteer-provided babysitting for toddlers during programs for older children so parents can have time to locate and check out wanted materials.[12]

CONCLUSION

In a "perfect" library, all patrons could quickly, easily, and comfortably obtain what they want, when and where they want it, without having to pay direct fees. They also would be able to keep materials as long as needed, returning them to a convenient location at their leisure. However, patrons' many, diverse demands and perceptions and libraries' limited budgets mean that this will not always occur. Therefore, library staff will want to reduce the cost of use as much as possible using these and similar innovative techniques before asking patrons to bear the rest of the cost, making allowances as possible for the fact that ability and willingness will vary with the individual.

NOTES

1. Uncited examples in this chapter come from Shay's observations, with the exception of the Park Ridge (Illinois) Public Library examples, which come from Karen's.

2. This distinction between basic and value-added services is frequently made (e.g., see Coffman 2000), and not just by librarians. For example, one management consultant firm that specializes in advising municipalities on cost-allocation plans told the New Mexico Municipal League that libraries should consider charging patrons for services that are "above and beyond what they normally provide." The firm recommended that fees be considered for such "extras" as adult education programs, story hours, and summer reading programs (Goldberg 1990).

3. Giacoma (1989) provides an excellent overview of the ethical issues involved in charging fees for public library use.

4. For example, one study found that 71 out of 139 California libraries surveyed charged for a reserve notice postcard (Strong 1984).

5. In fact, variables like these greatly influence the extent to which any media distribution outlet is used. For example, Gallup (1985) found that 38 percent of adult book buyers named location or hours as the factor that most influenced them to patronize a particular bookstore.

6. Little research has been conducted that relates specifically to library floor plans; however, various studies have indicated a strong correlation between the complexity of floor plans and user disorientation in general. See, for example, Weisman (1981).

7. Myers (1979) is one of the few authors who discusses, in a comprehensive manner, the principles of designing open stack areas from a user's point of view.

8. Various authors have described specific procedures for training and motivating shelvers, determining error rates, and reading shelves. Among the more useful are Kendrick (1991), Lowenberg (1989), and Schabo and Baculis (1989).

9. The same principle applies to items checked out as part of a reciprocal borrowing agreement made among a number of area library systems.

10. The same study also found that 83 percent of the libraries that had decreased the length of their loan periods allowed renewals, as opposed to only 33 percent of libraries with longer loan periods. This suggests that many libraries were trying to compensate for increasing patron costs in one area by decreasing them in another.

11. In the late 1980s, public libraries in Illinois gained access to this form of resource sharing by joining ILLINET Online. The database contains more than 5 million unique bibliographic records representing the OCLC cataloging activity of some 800 libraries of all types in the state. The system provides easy dial-up access to all libraries that can purchase microcomputer terminals to tap into the system and pay the telephone tolls. Titles are sent to participating libraries via a state-subsidized delivery system. For more information, see Sloan (1990, 1989) and Sloan and Stewart (1988).

12. For other suggestions about decreasing library anxiety, see Jiao and Onwuegbuzie (1997).

REFERENCES

"About Our Library." 2000. [Homepage of the Martinsburg-Berkeley County Public Library], [Online]. Available: http://tlc.library.net/martinsburg/default.asp (under About Us link) [Accessed September 28, 2001].

Adams, January. 1991. "A Year of Living Dangerously: Implementation of a No-Fine Policy at Somerville Free Public Library." *Public Libraries* 30, no. 6 (November/December): 346–49.

Adams, Sue. 1996. "Tales from the Front" (photo submission). *Public Libraries* 35, no. 6 (November/December): 346.

Anderson, Rick. 1999. "The Debate over Service Fees: What Was the Question Again?" *Library Collections, Acquisitions, & Technical Services* 23, no. 2 (Summer): 183–90.

"Barriers Get Removed." 1998. *Public Libraries* 37, no. 3 (May/June): 165.

Berry, Diana. 1990. "Creativity and Mobile Services." In *The Book Stops Here: New Directions in Bookmobile Services*, ed. Catherine Suyak Alloway, 253–61. Metuchen, NJ: Scarecrow Press.

"Best Sellers Are HOT and READY TO GO." 1999. *The Ho'ala News* (March) [Homepage of the State Public Library System], [Online]. Available: http://www.hcc.hawaii.edu/hspls/hotpicks.html. [Accessed September 28, 2001].

"Bestsellers Club." 1997. *Library PR News* 18, no 3/4 (March/April): 6–7.

"Book Return Locations." 2001. [Homepage of the Davenport Public Library], [Online]. (Updated September 26). Available: http://www.rbls.lib.il.us/dpl/return.htm [Accessed September 28, 2001].

"Borrower Information." 2000. [Homepage of Urbana Free Library], [Online]. (Updated May 23). Available: http://urbanafreelibrary.org//borrow.htm [Accessed September 28, 2001].

"Business Information Services." 1998. [Homepage of the County of Los Angeles Public Library], [Online]. Available: https://fyi.co.la.ca.us/bus/index.html (and linked pages) [Accessed October 5, 2001].

Carey, Robert F., and Lynne McKechnie. 1998. "Self-Service Circulation: An Exploratory Study." *Public Libraries* 37, no. 2 (March/April): 118–23.

Chadbourne, Robert. 1990. "A Friend Is a Friend." *Wilson Library Bulletin* 65, no. 1: 33.

Chute, Adrienne, and Elaine Kroe. 2001. *Public Libraries in the United States: Fiscal Year 1998.* Washington, DC: U.S. Department of Education/National Center for Education Statistics. NCES 2001-307.

"Circulation Fines, Fees and Charges." 2000. [Homepage of Westerville Public Library], [Online]. (Updated July). Formerly available: http://winslo.state.oh.us/publib/wplffcpl .htm [Accessed November 8, 2000].

Coffman, Steve. 1995. "Fee Based Services and the Future of Libraries." *Journal of Library Administration* 20, no. 3-4: 167–86.

———. 2000. " 'And Now, a Word from Our Sponsors . . .': Alternative Funding for Libraries." *Searcher* 8, no. 1 (January): 51–57.

Curry, Ann. 1997. "Seizing an Instructional and Marketing Opportunity: Audiocassette Tours in Public Libraries." *Public Library Quarterly* 16, no. 2: 5–16.

Eaton, Gale. 1991. "Wayfinding in the Library: Book Searches and Route Uncertainty." *RQ* 30, no. 4 (Summer): 319–27.

Fender, Kimber L. 1995. "Patron Initiated Interlibrary Loan Through FirstSearch: The Experience of the Public Library of Cincinnati and Hamilton County." *Journal of Interlibrary Loan, Document Delivery & Information Supply* 6, no. 1: 45–48.

"Food for Fines." 1999. *The Unabashed Librarian* no. 113: 26–27.

Freeland, Bayneeta. [1997]. "Re: Rental Books." [Homepage of Publib and Publib-Net], [Online]. (November 15). Available: http://sunsite.berkeley.edu/PubLib/archive .html [Accessed September 28, 2001].

"Friends of the Emporia Public Library." 2000. [Homepage of the Emporia Public Library], [Online]. (Updated August 6). Available: http://skyways.lib.ks.us/kansas/library /emporia/friends.html [Accessed September 27, 2001].

Gajerski, B. 1989. "Edmonton Public Library: 1989 User Survey." Edmonton, Alberta: Edmonton Public Library. ERIC ED327184.

Gallup Organization. 1985. *The Gallup 1985 Annual Report on Book Buying.* Princeton, NJ: Gallup Organization.

Giacoma, Pete. 1989. *The Fee or Free Decision.* New York: Neal-Schuman.

Gitner, Fred J. 1999. "New Americans Program: Part 2." *Reference and User Services Quarterly* 38, no. 3 (Spring): 243–44.

Goldberg, B. 1990. "Make Libraries Pay Their Way, Advises Consultant (at New Mexico Municipal League Seminar)." *American Libraries* 21, no. 1 (January): 13.

Goldhor, Herbert. 1988. "The Effect of Publicity on Interlibrary Loan Requests in Ten Illinois Public Libraries." *Public Libraries* 27, no. 4 (Winter): 184–87.

———. 1990. "Statistics of Renewals in Public Libraries." *Public Library Quarterly* 10, no. 2: 63–68.

Hébert, Françoise. 1994. "Service Quality: An Unobtrusive Investigation of Interlibrary Loan in Large Public Libraries in Canada." *Library and Information Science Research* 16, no. 1 (Winter): 3–21.

Hoffman, Rob. 1996. "Radical Overdue Technique." *The Unabashed Librarian* no. 100: 3.

Holt, Glen E. 1999. "Public Library Partnerships: Mission-Driven Tools for the 21st Century." [Homepage of Bertelsmann Foundation], [Online]. Available: http://www .bertelsmann-stiftung.de/documents/holt6en.pdf [Accessed September 28, 2001].

"The Hussey-Mayfield Memorial Public Library Celebrates Its First 10 Years." 2000. [Homepage of the Hussey-Mayfield Memorial Public Library], [Online]. (Updated October 29). Available: http://www.zionsville.lib.in.us/tenyear.htm#1995 [Accessed September 28, 2001].

Intner, Sheila S. 1987. *Circulation Policy in Academic, Public and School Libraries.* New York: Greenwood Press.

Jacobsen, Lynne. 1998. "Warren-Newport: Testing Innovative Design Concepts." *The Illinois Library Association Reporter* 16, no. 1 (February): 1, 3–4.

Jaeger, John. 1999. "User Fees, Community Goods, and the Public Library." *Public Library Quarterly* 17, no. 2: 49–62.

Jakobsen, V. G. 1996. "The Self-Service System in Toensberg Public Library, Norway." *Vine* no. 105: 33–35.

Jiao, Qun G., and Anthony J. Onwuegbuzie. 1997. "Antecedents of Library Anxiety." *Library Quarterly* 67, no. 4 (October): 372–89.

Joe, Ronald K. 1999. "Offering Assistance at the OPACs." *The Reference Librarian* no. 65: 137–59.

Keller, Shelly G. 1996. "The Secret Power of Community Connections." *The Reference Librarian* no. 54: 29–44.

Kendrick, Curtis L. 1991. "Performance Measures of Shelving Accuracy." *Journal of Academic Librarianship* 17, no. 1 (March): 16–18.

Kerr, George D. 1999. "Gaining and Retaining Customer Loyalty." [Homepage of Bertelsmann Foundation], [Online]. Available: http://www.bertelsmann-stiftung.de /documents/customer_loyality_englisch.pdf [Accessed September 28, 2001].

Kies, C. 1993. "Patron Rationales for Using Reciprocal Borrowing." *Resource Sharing & Information Networks* 9, no. 1: 11–32.

Kingma, Bruce R. 1998. "The Economics of Access Versus Ownership: The Costs and Benefits of Access to Scholarly Articles via Interlibrary Loan and Journal Subscriptions." *Journal of Library Administration* 26, no. 1-2: 145–57.

Kinnucan, Mark T., Mark R. Ferguson, and Leigh Estabrook. 1998. "Public Opinion Toward User Fees in Public Libraries." *Library Quarterly* 68, no. 2 (April): 183–204.

Kishimoto, T. 2000. "The Problem of User Fees in Public Libraries." *Toshokan-Kai* 51, no. 5 (January): 334–42.

Kobayashi, Z. 2000. "Examining the Introduction of Self-Issue Machine in a Public Library." *Toshokan Zasshi* 94, no. 3 (March): 194–95.

Lansdale, Metta. 1999. "Non-Resident Fees Text Only in Message." [Publib Archive], [Online]. [Homepage of Publib and Publib-Net], [Online]. (September 25). Available: http://sunsite.berkeley.edu/PubLib/archive.html [Accessed September 28, 2001].

Lay, Teresa M. 1999. "E-mail Reference in Ohio Public Libraries." Master's research paper, Kent State University. ERIC ED436190.

"Library Credits Net with Record Circ." 1999. *American Libraries* 30, no. 8 (September): 27.

"Library Goes 24 Hours." 1998. *Public Libraries* 37, no. 5 (September/October): 288.

Liu, Mengxiong. 1995. "Ethnicity and Information Seeking." *Reference Librarian* nos. 49/50: 123–34.

"Los Angeles County Public Opens Fee-Based Service." 1989. *Wilson Library Bulletin* 64, no. 1 (September): 18–19.

Lowenberg, Susan. 1989. "A Comprehensive Shelf Reading Program." *Journal of Academic Librarianship* 15, no. 1 (March): 24–27.

Lynch, Mary Jo. 1978. "Confusion Twice Compounded: Report of PLA Survey of Fees Currently Charged in Public Libraries." *Public Libraries* 17, no. 3 (Fall): 11–13.

Lynch, Mary Jo, ed. 1988. *Non-Tax Sources of Revenue for Public Libraries*. Chicago: American Library Association, Office for Research.

MacLeod, Leo. 1998. "BestSeller Blend: Starbucks and Library." *Public Libraries* 37, no. 2 (March/April): 102.

"Materials Recovery Service." 2001. [Homepage of the Seattle Public Library], [Online]. (Updated July 5). Available: http://www.spl.lib.wa.us/borrserv/recovery.html [Accessed September 28, 2001].

McNeely, Cate. 2000. "The Library of the Future: A Status Report." Presentation at *PLA 2000*, Public Library Association, Eighth National Conference, March 30.

Mellon, Constance A. 1986. "Library Anxiety: A Grounded Theory and Its Development." *College and Research Libraries* 47, no. 2 (March): 160–65.

Miller, Glenn. 1996. *Customer Service and Innovation in Libraries*. Fort Atkinson, WI: Highsmith.

Milner, Art. 1984. "Forgiveness Week." *Library Journal* 109, no. 6 (April 1): 627–30.

Mooers, Calvin N. 1960. "Mooers' Law or, Why Some Retrieval Systems Are Used and Others Are Not." *American Documentation* 11, no. 3 (July): ii.

Murphy, Molly, and Yang Lin. 1996. "How Much Are Customers Willing to Pay for Interlibrary Loan Service?" *Journal of Library Administration* 23, no. 1–2: 125–39.

Myers, Judy. 1979. "Designing Open Stack Areas for the User." In *Sign Systems for Libraries: Solving the Wayfinding Problem*, ed. Dorothy Pollet and Peter C. Haskell, 195–201. New York: R. R. Bowker.

National Commission on Libraries and Information Science. 1985. *The Role of Fees in Supporting Library and Information Services in Public and Academic Libraries*. Washington, DC. National Commission on Libraries and Information Science. ERIC ED258584.

Nelson, Susan, and Herbert Goldhor. 1987. "The Relationship Between the Length of Loan Period and Circulation in Public Libraries." *Illinois Library Statistical Report* 24 (August): 3-20.

"New Drive-Up Service Window at the Library Center Does 'Land-Office Business.' " 2000. *The Unabashed Librarian* no. 114: 9.

"News of Nebraska Libraries and People." 1997. *Ncompass* [Online] 4, no. 1 (Spring). Available: http://www.nlc.state.ne.us/public/archives/sprg97.html [Accessed September 28, 2001].

"Open Access." 2001. [Homepage of the State Library of Iowa], [Online]. (Updated August 24). Available: http://www.silo.lib.ia.us/Open%20Access.htm [Accessed September 27, 2001].

"Overdues." [2001]. [Homepage of the Mobile Public Library], [Online]. Available: http://www2.acan.net/~mplhp/faqo.html [Accessed September 28, 2001].

Oxford Dictionary of Quotations. 1980. 3d ed. reprinted with corrections. Oxford: Oxford University Press.

Peacocke, Andrew, and Jane Nees. 2000. "Beyond 'Cap in Hand' Funding of Rental Collections: The Establishment of High Demand Collections at Tauranga District Libraries." *Australasian Public Libraries and Information Services* 13, no. 3 (September): 102–5.

Phelan, Jody. 1985. "Fees for Services in Medium-Sized Public Libraries." *Iowa Library Quarterly* 23, no. 1 (Winter): 2–11.

"Policies and Procedures." [2001]. [Homepage of the Lewistown Public Library], [Online]. Available: http://www.lewistownlibrary.org (Under Policies) [Accessed September 27, 2001].

Potter, William Gray. 1986. "Creative Automation Boosts ILL Rates." *American Libraries* 17, no. 4 (April): 244–46.

Preece, Barbara G., and Thomas L. Kilpatrick. 1998. "Cutting out the Middleman: Patron-Initiated Interlibrary Loans." *Library Trends* 47, no. 1 (Summer): 144–57.

Public Library Association. 1991. *Public Library Data Service Statistical Report '91*. Chicago: Public Library Association.

———. 1998. *Public Library Data Service Statistical Report 1998*. Chicago: Public Library Association.

"Rainier Web-Index™ Management Survey." 2000. [Homepage of Rainier Corporation], [Online]. Available: http://www.rainierco.com/survey_2000/Management_Report .htm [Accessed September 28, 2001].

Ranganathan, Shiyali R. 1957. *The Five Laws of Library Science*. 2d ed. Bombay, India: Asia Publishing House.

Rollins, Gene. 1996. "Electronic Document Delivery: Impact and Implications for Library Services at Houston Public Library." *Resource Sharing & Information Networks* 11, no. 1–2: 17–25.

Ross, Catherine Sheldrick. 1999. "A Model of the Process of Choosing a Book for Pleasure." Presentation in *Growing Readers' Advisory Services* seminar at American Public Library Association Spring Symposium, Chicago, March 25–27.

Ross, Catherine Sheldrick, and Mary K. Chelton. 2001. "Reader's Advisory: Matching Mood and Material." *Library Journal* 126, no. 2 (February 1): 52–55.

Sarff, Meg. 1998. "Davenport Public Library Has a Hit with Bestsellers Club." *Footnotes: The Official Newsletter of the State Library of Iowa* 22, no. 6 (April): insert.

Schabo, Pat, and Diana Breuer Baculis. 1989. "Speed and Accuracy for Shelving." *Library Journal* 114, no. 16 (October 1): 67–68.

Schindler, Jo Ann. 2001. "A Summary of HSPLS Services." [Homepage of Hawaii State Public Library Service], [Online]. (Updated February 3). Available: http://www.hcc.hawaii.edu/hspls/sumserv.html [Accessed September 28, 2001].

Shontz, David. 1999. "Effect of Fines on Length of Checkout and Overdues in a Medical Library." *Bulletin of the Medical Library Association* 87, no. 1 (January): 82–84.

Sivulich, Kenneth. 1989. "How We Run the Queens Library Good (and Doubled Circulation in Seven Years." *Library Journal* 114, no. 3 (February 15): 123–27.

Sloan, Bernard G. 1989. "Resource Sharing at the Statewide Level: ILLINET Online." *Illinois Libraries* 71, nos. 3-4 (March-April): 185–89.

———. 1990. "Future Directions for ILLINET Online." *Illinois Libraries* 72, no. 1 (January): 40–44.

Sloan, Bernard G., and J. David Stewart. 1988. "ILLINET Online: Enhancing and Expanding Access to Library Resources in Illinois." *Library Hi Tech* 6, no. 3: 95–101.

Smith, Adam. 1937. *An Inquiry into the Nature and Causes of the Wealth of Nations.* New York: Modern Library.

Smith, Wendy. 1993. "Fee-Based Services: Are They Worth It." *Library Journal* 118, no. 11 (June 15): 40–43.

Spiller, David. 1980. "The Provision of Fiction for Public Libraries." *Journal of Librarianship* 12, no. 4 (October): 238–65.

Strong, Gary E. 1984. "Report on Fees and User Cost Sharing." *California State Library Newsletter,* no. 43 (July): 5–6.

Tilson, Yvette. 1995. "Income Generation and Pricing in Libraries." *Bottom Line* 8, no. 2: 23–36.

Underhill, Paco. 1999. *Why We Buy: The Science of Shopping.* New York: Simon & Schuster.

"Upfront News: Library Receives Entrepreneurial Loans." 1991. *Wilson Library Bulletin* 65, no. 7 (March): 12.

Van House, Nancy A. 1983a. *Public Library User Fees: The Use and Finance of Public Libraries.* Westport, CT: Greenwood Press.

———. 1983b. "A Time Allocation Theory of Public Library Use." *Library and Information Science Research* 5, no. 4 (Winter): 365–84.

Walker, Alice Sizer. 1989. *Making Money: Fees for Library Services.* New York: Neal-Schuman.

Weisman, Jerry. 1981. "Evaluating Architectural Legibility: Wayfinding in the Built Environment." *Environment and Behavior* 13, no. 2 (March): 189–203.

Welch, Alicia J., and Christine N. Donohue. 1994. "Awareness, Use, and Satisfaction with Public Libraries: A Summary of Connecticut Community Surveys." *Public Libraries* 33, no. 3 (May-June): 149–52.

Wessling, Julie, and Tom Delaney. 2000. "After the Flood, Colorado State Reaps a Harvest of Invention." *American Libraries* 31, no. 10 (November): 36–37.

CREATING ACCESS

"Do all the good you can, by all the means you can, in all the ways you can, in all the places you can"— John Wesley (Bartlett 1992, 309).

To be able to use items in a library's collection, a patron must first be able to access them, discovering where desired materials can be found and then obtaining them, whether physically or digitally. Unless immediately obtainable online (e.g., an article from a full-text database available through the library's Web site or dial-in access), collection products are removed in space from the patron; they may also be removed in time, when a patron wants an item after library hours. Determining what methods of distribution will best resolve space and time issues requires consideration of at least four major questions:

- What collection distribution outlets will the library use?
- How will staff distribute items among these outlets?
- How will staff distribute items among collections in a single library facility?
- How can the interior be designed for maximum distribution effectiveness?

WHAT COLLECTION DISTRIBUTION OUTLETS WILL THE LIBRARY USE?

We think immediately of the three "laws" of real estate: location, location, location. Which location(s) will optimally meet community needs? Primary elements that influence this decision include the geographic area served, the distribution of the population within it, the nature of the library's clientele (including their ability and/or willingness to travel to use the collection), and the costs and benefits of each option. Studies have consistently shown that overall library use is highest when patrons have convenient, ready access to the collection. Our challenge is finding affordable ways to accommodate this need.

Eight major distribution options exist: main libraries, full-service branches, remote electronic access, mini-branches, bookmobiles, deposit collections, home delivery services, and materials-by-mail services.

Main Libraries

A single main library, which reduces the need for duplicate collections, provides a highly economical choice.[1] With personnel and operating expenditures in only one building, the library may be able to stay open longer, making it more accessible to patrons who need early, late, or weekend hours. Main libraries also usually house larger, more diverse collections than other library outlets and may offer additional amenities, such as spacious computer labs or meeting rooms. Particularly when the building is attractive, these features can attract patrons. When the San Antonio (Texas) Public Library built a new central facility twice the size of the old, the number of visitors tripled. A year after the Charleston County (South Carolina) Public Library opened its new main library circulation had increased 250 percent, visits 184 percent, and new registered borrowers 177 percent ("Renaissance" 1999). Patrons who read voluminously in one subject area, extensively use a particular audiovisual format, seek more sophisticated or uncommon items, or have other specialized needs, especially those associated with a formal educational program or career, will frequently travel farther to use a main library rather than limit themselves to the materials available at their local branch (Gajerski 1989; Gallup 1976).

Nevertheless, for many day-to-day needs, patrons may find main libraries inconvenient to reach, particularly in larger communities, and prefer to pick up an audiobook or read the newspaper at a location close to where they work, shop, or, especially, live. Casual users are often unwilling to travel more than five miles out of their way to reach a library outlet (Childers and Van House 1989; Hayes and Palmer 1983; Palmer 1981). Lack of transportation encourages nonuse (D'Elia 1980; Gallup 1976), making library proximity particularly crucial for youth (Ballard 1986; Fry 1989) and those living in areas where many residents do not own cars or have little background in using libraries (Shoham, Hershkovitz, and Metzer 1990). Indeed, Jue et al. (1999) found library outlets underrepresented in areas with poverty rates exceeding 40 percent. As of 1993, 3 million people living in poverty in the

United States did not have ready access to a library, a situation contributing to that invisible yet real division between the information rich and poor.

Even people who own an automobile may be discouraged from using main library facilities when they lack free or easily accessible parking. When asked to rate the importance of 61 separate indicators of a library's overall effectiveness, users ranked adequate parking as the 11th most significant factor that influences use. In contrast, library managers ranked it 38th and librarians ranked it 45th (Van House and Childers 1993). We encourage as many librarians as possible to seek innovative ways to address this issue. For example, the Grand Rapids (Michigan) Public Library assumed ownership of and responsibility for operating the lot next to it, previously run by the city and only available for those with monthly passes. Patrons can now validate their tickets at the circulation desk to receive an hour of free parking on weekdays and unlimited free parking on weekends ("Library Offers" 1995).

Full-Service Branch Libraries

Medium-sized and larger communities in particular can minimize patron travel time by supplementing a centrally located main library with full-service branches built near residential, shopping, and work areas.[2] Currently, 16.6 percent of libraries in the United States do this, as table 6.1, page 124, shows (Chute and Kroe 2001).

Compared to the main library, branch libraries usually offer substantially smaller collections, which can minimize library anxiety and overload issues. Staff can also tailor branch collections to satisfy the unique needs of area residents. For example, the Queens Borough (New York) Public Library (QBPL) designed a collection of popular and traditional Spanish-language materials for patrons at its Corona Branch, which serves a predominantly Hispanic clientele (Sivulich 1989).

Nevertheless, the relatively small square footage in branches can limit the breadth of subjects and formats available. For example, the New York Public Library features an extensive collection of CDs, music on tape, audiobooks, and videos at two central libraries, a research library, and two borough centers and offers much smaller nonprint collections at most neighborhood branches ("Branch" 1999). Such smaller collection sizes can decrease use. Indeed, Detweiler (1986) found that the circulation per volume falls off sharply when the size of a library's collection drops below 50,000 volumes.

Online resources available at all library outlets can increase branch collections in a space-efficient manner. Staff can further offset the smaller size of branch collections by sending an item from another location to a patron's branch upon request. The Williamson County (Tennessee) Public Library makes this option more attractive by offering next-day delivery, Tuesday through Saturday, whenever patrons request "on shelf" items from another branch ("Services" 2001). Patrons willing to travel to other facilities can also benefit from maps showing all branch locations and hours, automated catalogs that clearly indicate all locations of owned items, and a phone so that a patron or staff member can call ahead and have the material held.

TABLE 6.1. Number of Public Libraries and Their Branches in the United States, Cross-Analyzed by Size of Population Served.*

Size of Population Served	Number of Libraries Responding to Outlet Count	Number of Libraries with a Branch Library**	Percentage of Libraries with a Branch Library	Total Number of Branch Libraries	Average Number of Branch Libraries***
Total	8,964	1,513	16.9%	7,293	4.8
1,000,000 or more	20	20	100.0%	854	42.7
500,000 to 999,999	54	54	100.0%	1,124	20.8
250,000 to 499,999	94	90	95.7%	980	10.9
100,000 to 249,999	323	289	89.5%	1,662	5.8
50,000 to 99,999	513	335	65.3%	1,108	3.3
25,000 to 49,999	860	304	35.3%	790	2.6
10,000 to 24,999	1,716	263	15.3%	527	2.0
5,000 to 9,999	1,475	109	7.4%	179	1.6
2,500 to 4,999	1,326	32	2.4%	45	1.4
1,000 to 2,499	1,638	16	1.0%	22	1.4
Fewer than 1,000	945	1	0.1%	2	2.0

*Table compiled from figures reported in *Public Libraries in the United States: Fiscal Year 1998* (Chute and Kroe 2001).

**No distinction was made in this survey between full-service branch libraries and minibranches.

***Among libraries that possess branch libraries.

To meet the long-term needs of branch patrons, staff may supplement "fixed" collections with rotating sets of more specialized materials. QBPL has used this strategy to expand video selections at 17 branches, cycling supplemental collections of 300 specialized videos among the locations (Sivulich 1989). QBPL also encourages branches to test the market for foreign-language materials by borrowing a collection in one of 50 languages from the central library (Gitner 1998).

Branches can also choose to buy a core of classics, best-selling materials (discarded when demand passes), basic reference works, and the unique items needed for the neighborhood clientele. All other works can be purchased centrally and moved frequently between different branches so that each has a continually renewed collection (Savage 1946). In 1992 the Norfolk (Virginia) Public Library followed a modified version of this approach, purchasing a rotating collection of story-hour books for the library's 11 neighborhood branches to refresh the children's collections, a practice repeat patrons appreciated. As an added benefit, the library received an $1,800 productivity award from the city of Norfolk for meeting a broad range of needs while saving taxpayers' money (Murray 1992). The Pine Rivers Shire (Australia) Library Service has also employed this tactic successfully, rotating book group kits, which contain multiple copies of a single title, among branches twice a year (Bolin 2000).

In the past several decades, use of rotating collections was often limited by the time-consuming nature of changing catalog records when a work moved from branch to branch. Librarians today have options other than simply leaving these works uncataloged. First, they can prepackage collections so that an entire set of items rotates together. For example, a large library might have 15 different collections of DVDs that rotate on the first day of every other month to a different branch. Patrons could determine the titles currently housed at their branch by consulting a print catalog—inexpensive to maintain in this automated age—that travels with each unit. Additionally, an automated circulation system can be programmed to indicate that a desired title belongs to DVD collection number 12 and to seamlessly link that collection number to its current location at PQR branch.

In the Province of Quebec (Canada), which has many small, isolated communities, collections rotate from regional to member libraries. Local libraries buy their own reference items, bestsellers, and other popular titles and supplement their purchases with materials borrowed from their regional library, which has 40,000 to 50,000 titles available for such loans. Normally, librarians exchange these borrowed materials three times a year (Fink and Boivin 1988). Similarly, the New Jersey State Library's Multi-Lingual Materials Acquisition Center has thousands of fully-cataloged and annotated books, magazines, videos, and newspapers in a number of foreign languages, including Arabic, Hindi, Korean, Mandarin Chinese, Vietnamese, Gujarati, Haitian French, Tagalog, Polish, Russian, and Spanish, available free of charge for three-month bulk loans to libraries in the state (*Multi-MAC* 1998).[3]

Branches, particularly those located in easily accessible places, can reduce patron travel costs so much that people who would not normally do so start to use the library. For example, the Fort Vancouver (Washington) Regional Library District's shopping mall branch, open 71 hours per week plus extra hours during the

Christmas season, does such brisk business that 60 percent of the children's collection is always checked out, many by nontraditional users (Behrman and Conable 1989). Such heavy use, when combined with smaller size and operating costs, allows branches to circulate materials at a reduced cost per item. Rawlinson (1990) quotes statistics that show that branches account for 82 percent of the circulation of library systems, even though they receive only about 54 percent of book funds and 57 percent of total operating expenditures.

As metropolitan areas and their suburbs continue to expand, the need for branches will increase. Yet building new branches can be quite expensive. Joint-use facilities provide one cost-saving approach to providing branch service. In Australia, they represent 8 percent of all public library outlets (Bundy 1998). Public libraries may share space with numerous other agencies, including schools, colleges and universities, municipal governments, museums, and even other library systems.

Successful joint-use endeavors require careful planning, strong communication between institutions, and an enduring commitment to all client groups. Therefore, librarians considering entering into a joint-use agreement may want to consult others with similar arrangements.[4] Karp (1996) and Bundy (1998) look at the history and future of joint-use libraries, review the pros and cons of them, describe the most common kinds of partnerships, and note many recommendations for success. Recurring themes include the importance of

- establishing clear, formal guidelines during the planning process, such as spelling out who will provide what services to which user populations. For example, Conaway (2000) details the process used by the San Jose (California) Public Library and San Jose State University, whose joint-use library is scheduled to open in 2003.

- providing central, convenient locations that meet the needs of all user groups;

- considering the unique circumstances of a proposed joint-use arrangement as well as learning from others. For example, the experiences of the Washoe County (Nevada) Library System suggest that a public library sharing space in a school media center can encourage adult visits by having an outside entrance into the library as well as the entry from the school (Goldberg 1996).

- involving administrators, staff who will be working on site, and community representatives in the planning process and continuing to consult with all relevant parties; and

- offering at least the same level of service separate facilities would offer and evaluating the library regularly.

Remote Electronic Access

Superior service in this digital age implies that libraries offer remote bibliographic access to their collections through such means as dial-in or Internet catalog connections. The number of U.S. libraries doing this continues to increase. So does the number of institutions offering dial-in or Internet access to full-text databases or CD-ROMs—36.1 percent of all public library outlets as of 2000 (Bertot and McClure)—and other electronic access to the content of their collections, as copyright restrictions allow. When digitized and mounted on a Web page, library materials can be accessed by anyone, anywhere in the world, with the use of an Internet-connected computer.[5] In 1999, Scally found 14.2 percent of U.S. public libraries involved in a digitization project, 14.3 percent had one planned in the next three years, and 2.5 percent had completed one within the last three years. Large libraries (service populations exceeding 100,000) have been particularly likely to undertake such projects; 81.3 percent had one in the works. Scally also identified the most commonly digitized items: photograph collections (in 77.1 percent of libraries with digitization projects), manuscripts (31.4 percent), books and diaries (28.6 percent each), postcards (25.7 percent), maps and newspapers (14.3 percent), and sound recordings (2.9 percent). Examples of digitization projects include the Mount Prospect (Illinois) Public Library's effort, done jointly with the village's historical society, to digitize the oral histories of 28 longtime residents and the Chicago Public Library's digitization of photographs from its African-American history and literature collection (Filipek 1998).

Public libraries can also use their Web sites to integrate their digital, audiovisual, and print resources, providing an organized information gateway. For example, the Santa Fe (New Mexico) Public Library's site features a page offering access to its magazine resources, including indexes (many full-text), a periodicals holdings list, and an explanation of interlibrary loan ("Magazines" 2001).

What of the person who does not want or cannot afford to own a computer or pay for an Internet connection? A growing number of libraries offer public Internet access within their buildings. Bertot and McClure (2000) found that 94.5 percent of all U.S. public libraries do so, up from the 73.3 percent figure noted in 1998. Moreover, a few libraries have placed electronic kiosks at public locations beyond the library to offer access to their catalog, the Internet, and other resources, a trend we find encouraging and anticipate will grow. Designed for durability and unattended use, these kiosks reside in such locations as shopping malls, grocery stores, and community centers (e.g., DataDepot 2000; "Information" 2001; "Visit" 1997).

Mini-Branches

A library that cannot afford a full-service branch providing story hours and similar services may consider establishing a mini-branch that primarily supplies browseable materials for checkout. We suggest supplementing a small collection of current and popular titles with high-quality works, such as a carefully selected set of classics and current award winners. Especially when equipped with a telephone hotline to the main reference desk for tough questions, such facilities may be staffed inexpensively by employees without library degrees.

Rapid transit stations, which offer service in the day-to-day path of potential users, are one popular location for mini-branches. The Montreal Public Library installed one of the first rapid transit libraries in the McGill metro station in 1981. During its first year of operation, almost 7,000 patrons (68 percent new borrowers) used this branch (Lavigne 1984). By its eighth year of operation, McGill's branch was circulating approximately 200,000 items per year. The DeKalb County (Georgia) Public Library has experienced similar success in reaching new patrons, opening its first train station kiosk in 1986 and its second in 1993. After one year of operation, the first location had issued more than 1,750 new cards; soon after opening, the second kiosk was averaging one to three new card issues per day ("First" 1987; "GA" 1993). Other public libraries that have operated mini-branches in rapid transit centers include the Paris (France) Public and the Miami-Dade (Florida) Public Library System, the first to install a mini-branch on the platform of an elevated transit system ("World's" 1992; "Reading on the Rails" 1999).

Libraries can also situate mini-branches in shopping centers. The Wichita (Kansas) Public Library and the Adams Memorial (Latrobe, Pennsylvania) Library provide such facilities in area supermarkets ("Supermarket" 1986; Commings 1996). In 1979 the Public Library of Cincinnati and Hamilton (Ohio) County launched a mall mini-branch, offering uncataloged books arranged by reader-interest categories (discussed in detail in Chapter 10); by 1985, it boasted the greatest circulation per square footage of any of the library's branches (Singh 1985). Likewise, the Hayner (Alton, Illinois) Public Library District opened its mall mini-branch in 1985 to booming circulation, which at times exceeded that of the main library. By 1997, circulation had more than tripled from the opening year's figures; the library board decided to purchase the empty retail space next door, creating facilities for children's programming, additional computer workstations offering Internet and word processing access, and a leisure reading area (Schoeberle and Reid 1998). We suspect this facility enjoys considerable usage from spouses, friends, and relatives accompanying shoppers engaged in long sprees.

Because malls charge a great deal to rent store space, libraries may be able to establish a long-term presence at a more reasonable cost by setting up a mini-branch along the mall walkway. Lockable, portable kiosks can house these branches, which have been used successfully by the Fairfax County (Virginia) Public Library, the St. Paul (Minnesota) Public Library, and the Public Library of Cincinnati and Hamilton County (Ohio) (Wagner 1987; Paine 1985).

Portable library structures may also prove cost-effective choices for other locations; they have achieved success in residential neighborhoods, at air force bases, and on elementary school grounds (Akin and Dowd 1993). The Comfenalco Family Compensation Bureau Libraries serving Antioquia in Colombia house 300-book collections in weather-resistant metallic structures in parks and other out-of-door public spaces (Rodríguez 1998).

Mini-branches set up as experimental facilities can also measure the potential demand for services among a particular group. The Livermore (California) Library tried this strategy in the late 1980s when it began offering summer-only service out of a 12-foot-square metal box of the type used at construction sites. Staff built a ramp up to the box and installed free-standing metal shelving around the perimeter. The library opened a branch there in 1992 and has since moved the box to other locations. Staffed by a library assistant, a clerk, and volunteers and open 20 hours a week from June until August, the "Library in a Box" has a higher turnover rate than the library's two traditional branches ("A Library in a Box" 1998).

Bookmobiles

As table 6.2, page 130, shows, 9 percent of the libraries in the United States currently use mobile facilities to provide a traveling collection of books and other materials (Chute and Kroe 2001). Many libraries arrange bookmobile stops at senior citizen complexes, child care facilities, schools, correctional institutions, and other establishments that house potential users for whom it might be inconvenient or impossible to reach other library facilities.

Bookmobiles can bring service to locations far from the main library. East Gippslandshire (Australia) Library Service bookmobile staff spend the night on the vehicle several times every two weeks to offer stops more than three or four hours from the library (Kenneally and Payne 2000). The Kenya (Africa) National Library Service serves people in locations so difficult to reach that camels, rather than motor vehicles, transport the books (Atuti and Ikoja-Odongo 1999). Thailand has three boat libraries that each carry 5,000 books and 100 videos (Sorensen 1999), and an IFLA survey suggests that other libraries may use wagons, motorcycles, helicopters, trains, and donkeys, among other mechanisms, to bring library materials out into the community (Stringer 1999).

Even in less isolated areas, some people may quit using the library entirely if it eliminates bookmobile service. Bolt (1984) documented that 39 percents of students served by one public library in rural Ohio quit checking out materials when their school's bookmobile stop was discontinued; the cost of travel to the main library was too high.

Because bookmobiles offer personalized services on a relatively small scale, they can also help ease patrons' potential fears of using large facilities. Staff at the Fresno County (California) Library schedule bookmobile stops at the camps of migrant workers. They reasoned that many workers, currently or once illegal aliens, are leery of large governmental institutions, work long hours, and have little or no tradition of library use, and therefore would be unlikely to bring their children to the library (Naismith 1989). Similarly, the Mitchell Shire (Australia) Library has offered service to Kosovar refugees (Kenneally and Payne 2000). Other individuals who have responded well to bookmobile visits include older persons who have not previously used the library, more conservative residents of highly rural areas (Philip 1990), and Native Americans (Skrzeszewski, Huggins-Chan, and Clarke 1990).

TABLE 6.2. Number of Public Libraries with Bookmobiles in the United States, Cross-Analyzed by Size of Population Served.*

Size of Population Served	Number of Libraries Responding to Outlet Count	Number of Libraries with a Bookmobile	Percentage of Libraries with a Bookmobile	Total Number of Bookmobiles	Average Number of Bookmobiles**
Total	8,964	792	8.9%	933	1.2
1,000,000 or more	20	11	55.0%	27	2.5
500,000 to 999,999	54	36	66.7%	75	2.1
250,000 to 499,999	94	49	52.1%	71	1.4
100,000 to 249,999	323	152	47.1%	185	1.2
50,000 to 99,999	513	168	32.7%	189	1.1
25,000 to 49,999	860	164	19.1%	168	1.0
10,000 to 24,999	1,716	141	8.2%	146	1.0
5,000 to 9,999	1,475	46	3.1%	46	1.0
2,500 to 4,999	1,326	14	1.1%	14	1.0
1,000 to 2,499	1,638	7	0.4%	8	1.1
Fewer than 1,000	945	4	0.4%	4	1.0

*Table compiled from figures reported in *Public Libraries in the United States: Fiscal Year 1998* (Chute and Kroe 2001).

**Among libraries that possess bookmobiles.

Bookmobiles may target only one service population, offering very specialized collections and services. Examples follow.

- The Columbus (Ohio) Metropolitan Library's MetroMouse Mobile serves Head Start daycare centers. Bookmobile staff members carry picture books and audiovisual materials suitable for preschoolers and present a program at each visit ("Reading Rodent" 1996).

- The Espoo City (Finland) Library Peikonpoika-Trollungen [6] bookmobile stops at primary schools and daycare centers. It features modular shelving that allows librarians to make space for story time or switch collections quickly to suit the language (Finnish or Swedish) of the site they will visit (Laitinen 1998).

- The Memphis/Shelby County (Tennessee) Public Library and Information Center provides a mobile service called JOBLINC designed to help job seekers. The JOBLINC bookmobile offers work and career materials, a list of state job openings, a phone, computers, and a staff trained to help with job and career counseling and reference (Drescher 1995, 1998). The library also has a mobile library serving daycare centers (dubbed "Training Wheels") and an InfoBus serving immigrants (King and Shanks 2000).

- The District of Columbia Public Library offers special mobile service to inner-city elderly with a bookmobile equipped with a wheelchair lift and a retractable step, large print books, Braille magazines, and magnifying glasses (Boyce and Boyce 1990).

- The Springfield-Greene (Missouri) County Library District's Mobile Learning Center visits homebound literacy students and serves as a literacy tutor training site. Their bookmobile—a customized van—carries a computer, television, and tape recorder as well as literacy materials (Miller and Smith 1988).

Bookmobiles can also be used to reach out to more general populations. For example, within neighborhoods or rural areas that lack branches, librarians may schedule regular stops at apartment buildings, trailer courts, shopping malls, schools, housing projects, and manufacturing plants.

Bookmobile disadvantages include the often short stops, ranging from one-half to two-and-one-half hours and repeated an average of once every two weeks (Vavrek 1990b), which provide intermittent access to the collection, and space limitations that curtail collection diversity and depth as well as the potential for reference services.

This latter situation is changing as technology allows bookmobiles to offer access to databases (including the library's catalog), CD-ROMs, and the Internet (Monley and Pestell 1996). In Australia, 25 percent of bookmobiles offer online catalog access and 14 percent provide access to the Internet and e-mail, CD-ROMs, and computers with word processing and similar applications (Kenneally 1998). In the United States, numerous public libraries have bookmobiles that offer Internet access as well as online circulation, including public libraries in Des Plaines (Illinois), Memphis, San Francisco, and Topeka. Muncie (Indiana) Public Library's Cybermobile boasts six Internet workstations (King and Shanks 2000; Schneider 1998). We anticipate that this trend will continue as cellular, and other technologies enabling this access, continue to develop and become more affordable.

Bookmobiles can be used to whet patrons' appetites for library service, encouraging them to visit another, non-mobile outlet. This idea lies behind the Sacramento (California) Public Library's WonderWagon service, which visits special events and Head Start programs, registering patrons, letting them check out books, and encouraging them to go to their neighborhood library (Dukelow 1999). Bookmobile service may also temporarily substitute for a branch, as one did at the Williamsburg (Virginia) Regional Library when it closed its children's facility for renovation (Kurzeja and Charbeneau 1999), or even pave the way to the eventual establishment of a branch. In the latter instance, we suggest parking in a growing neighborhood for at least an entire day once a week to meet the demands of an expanding population and provide usage statistics to help demonstrate to funding bodies the need for a non-mobile branch. For example, the Chinatown branch of the Los Angeles Public Library, now one of the busiest in that city, began as a bookmobile stop (Mathis 1990).

Deposit Collections

Deposit collections can also bring library materials to community residents who find it highly inconvenient to travel to the library. For example, the library can provide a small group of desirable materials to residents of a senior citizen complex who can no longer drive and could find the time and the physical costs of visiting the library on a bus prohibitive.

Librarians may make deposit collections available for the general public, as does the Beauregard Parish (Louisiana) Library, which provides them in selected stores and community service buildings throughout its service area ("Community" 2000). They may also establish deposit collections for a specific clientele, as do

- the Onondaga County (New York) Public Library, providing rotating deposit collections of read-aloud books to area preschools (Wyker 1988) and adult new reader titles to the waiting rooms of health and welfare organizations ("Outposts" 1988);

- the Comfenalco Family Compensation Bureau Libraries in Medellín, Colombia, offering "traveling boxes" of at least 50 books to companies for their employees' recreational reading needs (Rodríguez 1998);

- the New York Public Library, furnishing deposit collections for homeless shelter residents of all ages (Behrmann, Bonitch, and Gottfried 1988; Gonzalez and Gottfried 1988);

- the Medina County (Ohio) District Library, supplying the local hospital with a "comedy cart" collection of uplifting and humorous items that volunteers wheel to patients' rooms (Nelson and Solecki 1998);

- the public library serving Nonantola, Italy, which offers the "BiblioVox" deposit collection in a popular discotheque in an effort to reach 20-30 year-olds, about 7,500 of whom visited the BiblioVox in its first eight months of existence (Betti 1996);

- the numerous libraries that offer deposit collections at correctional facilities (Herald 1995; "Brooklyn" 1999); and

- the Waterford (New York) Public Library, preparing various story kits (each containing two picture books and an activity) for preschool and childcare centers, for direct loan to the children they serve. Over the course of one school year, 70 percent of these children and their parents borrowed at least five kits and 95 percent borrowed at least one (Bagley 2000).

In each of the listed cases, librarians tailor the small deposit collections to meet the special needs of the client group and (optimally) rotate them frequently to ensure that patrons have access to diverse choices over time. For example, a collection at a jail might include books and magazines for recreational reading as well as a range of legal information. Nonprint formats may also be relevant, as in the case of a senior center collection that includes videos, DVDs, and audiobooks as well as large print newspapers, magazines, and books.

Libraries may also provide deposit collections on an as-demanded, rather than ongoing, basis. For example, on request, the Park Ridge (Illinois) Public Library will loan local teachers up to 35 items as a classroom collection for their students' use. These loans supplement school media center resources and may save students a trip to the public library (*Teacher's* 1997).

In addition to increasing access to library materials, deposit collections can promote the library. The Westport (Connecticut) Public Library provides several local doctors' offices with rotating collections of children's books, each containing a letter inviting the reader to the library for "more good books just like this one" and an evaluation form. Data collected on these forms show that after being exposed to the collection in their doctor's waiting room, 85 percent of adults who did not visit the public library at least once a month intended to visit in the future (Fader 1991).

Following the lead of the Orange (New Jersey) Public Library (OPL), a number of libraries have also tried "read-and-return" collections of books that the library would otherwise discard. OPL staff members mark former bestsellers, mysteries, and other titles likely to appeal to casual readers with a label that invites residents to take and read the title, returning it to the library when finished. Distributed in a range of outlets around the community (such as banks, beauty parlors, and doctors' offices), read-and-return titles are displayed in a simple rack with an accompanying sign and changed as frequently as demand indicates (Scilken 1971). The Montgomery County (Maryland) Public Libraries have placed books in the county courthouse for use by citizens called to jury duty ("AL" 1991). And one

New York library system supplies a local hospital's admissions waiting room with paperbacks that can be returned to any area library or simply left in the patient's room ("Libraries" 1996). (We suggest that this practice could also be applied to emergency rooms, where noncritical patients and their families often wait several hours for treatment.) The Cambridge (Massachusetts) Public Library established an expansive program that placed thousands of donated paperbacks in a subway station and invited riders to borrow the books on the honor system (Watson 1988).

Obviously, patrons never return some of the materials borrowed from read-and-return collections. For example, when OPL began its collection, it tracked this and noted a return rate of 65 percent (Scilken 1971); Senior Reference Librarian Alice McMillan estimates a current return rate as high as 80 percent (1999). Nevertheless, when librarians use donations or discards as stock, they can raise community awareness about the collection at a relatively low cost. To this end, the Friends of the Vernon Area (Illinois) Public Library District stock shelves at two local train stations with paperbacks intended to be taken by commuters but not necessarily returned ("All" 2000). We suspect that even those who take and do not return materials remember the library—and may demonstrate this when voting for referenda.

Personal Delivery Services

Many public libraries offer delivery to patrons' homes, offices, hospital beds, jail cells, and so forth. Homebound delivery, a commonly offered service of this kind, is widely available, especially in larger communities. In Northeastern Ohio, 92 percent of public libraries serving over 50,000 patrons and 76 percent of those serving communities of less than 20,000 offer homebound delivery (Hartman 1995). Libraries can help ensure quality service by sending professionals to interview patrons and determine their requirements before making and delivering the highly individual selections.

A number of libraries in the United States and elsewhere use specially designed vans to serve the homebound. For example, the Broughton (Salford, England) Library purchased a van; added shelving, lights, and a small but choice collection of materials; and staffed it with professional librarians who visited patrons in their homes. The van, equipped with a hydraulic lift and non-slip flooring, was accessible to people in wheelchairs, who appreciated being able to supplement the librarian's recommendations with their own choices (Haydon 1989). With the warden's cooperation and following relevant security measures, this method could be adapted to serve inmates at local jails. The King County (Washington) Public Library, among others, even uses low-cost vans instead of expensive, hard-to-maneuver bookmobiles (Hawkins 1980).

Personalized, professional home delivery services can be costly (the Broughton Library reported serving 300 individuals per month with a staff of three professionals and one part-time clerk). The Arlington Heights (Illinois) Memorial Library reduces costs by having librarians telephone patrons and select relevant materials and paraprofessional staff members or volunteers deliver them (Voss

1998). Librarians can obtain feedback, via phone, e-mail, notes, or messages sent through the deliverers, about how well the selections met patrons' needs.

Other libraries reduce costs by offering a delivery service completely staffed by volunteers, an option effective when it meets the following two conditions:

- Reliable volunteers can be recruited.

- Volunteers have the necessary talent, knowledge, and training to perform the professional work of interviewing patrons and selecting relevant materials. We highly recommend seeking retired librarians, educators, and avid readers and media users for these tasks.

McCune and Nelson (1995) and Burke and Liljenstolpe (1992) discuss ways to identify, recruit, and develop community members well suited for specialized volunteer tasks. Both training and technology can enhance the quality of service provided. For example, King County (Washington) Public Library volunteers bring a laptop loaded with the reader's advisory software NoveList when they visit homebound patrons for the first time. This tool assists them in learning more about patron tastes in fiction and in identifying specific genres, authors, and titles desired (Smith 2000).

Libraries can also keep delivery costs low by limiting full-delivery services to patrons physically unable to travel to the library, such as the homebound and the incarcerated, or charging other patrons, in part or full, for delivery. For example, the Hawaii State Public Library System will fax up to five pages of legislative testimony to any location in the state for free, and within copyright restraints, will fax information from reference materials for a charge of $2.50 per page (Schindler 2001).

Materials-by-Mail Services

These services use the mail both to deliver materials to patrons and return them to the library. For example, the Library of Congress's National Library Service for the Blind and Physically Handicapped mails qualified patrons record players or special four-track tape players along with books and magazines recorded on record or four-track cassette. In this program, fully subsidized by Congress, patrons do not even bear the monetary costs of returning materials, posting them with the "free matter for the blind and physically handicapped" label.

Most public libraries that send patrons materials by mail on a regular basis serve very large communities or highly rural areas with a widely dispersed population. The Juneau (Alaska) Public Libraries, which serves a region larger than Oregon, Washington, and California combined, mails library materials to more than 500 patrons who need only pay for return postage (Ferrell 1983; Bishop 1999). Libraries may provide a printed bibliography (preferably annotated) to their materials-by-mail customers, as well as dial-in or Internet access to a catalog of loan holdings. Member libraries can contract with the Ohio Valley Area Libraries

(OVAL), a chartered regional library system, on a fee-basis to provide a books-by-mail service for any of their patrons. OVAL staff members send everyone with a mailing address a mile or more from their local public library two catalogs each year that describe the 700 to 1,200 titles available for loan through the service and includes an order card. Registered users also receive an annotated new title list on a monthly basis and postage-paid return envelopes ("Books" 2001; Anderson 1999).

Although most public libraries once limited materials-by-mail services to patrons unable to travel to a library facility, this practice is changing as patrons with limited time and more discretionary income express a willingness to pay for such services. Currently the Multnomah County (Oregon) Public Library delivers books, videos, and other materials by mail to patrons who request them using the library's catalog, accessible via dial-in and the Internet. The service, free to home-bound patrons, costs all others $2.00 per item for shipping ("Books" 2000). The Count of Los Angeles Public Library offers a specialized service, Audio Express, that provides a shop-at-home catalog featuring a large selection of audiobooks: bestsellers, classics, mysteries, general fiction, and nonfiction titles, including business and language-instruction tapes. The library charges $10 per item for a 30-day rental; allows customers to place orders by mail, telephone, or fax; and accepts cash, checks, and major credit cards ("County" 1992; "Drive" 2001).

The Problem of Two-Way Distribution Channels

Although most organizations' products regularly flow only one way (from the organization to the consumer), which simplifies distribution, library materials of necessity routinely flow in both directions. Libraries may make returning materials convenient in a variety of ways, including

- allowing materials borrowed at any library facility to be returned to any other one;
- setting hours of operation convenient for the patron;
- installing outside returns where as many forms of materials as possible can be brought back even when the library is closed; and
- reducing or eliminating fines for overdue materials.

Chapter 5 considers these strategies.

Are Librarians Making Effective Choices About Their Collection Distribution Options?

Selecting distribution outlets requires contemplating which option(s) will best meet community needs, then evaluating and modifying these decisions, as relevant. Overlooking important issues during this process could reduce the cost-effectiveness of services, a serious problem during any time of limited funding, especially given that some distribution decisions can be more easily modified than others. For example, a library can change a poorly selected deposit collection site relatively easily, whereas correcting for a poorly sited branch may cost the library more than it can afford, in terms of both dollars and political capital. The difficulty of remedying bad distribution decisions underscores the importance of careful planning. Research data on the bookmobile, one of the most studied distribution outlets, illustrates these points.

Although the costs of circulating works can vary significantly among different outlets (Tutton 1990; Vavrek 1990a), many libraries may not be collecting the budget statistics necessary to calculate cost-effectiveness figures. For example, Kennedy's (1997) survey of a national sample of public libraries with bookmobiles revealed that only 20 percent of them have separate bookmobile budgets, which would readily allow this calculation.

Moreover, the literature (admittedly an incomplete representation of practice) does not indicate that libraries weigh cost-effectiveness figures against indicators of the benefits received from each outlet. Indeed, several nationwide studies conducted by the Center for Rural Librarianship found that 70 percent of libraries with bookmobiles have not surveyed their users to determine the extent to which the collection meets their needs (Vavrek 1990a).

Further, everyday matters pertaining to each outlet may not be optimally considered. In the United States, two-thirds of public libraries with bookmobiles have no formal long-range plans guiding that service (Vavrek 1990a). One of the few studies to formally explore bookmobile scheduling showed that only 27 percent of North Carolina libraries used population and census tract maps to help schedule stops. Furthermore, although patrons in both suburban neighborhoods and rural communities wanted evening and weekend stops, fewer than 5 percent of bookmobiles offered such services (Abel 1986). Yet elements such as these are crucial when considering the potential impact of even a small change in the timing of bookmobile stops. For example, when the Alameda County (California) Library bookmobile changed a stop by a mere 15 minutes, circulation at that location doubled (Overmyer 1987).

In short, both the evidence and lack of it suggests that libraries may not always weigh decisions about distribution outlets as thoughtfully as they could. We applaud the publication of relevant literature from researchers and practitioners, such as the criteria the Middletown (Ohio) Public Library routinely consider when scheduling bookmobile stops (Mort 1990) and the in-depth procedures the Warren-Newport (Illinois) Public Library District use to determine cost-effectiveness for its bookmobile (Tutton 1990).

HOW WILL THE LIBRARY
DISTRIBUTE ITEMS
AMONG ITS OUTLETS?

Librarians must make tough choices about how many copies of (or licenses to) a work to purchase and in which outlets to place these (or, in the case of computerized resources, where to locate these on the library's network to allow users optimum access).

A societal-marketing orientation suggests beginning with two primary factors when determining how to distribute items among various outlets. First, librarians can examine the use that similar products or product lines have received or will likely receive at different distribution outlets. In general, items that receive little use may best be housed only at the main library or at large branches. Betts suggests that for most public libraries these include "original works of literature by minor authors, science and technology beyond the general interest and practical level, academic social science, philosophy and religion (other than 'personal' religion)" (1986, 45). We recommend here, however, that each library examine its own use data to determine whether these subjects actually do receive little use (and why) and what other kinds of materials may be added to this list. When one outlet depends heavily on another for materials in certain subjects, genres, or formats, librarians will want to monitor infrasystem and interlibrary loan statistics for these categories; significant borrowing presumably will warrant a change in purchasing or distribution patterns.

Once locally relevant decisions have been made, the process of placement will usually be fairly straightforward. For example, the head of collection development may send several copies of the latest animated video in a popular children's series to a suburban branch with consistently heavy circulation for such works and no copies of the same video to a mini-branch in the midst of the city's financial district.

Second, librarians may consider the short- and long-term needs of target markets. For example, inmates served by a prison deposit collection may benefit from materials that include information about legal matters, drug rehabilitation programs, career options, and, according to at least one study (Hardy 1998), art instruction. A large group of Korean immigrants served by a library may require information on learning English as a foreign language and obtaining citizenship.

Consider the following hypothetical case: ABCD library serves 50,000 residents in the Midwest. It has its main building in the county seat, three branch libraries in neighboring towns, a bookmobile, and deposit collections at the jail and the senior citizens' center. The head of collection development chooses to handle each of the following purchases differently, keeping in mind both past and potential use and the needs of different client groups:

- The selector buys seven copies of a new edition of a cookbook that has circulated steadily in the past, placing three in the main library, one in the bookmobile, and one at each branch.

- The selector purchases four copies of a new book about living well during one's retirement years. She places one in the main library, one in a branch serving a large elderly population, one in the deposit collection at the senior center, and one on the bookmobile, which stops at three housing complexes for the elderly.

- Because demand for very specialized career development books has been relatively low, the selector purchases only one copy of a recent book on careers in psychology, placing it in the main library.

Although ABCD Library's placement decisions seem reasonably effective, some potential use will be lost by not having a work at a particular outlet the day a patron seeks it, given that not every patron will be willing to bear the cost of obtaining a work from a different facility.

Staff can keep the likelihood that patrons will be able to obtain desired items when needed high by adopting a three-tiered distribution strategy. First, the library can establish a centralized program to do formula buying of materials likely to be in heavy demand by patrons and process and distribute them to relevant outlets as quickly as possible. Second, the library can ask its professional selectors to develop local collections to meet the special needs of their clientele. (Chapter 9 explains both of these strategies in more detail.) Third, the library can design a cost-effective delivery system to link distribution outlets.

HOW WILL STAFF DISTRIBUTE ITEMS AMONG COLLECTIONS IN A SINGLE FACILITY?

A fully integrated collection would contain materials of all types (for all ages, of all formats, on all subjects, etc.) housed in a single shelving range; at the other extreme each different type of collection is shelved separately. Either option can potentially cause confusion.

Successful decisions about integration and separation require consideration of six questions related to both patron needs and standard operational practices:

- Do patrons have special needs that an integrated collection might hinder?

- Will the size of an integrated collection assist or encumber patrons?

- Will patrons need special help using a collection due to the complexity of accessing information in it?

- Will housing other collections separately result in quick, convenient access?

- Do librarians need ready access to a subset of the collection so they can help other patrons?

- Do the physical characteristics of certain materials allow them to be interfiled?

Do Patrons Have Special Needs That an Integrated Collection Might Hinder?

Separate collections may better meet patron needs than integrated ones. For example, libraries usually subdivide children's collections to meet the needs of youth in various developmental stages.[7] Picture books expose young children to the wonders of reading and may teach basic concepts like shapes, colors, and the letters of the alphabet. Easy readers use simple vocabularies to encourage children just beginning to read; juvenile fiction and nonfiction serve more advanced readers.

Separate collections also permit libraries to establish distinct spaces for different user groups, which can encourage use. Consider that the number of U.S. public libraries offering separate young adult collections (whether housed in their own distinct space or not) has decreased in recent years from 84 percent in 1988 to 58 percent in 1997 (Chelton 1997).[8] This may reflect, at least in part, the speed at which some teenagers bypass young adult reading and dive into adult books. Nevertheless, a few libraries, recognizing that teenagers feel more comfortable when they have their own area in libraries (Meyers 1999; Maughan 1999), have increased usage in innovative ways. The Renfrew (Scotland) Library District opened a separate facility for teens replete with popular books and magazines, computer games, compact discs, and music on tape in an inviting atmosphere that includes movie and music posters and music (MacRae 1996). And the Salem (Oregon) Public Library offers the Teen Scene, featuring materials of interest to middle and high school students, futon chairs, ample space to study, and posted signs indicating that adults unaccompanied by a teen should not stay longer than 15 minutes (Young 2000).

Similarly, many patrons want public libraries to offer a technology-free, quiet, comfortable area to read and study. Libraries meeting this demand include the Maple Grove and Plymouth Community Libraries of the Hennepin (Minnesota) County Library System and the Thomas Ford (Western Springs, Illinois) Memorial Library, which has a quiet room featuring a fireplace and a browsing collection (Jacob and Morphew 1997).

Works suitable for more than one collection, such as Ursula LeGuin's Earthsea Trilogy, which can be enjoyed by both teenagers and adults, can be placed in each. Such multiple placement will increase the likelihood that patrons, particularly browsers, will find and enjoy these titles.

Staff may also consider housing materials for adult new readers and foreign-language works in separate collections. Interfiling these works with the regular collection potentially limits their use because those just learning to read or speak English may be unable to search the catalog successfully and may be reluctant to ask for help. Marking each of these sections with multilingual or word-and-picture signs allows those who have difficulty reading English to find materials easily.

Separate large print collections also appeal to most patrons, who often request these works only when impaired vision inhibits their enjoyment of standard size print or when they want to read while using an exercise machine. Separating these materials makes them more convenient to find and also allows the library to add special features, like additional lighting, to further assist patrons. (It also reduces the chance that other patrons, who may find the type size bothersome, will accidentally choose these.)

Will the Size of an Integrated Collection Help or Hinder Patrons?

Occasionally, a library's size may influence the number and types of collections housed together. For example, branches with very limited resources frequently place their collections of juvenile, young adult, and adult nonfiction in one integrated section, increasing the likelihood that patrons will find at least one work on each desired subject.[9] This practice allows older patrons to choose works of a simpler style without embarrassment and encourages younger people to select works in line with their reading skills, even if these may officially be "adult" works. Interfiling nonfiction for all ages also helps meet the needs of students writing reports, who can find both simple and complex topical works in a single location. Libraries will, however, need to house such collections on shelves that both children and adults can reach or provide step-stools as needed.

Subdividing collections in large libraries can also potentially alleviate information overload. When does a collection grow large enough to warrant subdivided collections? Two studies address this briefly in the context of fiction collections. The first found significant information overload in a library with approximately 4,700 adult fiction books but not in a library with 1,300 (Baker 1986). The second found a majority of patrons in a library with 6,000 works of fiction experienced information overload, whereas most patrons in a library with 2,500 books did not (Baker 1988). These findings suggest that libraries with collections smaller than 2,500 books may not need to categorize fiction by genre, but those with collections larger than 4,700 items can help patrons by doing so, at the very least speeding search time.

Will Patrons Need Special Help Using a Collection Due to the Complexity of Accessing Information in It?

Evidence also supports separating collections when the methods used to access them are particularly time-consuming or confusing. For example, maintaining separate local history or genealogical collections, which may not be indexed anywhere, can facilitate access, especially when libraries provide a knowledgeable staff member to assist patrons in using them. Librarians can also create electronic or print finding aids for these works, using qualified volunteers as relevant.

Will Housing Other Collections Separately Result in Quick, Convenient Access?

Most patrons want new works of all types housed separately, so they can browse quickly among recent titles. This preference has been documented by studies that show:

- significant circulation increases when staff members display new titles in a separate section; and

- immediate and significant declines in use when staff members ultimately move these same titles to the regular stacks (Baker 1988; Spiller 1980; Briggs 1973; Borden 1909).

Because many patrons, particularly browsers, have difficulty locating fiction and biographies classified within the Dewey Decimal System, most public libraries separate these collections, shelving fiction alphabetically by the author, then title, and biographies alphabetically by the subject of the work, then author.

Many patrons also prefer that libraries separately house audiovisual materials because they often seek a particular format, then determine the genre or subject sought. That is, patrons who come to the library specifically seeking an entertaining video to watch will likely not be as satisfied with an amusing audiobook. Staff at the Dover (New Hampshire) Public Library discovered this when they tried interfiling nonfiction videos with nonfiction books. After a six-month trial period, they stopped this experiment due to extremely negative patron response. Most patrons who checked out videos did not seek topical information; they came into the library to borrow something on video and wanted all videos, fiction and nonfiction, housed in one area for easy browsing ("Action" 1989). An enterprising librarian may want to formally test patron use of and satisfaction with multimedia interfiled collections for select subjects, such as language instruction, which we believe would circulate particularly well interfiled. As a general practice, we recommend that libraries use a combination of surveys and experimentation to determine when specific collections will better serve patrons separated or integrated and then publish their findings.

Do Librarians Need Ready Access to a Subset of the Collection So They Can Help Patrons?

Maintaining a separate collection of reference works located near the reference desk can provide staff with ready access to materials needed to assist patrons. The growing number of online reference resources allows these to be made available from multiple locations throughout a library or system, thus easing the placement decision. For print resources, we do not recommend maintaining large collections of either ready or regular reference materials, which make it awkward or inconvenient for patrons, particularly the large number who bypass the catalog, to find the information they need. Large reference collections may also inhibit librarians' in-depth knowledge of specific materials, which can decrease search efficiency[10] and increase time required for collection maintenance and thus the percentage of dated materials in the collection.

Nolan (1991) suggested that assigning someone to oversee the nonfiction selection and de-selection process (and establishing formal criteria for what items belong in the reference collection) will facilitate ordering all necessary items and making consistent decisions about placement. In general, says Nolan, the size of the reference collection will be manageable when reference works

- have a format that makes them convenient to use for looking up information quickly,
- are used frequently by reference librarians,
- are authoritative,
- are current, and
- have unique coverage.

Do the Physical Characteristics of Certain Materials Allow Them to Be Interfiled?

At times the physical characteristics of specific works make interfiling unfeasible. For example, public libraries handle "oversized" items in various ways. Heavily weeding dated collections so that shelf heights can be adjusted to accommodate materials of all sizes presents a tidy solution to this challenge. However, many libraries cannot afford to sacrifice shelf space in this way. Turning oversized items spine up and interfiling them with other, similar materials can save patrons the additional cost of checking a second location for works on a particular subject. However, because this practice will eventually damage most items, it works well only for ephemeral items that will be discarded in a few years anyway. Shelving oversized works separately at the end of each range or on a separate range at the end of the entire collection requires higher short-term costs for patrons but preserves materials for future use. As a compromise position, libraries with some extra shelf space may store oversized books flat on the lowest shelf of the relevant stack, reasoning that patrons will not browse there anyway. Wherever libraries shelve oversized items, they will want to communicate through clear signage in the stacks at those points at which location errors could occur. For example, in areas with many oversized books, such as art, labels affixed to the front of the shelves may remind individuals of the location of these works.

Final Comments on Integration

However a library chooses to shelve its materials, we recommend integrating all types of materials in a single catalog whenever possible. In 1984 only 38 percent of public libraries had an integrated, multimedia catalog (Intner 1984), a percentage we suspect to be significantly higher today due to the relative ease of integrating online catalogs and the ever-increasing popularity of audiovisual formats.

For those who bypass the catalog libraries may judiciously place dummies—materials often made of wood that "stand-in" for an item on the shelf and indicate where it is—or small signs in the collection to alert patrons to materials they might find intriguing. For example, a shelf dummy placed next to Frank McCourt's lyrical book *Angela's Ashes* might refer patrons to the audiobook of the same title, housed elsewhere. A shelf dummy can refer those browsing among books on baroque music to related compact discs. Signs and dummies can also inform patrons when a library has temporarily removed works in a particular subject area to a display.

HOW CAN THE INTERIOR BE DESIGNED FOR MAXIMUM DISTRIBUTION EFFECTIVENESS?[11]

One comprehensive article on the topic of people's orientation needs notes that: "Unfamiliar environments make special demands upon us. Even the simplest of settings can involve a jumble of information that has to be sorted and processed before it becomes meaningful" (Pollet and Haskell 1979, 3). Even the smallest public libraries can be frustrating for a patron. They contain many kinds of collections, organized in different fashions; storage units of all sizes and shapes to house these; furniture for lounging and studying; service desks of all kinds; and dozens of miscellaneous items like signs, computers designated for various use, photocopy machines, plants, vending machines, and coat racks. Although these items serve important functions, their accumulated mass potentially contributes to a sense of disorientation.

As a library grows in size and the number of separate collections proliferates, the cost involved in finding desired items also increases. Both time and psychological costs will eventually decline as the patron becomes familiar with the library's layout. An inviting, intuitive design and clear signage particularly help new or infrequent users as well as patrons reluctant to ask for help.

Although outside the scope of this chapter, librarians planning their building interiors, particularly those constructing new facilities, will also want to consider a host of other issues and related studies from multiple disciplines. For example, libraries offering coffee shops or cafés (Boehning 1995; Reese 1999) are responding to retail-oriented research indicating that the amount of time people spend in a store greatly affects, and may be the single largest factor influencing, the amount they purchase and their satisfaction levels (Underhill 1999). Librarians interested in space planning may wish to consult Sannwald (1997) and McCabe (2000) or refer to the "The Librarian's Bookshelf" bibliography in the *Bowker Annual Library and Trade Book Almanac*, which includes a section entitled "Library Buildings and Space Planning" (Bogart 2000). As a supplement, we recommend that those interested in facility design read *Why We Buy*, which presents the knowledge retail anthropologist Paco Underhill (1999) has gleaned in almost 20 years of systematically studying shoppers' behavior. The book presents strategies for minimizing transition zones in public buildings, areas just inside the entrance to which people pay little attention as they adjust to their new environment, important because most libraries can't afford to waste an inch, let alone several feet or yards. Underhill also introduces the "butt-brush effect," wherein people brushed from behind will abandon merchandise that interests them to avoid being touched (1999, 17); this supports the argument that maintaining wide aisles can increase patrons' comfort and circulation as well as meeting ADA requirements. The book also leads the reader through an evaluation of a bookstore's physical attributes—including signage, layout, displays, and more—starting from a half-block away and moving throughout the store. Librarians can easily adapt this sample self-assessment to their own facilities to better see them through a patron's eyes.

To What Extent Does Placement of Collections Influence Their Use?

Evidence shows that collections located near the entrance of a building often receive significantly more use than those housed farther away (e.g., Harris 1966). In one of the earliest studies on the subject, Carnovsky describes the way that physical location of books in a small browsing library influences use: "[O]ne section of shelving . . . directly confronts the student when he enters the room. During the first month of . . . operation, I placed the fiction in this section. During the second month I . . . substituted non-fiction on the more accessible shelves. In spite of the fact that fiction was still quite accessible, there was . . . a noticeable drop in the proportion of fiction circulated as compared with the period when fiction was on the section more easily accessible. At the end of the second month, I . . . restored the books to their original sections and once again the fiction resumed a circulation very similar to that of the first month" (1935, 474).

To maximize use, staff can scrutinize past circulation records, determine which kinds of items receive the most use, and place these by the front door. The Phoenix Public Library (PPL) has successfully used this strategy, housing its "Popular Library" of new books, bestsellers, paperbacks, popular magazines, and a rental collection immediately inside the main entrance and adjacent to the circulation desk in its central library. The first stop in the library's traffic pattern, it accommodates the needs of browsers, who constitute a large part of PPL's clientele. As Webb notes, "A person who requires specific information—a researcher or an independent learner—passes through the Popular Library to the subject departments where the bulk of the library's collection [is] located, including the reference tools, the scholarly journals, the older, more technical books, books on specialized topics, and educational books such as test tutors and licensing exams" (1985, 64).

Although positioning popular works near the entrance can increase circulation by making it more convenient for patrons to access these, such prominent placement risks increasing competition for already popular titles, potentially decreasing the patron's chances of finding desired items on the shelves. The long-term result may be lower user satisfaction unless the library adopts corrective strategies, such as purchasing more copies of these works or assigning them shorter loan periods. (Chapter 9 discusses considerations surrounding these decisions.)

Locating the most-used items near the door may also reduce the likelihood that patrons will venture farther into the building to seek other, less popular materials. One bookstore experienced this phenomenon when it placed one popular collection—discounted books—just inside its doors. Careful tracking of shoppers' behavior found that almost everyone stopped at the table to browse, and a high percentage purchased at least one title, yet visits to other sections of the store uniformly dropped (Underhill 1999).

As an alternative, libraries can entice patrons farther into the building by placing popular items at the back of the facility, a strategy quite familiar to groceries, which often house staples like milk and bread at the rear of the store (Green 1995). Libraries have also used this tactic. For example, reasoning that patrons would be willing to take extra time and effort to retrieve highly popular items, staff at the Woodlawn Branch of the Baltimore County (Maryland) Public Library placed two of their most used collections, new books and videos, at the back of the library, marking the path to these items with brightly colored footsteps. They then chose worthy, lesser-known items and arranged them along this path in special subject displays angled for maximum visibility. This placement technique increased the use of displayed materials without significantly decreasing the use of the new fiction or videos.

As librarians plan placement of collections, signage, and displays (what will browsers ideally see first? next?), it may help to know how people usually navigate a public space without footsteps or other cues to direct them. Research shows that in the United States they walk forward, moving slightly toward the right, a pattern that driving may help establish, because in Great Britain and Australia, people move toward the left (Underhill 1999).

How Might the Library's Collections Be Arranged to Minimize Patron Costs of Locating Items?

Although relatively little research to date has explored user-friendly shelving arrangements in public libraries, we recommend that, as the building's architecture and the need for clear sight lines permit, librarians follow a few basic principles for arranging shelving of all types.[12]

First, group like collections together so that patrons can browse among them quickly. For example, we recommend placing general and genre fiction collections in roughly the same area. The side-by-side placement of collections likely to attract the same, or an overlapping, primary audience, can be especially effective. In this context, the Gallup Organization's (1985) identification of fiction and nonfiction materials with overlapping clientele, as shown in tables 6.3 and 6.4, pages 147 and 148, suggests particularly intriguing possibilities for collection arrangement.

TABLE 6.3. Fiction Categories Book Buyers Were Most Likely to Buy.*

Fiction Categories Almost Always Checked	Most Likely Category to Check Also	Second Most Likely Category to Check Also	Least Likely to Check Also
Action/Adventure	Mystery/Suspense/Spy	Popular Fiction	Occult/Supernatural
Historical Fiction	Autobiography/Biography	Historical Nonfiction	Occult/Supernatural
Humor	Autobiography/Biography	Popular Fiction	Western; Investment/Economics/Income Tax
Mystery/Suspense/Spy	Popular Fiction	Action/Adventure	Investment/Economics/Income Tax
Occult/Supernatural	Mystery/Suspense/Spy	Popular Fiction	Western
Popular Fiction	Autobiography/Biography	Mystery/Suspense/Spy	Western
Romance	Mystery/Suspense/Spy	Cookbooks	War/Military
Science Fiction	Action/Adventure	Popular Fiction	Investment/Economics/Income Tax
War/Military	Historical Fiction	Historical Nonfiction	Romance; Cookbook
Western	Action/Adventure	Historical Fiction	Occult/Supernatural

*Reprinted with permission from the Gallup Organization (1985, 127).

TABLE 6.4. Nonfiction Categories Book Buyers Were Most Likely to Buy.*

Nonfiction Categories Almost Always Checked	Most Likely Category to Check Also	Second Most Likely Category to Check Also	Least Likely to Check Also
Autobiography/ Biography	Historical	Popular Fiction	Western
Cookbook	Home and Garden/ How-To-Do-It	Autobiography/ Biography	War; Western
Health/Diet/Exercise	Home and Garden/ How-To-Do-It	Cookbook	Western
Historical Nonfiction	Historical Fiction	Autobiography/ Biography	Occult/Supernatural
Home and Garden/ How-To-Do-It	Cookbook	Health/Diet/Exercise	Western
Investment/Economics/ Income Tax	Home and Garden/ How-To-Do-It	Autobiography/ Biography	Western
Leisure	Popular Fiction	Humor	Occult/Supernatural
Reference/Instruction	Home and Garden/ How-To-Do-It	Autobiography/ Biography	Occult/Supernatural
Religious	Home and Garden/ How-To-Do-It	Autobiography/ Biography	Occult/Supernatural

*Reprinted with permission from the Gallup Organization (1985, 129).

Second, group all items in a collection within a single range of shelves. This will eliminate the confusion that can result when furniture, equipment, or service areas break up a range of similar materials. Occasionally, a library must violate this tenet. For example, one Midwestern public library has split its range of juvenile nonfiction into two sections to allow the personnel at the service desk to see the entire children's room. When structural considerations make it necessary for a library to divide stacks, staff can post signs at the point of the split, to inform patrons where the shelving continues. The larger the split—for example between floors—the more likely patrons will become frustrated, annoyed, or lost in the stacks without guidance.

Third, avoid placing shelving around the perimeter of the stacks, perpendicular to the regular ranges of shelves. Again, when structural considerations make this necessary, staff can post signs explaining this arrangement to patrons.

The second and third shelving principles do not preclude arranging materials in wide U-shaped bays, which may invite patrons into their depths and so encourage browsing, as well as minimizing the butt-brush effect. Such nooks have been used, for example, at the Cockeysville and Pikesville branches of the Baltimore County (Maryland) Public Library. They also do not inhibit using unique shelving configurations, such as those required in a small X-shaped branch with a circulation/information desk located in the center.

Fourth, use color cues to alert patrons to the location of separate collections. A library may use floor tiles of different colors to mark the paths to various collections or paint the shelves that hold easy readers bright yellow, juvenile nonfiction red, and juvenile fiction blue.

Finally, use effective sign systems to mark the location of collections. Signs for each major collection will optimally be large enough to read from just inside the door. Stack sections with labels that indicate the call number ranges they house and corresponding subject headings (e.g., 747—Interior Design) also help patrons locate materials. These encourage browsing when they are large enough to read easily (those currently offered by many U.S. vendors are very small), use natural language terms (these may or may not be the Library of Congress's), and are of medium specificity (e.g., South American history rather than Brazilian history, 1901–date).

As with all forms of communication, the intended audience must be considered when designing, phrasing, and positioning signs. Children may respond well to bright signs in primary colors; a moderate look may give messages credence with executives. In general, signs that use upper- *and* lowercase letters, high contrast colors, and a simple, fairly large font will be particularly readable. We also recommend that libraries invest in some combination of professional signs, well-designed, laminated, computer-generated signs, as well as intriguing artistic ones.

When wording signs, we advocate interesting yet simple messages, although the optimal number of words depends on where a sign hangs. Signs must be evaluated in context; it will not work to "just look around . . . see where there are empty spots on the walls and put the signs there" (Underhill 1999, 63). In part, this is because people will not usually stop just to read a sign; "putting a sign that requires twelve seconds to read in a place where customers spend four seconds is just slightly more effective than putting it in your garage" (Underhill 1999, 63).

Librarians need to determine how much time people will spend in a particular location, what they will be doing and thinking about there, and where their eyes will be focused; optimal sign placement interrupts "the existing natural sight lines in any given area" (Underhill 1999, 64). Thus, the most effective sign placement will be as close to eye level as possible, perpendicular to the line of vision of the person approaching the sign, and multi-sided, as necessary. Given (U.S.) patrons' natural inclination to move forward and toward the right, optimal positioning may well be canted to the left (Underhill 1999), unless current layout has trained patrons to follow other paths, in which case libraries will need to adjust accordingly.

Guides to designing effective sign systems include Ruderman and Ruderman (1998), Mallery and DeVore (1982), and Reynolds and Barrett (1981). Lubans and Kushner (1979) also spell out principles that can be used to evaluate the effectiveness of existing sign systems.

CONCLUSION

Distribution and placement decisions can either encourage use, making collection access easy and as trouble-free as possible, or discourage use, making access a chore. Librarians can both review distribution principles and research and also study the community to determine which outlets and collection arrangements will facilitate, or even invite, use. We also encourage librarians to experiment with and publish the results of studies of library placement issues, such as the cost-effectiveness of various distribution outlets, the effects that separation and integration have on use of the collection, and the effectiveness of various collection layout arrangements within existing buildings. Finally, exploring the literature beyond that reported in the library press can yield a wealth of relevant scientific findings from related disciplines.

NOTES

1. In 2001, there were 9,415 main library facilities in the United States (*American* 2001).

2. It is beyond the scope of this book to consider the historical development of branch libraries or the particulars of choosing the best site for a branch. See Koontz (1990,1994) for a review of the general literature on site location and a description of market-based models for predicting the use of new or relocated public library facilities, or Ballard (1986) for a description of branch library theory and its implementation.

3. The Center also offers other assistance to libraries developing collections, services, and programs for multilingual communities, such as translating signage, forms, and other materials; evaluating foreign-language circulating and reference collections; offering workshops on serving multicultural groups; and sending monthly annotated catalogs of recommended purchases that list ISBN, price, vendor, Dewey number, and subject headings (*Multi-MAC* 1998; "Multi-MAC" 1999).

4. The ALA Web site offers a bibliography of books and articles discussing public libraries sharing space with either school media centers or university/community college libraries ("Combined" 2000).

5. For more information about digitization, see Falk (1999) and Maxymuk (1999).

6. Peikonpokia and Trollungen are the Finnish and Swedish words for a young troll, considered to be mischievous but friendly.

7. Birckmayer (1988) provides a brief introduction to the developmental stages that children pass through and gives suggestions for how librarians can respond to these stages.

8. See Byczek and Vaillancourt (1998) for more information on serving teens.

9. Kralick (1977) found that although patrons accept the practice of interfiling nonfiction works for all ages, they are not as comfortable with the idea of interfiling fictional works for all ages. They felt that many adult novels were (because of subject matter and language) unsuitable for non-adults.

10. This problem is discussed in some detail in chapter eight of Baker and Lancaster (1991).

11. This section limits itself to discussing how the interiors of main, full-service-branch, and mini-branch libraries might be designed to improve distribution effectiveness. Readers who are interested in designing the interiors of bookmobiles may wish to refer to Hole and Topping (1990).

12. Academic libraries have explored the matter in a bit more detail. See, for example, Myers (1979).

REFERENCES

Abel, Joanne. 1986. "A Survey of Bookmobile Service in North Carolina." *North Carolina Libraries* 44, no. 4 (Winter): 225–29.

"Action Exchange: Self-Service AV Collections; Software to Track Attendance." 1989. *American Libraries* 20, no. 1 (January): 30.

Akin, Lynn, and Frances Smardo Dowd. 1993. "A National Survey of Portable Library Structures: What Works and Why." *Public Libraries* 32, no. 5 (September/October): 267–69.

"AL Aside—Ideas." 1991. *American Libraries* 22, no. 2 (February): 123.

"All Aboard." 2000. *FOIL (Friends of Illinois Libraries) Newsletter* 2, no. 1 (Spring): 3.

American Library Directory 2001-2002. 2001. 54th ed. Vol. 1, *Libraries in the United States.* New Providence, NJ: R. R. Bowker.

Anderson, Eric S. 1999. (Former Director, Ohio Valley Area Libraries). "Re: Books By Mail." E-mail to Karen Wallace, August 31.

Atuti, Richard Masaranga, and J. R. Ikoja-Odongo. 1999. "Private Camel Library Brings Hope to Pastoralists: The Kenyan Experience." *Library Review* 48, no. 1 and 2: 36–42.

Bagley, Norman E., IV. 2000. "Making Connections: Outreach to Preschoolers through Satellite Library Connections." *Journal of Youth Services* 13, no. 3 (Spring): 16–18.

Baker, Sharon L. 1986. "Overload, Browsers and Selections." *Library and Information Science Research* 8, no. 4 (October-December): 315–29.

———. 1988. "Will Fiction Classification Schemes Increase Use? Results of an Experimental Study." *RQ* 27, no. 3 (Spring): 366–76.

Baker, Sharon L., and F. Wilfrid Lancaster. 1991. *The Measurement and Evaluation of Library Services*. 2d ed. Washington, DC: Information Resources Press.

Ballard, Thomas H. 1986. *The Failure of Resource Sharing in Public Libraries and Alternative Strategies for Success*. Chicago: American Library Association.

Bartlett, John. 1992. *Familiar Quotations: A Collection of Passages, Phrases, and Proverbs Traced to Their Sources in Ancient and Modern Literature*. 16th ed., revised and enlarged, ed. Justin Kaplan. Boston: Little, Brown.

Behrman, Sara, and Gordon Conable. 1989. "There's a Library at the Mall." *Wilson Library Bulletin* 64, no. 4 (December): 31–33.

Behrmann, Christine, Yolanda Bonitch, and Harriet Gottfried. 1988. "The Library Serves Homeless Children." *The Bookmark* 46, no. 3 (Spring): 198–99.

Bertot, John Carlo, and Charles R. McClure. 2000. "Public Libraries and the Internet 2000: Summary Findings and Data Tables." [Homepage of the National Commission on Libraries and Information Science], [Online]. (Copyright September 7). Available: http://www.nclis.gov/statsurv/2000plo.pdf [Accessed September 28, 2001].

Betti, D. 1996. "BiblioVox, Uno Spazio per i Libri In Discoteca [BiblioVox, a Readers' Corner Inside a Discotheque.]" *Biblioteche Oggi* 14, no. 8 (October): 25–26.

Betts, Doug. 1986. "Public Library Bookstock Management." *Library Review* 35 (Spring): 39–51.

Birckmayer, Jennifer. 1988. "Developmental Needs of Youth in These Changing Times." *The Bookmark* 46, no. 3 (Spring): 161–65.

Bishop, Beth. 1999. (Supervisor of Regional Services and Interlibrary Loans, Juneau [Alaska] Public Library). "Re: Mail Services." E-mail to Karen Wallace, May 18.

Boehning, Julie C. 1995. "Libs. Brew Bookstore Trend." *Library Journal* 120, no. 12 (July): 21.

Bogart, D., ed. 2000. *The Bowker Annual Library and Trade Book Almanac*. 45th ed. New Providence, NJ: R. R. Bowker.

Bolin, Sheryl. 2000. "Public Libraries and Reading Groups." *Australasian Public Libraries and Information Services* 13, no. 1 (March): 21–24.

Bolt, Nancy M. 1984. *Brown County, Ohio, Need for Library Service and Cooperation Among Libraries*. Columbus: State Library of Ohio.

"Books by Mail." 2000. [Homepage of Multnomah County Library], [Online]. (Updated July 23). Available: http://www.multnomah.lib.or.us/lib/about/mcl-bkmail.html [Accessed September 28, 2001].

"Books By Mail." 2001. [Homepage of Ohio Valley Area Libraries (OVAL)], [Online]. (Updated September 25). Available: http://www.oval.lib.oh.us/bbm [Accessed September 28, 2001].

Borden, William A. 1909. "On Classifying Fiction." *Library Journal* 34, no. 6 (June): 264–65.

Boyce, Bert R., and Judith I. Boyce. 1990. "Bookmobiles and Adults Services." In *Adult Services: An Enduring Focus for Public Libraries,* ed. Kathleen M. Heim and Danny P. Wallace, 314-26. Chicago: American Library Association.

"Branch Collections." 1999. [Homepage of The New York Public Library], [Online]. (Updated August 11) Available: http://www.nypl.org/branch/services/collect.html [Accessed September 28, 2001].

Briggs, Betty S. 1973. "A Case for Classified Fiction." *Library Journal* 98, no. 22 (15 December): 3694.

"Brooklyn PL's Unique Programs Reach Prison, Day-Care Sites." 1999. *Library Hotline* 28, no. 13 (April 5): 6, 8.

Bundy, Alan. 1998. "Widening Client Horizons: Joint Use Public Libraries in the 1990s." *Australasian Public Libraries and Information Services* 11, no. 1 (March): 4–16.

Burke, Mary Ann, and Carl Liljenstolpe. 1992. *Recruiting Volunteers: A Guide for Non-Profits.* Los Altos, CA: Crisp.

Byczek, Jane R., and Renee J. Vaillancourt. 1998. "Homework on the Range: Public Librarians Can't Afford to Be Lone Rangers." *Voice of Youth Advocates* 21, no. 3 (August): 183–86.

Carnovsky, Leon. 1935. Personal correspondence, cited in Harriet R. Forbes. "The Geography of Reading." *ALA Bulletin* 29, no. 8 (August): 470–76.

Chelton, Mary Kay. 1997. "Three in Five Public Library Users are Youth: Implications of Survey Results from the National Center for Education Statistics." *Public Libraries* 36, no. 2 (March/April): 104–8.

Childers, Thomas, and Nancy A. Van House. 1989. *The Public Library Effectiveness Study: Final Report.* Philadelphia: Drexel University, College of Information Studies.

Chute, Adrienne, and Elaine Kroe. 2001. *Public Libraries in the United States: Fiscal Year 1998.* Washington, DC: U.S. Department of Education/National Center for Education Statistics. NCES 2000-316.

"Combined Libraries: A Bibliography." 2000. [Homepage of the American Library Association], [Online]. (Updated April 6). Available: http://www.ala.org/library/fact20.html [Accessed September 28, 2001].

Commings, Karen. 1996. "New Library Locations: Go Where the Patrons Are." *Computers in Libraries* 16, no. 10 (November-December): 24–26.

"Community Book Center Locations." 2000. [Homepage of Beauregard Parish Public Library], [Online]. (Updated March 31). Available: http://www.beau.lib.la.us/lib/rural_services.html [Accessed September 28, 2001].

Conaway, Peggy. 2000. "One Reference Service for Everyone?" *Library Journal* 125, no. 12 (July): 42–44.

"County of Los Angeles Public Library Offers New Service to Los Angeles County Commuters." 1992. *Public Libraries* 31, no. 1 (January/February): 9.

"DataDepot." 2000. [Homepage of Howard County Central Library], [Online]. (Updated June 21). Available: http://www.howa.lib.md.us/library/locations_datadepot.html [Accessed September 28, 2001].

D'Elia, George. 1980. "The Development and Testing of a Conceptual Model of Public Library User Behavior." *Library Quarterly* 50, no. 4: 410–30.

Detweiler, Mary Jo. 1986. "The 'Best Size' Public Library." *Library Journal* 111, no. 9 (May 15): 34–35.

Drescher, Judith. 1995. "Providing Mobile Library Services in Memphis, Tennessee: An Urban Perspective." *Public Libraries* 34, no. 5 (September/October): 271–72.

———. 1998. "Outreach and the Public Need." *Bookmobile and Outreach Services* 1, no. 1: 36–42.

"Drive to Work with Leo Tolstoy . . . For Only 33 Cents a Day." 2001. [Homepage of the County of Los Angeles Public Library], [Online]. (Updated March). Available: http://www.colapublib.org/services/audio/index.html [Accessed September 28, 2001].

Dukelow, Rosemary. 1999. "Sacramento Public Library's Wonderwagon: Not the Same Old Bookmobile You Know and Love." *The Unabashed Librarian* no. 112: 26.

Fader, Ellen G. 1991. "The Doctors' Office Collection." *School Library Journal* 37, no. 6 (June): 48.

Falk, Howard. 1999. "Storing and Viewing Electronic Documents." *Electronic Library* 17, no. 1 (February): 40–44.

Ferrell, Nancy. 1983. "Alaska's Flying Library." *Library Journal* 108, no. 6 (March 15): 554–55.

Filipek, Deborah. 1998. "Library Archives Becoming Digitized." *Park Ridge Herald-Advocate* 65, no. 42 (July 16): 19–20.

Fink, Norman A., and Richard Boivin. 1988. "MultiLIS Book Exchange Process: A 'Shuttle' Approach to Collection Development." *Library Hi Tech* 6, no. 2: 63–70.

"First Commuter Library Celebrates One Year of Successful Service." 1987. *Library Journal* 112, no. 17 (October 15): 20.

Fry, Ray M. 1989. "Services and Resources for Young Adults in Public Libraries: Report of the NCES Survey." In *Bowker Annual: Library and Book Trade Almanac, 1989-1990,* 34th ed., ed. Filomena Simora, 414–23. New York: R. R. Bowker.

"GA Rapid Transit Lib." 1993. *Library Journal* 118, no. 5 (March 15): 19.

Gajerski, B. 1989. "Edmonton Public Library: 1989 User Survey." Edmonton, Alberta: Edmonton Public Library. ERIC ED327184.

Gallup Organization, Inc. 1976. *The Role of Libraries in America: A Report of the Survey Conducted by the Gallup Organization, Inc. for the Chief Officers of State Library Agencies of Arizona, Florida, Idaho, Illinois, Iowa, Kentucky, Maryland, Massachusetts, Mississippi, Nevada, New York, North Carolina, Pennsylvania, South Dakota, Wisconsin, Wyoming, and the American Library Association.* Frankfort: Kentucky Department of Library and Archives.

———. 1985. *The Gallup 1985 Annual Report on Book Buying.* Princeton, NJ: Gallup Organization.

Gitner, Fred J. 1998. "The New Americans Program: Twenty-One Years of Successful Partnerships Serving Diverse and Changing Communities." *Reference & User Services Quarterly* 38, no. 2: 143–45.

Goldberg, Beverly. 1996. "Public Libraries Go Back to School." *American Libraries* 27, no. 11 (December): 54–55.

Gonzalez, Mario, and Harriet Gottfried. 1988. "Library Service to the City's Homeless." *The Bookmark* 46, no. 4 (Summer): 223–31.

Green, Mark. 1995. *The Consumer Bible: 1001 Ways to Shop Smart*. New York: Workman.

Hardy, Ronald. 1998. "Library Materials Prisoners Want and Need: A Case Study of the Jail Population in Iowa City, Iowa." Unpublished student paper, University of Iowa, School of Library and Information Science.

Harris, Ira. 1966. "The Influence of Accessibility on Academic Library Use." Ph.D. diss., Rutgers University.

Hartman, Rachael A. 1995. "Public Library Services to Older Adults in Northeastern Ohio." Master's research paper, Kent State University. ERIC ED390415.

Hawkins, Marilyn. 1980. "Seattle's Bookmobile Metamorphis." *Wilson Library Bulletin* 54, no. 7 (March): 442–46.

Haydon, John. 1989. "Salford's Mobile Service for the Homebound." *Library Association Record* 91, no. 1 (January 27): 42.

Hayes, Robert M., and E. Susan Palmer. 1983. "The Effects of Distance Upon Use of Libraries: Case Studies Based on a Survey of Users of the Los Angeles Public Library." *Library and Information Science Research* 5, no. 1 (Spring): 67–100.

Herald, Diana Tixier. 1995. "Booktalking to a Captive Audience." *School Library Journal* 41, no. 5 (May): 35–36.

Hole, Carol, and Russ Topping. 1990. "Designing Bookmobile Interiors." In *The Book Stops Here: New Directions in Bookmobile Service*, ed. Catherine Suyak Alloway, 135–56. Metuchen, NJ: Scarecrow Press.

"Information Kiosk: Your Electronic Library." 2001. [Homepage of the Davenport Public Library], [Online]. (Updated September 28). Available: http://www.rbls.lib.il.us /dpl/kiosk.htm [Accessed September 28, 2001].

Intner, Sheila S. 1984. "Access to Media: Attitudes of Public Librarians." *RQ* 23, no. 4 (Summer): 424–30.

Jacob, Bernard, and Carol Morphew. 1997. "The Quiet Room: A Cyber-Free Haven in the Community Library." *Public Libraries* 36, no. 4 (July/August): 216–17.

Jue, Dean K., et al. 1999. "Using Public Libraries to Provide Technology Access for Individuals in Poverty: A Nationwide Analysis of Library Market Areas Using a Geographic Information System." *Library and Information Science Research* 21, no. 3: 299–325.

Karp, Rashelle S. 1996. "The Literature of Joint-Use Libraries." *Advances in Library Administration and Organization* 14: 227–71.

Kenneally, Adele. 1998. "Mobile Services: Australian Style." *Bookmobile and Outreach Services* 2, no. 1: 26–38.

Kenneally, Adele, and Christine Payne. 2000. "Mobile Library Services: Australian Trends." *Australasian Public Libraries and Information Services* 13, no. 2 (June): 63–71.

Kennedy, Liam. 1997. "Bookmobile Survey." *Rural Libraries* no. 1: 41-50.

King, Bobby, and Todd Shanks. 2000. "This Is Not Your Father's Bookmobile." *Netconnect* supplement to *Library Journal* (Summer): 14–17.

Koontz, Christine M. 1990. "Market-Based Modelling for Public Library Facility Location and Use-Forecasting." Ph.D. diss., Florida State University.

———. 1994. "Retail Location Theory: Can It Help Solve the Public Library Location Dilemma?" In *Research Issues in Public Librarianship: Trends for the Future*, ed. Joy M. Greiner, 171–87. Westport, CT: Greenwood Press.

Kralick, John E. 1977. "The Integration of Non-Fiction Collections." Master's research paper, University of California at Los Angeles.

Kurzeja, Karen, and Brett Charbeneau. 1999. "Remote But Not Alone." *Computers in Libraries* 19, no. 4 (April): 20–22, 24–26.

Laitinen, Eeva, and Maija Kivekäs. 1998. "Children's Libraries-on-Wheels in Espoo . . . and in Lahti." *Scandinavian Public Library Quarterly* 31, no. 2: 19–22.

Lavigne, Nicole. 1984. "International Developments: A Library in the Metro Station." *Public Library Quarterly* 5, no. 2 (Summer): 47–57.

"Libraries Reach Out to Hospital Patients." 1996. *Library PR News* 17, nos. 7 and 8 (July/August): 10.

"A Library in a Box." 1998. *Library PR News* 19, nos. 3 and 4 (March/April): 3–5.

"Library Offers One Hour Free Parking." 1995. *The Unabashed Librarian* no. 96: 6.

Lubans, John, Jr., and Gary Kushner. 1979. "Evaluating Signage Systems in Libraries." In *Sign Systems for Libraries*, ed. Dorothy Pollet and Peter C. Haskell, 115-23. New York: R. R. Bowker.

MacRae, Cathi Dunn. 1996. "A Library Where Silence Is Banned." *Voice of Youth Advocates* 19, no. 1 (April): 7–12.

"Magazines and Full-Text Magazine Databases." 2001. [Homepage of the Santa Fe Public Library], [Online]. (Updated September 7). Available: http://www.ci.santa-fe.nm.us/sfpl/gate.html [Accessed September 28, 2001].

Mallery, Mary S., and Ralph E. DeVore. 1982. *A Sign System for Libraries: Solving the Wayfinding Problem*. Chicago: American Library Association.

Mathis, Marie. 1990. "Bookmobile Service in an Urban Area." In *The Book Stops Here: New Directions in Bookmobile Service*, ed. Catherine Suyak Alloway, 276–83. Metuchen, NJ: Scarecrow Press.

Maughan, Shannon. 1999. "Making the Teen Scene." *Publishers Weekly* 246, no. 42 (October 18): 28–31.

Maxymuk, John M. 1999. "Internet: Counting by Ones and Zeroes." *Bottom Line* 12, no. 1: 41–44.

McCabe, Gerard B. 2000. *Planning for a New Generation of Public Library Buildings*. Westport, CT: Greenwood Press.

McCune, Bonnie F., and Charleszine "Terry" Nelson. 1995. *Recruiting and Managing Volunteers in Libraries: A How-to-Do-It Manual*. New York: Neal-Schuman.

McMillan, Alice. 1999. (Senior Reference Librarian, Orange [New Jersey] Public Library). Telephone conversation with Karen Wallace, August 27.

Meyers, Elaine. 1999. "The Coolness Factor: Ten Libraries Listen to Youth." *American Libraries* 30, no. 10 (November): 42–45.

Miller, Betty, and Ray Smith. 1988. "Literacy Update: Springfield-Greene County Library District." *Show-Me Libraries* 40 (Fall): 30.

Monley, Bruce, and Robert Pestell. 1996. "Mobile Libraries in the Age of Technology." *Aplis* 9, no. 2 (June): 78–82.

Mort, Ann. 1990. "Scheduling: Where and When." In *The Book Stops Here: New Directions in Bookmobile Service*, ed. Catherine Suyak Alloway, 74–79. Metuchen, NJ: Scarecrow Press.

Multi-MAC BOOKLIST. 1998. no. 19 (Spring): 1–20.

"Multi-MAC: Multi-Lingual Materials Acquisition Center." 1999. [Homepage of New Jersey State Library], [Online]. (Updated November 1). Available: http://www2.njstatelib.org/njlib/multimac.htm [Accessed September 28, 2001].

Murray, Martin S. 1992. "In the News." *Bottom Line* 6 (Summer): 6.

Myers, Judy. 1979. "Designing Open-Stack Areas for the User." In *Sign Systems for Libraries: Solving the Wayfinding Problem*, ed. Mary S. Mallery and Ralph E. DeVore, 195–201. New York: R. R. Bowker.

Naismith, Rachael. 1989. "Library Service to Migrant Farm Workers." *Library Journal* 114, no. 4 (March 1): 52–55.

Nelson, Judy, and Beverly Solecki. 1998. "Outreach Services from the Bookmobile." *Bookmobile and Outreach Services* 2, no. 1: 21–22.

Nolan, Christopher W. 1991. "The Lean Reference Collection: Improving Functionality through Selection and Weeding." *RQ* 52, no. 1 (January): 80–91.

"Outposts for New Reader Books." 1988. *The Unabashed Librarian*, no. 66: 11.

Overmyer, Elizabeth. 1987. "Booklegging: Community-Wide Booktalking through Library-Trained Volunteers." *Journal of Youth Services in Libraries* 1, no. 1 (Fall): 82–86.

Paine, Anne W. 1985. "Consideration of Portable Structures in Meeting Library Needs." *Illinois Libraries* 67, no. 9 (November): 813–15.

Palmer, E. Susan. 1981. "The Effect of Distance on Public Library Use: A Literature Survey." *Library Research* 3, no. 4 (Winter): 315–54.

Philip, John J. 1990. "Bookmobile Service: Justification to the Nonbeliever (Or to the Weak of Heart)." In *The Book Stops Here: New Directions in Bookmobile Service*, ed. Catherine Suyak Alloway, 1–7. Metuchen, NJ: Scarecrow Press.

Pollet, Dorothy, and Peter C. Haskell, ed. 1979. *Sign Systems for Libraries: Solving the Wayfinding Problem.* New York: R. R. Bowker.

Rawlinson, Nora. 1990. "The Central Library: A Fatal Attraction." *Library Journal* 115, no. 10 (June 1): 6.

"Reading on the Rails." 1999. *Public Libraries* 38, no. 1 (January/February): 16.

"Reading Rodent." 1996. *American Libraries* 27, no. 2 (February): 12.

Reese, Noreen. 1999. "Café Service in Public Libraries: Survey of 19 Public Libraries Offering Coffee Service." *Public Libraries* 38, no. 3 (May/June): 176–78.

"Renaissance in Public Libraries." 1999. [Homepage of the American Library Association], [Online]. (Copyright March). Available: http://www.ala.org/pio/factsheets/renaissance.html [Accessed September 28, 2001].

Reynolds, Linda, and Stephen Barrett. 1981. *Signs and Guiding for Libraries*. London: Clive Bingley.

Rodríguez, Gloria María. 1998. "The Public Library: A Proposal for Creating Equitable Access." [Homepage of the International Federation of Library Associations and Institutions], [Online]. Presented at 64th IFLA General Conference, August 16–August 21. Available: http://www.ifla.org/IV/ifla64/093-105e.htm [Accessed September 28, 2001].

Ruderman, Larry, and Arthur Ruderman. 1998. *In-Store Signage and Graphics: Connecting with Your Customer*. Cincinnati: ST Publications.

Sannwald, William W., ed. 1997. *Checklist of Library Building Design Considerations*. 3d ed. Chicago: American Library Association.

Savage, Ernest A. 1946. *Manual of Book Classification and Display for Public Libraries*. London: Allen & Unwin.

Scally, Patricia H. 1999. "Digital Technology Projects Already Thriving in Public Libraries." *Public Libraries* 38, no. 1 (January/February): 48–50.

Schindler, Jo Ann. 2001. "A Summary of HSPLS Services." [Homepage of Hawaii State Public Library Service], [Online]. (Updated February 3). Available: http://www.hcc.hawaii.edu/hspls/sumserv.html [Accessed September 28, 2001].

Schneider, Karen. 1998. "Internet Librarian—The Cybermobile: A Groovy Set of Wheels." *American Libraries* 29, no. 8 (September): 76.

Schoeberle, Beverly, and Joyce Reid. 1998. "The First Mall Library in Illinois." *Illinois Libraries* 80, no. 3 (Summer): 115–16.

Scilken, Marvin H. 1971. "The Read and Return Collection: A Scheme for Overcomig Librarians' Reluctance to Buy Multiple Copies of Popular Books." *Wilson Library Bulletin* 46, no. 1 (September): 104–5.

"Services and Guidelines." 2001. [Homepage of the Williamson County Public Library], [Online]. (Updated July 19). Available: http://lib.williamson-tn.org/general.htm [Accessed September 28, 2001].

Shoham, Snunith, Sara Hershkovitz, and Dalya Metzer. 1990. "Distribution of Libraries in an Urban Space and Its Effects on Their Use: The Case of Tel Aviv." *Library and Information Science Research* 12, no. 2 (April/June): 167–81.

Singh, Sharon R. 1985. "Happy Mall Fellows: Libraries and Bookstores are Great Neighbors." *American Libraries* 16, no. 3 (March): 154.

Sivulich, Kenneth G. 1989. "How We Run the Queens Library Good (and Doubled Circulation in Seven Years)." *Library Journal* 114, no. 3 (February 15): 123–27.

Skrzeszewski, Stan, June Huggins-Chan, and Frank Clarke. 1990. "Bookmobile Services to Native Peoples: An Experiment in Saskatchewan." In *The Book Stops Here: New Directions in Bookmobile Service*, ed. Catherine Suyak Alloway, 312–21. Metuchen, NJ: Scarecrow Press.

Smith, Duncan. 2000. (NoveList Product Manager, Carl Corporation). Conversation with Karen Wallace, March 30.

Sorensen, B. 1999. "Er der Folkebiblioteker I Thailand? [Are There Public Libraries in Thailand?]" *Bibliotekspressen* 19, no. 26 (October): 622–23.

Spiller, David. 1980. "The Provision of Fiction for Public Libraries." *Journal of Librarianship* 12, no. 4 (October): 238–66.

Stringer, Ian. 1999. "IFLA." *Service Point* no. 76 (December): 20.

"Supermarket Libraries Appeal to Customers." 1986. *Library Journal* 111, no. 20 (December): 30.

Teacher's Guide to the Park Ridge Public Library. 1997. Rev. ed. Park Ridge, IL: Park Ridge Public Library.

Tutton, Mary. 1990. "A New Perspective on Bookmobile Costs." In *The Book Stops Here: New Directions in Bookmobile Service*, ed. Catherine Suyak Alloway, 32–38. Metuchen, NJ: Scarecrow Press.

Underhill, Paco. 1999. *Why We Buy: The Science of Shopping*. New York: Simon & Schuster.

Van House, Nancy, and Thomas A. Childers. 1993. *The Public Library Effectiveness Study: The Complete Report*. Chicago: American Library Association.

Vavrek, Bernard. 1990a. "Mapping the Bookmobile: Recent Surveys." In *The Book Stops Here: New Directions in Bookmobile Service*, ed. Catherine Suyak Alloway, 9–15. Metuchen, NJ: Scarecrow Press.

———. 1990b. "Rural Road Warriors." *Library Journal* 115, no. 5 (May 15): 56–57.

"Visit the Electronic Kiosk at Park Ridge Recreation and Park District Park Ridge Community Center." 1997. [Homepage of the Park Ridge Public Library], [Online]. (Updated December 17). Available: http://www.park-ridge.il.us/library/kiosk.html [Accessed September 28, 2001].

Voss, Joyce. 1998. "Bookmobiles in the Burbs." *Bookmobile and Outreach Services* 1, no. 1: 43–46.

Wagner, Elaine. 1987. "A Library in a Skyway." *Minnesota Libraries* 28, no. 10 (Summer): 324–28.

Watson, Tom. 1988. "Read and Return." *Wilson Library Bulletin* 62, no. 9 (May): 53–54.

Webb, T. D. 1985. *Reorganization in the Public Library*. Phoenix: Oryx Press.

"World's First Library in an Elevated Transit System Opens in Miami." 1992. *Public Libraries* 31, no. 1 (January/February): 8–9.

Wyker, Shirley. 1988. "Welcome to the Public Library: Serving Children in Day-Care." *The Bookmark* 46, no. 3 (Spring): 193–94.

"Young Adult Home Page." 2000. [Homepage of Salem Public Library], [Online]. (Updated August 31). Available: http://www.open.org/~library/teen.html [Accessed September 28, 2001].

CREATING RECOGNITION OF COLLECTION-USE BENEFITS

> "Irish poets, earn your trade, sing whatever is well made"—William Butler Yeats ("Under" 2001).

Designing collections to meet community needs, setting low monetary and psychological prices for using collections, and making effective placement decisions lay the groundwork for effective promotion. Almost all libraries receive feedback, both anecdotal and statistical, reinforcing the need to continually publicize what we offer. To attract and retain patrons, staff members must consciously and actively inform them about the existence of an affordable collection matched to user needs and the benefits of using it. Individual patrons digest this information, weighing the highly idiosyncratic benefits of using a particular public library's collection against the costs (real and perceived) when selecting whether or how much they will use the library or other sources of materials and information.

Broad questions that library staff may consider when developing promotional campaigns include the following:

- What target market(s) will the library try to reach with a particular promotional effort?
- What aspects of the collection can libraries promote?

- When can promotion occur?
- What response(s) does the library seek from the target market?
- What message(s) will the library try to convey to the target market?
- What factors influence the optimum frequency of promotion?
- What techniques can the library use to promote its products?
- How will the library evaluate the results of its promotional efforts?

WHAT TARGET MARKET(S) WILL THE LIBRARY TRY TO REACH WITH A PARTICULAR PROMOTIONAL EFFORT?

Chapters 2 and 3 introduce the idea that, for optimal efficiency and effectiveness, librarians must both consider the full range of patrons and try to understand targeted users to communicate successfully. This becomes particularly clear when viewed through the lens of the basic communication model.

Communication Model

As figure 7.1 indicates, the source (in our case, one or more library staff members) will, directly or through an intermediary, encode the relevant message into words, pictures, or the like, then direct it to one or more people via a channel: a mass medium such as a newsletter, radio, or Web site, or interpersonal communication, such as speech, writing, or pantomime. When a receiver obtains the message, he or she decodes it to determine both the objective meaning and any personal implications. During this process, outside sources may introduce "noise" that can interfere with the receipt or quick decoding of the message or even distort its meaning. To ensure that the receiver understands the intended message, library staff members can pay close attention to verbal and non-verbal feedback, correcting any confusion that may arise.[1]

To minimize the chance of miscommunication when composing clear and enticing messages, superior librarians will consider knowledge they possess about individuals within the target market(s), including their language, vocabulary, age, frames of reference, culture and ethnicity, beliefs and values, habits, pastimes, and abilities. For example, messages directed at kindergartners may use fairly simple sentence structure and be participatory. Messages intended for people with macular degeneration would be verbal or printed in high contrast using a simple font and large type.

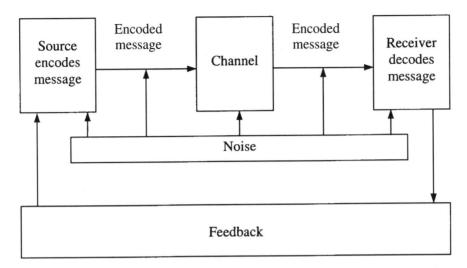

FIGURE 7.1. **Communication Model.** Derived from the work of Claude Shannon, Warren Weaver, and Norbert Wiener.

How Consumers Process Promotional Information

Adding the four steps of consumer information processing, as noted in the classic work by Engel, Kollatt, and Blackwell (1973), to the basic communication model provides an enriched means of thinking about promotional communication (see figure 7.2, page 164):

- Exposure to different stimuli—in this case, the promotional messages libraries send—activates consumer senses.

- For the exposure (promotion) to be effective, it must capture the consumer's attention. In terms of the communication model, the message must reach the receiver. If, for example, the local newspaper runs a feature story on the library's collection of travel books, the consumer/receiver must glance through the paper and also notice this particular story.

- The consumer must then comprehend the stimulus. That is, he or she must take in and make some attempt at understanding (i.e., decode) the promotional message. For example, the consumer can read the travel book article and notice the types of resources that he or she would find of benefit.

- Finally, the consumer must retain the promotional information long enough for it to aid in the decision to use library resources, which will involve weighing information about the benefits of library use against information about the costs.

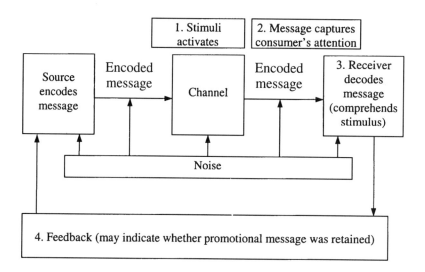

FIGURE 7.2. **Combination of Communication Model** (derived from the work of Claude Shannon, Warren Weaver, and Norbert Wiener) and **Consumer Information Processing Model** (derived from the work of James Engel, David Kollatt, and Roger Blackwell).

Looking again at the communication model, direct and indirect customer feedback, such as patron comments on the newspaper article or an increase in the use of the travel book collection, indicates correct receipt and decoding of the message. Lack of such feedback presents a puzzle to be solved. The medium might be flawed (e.g., as when a Web site crashes for several days). The receiver may have been confused by the message; deemed it irrelevant; or decided that a shortage of time, library parking, or other considerations outweighed whatever interest in using the collection the message sparked. Other possible explanations may also exist.

These explanations often relate to three major concerns. First, capturing the patron's attention may be difficult. Prospective patrons receive much more promotional information than they retain, because they selectively filter out information they do not want, need, or understand (Bettman 1979). For example, an adult with no children may ignore displays, booklists, news stories, and similar items that feature picture books and easy readers. People may also ignore information presented in dry or unappealing formats. Although the overwhelming amount of information patrons receive largely lies beyond our control, we can make a difference in the way we present our own messages.

Second, in many situations, consumers have relatively little motivation to acquire and process promotional information that they did not seek out (Bettman 1979). In these instances, motivation may be greatest for items high in cost and, therefore risk, like a new car. However, risk is less for items low in monetary cost (to the patron), such as most library materials. Librarians can offer patrons an incentive to pay attention to promotional information by showing, in a winning and persuasive manner, how library services and resources will benefit them.

Finally, time constraints can negatively affect consumer information processing (Wright and Weitz 1977). That is, consumers with very limited time may not always process promotional information effectively. Thus, whenever possible, librarians may wish to design promotional techniques that patrons find quick and easy to understand and use.

Taken together, these research findings suggest that librarians can increase awareness or use of library materials by employing promotional techniques that capture consumers' attention, require little effort to decode, and show the benefits of use. The findings also imply that promotions noted by large numbers of people will increase awareness and use levels significantly more than those that catch the attention of a smaller audience.

Determining Whom to Woo

The library may direct its promotional efforts toward

- community residents in general, for example, promoting its leisure reading collections via the newsletter it sends to all the postal customers in town or a public service announcement sent to all area radio stations.

- library users in general, by such means as mailing or e-mailing all registered borrowers a brochure explaining the new e-book collection or arranging different displays within the library that highlight classical music, travel videos, dinosaur books, or other subsets of the collection;

- individual patrons, for example, through personalized readers' advisory services to promote the collection, one work at a time, to those trying to find items that they would like to read, watch, or listen to, or through selected distribution of relevant governmental information to the mayor and city council members; and

- one or more groups of community residents with a common bond, such as interest, membership, or stage of life.[2] A library might advertise its young adult collection in the junior high school newspaper or host a program for engaged couples illustrating resources that can help them plan their weddings and honeymoons.

Knowledge about the community as a whole informs the process of identifying target markets. A library that has followed the strategic planning and marketing procedures suggested in Chapter 3 to decide which markets to pursue can quickly craft thoughtful promotional goals and objectives and design cost-effective activities to meet these.

WHAT ASPECTS OF THE COLLECTION CAN LIBRARIES PROMOTE?

Over the years, mounting evidence has shown that librarians can increase patron awareness and use of many different kinds of materials by using tried-and-true promotional techniques. For example, Baker's (1986) review documented that properly designed booklists and displays have increased the circulation of old books, new books, biographies, randomly selected fiction and nonfiction titles, works on both general and specialized topics, popular titles, and works that have not circulated in years. These findings suggest that librarians can choose which aspects of their collections they want to promote: the collection as a whole, specific product lines and items within the collection, collection-related events, or changes in the cost of using library resources.

Promoting the Collection as a Whole

Many libraries have chosen to promote a broad spectrum of materials in the collection to a specific target market or an entire community of prospective users. For example, the Kansas City (Missouri) Public Library illustrated the range of its collection with a marketing campaign casting the library as an "Information Playground." The library included the logo from its redesigned, neon cards on its homepage; coffee mugs, book bags, mouse pads, and other merchandise, as well as all its publications. One sign featured the new library card centered against a background listing a broad sample of the items available in the collection: "How-To, Hopi Indian History, Hispanic Heritage Month, Investment Guides, Comics, Steamy Romances," and so forth (Volpe 1996, 21).

Promoting a Specific Product Line

A library can also promote product lines, or groups of works that have a common

- *subject or theme*. For example, supported by a $135,000 grant from the National Endowment for the Humanities, the Houston (Texas) Public Library offered an adult learning and reading program called CITY! and publicized related works through press releases, television public service announcements, flyers, calendars, and posters, including one that read, "Loving, Warring, Lying, Scheming, Building, Coping, Dreaming—The City in Fiction and Film" (Tuggle and Heller 1987).

- *genre or sub-genre*. The library might distribute lists of short story audiobooks, Christian romances, cleric detective stories, or science fiction videos.

- *format*. For example, in conjunction with the local Society for the Blind and Visually Impaired, the St. Louis (Missouri) Public Library offered free monthly screenings of films in Descriptive Video Service (DVS) format, as well as special screenings of DVS movies adapted from books followed by a discussion of both the book and movie ("DVS" 1997).[3]

- *author*. In a monthly 15-minute radio interview, the readers' adviser might discuss the life and writings of a prolific author.

- *title*. Staff members might create a small display near the circulation desk that includes all versions of an especially worthy title, regardless of format. For example, they could feature Jane Austen's *Pride and Prejudice* in hardback, paperback, large print, e-book, audiobook, "classic comic," video, and DVD forms, as well as a bookmark listing Web sites for Austen fans.

- *audience*. Librarians may publicize all materials appealing to a particular target market. For example, Danish public libraries actively promote their audiobooks, easy readers, reading service, and assistive technologies to those with dyslexia (Nielsen 1998).

- *other commonality*. For example, staff at one elementary school promoted Newbery Award winners to fourth and fifth grade classes through booktalks, Newbery reading clubs, in-class reading, contests, and games. In the three months prior to the promotion, no student had checked out a Newbery winner from the school media center; during the promotion 87 percent of the students involved checked out at least one Newbery title from the school library, and the local public library also noted an increased circulation of Newbery books (Gunter 1994). The library might also create a display of local authors' works, books over 500 pages, fiction set in the South, or even "good books with red covers."

Promoting a Specific Item

The possibilities for promoting specific items are legion. For example, on a weekly basis, one public radio station aired reviews taped by librarians from the Fairbanks North Star Borough (Alaska) Public Library in five fields: best-selling fiction, nonfiction, children's books, homemaking books, and technical books for the layperson (Sherman 1980).

Promoting a Collection-Related Event

Talks by local authors and other collection-related events also merit promotion. In fact, many libraries create various eye-catching events that will allow a series of stories to be generated in the local media, as well as providing interesting or entertaining experiences for participants. For example, librarians from the Springfield (Massachusetts) Library worked with community leaders and city schools to celebrate the 350th birthday of the city. Because Theodor Geisel (Dr. Seuss) hails from Springfield, the library decided to sponsor a four-month "Seussamania" festival. Librarians dressed up as the Cat in the Hat or Sneetches and visited each classroom in nine elementary schools to introduce the less-familiar Seuss books. The library displayed hundreds of pieces of sculpture and other children's artwork portraying Seuss characters, hosted a performance of *The Lorax* by a children's theater group, and held a Seuss-fest of singing. Circulation of children's books increased 50 percent systemwide during the festival, which received extensive media coverage ("Youthreach" 1986).

Libraries can also create collection-related events around established occasions. For example, in 1997 the Carson City (Nevada) Library sponsored hourly programs throughout National Library Week. Staff publicized these through word-of-mouth, flyers, posters, articles in the local newspaper and the city's parks and recreation newsletter, mailings to other city departments and area libraries, and public service announcements on radio and television, including a rap aired on the local cable channel. During the week, library attendance increased to 133 percent of average (Fakolt 1998). The Birmingham (England) Libraries also planned an elaborate celebration of Britain's National Libraries Week, offering 210 events, including quizzes, parties, tours, and giveaways. Working with Dillons, a local bookstore, the library promoted the festivities with 300 street signs; 28 radio ads; and television, radio, and newspaper coverage. In addition, both bookstore and library staff wore sweatshirts emblazoned with their slogans for National Libraries Week: "Libraries. The Future. Literally." and "Dillons, simply all the books you need." During the week the number of patrons registering increased by as much as 100 percent at some library locations, and over 50 percent of those surveyed at non-library locations knew it was National Libraries Week (Rock 1998), percentages we challenge other libraries to duplicate.

With much less effort, librarians can also promote materials related to non-library events. A simple topical booklist or display can capitalize on patron interest in current affairs. Materials about the U.S. political process and the electoral college, including those that might have had little past use, became ripe for promotion in November and December 2000, as people waited to see whether George W. Bush or Al Gore would become the 43rd president of the nation. Similarly, the Lane (Hampton, New Hampshire) Memorial Library promotes materials related to a highly local current "event," homework assignments. Their Web page offers lists of print, computer, and audiovisual resources to assist with currently assigned projects and papers ("Lane" 2001b).

Promoting a Change in the Cost of Using the Collection

Libraries will need to inform patrons whenever the cost of using a collection significantly decreases (e.g., a two-for-one special on a rental collection of popular materials) or increases, as when the library reduces the loan period to stretch a limited collection to better meet patron demands.

Publicizing these changes allows patrons to decide for themselves whether the benefits of using the collection continue to outweigh the costs. Moreover, when the library takes the time to explain why costs are rising or falling, patrons may better understand the need for the change. For example, the Duke University (North Carolina) Medical Center Library created an informational banner, posters, and flyers featuring the slogan, "Save trees, paper and our budget," when it began charging for printing. When staff members explained the fee on the library's Web site, in its newsletter, and in the medical center's newsletter, and visually illustrated the extent of the problem by mounting a (large!) display of a month's worth of scrap and recycled paper, patrons indicated that they recognized the need to start charging for printing (Murphy, VanDyke, and Vines 1998).

WHEN CAN PROMOTION OCCUR?

Small-scale promotional efforts can occur every day. The librarian who takes a reserve request for a particular work may also stir the patron's interest in lesser-known titles in the collection by suggesting readalikes to sustain him or her through the wait. Similarly, a librarian helping an expectant mother find baby name books can also volunteer information about the library's collections of board books and parenting resources. The library Web site can note call number ranges for subjects that tie in with holidays or local events. For example, an "ad" on the Web site could say, "Dream it at the garden show this weekend, and then do it with help from our collection. Check out Dewey numbers 635, 712, and 716 in the video, DVD, CD-ROM and book collections." Staff can seize such "on-the-spot" promotional opportunities outside the library during personal time as well as while at work (Krieg-Sigman 1995).

Ready-made promotional opportunities can involve mass, as well as interpersonal, communication. For example, the library's annual report might serve as the basis for press releases, targeted mailings, and a newsletter article; used in this manner, it will have much more impact than if it is only made available to the public by request at the reference desk.

To optimize promotional efforts, staff members first must lay the necessary internal groundwork. This may be as simple as letting the entire staff know that the current feature display celebrates International Mirth Month and securing an adequate supply of attractive, humorous materials to showcase. In other instances, a library may need to dedicate significant resources to ensure a high-quality, diverse collection and a staff that values and provides outstanding service prior to promotion. In other words, before undertaking a massive promotional campaign, the library must guarantee that collection and services are truly "efficient, reliable, and responsive to identified need" (Krieg-Sigman 1995, 420).

Patron satisfaction results when the user's actual experience meets expectations. When the experience exceeds expectations, patrons may be delighted; if, however, it falls short, patrons will likely feel dissatisfied (Kotler and Armstrong 1999; Hernon and Whitman 2001). Ideally, libraries will aim to delight, thereby fostering patron loyalty. One study indicated that completely satisfied customers are almost 42 percent more likely to be loyal than satisfied customers (Kotler and Armstrong 1999). Moreover, libraries will want to guard against creating false expectations and avoid bringing customers to the library if the library is not equipped "to provide the level of service necessary to meet an identified need [or to] absorb or handle a major increase in work activity within the service area" (Krieg-Sigman 1995, 420). Imagine a patron attracted to the library by a poster she saw at her health club that advertised the collection of workout videos. If she finds that the library owns only seven such videos—all checked out with waiting lists—she'll likely feel dissatisfied. Furthermore, even if the collection pleases the patron, she still may not leave with a positive image of the library if she perceives the staff member who helped her find the tapes as unfriendly and slightly patronizing. As Sherman notes, "Marketing money might as well be shredded if customer service isn't up to snuff" (1994, 24).

Librarians can also avoid creating demand they cannot meet by paying attention to a particular product's life cycle. As Chapter 4 explains in some detail, although a few products have faddish (very rapid) or cyclical (seasonal) life cycles, most experience four stages:

> The introductory stage, in which demand for an item is slow
>
> The growth stage, in which demand for the product increases rapidly
>
> The maturity stage, in which demand levels off, then wanes
>
> The decline stage, in which demand falls sharply

Librarians may want to promote products in the introductory stage of their life cycles as these are acquired. Most public libraries display new materials prominently within the building, a tactic that significantly increases their average use (e.g., Mueller 1965). But a library can also promote these works outside its doors. For example, the Lane (Hampton, New Hampshire) Memorial Library allows patrons to sign up for an e-mail newsletter to alert them about new acquisitions in areas of interest (Lane 2001a). The director of the Hobbs (New Mexico) Public Library promotes new materials in a weekly column published in the local paper and on the library Web site ("Library" 2001). Products particularly well suited for promotional efforts include works in new formats, by first-time authors, or with local interest, such as a newly published book featuring historical maps of the area.

Bookstores and other for-profit media distributors also heavily promote products in the growth stage of the life cycle, such as many works currently featured on radio and television talk shows, or those that, like exposé books, have a faddish life cycle. However, most public libraries do not have enough money to purchase unlimited quantities of works in high demand (a topic covered in more detail in Chapter 9) and will want to promote these titles only if

- such promotion supports its selected service responses (e.g., current topics and titles) and

- it allocates additional resources for meeting the resultant demand.

Libraries that do not purchase extra copies of popular items may choose to promote readalikes instead. For example, the Lucius Beebe (Wakefield, Massachusetts) Memorial Library offers its patrons lists of "Oprahlikes," readalikes for the popular titles selected by Oprah Winfrey for her television book club ("Oprahlikes" 1999).

Many libraries will also find it valuable to promote products in the mature stage whose use has waned. As these materials age and publicity fades, so does patron awareness of them; they become "lost" on the shelves and their circulation declines. Thus, inventories of mature works, which make up the bulk of the collection in many public libraries, build up unless staff members increase patron knowledge of these items.

Although librarians will want to remove some mature items from the collection (e.g., out-of-date materials), they can effectively publicize the remaining ones of good quality (e.g., classic videos) and general interest, those neither too esoteric nor too technical to appeal to a wide audience. However, librarians will want to observe the results of their promotional efforts closely; despite our best wishes and efforts, some mature products may have outlived their usefulness even if they do not contain obsolete information.

Finally, librarians will want to weed, rather than promote, most items in the decline stage, unless an overriding reason for keeping them exists (e.g., they are unique local history materials).

WHAT RESPONSE(S) DOES THE LIBRARY SEEK FROM THE TARGET MARKET?

When an organization overstates a product's benefits; presents intense, slick, "one-size-fits-all" sales pitches; makes disparaging comments about competitors' products; or uses other hard-sell promotional techniques, it risks offending, or even repelling, customers. Most businesses that employ these kinds of pressure-selling tactics intend to maximize their immediate sales. However, libraries aim to maximize user satisfaction and the number of repeat customers, a goal better achieved by studying and trying to anticipate customers' requirements, then suggesting works that will meet them.

Getting to Know You: Relationship Marketing

This soft-sell approach encourages the library to build long-term relationships with its customers, "staying in touch with people's changing needs and ensuring the [library's] ability to fulfill those needs with new product lines and marketing strategies" (McDonald and Keegan 1997, 9). To understand customers' needs, a library must foster ongoing dialogue with its patrons, or, in terms of the communication model presented in figures 7.1 and 7.2 (see pages 163 and 164), seek feedback.

Libraries can obtain customer input in many ways, such as by surveying patrons or conducting focus groups, techniques discussed in more detail later in this chapter and in Chapter 8. They can also supplement formal methods with simpler, but continuous, means of obtaining customer opinion. Front-line staff invite feedback when asking questions such as, "What haven't we done yet today to serve your needs?" Making comment cards widely available and encouraging patrons to fill them out offers another proven method of capturing a significant amount of information. For example, in 1996 the Fuji (Japan) Municipal Central Library received 1,683 opinions in its suggestion box (Yamamoto 1998). Staff or volunteers can also seek input outside the library by attending community meetings and asking others present about their experiences with and impressions of the library. Trustees at the Newport Beach (California) Public Library have even directly phoned cardholders and established a telephone hotline to elicit customer feedback ("Briefly" 1999).[4]

Customer dissatisfaction constitutes another potential source of valuable customer feedback. Libraries often try to measure satisfaction levels through formal surveys. However, Cramer (2000) notes that these frequently yield inflated results because patrons keep their complaints to themselves for a variety of reasons:

- They don't want to seem ungrateful about a "free" service.

- They believe libraries are supposed to be somewhat challenging to use ("no pain, no gain").

- They perceive the library as a "good" place and hold it to lower standards than a for-profit enterprise.

- They do not know what they could be getting and just expect what they've always had.

A patron will be most likely to complain at the point at which he or she experiences the disappointment; as time passes the likelihood of the patron raising the issue will decline.

Remembering that complaints can identify problems and ultimately strengthen service, libraries can try "to create a climate in which aggrieved users are encouraged to complain" (Pluse 1991, 4). Such an environment can be achieved through diligent, ongoing attempts to gather feedback, combined with a staff trained (and empowered) to put unhappy patrons at ease, and an administration committed to using patron input to improve the library. The Odum Library at Valdosta State University (Georgia) demonstrates this commitment by posting user comments and questions from its online suggestion box together with staff responses on a bulletin board hung in a visible location (Davis and Bernstein 1997).

By encouraging and mindfully considering patron feedback—even when it is negative—libraries show customers that they care about their opinions and needs. As Robinson states, "When patrons feel comfortable about complaining, the library is developing a good relationship with its users. In fact, the absence of complaints is much more likely to indicate error or failure" (1984, 14). In terms of the findings presented in Chapter 1—that dissatisfied patrons make conscious choices to either remain loyal to the library, voice their complaints in an effort to resolve the concern, neglect their relationship with the library, or return sporadically or not at all—patrons may be exiting without first giving voice to their concerns. Conversely, patrons who believe they can work with staff to fix problems, because they know that staff constantly seek to improve the library's shortcomings and service lapses, will much more frequently opt to continue using the library.

Staff adept at resolving complaints can greatly improve the relationship between the library and the (formerly) dissatisfied patron. As Tax, Brown, and Chandrashekaran (1998) note, successful service recovery can lead to even higher customer satisfaction than if there had been no complaint in the first place. Conversely, patrons who remain unhappy can create a ripple effect of ill will toward the library. Studies show that, on average, customers share a negative experience with eleven others, who in turn may each tell five more people (Timm 1995).

We recommend that the administration empower front-line staff to resolve as many complaints as possible themselves and encourage them to suggest ways in which the library could prevent the problem from recurring. Consider the high likelihood that for every patron who makes the effort to complain about something, a number of others quietly share this dissatisfaction; studies in the for-profit environment indicate that less than 5 percent of dissatisfied customers will make the effort to complain (Kotler and Armstrong 1999).

Milner (1996) notes that unless patrons record their dissatisfaction in writing, their comments frequently vanish without changes being made on an institutionwide basis. Therefore, staff need to direct written comments to the person responsible for overseeing operations in the relevant part of the library and also share oral comments by writing in a logbook; sending a note or e-mail message; or following some other quick, easy process that maximizes the amount of feedback shared.[5] Staff will also be more likely to forward complaints when managers offer assurance that they will not slaughter the messenger but intend to find ways to improve service.

We concur with Robinson's (1984) recommendation that a library commit to a complaint handling program. We further urge that, at a minimum, this program must explain the importance of complaints and the way they will be addressed (again, not retributively!) and train staff to

- remain calm, without taking the complaint personally or arguing with the patron (Robinson 1984; Rubin 2000);

- exhibit good interpersonal skills, such as listening well, maintaining eye contact, and being patient (Rubin 2000);

- offer an apology when the library has made an error and try to rectify the situation, working with the patron to try to achieve a mutually satisfactory solution (Anderson and Zemke 1998; Rubin 2000); and

- consider offering a care token to tangibly express the library's regret that it disappointed the patron (Leland and Bailey 1999; Bessler 1994). For example, the Wright Memorial (Oakwood, Ohio) Public Library presents a card and a brass bookmark to patrons as compensation for a mistake (Walder 1999).[6]

Clearly, front-line staff members play a pivotal role in the library's endeavor to understand and build mutually beneficial relationships with patrons. This underscores the importance of smart hiring practices and effective training programs. In fact, investing resources in customer service programs can be seen as a form of promotion. For example, Ukrop's, a retail food store chain in the eastern United States, reallocated money from its advertising and sales promotional budget into training when it discovered that its checkout clerks and baggers had the greatest influence on customer relationships (Duncan and Moriarty 1998). Such training programs must extend beyond the front lines because everyone in the library, including technical services staff, maintenance department members, and administrators, can directly affect patron satisfaction.

It bears mention that although we support policies flexible enough that staff (including those on the front lines) can make reasonable, or even generous, accommodations for patrons, we do not recommend an approach wherein the person complaining automatically receives whatever he or she requests. Such an approach builds staff resentment, fostering a deadly "us-versus-them" mentality, and rewards vocal patrons at the expense of others. Nevertheless, complaints present an opportunity for staff to work directly with patrons to seek ways to meet everyone's needs; at times this will require tact, a willingness to listen, and creative problem solving on both sides.

Of course, certain individuals can be difficult to please. A for-profit company would willingly let these customers switch to a competitor because they require an inordinate amount of time to serve (Kotler and Armstrong 1999). As Hernon and Whitman observe, libraries cannot rebuff their "chronic complainers" but must find ways to handle "a certain element of disgruntlement . . . sensitively and diplomatically" (2001, 35).

In all its forms, feedback can help the library better understand patron requirements and get to know the individual users and what they deem important. Note that customers do not measure value simply by the service quality in the abstract; rather, they combine that measure with the quality of the result they receive (Sweeney 1997). Cultivating relationships between customers and "the library," usually represented through individual employees, often very effectively enhances a patron's experience and helps ensure repeat visits and use (Besant and Sharp 2000; Gupta 1999).[7]

Getting to Know All About You: Relational Databases

Many businesses use technology to try to increase the likelihood that staff will offer patrons positive encounters. Relational databases provide information on an organization's customers and a history of each client's transactions. For example, if a customer calls a home furnishings company to order sheets for the second time, the salesperson can ask if he or she would like the same size, thread count, and color as ordered last time. Thus, relational databases allow a personal touch akin to that of a waitress asking a regular customer if he or she wants "the usual." This permits staff to provide meaningful value at every interaction (Levins 1998), fostering personal connections with even large numbers of customers, regardless of whether they interact with a computer interface or a different representative each time.

Although libraries already have databases that provide patron registration information and track circulation, they usually do not retain as much data about patron behavior and tastes as they could be programmed to provide, due largely to very real privacy concerns. As Estabrook observes, "In the name of one good—keeping patron records confidential—we are sacrificing another: targeted and tailored services to library users" (1996, 48).[8] To balance privacy and service issues, libraries could follow Levins's (1998) advice for the responsible use of relational databases in the healthcare profession. This would involve asking card holders' permission to keep and use their circulation data, explaining exactly how the data will be used and by whom, and providing a ready means for opting out of the program.

Should libraries work with automation vendors to establish such capabilities in a way that would honor patron privacy (including guaranteeing that patron data would not be sold!), the rewards could be tremendous. For example, a library could generate a mailing list of all its cozy mystery readers and send them an annotated bibliography of the latest Agatha nominees and past winners, including the call numbers for all the titles the library owns.[9] Internet bookstores routinely take advantage of this kind of customized promotion. When Barnes & Noble's electronic customers log on, the company asks them about their reading preferences and then uses the data to send e-mails describing special offers (Grossman 1998).

Academic libraries are leading the way in another arena of electronic personalization, offering patrons the ability to easily create a Web page that customizes their access to the library's automated resources. Similar to My Yahoo!, users can choose which sources will appear on the screen and how they will be organized, if they want to receive notification of new purchases in certain areas of the collection, and so forth. Libraries offering such services include those at North Carolina State University, Virginia Commonwealth University, Cornell (New York), the University of Washington, and California Polytechnic State University/San Luis Obispo. The response has been tremendous. Almost 100 percent of students have created their own pages on a similar system UCLA offers that allows tailored access to campuswide event, academic, and time-management resources, and 90 percent of freshmen use their pages at least once a week (Winter 1999).[10]

Both high-tech and high-touch relationship marketing techniques can help the library retain its customers and thus may prove to be very cost-effective over the long run. Research indicates that attracting a new customer costs significantly (three to nine times) more than retaining a current customer (Duncan and Moriarty 1998; Geller 1997). Moreover, loyal patrons may exponentially increase their use of the library. After raising their customer retention rates by 5 percent, some for-profit organizations have noted increases in profit between 25 and 100 percent (Crandall 1998). With this knowledge, the West Lothian (Scotland) Public Library Service has tried to reach out to lapsed borrowers in a variety of ways. For example, when two branches were ready to re-open after being closed for renovation, the library sent a special welcome pack, including a letter, schedule of events, bookmarks, booklists, and balloons, to registered borrowers who had not used the library during the six months prior to closing. As a control, librarians also tracked use among a group of borrowers at another library who also had not used the collection during the same period. The measure proved successful. Of the two groups of borrowers who received packs, 32.5 percent and 25.1 percent returned to the library; of the control group, only 4.2 percent came back (Kerr 1999).

Buyer Readiness Stages

In their promotional ventures, librarians seek to increase collection use by communicating to patrons that the library can meet their needs. However, this may not be the immediate result. As Kotler and Armstrong (1999) observe, before use will occur, customers of any organization usually move (sometimes in a split second) through six different buyer readiness stages: awareness, knowledge, liking, preference, conviction, and purchase (or action). Staff members will be able to promote the library most effectively if they determine which stage(s) best describe(s) a majority of individuals in each target market and focus their promotional efforts accordingly.

Staff will wish to build name recognition and provide information about specific services whenever the target market has little awareness of the library's existence or knowledge of its collection. For example, transfer students who attend rural high schools may not be aware that the public library in the county seat serves the entire region. Librarians may want to purchase ads in the school newspaper, featuring such basic information about the library as its location, hours, and the fact that students can register for a free card. For example, the Coppell (Texas) Public Library informs new residents about the library's collections and services via a visiting service similar to Welcome Wagon ("Action" 1992), and the West Lothian (Scotland) Public Library Service has measured a 13.9 percent response rate to welcome packs mailed to new residents (Kerr 1999).

If target audience members know about but do not "like" the library, staff members must find out why before they can build up favorable and lasting feeling (Kotler and Armstrong 1999). Again, this dislike may be related to cost-benefit considerations. In such instances, staff may stress the benefits of collection use in a straightforward fashion, as the County of Los Angeles Public Library did when it launched a major publicity drive under one unifying slogan: "The best things in life are still free" ("Los Angeles" 1991). Five public library districts near Stockholm, Sweden, took a more targeted approach, publishing a newspaper for commuters, *LÄSENÄREN (The Traveling Reader)*, that described the benefits of library use. Staff distributed 80,000 copies of it at railway and bus stations, and, according to data collected several weeks later, over 30 percent of commuters received the paper, over 80 percent of these took it with them to their home or work, and 20 percent discovered new library services through it. The promotion has been repeated on several occasions, with more library districts joining each time (Rydquist 1992).

If a target audience prefers the library to other information outlets but has not developed the conviction to use it, librarians can emphasize the ways in which use will help meet patron needs. Again, convincing hard-core nonusers that they will benefit from using materials in the library's collection will require a more long-term (frequently questionable) effort.

Finally, some members of a target market, although believing that they should use the library's collection, fail to act on this conviction. The marketing task thus becomes tactfully urging the potential patron to act. For example, the library may reorganize titles in the Dewey 800s into an easy-to-browse, multicultural literature collection or reduce the costs of use in other ways.

Librarians can determine the buyer awareness stage of a target market in a variety of ways. Many librarians maintain regular contacts with individuals in these groups, obtaining a very rough idea of the buyer readiness stage of children, for example, by talking with kids who already visit the library or with area elementary school librarians and teachers. Although such informal information gathering costs little money, it may not fully reflect the potential user base. Juveniles who visit the library have already decided to use it and therefore do not truly represent all children in the community. Likewise, school librarians and teachers do not belong to the target group, and their analysis of it may be slightly skewed or outdated.

More formal marketing research can help resolve this problem. One popular research method involves organizing one or more focus groups consisting of six to ten members of each target market, then probing these individuals' knowledge of library resources. Chapter 8 presents detailed instructions for conducting focus group research, but we briefly suggest here that libraries

- use multiple focus groups to obtain an in-depth look at a broad spectrum of the target market;
- include both users and nonusers in these discussions; and
- use moderators who have a broad knowledge of both public libraries and marketing practices to guide the discussions.

The Iowa City (Iowa) Public Library (ICPL) followed these principles when it sponsored a series of focus groups to determine how it could better serve the needs of area business people. Sixty-eight business people attended, representing six different kinds of businesses from nonprofit agencies and service enterprises to large manufacturing companies. ICPL found that business people were using few library resources, primarily because group members, aware of the library as a whole, lacked in-depth knowledge about how its collections could meet their needs. These business people strongly urged the library to publicize its business services in a more concentrated fashion, working closely with the Chamber of Commerce, heads of local government agencies, and trade associations like the area Board of Realtors. Participants felt that the two most effective means of promotion would be press releases in the Chamber of Commerce newsletter and small group tours targeted to specific types of businesses (Baker 1991).

A library may also employ a well-designed survey, combining sophisticated research design with knowledge of potential patron behavior patterns, to measure the exact buyer awareness stage of a large number of persons in the target market. Determining why certain attitudes exist allows causal factors to be addressed during promotional efforts. A library may keep costs of such surveys down by persuading market researchers or graduate marketing students to donate their time to the effort or by hiring these specialists to review surveys librarians have drafted, explain data collection procedures to volunteers who will gather the data, help libraries analyze and interpret the results, and suggest creative solutions for the problems identified.[11]

WHAT MESSAGE(S) WILL THE LIBRARY TRY TO CONVEY TO THE TARGET MARKET?

Libraries can relate three broad types of promotional messages: information, persuasion, and reminder. The choice depends in part on the buyer readiness stage of the bulk of the target market.

Information messages can attract the attention of potential customers and inform target markets about the services and materials the library offers. For example, as part of a library card campaign, the King County (Washington) Library System informed patrons of its Web address, printed on each of its five new card designs. Use of the library's homepage increased by 500 percent (St. Lifer 2001; "King County Library System" 2001; "Library Cards" 2000). Information messages may also be used to clarify the library's image, correct false impressions, reduce consumer fears, or publicize changes. For example, after a property-assessment hike increased its annual budget by 50 percent and doubled its book budget, the Sacramento (California) Public Library informed patrons of the changes it was making by proclaiming "Got Hours! Got Books!" on banners, trucks, and other promotional materials ("Got" 1998).

As noted above, patrons may not always take note of the messages a library sends, particularly if they do not immediately need the information. Therefore, librarians may need to check their beliefs that "everyone knows that" and publicize basic information regularly. For example, Karen worked at one library that had offered online catalog classes for years, advertising them regularly in a variety of ways, yet patron surveys would invariably yield requests to begin offering such classes. Hernon and Whitman (2001) suggest that libraries create "if only the customer knew" lists that begin "Do you know that . . ." and briefly state library offerings that may be misunderstood or unknown, then distribute these lists widely to improve patron satisfaction.

Persuasion messages, designed to help convince customers to engage in library use now, state the benefits of such use. For example, the Woodson Regional Branch of the Chicago Public Library encouraged teen parents to attend a 25-week parenting program that promised to teach them "how to keep [their] child from becoming another statistic" by focusing on such issues as discipline, building self-esteem, and proper nutrition (Chelton 1997, 20). Thirty-one mothers between the ages of 14 and 16 registered, 20 graduated, and a significant number now bring their children to use the library.

Reminder messages can jog patrons' memories about the kinds of works available and the benefits of using them. For example, the Manatee County (Florida) Public Library System reminds county residents of the diversity of works in the library's collection with a weekly column written by staff and published in the local newspaper. Each column briefly highlights library resources in a featured subject area, and over the years staff have covered hundreds of topics, including medieval British history, Laura Ingalls Wilder, and UFOs (Sabin 1998).

For each promotional undertaking, library staff may develop creative messages that attract potential users' attention, hold their interest, arouse their desires, and encourage them to act. We recommend that librarians who wish to explore ways to generate memorable, attention-getting messages likely to appeal to the target market refer to standard public relations texts. Recent books that discuss these matters in some detail are Kohl (2000), Marconi (1999), Salzman and Salzman (1998), and Thompson (1996). Works by Balas (1998), Wolfe (1997), Karp (1995), Field and Field (1993), Leerburger (1989), and Tuggle and Heller (1987) address the subject from a library perspective, as do three excellent, well-established marketing newsletters (*Library PR News*, *Marketing Library Services*, and *Marketing Treasures*), one promising newcomer (*The Shy Librarian*), and the ALA electronic mailing list, PR-Talk, for which subscription information can be found at http://lp-web.ala.org:8000/.

WHAT FACTORS INFLUENCE THE OPTIMUM FREQUENCY OF PROMOTION?

The buyer awareness state of the target audience helps determine the optimum frequency of promotion; it requires stronger and more frequent promotion to convince people who have little awareness of, knowledge of, or liking for the library's collection to use it. An astute group of public, school, university, and special librarians from Fairbanks, Alaska, recognized this principle more than 25 years ago when they organized a joint, year-long effort to increase community awareness of the cramped, underused, and understaffed public library. They produced photographic spreads of library facilities for area newspapers; aired film and sound clips advertising library services and collections via local movie theaters, television stations, and radio stations; featured weekly reviews of works in the collection in area newspapers and on the radio; set up twentieth-century bestseller exhibits in the library and at the Fairbanks International Airport; and distributed lists of works about Alaska. The promotions increased community knowledge and use of the library and its collection and helped convince the city of Fairbanks to fund a new library building (Sherman 1980).

The extent to which a product's use varies seasonally also affects the optimum frequency of promotion. For example, works on gardening, cross-country skiing, fossil collecting, and holidays may show high use during one part of the year and very low use during others. It will be most cost-effective for libraries to time promotion of seasonal works as natural interest in the product ripens.

A library may follow several other promotional patterns. It could use burst advertising—heavy publicity over a brief period—to obtain maximum attention. For example, when Free Library of Philadelphia staff began visiting every local school at the end of each academic year to distribute brochures, stickers and other publicity materials about the summer reading program, program participation increased from between 3,000 and 6,000 to 30,000 children over a four-year period (Nataloni 1994). Burst advertising often achieves only temporary results, so it is best used for short-term efforts.

Science fiction books, investment resources, and other materials used on a regular basis can benefit from continuous promotion, which recurs at regular intervals (e.g., once a quarter) to remind potential patrons of a particular collection. Because such promotion may be ignored by both the media and the public when used too frequently, librarians may also consider using intermittent promotion, publicizing a particular collection in small bursts on an irregular, yet ongoing, basis.

WHAT TECHNIQUES CAN THE LIBRARY USE TO PROMOTE ITS PRODUCTS?

Librarians have issued public service announcements, disseminated information on Web sites and newsletters, printed their logos on the side of book bags, and employed similar tried-and-true methods of promotion. They have also advertised their wares on matchbook covers, parade floats, rapid-transit vehicles, and hot-air balloons and sought other innovative ways to reach their public.

Common promotional methods include

- *personal selling*, wherein a staff member uses her personal influence to promote materials, for example, suggesting specific titles suited to a patron's needs or presenting a booktalk;

- *promotional activities*, such as talks by local authors or strategically located displays, which inform patrons of the range and depth of the collection;

- *mass-media promotion*, which features the library's products in local media or on the Internet; and

- *targeted information pieces*, such as brochures, materials lists, posters, signs, or newsletters distributed within or outside the library building, to spotlight intriguing product items or lines.

Promotional Medium Selection

As Wood (1988, 11) has so cogently noted, although media selection has few "rules whose faithful, mechanical application assures success," librarians who strive to choose the promotional medium, or media mix, that will most effectively achieve the campaign's objectives and satisfy budgetary constraints will consider, at a minimum, three broad factors:

The target market

The message content

The cost

Table 7.1, pages 182–85, shows the relationship between each of these factors and commonly used promotional media.

Target market issues include such broad considerations as the size and diversity of the market as well as the specific characteristics of individuals within it. Although advertisements in the local newspaper will reach a bigger, more heterogeneous audience than a public service announcement aired on a local country music station, the latter may be an effective venue to extol the library's selection of Country Music Association Award winners. Awareness of the extent of library use, lifestyle, leisure interests, and other psychographic and demographic elements of the target market may facilitate the library's decisions to tantalize train commuters with posters on audiobooks and buy ads on a rock-and-roll radio station to stimulate teenagers' interest in its music collection. Buyer readiness stages may also affect choice of promotional technique. For customers in the preference, conviction, and action stages, personal selling, with its immediacy, interactivity, and the interpersonal relationship it fosters, can be an organization's most effective tool (Kotler and Andreasen 1996).

Message content also influences media selection in at least two important ways:

- the degree of timeliness necessary. Bibliographies and similar media with a long shelf-life can effectively publicize classic fiction and other materials of ongoing interest; conversely, current events materials and collection-related programs require a medium, such as e-mail, that will reach people while their interest is piqued.

- the complexity of the message. Although posters and signs can feature short messages, a news article or an information brochure will better convey detailed technical information, such as the types of collection sources area businesses may find useful.

Finally, librarians can consider the actual out-of-pocket expense to the library associated with different advertising (paid forms of promotion by identified sponsors) and publicity techniques (planting commercially significant news in a medium not paid for by the sponsor). When a library uses publicity, it finds or creates eye-catching, timely, well-written news stories related to the collection, then tries to persuade the news media to use these. Publicity's advantages are its high potential for dramatization when it arouses interest in a forthcoming noteworthy event and its higher appearance of veracity (over paid advertising, which places no reliance on media producer goodwill) (Kotler and Armstrong 1999).

TABLE 7.1. Promotional Techniques Commonly Used by Libraries.

- **Newspaper** feature stories, photographs, or advertisements;

- **Magazine/newsletter** feature stories, photographs, or advertisements;

- **Television or cable television** feature stories, advertisements, or public service announcements;

- **Radio** feature stories, advertisements, or public service announcements;

- **Direct mailings** (newsletters, information brochures, booklists, or posters);

- **Web site** announcements, articles, photographs, or forms;

- **Posters and signs** placed within the building;

- **Bookmarks or flyers** available within the building;

- **Displays** within the building;

- **Speeches or booktalks** presented to the target market, inside the library or outside its doors; and

- **Individual suggestions** given by readers' advisers and reference librarians.

Target Market	Message Content	Types of Costs Incurred
Newspapers provide good market coverage for community residents in general. Special audience newspapers, such as foreign-language or school newspapers, can effectively reach target markets.	• Messages in news stories can range from simple to complex; they can inform, persuade, or remind. • Messages in advertisements should be simple and capture attention immediately; they can inform, persuade, or remind. • The message is very timely and therefore especially useful for promoting current collection-related events or for informing the public about recent changes in the cost of using the collection. • The medium is fairly transient, so messages about on-going features of the collection should be repeated periodically. • Effective graphic design may be used to help gain attention	• Staff time: to write stories or press releases, design copy, take photographs, develop graphic materials, and work with media representatives to ensure good coverage and placement. • Advertising: purchased by the column inch. • Equipment and supplies

Target Market	Message Content	Types of Costs Incurred
General interest magazines can provide average to good market coverage for the general community. Special interest magazines, such as a club newsletter, can effectively reach highly specialized target markets.	• Messages in news stories can range from simple to complex; they can inform, persuade, or remind. • Messages in advertisements should be simple and capture attention immediately; they can inform, persuade, or remind. • The medium can be used to convey messages about current collection-related events if the marketer allows for the lead time required for publication. • Because the medium is fairly transient, messages about on-going features of the collection should be repeated periodically. • Effective graphic design may be used to help gain attention	• Staff time: to write stories, design advertising copy, take photographs, develop graphic materials, and work with media representatives to ensure good coverage and placement of material. • Advertising: purchased by the column inch (may be free in some special interest publications). • Equipment and supplies
Television can provide average to good market coverage for community residents in general	• Messages in news stories can be simple or of medium complexity; they can inform, persuade, or remind. • Messages in advertisements and public service announcements should be simple and capture attention immediately; they can inform, persuade, and remind. • Messages are timely and thus especially useful for promoting current collection-related events or for informing the public about recent changes in the cost of using the collection. • The medium is fairly transient, so messages about on-going features of the collection should be repeated periodically.	• Staff time: to plan stories, develop advertising copy or script, design graphic materials, and work with media representatives to ensure good coverage and placement of material. • Advertising: may be purchased by the minute. • Equipment and supplies.
Radio can provide average to good coverage for the general community. Radio stations of a specific format (e.g., rock, classical music, information) can reach highly selective target audiences.	• Messages in news stories can be simple or of medium complexity; they can inform, persuade, or remind. • Messages in advertisements and public service announcements should be simple and capture attention immediately; they can inform, persuade, or remind. • The message is very timely and therefore especially useful for promoting current collection-related events or for informing the public about recent changes in the cost of using the collection. • Because the medium is fairly transient, messages about on-going features of the collection should be repeated periodically.	• Staff time: to plan stories, develop advertising copy or script, and work with media representatives to ensure good coverage and placement of material. • Advertising: may be purchased by the minute. • Equipment and supplies.

(Table 7.1 continues on page 184.)

TABLE 7.1—*Continued*

Target Market	Message Content	Types of Costs Incurred
Direct mail (conventional or e-mail) can provide average to good market coverage for the general community, library patrons, or a small, targeted group. Target markets may vary greatly in size.	• Messages in newsletters, brochures, and book lists can range from simple to complex; they can inform, persuade, or remind. • Messages on posters should be simple and capture attention immediately; they can inform, persuade, or remind. • The medium can be used to convey messages about current collection-related events if the marketer allows for the lead time required for publication and mailing. • Because the medium is fairly transient, messages about on-going features of the collection should be repeated periodically. • Effective graphic design should be used to help gain attention.	• Staff time: to write copy, take photographs, develop graphic materials, compile mailing list, and mail materials. • Printing costs. • Equipment and supplies. • Postage.
Web sites can reach current and potential users who visit the site. Links from related sites may increase the number of visitors	• Messages on web sites can range from simple to complex; they can inform, persuade, or remind. • The message can be timely and therefore especially useful for promoting current collection-related events. • The message can also be enduring and therefore especially useful for promoting on-going features of the collection or the costs of using various materials. • Effective graphic design should be used to help gain attention, keeping in mind the needs of those using slow or text-based browsers. • The message may be interactive, providing a means for users to supply feedback, contact staff, or immediately access services or materials.	• Staff time: to develop content, design pages, and code them in the appropriate computer language(s). • Server space to host web site. • Equipment and supplies.
Posters and signs, if appropriately designed and positioned, can reach library users effectively.	• Messages on signs and posters should be simple and capture attention immediately; they can inform, persuade, or remind. • The message can be timely and therefore especially useful for promoting current collection-related events. • The message can also be enduring and therefore especially useful for promoting ongoing features of the collection or the costs of using various materials. • Effective graphic design can help gain attention.	• Staff time: to write message and develop graphic materials. • Printing costs. • Equipment and supplies.

Target Market	Message Content	Types of Costs Incurred
Bookmarks and flyers, if appropriately designed and positioned, can reach library users effectively. They can be put out for those who choose to pick them up, given to patrons in response to questions, or given to everyone who checks out an item.	• Messages on bookmarks and flyers can range from simple to complex; they can inform, persuade, or remind. • The message can be timely and therefore especially useful for promoting current collection-related events. • The message can also be enduring and therefore especially useful for promoting on-going features of the collection or the costs of using various materials. • Effective graphic design should be used to help gain attention.	• Staff time: to write message and develop graphic materials. • Printing costs. • Equipment and supplies.
If appropriately designed and positioned, **displays** can reach library users effectively.	• Messages on accompanying signs should be simple and capture attention immediately; they can inform, persuade, or remind. • Effective graphic design may be used to help gain attention.	• Staff time: to pull materials for the display, refill the display as it empties, and develop graphic materials. • Furniture to house the display. • Equipment and supplies.
Speeches and talks can reach specially targeted groups of community residents and library patrons.	• If carefully designed and delivered, message can effectively promote collection-related events, the collection as a whole, or individual product lines or items. • Slides and graphics can accompany talk to help gain attention. • Message may be interactive, giving audience members a chance to provide feedback or immediately access materials or services.	• Staff time: to prepare and deliver talk, develop graphic materials, and travel to group meeting places. • Equipment and supplies.
Suggestions are designed to reach individual patrons rather than targeted groups of users.	• Messages can promote individual product items or lines in the collection. • Message is interactive, requiring a dialogue between user and staff member.	• Staff time: to help patrons on an individual basis.

Publicity efforts do have a hidden cost, however: The library's marketing representative(s) must gain the goodwill of the media and their willingness to air public service announcements, take publicity photographs, cover newsworthy events, or print library press releases. To gain more control over the frequency, size, and placement of their promotional efforts and repay the media for providing free promotion at other times, a library may budget money for paid advertising. For example, in recent years the St. Louis (Missouri) Public Library has allotted $100,000 annually for advertising, which has also helped the library gain over $260,000 per year of in-kind contributions from media outlets (Holt 1999). In 1991, the County of Los Angeles Public Library allocated $600,000 for a two-year campaign designed to increase library use and the number of card holders—a campaign conducted during prime time, when stations usually do not air public service announcements ("Los Angeles" 1991). Such examples are not isolated; a 1998 American Library Association survey found that 53 percent of responding libraries had paid for advertising in the prior year ("1998 ALA" 1999).

Budgeting

As a library formulates activities to meet its goals and objectives, it must also earmark resources to allow for their implementation. Developing strategies to create a superior collection without also providing sufficient resources to ensure that effective promotion occurs erroneously assumes that the *Field of Dreams* motto, "If you build it, they will come," works for libraries as well as baseball.[12] In fact, many libraries recognize the fallacy of this belief; a 1998 American Library Association survey indicates that 62 percent of libraries have funds specifically allocated to PR activities ("1998 ALA" 1999).

No simple formula defines what constitutes sufficient resources for effective promotion. Librarians must rely on informed estimates to allocate money to different promotional activities, considering the particulars of each situation, among them the desired result (Graham 1995), the local costs of various publicity techniques, and other factors described in this chapter. In turn, evaluative observations and other data collected on a particular promotional initiative can inform future allocation decisions.[13]

The most cost-effective promotional choice will not always be the least expensive. Suppose that a library wants to increase awareness of its parenting collection among parents of elementary school students. It could create an in-library display of these materials fairly inexpensively. However, if many of the parents do not currently come to the library, such a display will miss a significant portion of the target audience. A resource-heavy choice, such as creating a parents' collection brochure and distributing it through the schools or the mail (virtual or otherwise), may promise a greater potential return on investment over the long run.

Libraries may also be able to stretch precious funds by recruiting volunteers, particularly public relations students, professional graphic artists, and others with specialized skills and talents, to help with promotional efforts. University of Illinois/Chicago design students helped the American Library Association create a series of advertisements intended to portray libraries as fun, exciting places

(Kelly 1997). The Boston Public Library recently purchased television time and newspaper, billboard, and public transit space for ads created pro bono by an advertising/public relations agency ("Boston" 2000).

HOW WILL THE LIBRARY EVALUATE THE RESULTS OF ITS PROMOTIONAL EFFORTS?

Because not all methods of promotion will significantly increase the target market's awareness of, use of, or satisfaction with the collection, a library will want to consider modifying or dropping ventures that have little effect on user behavior and trying them again only if circumstances change.

Exposure count, which quantifies the relationship between the news media coverage received and the estimated audience contacted, provides one method of assessing the reach of promotional techniques. For example, the Morris County (New Jersey) Library knows that the radio spot it has been airing for about 10 years during morning drive time reaches approximately 110,000 listeners for two minutes once a week (Roukens 1999). Another library might note that coverage of its new CD book collection included 200 column inches of news and photographs in the local newspaper with a circulation of 8,500 and one minute of air time on the local television station watched by an estimated 12,800 persons. Such figures estimate the maximum number of people a particular promotional effort could reach and the length of their exposure to it; as noted previously, the number who actually pay attention to the stimulus will be smaller and influenced by such factors as design, content, placement, and timing. Formal surveys can more accurately determine the number of people aware of a message. For example, when a professional research firm evaluated the San Diego Public Library's "Check it out" television spots, it found that almost 60 percent of those surveyed knew of the campaign ("San Diego" 2000).

Ultimately, staff will want to assess the effectiveness of a promotional technique as well as its reach, measuring such aspects as the extent of the change of the target market's awareness of and satisfaction with the library. If a library has already formally surveyed the target market, it can re-survey to determine the extent to which an attitude change has occurred.

Formal or informal experimentation can also determine whether, or which, promotional efforts significantly affect satisfaction with and use of the collection. The formal, rigorous experiments with scientific controls that yield rich, relevant data require resources and special knowledge to conduct. The library must identify staff members, consultants, or other specialists conversant with the principles of hypothesis testing, causality, study design, and statistics and also available and willing to conduct the research. Faculty or students in marketing, information science, or library science, or mathematically adept staff members, may be willing sources of expertise when given economic support. If these prerequisites can be fulfilled, libraries will particularly want to consider using controlled experiments when

- the change has the potential to greatly improve satisfaction or use or save a large sum of money over time;

- the library will willingly endure the inconvenience of changing its procedures for a short time and collecting statistics associated with the study; and

- the library makes a commitment to use results of the study to effect changes.

We recommend that libraries that cannot comfortably coordinate such efforts employ one or both of the following methods. First, they can closely examine research literature documenting the conditions under which promotional efforts are effective. For example, booklists are generally effective as long as they receive wide distribution within the library; that is, staff consistently place them in works that patrons check out, continually promote them, or prominently display them in high-traffic areas (Baker 1986).

They can also use quick, creative techniques to estimate the success of their promotional efforts. For example, at the beginning of each month one manager placed two mason jars in the circulation area, filling the first with 300 pennies and leaving the second empty. Each time a staff member convinced a patron to borrow an additional work or file a reserve, he or she moved a penny from the first to the second jar. At the end of the month, the manager counted the pennies in the second jar and informed staff how much of the monthly circulation total was due to these individual promotional efforts. If use had increased significantly, he rewarded them by taking them out to lunch (Smith 1992).

Another simple measurement methodology compares the results of the test case, where the promotion occurs, with one or more unchanged control cases. For example, when staff at one branch of the Cumberland County (North Carolina) Public Library and Information Center displayed related fiction and nonfiction categories next to each other, fiction circulation at that branch increased significantly more than at three other libraries in the system that did not employ the new technique (Cannell and McCluskey 1996).

CONCLUSION

A library promotes itself most effectively when staff members consider the many, varied ways in which the library communicates with its customers and potential patrons and try to ensure that each encounter reflects the library's mission, goals, and objectives. A library that carefully determines the specific products or collection-related events it will spotlight, the target markets it will court, the best techniques for attracting these audiences, and the optimum frequency of its promotional efforts, while also maintaining outstanding customer service, will have a strong potential for increasing awareness and use of the collection and winning the affection and loyalty of the community.

NOTES

1.   The work of mathematicians Claude Shannon and Warren Weaver in the late 1940s forms the basis for most of the communication model described in this chapter. The feedback portion of the model comes from the work of Norbert Wiener, another mathematician and a contemporary of Shannon and Weaver. An encyclopedia can provide a more detailed overview of the development of this communication model. See, for example, "Communication" (1991).

2.   See Chapter 3 for a more detailed discussion of segmentation strategies.

3.   DVS videos present a descriptive narration of a film's visual elements (scenery, action, etc.) to make the movies more accessible to people with visual impairments.

4.   For other methods of obtaining feedback, see Hernon and Altman (1998), Alexander, Goodyear, and Kellum (1997) and Todaro (1995).

5.   See Hernon and Altman (1998) for detailed advice on establishing compliment and complaint tracking systems.

6.   For in-depth views of elements to include in complaint handling and conflict-resolution training, consult Robinson (1984), Bessler (1994), Anderson and Zemke (1998), Zemke (1995), and Leland and Bailey (1999).

7.   For a more in-depth look at relationship marketing, see Gordon (1999), Peppers and Rogers (1999), Payne et al. (1998), Vavra (1995), and Christopher, Payne, and Ballantyne (1993).

8.   Sweeney (1997) also advocates using technology to offer more customized library services.

9.   Reading (1997) suggests numerous ways that libraries can use e-mail to promote services and collections; many could also be adapted to other forms of communication.

10.   The December 2000 issue of *Information Technology and Libraries* includes several related articles on this issue.

11.   Mueller-Alexander (1991) lists the advantages and disadvantages of using these and other alternative sources for marketing research.

12.   The original quote, "If you build it, he will come," from the novel *Shoeless Joe* (Kinsella 1982) doesn't illustrate the argument as well as the film version.

13.   For an example of the manner in which one library has tied its promotional budget allocation into its overall planning and marketing process, see Eisner (1990).

REFERENCES

"Action Exchange: Promoting the Library to New Residents. 1992." *American Libraries* 23, no. 5 (May): 371–72.

Alexander, Adrian W., Mary Lou Goodyear, and Cathy Kellum. 1997. "Voice of the Customer: Feedback Strategies for Libraries and Vendors." *The Serials Librarian* 31 nos. 1/2: 289–94.

Anderson, Kristin, and Ron Zemke. 1998. *Delivering Knock Your Socks Off Service*. Rev. ed. New York: American Management Association.

Baker, Sharon L. 1986. "Overload, Browsers, and Selections." *Library and Information Science Research* 8, no. 4 (October-December): 315–29.

———. 1991. "Improving Business Services Through the Use of Focus Groups." *RQ* 30, no. 3 (Spring): 377–85.

Balas, Janet L. 1998. "Using the Web to Market the Library." *Computers in Libraries* 18, no. 8 (September): 46.

Besant, Larry X., and Deborah Sharp. 2000. "Upsize This! Libraries Need Relationship Marketing." *Information Outlook* 4, no. 3 (March): 17–22.

Bessler, Joanne M. 1994. *Putting Service into Library Staff Training*. Chicago: American Library Association.

Bettman, James R. 1979. *An Information Processing Theory of Consumer Choice*. Reading, MA: Addison-Wesley.

"Boston PL Launches Ad Campaign." 2000. *American Libraries* 31, no. 9 (October): 22, 24.

"Briefly Noted." 1999. *Library Hotline* 28, no. 24 (June 21): 6.

Cannell, Jeffrey, and Eileen McCluskey. 1996. "Genrefication: Fiction Classification and Increased Circulation." In *Guiding the Reader to the Next Book*, ed. Kenneth D. Shearer, 159–65. New York: Neal-Schuman.

Chelton, Mary K., ed. 1997. *Excellence in Library Services to Young Adults: The Nation's Top Programs*. 2d ed. Chicago: American Library Association.

Christopher, Martin, Adrian Payne, and David Ballantyne. 1993. *Relationship Marketing: Bringing Quality, Customer Service, and Marketing Together*. Woburn, MA: Butterworth-Heinemann.

"Communication." 1991. In *New Encyclopaedia Britannica Macropaedia*. 15th ed. Vol. 16, 623–28. Chicago: Encyclopaedia Britannica.

Cramer, Dina. 2000. "How Are We Treating Our Customers?" *Public Libraries* 39, no. 2 (March/April): 67–68.

Crandall, Rick. 1998. *1001 Ways to Market Your Services: Even If You Hate to Sell*. Lincolnwood, IL: Contemporary Books.

Davis, Deborah S., and Alan M. Bernstein. 1997. "From Survey to Service: Using Patron Input to Improve Customer Satisfaction." *Technical Services Quarterly* 14, no. 3: 47–62.

Duncan, Tom, and Sandra E. Moriarty. 1998. "A Communication-based Marketing Model for Managing Relationships." *Journal of Marketing* 62, no. 2 (April): 1–13.

"DVS-Formatted Film Series Planned." 1997. *Public Libraries* 36, no. 5 (September/October): 275.

Eisner, Joe. 1990. "The Marketing Budget: How Much Is Enough?" *The Bottom Line* 4, no. 2 (Spring): 33–34.

Engel, James F., David T. Kollatt, and Roger D. Blackwell. 1973. *Consumer Behavior*. 2d ed. New York: Holt, Rinehart & Winston.

Estabrook, Leigh S. 1996. "Sacred Trust or Competitive Opportunity: Using Patron Records." *Library Journal* 121, no. 2 (February 1): 48–49

Fakolt, Jennifer. 1998. "Everybody Wins! Carson City Public Library Pulls Out All the Stops for National Library Week." *Public Libraries* 37, no. 3 (May/June): 190–94.

Field, Selma G., and Edwin M. Field. 1993. *Publicity Manual for Libraries*. Monticello, NY: Knowledge Network Press.

Geller, Lois. 1997. "Customer Retention Begins with the Basics." *Direct Marketing* 60, no. 5 (September): 58–62.

Gordon, Ian. 1999. *Relationship Marketing: New Strategies, Techniques, and Technologies to Win the Customers You Want and Keep Them Forever*. Toronto: Wiley.

"Got Hours! Got Books!" 1998. *American Libraries* 29 no. 4 (April): 28.

Graham, John R. 1995. "How Much Should a Company Spend on Marketing?" *American Salesman* 40, no. 6 (June): 13–15.

Grossman, Aaron. 1998. "One-to-One: Net Marketing Opportunities Can Heighten Customer Loyalty, Satisfaction." *Marketing News* 32, no. 2 (January 19): 13.

Gunter, Dorothy. 1994. "Introducing Newbery Winners and Honor Books to Hispanic Fourth and Fifth Graders through a Recreational Reading Program." Fort Lauderdale, FL: Nova Southeastern University. ERIC ED369042.

Gupta, Dinesh K. 1999. "User-Focus Approach: Central to Ranganathan's Philosophy." *Library Science with a slant to Documentation and Information Studies* 36, no. 2: 123–28.

Hernon, Peter, and Ellen Altman. 1998. *Assessing Service Quality: Satisfying the Expectations of Library Customers*. Chicago: American Library Association.

Hernon, Peter, and John R. Whitman. 2001. *Delivering Satisfaction and Service Quality: A Customer-Based Approach for Libraries*. Chicago: American Library Association.

Holt, Glen E. 1999. *Public Library Partnerships: Mission-Driven Tools for the 21st Century*. [Homepage of Bertelsmann Foundation], [Online]. Formerly available: http://www.stiftung.bertelsmann.de/english/netz/publib/themen/index.htm [Accessed September 28, 2001].

Information Technology and Libraries. 2000. 19, no. 4 (December): entrie issue.

Karp, Rashelle S., ed. for the Publications Committee of the Public Relations Section, Library Administration and Management Association. 1995. *Part-time Public Relations with Full-time Results: A PR Primer for Librarians*. Chicago: American Library Association.

Kelly, Joyce. 1997. "Generation Xers Create a Campaign for the Libr@ry." *American Libraries* 28, no. 2 (February): 60–62.

Kerr, George D. 1999. Gaining and Retaining Customer Loyalty. [Homepage of Bertelsmann Foundation], [Online]. Formerly available: http://www.stiftung.bertelsmann.de /english/netz/publib/themen/index.htm [Accessed September 28, 2001].

"King County Library System Annual Report 2000." 2001. [Homepage of the King County Library System], [Online]. (Updated September 25). Available: http://www.kcls.org /kcls/annualreport2000.html [Accessed September 28, 2001].

Kinsella, W. P. 1982. *Shoeless Joe*. New York: Ballantine.

Kohl, Susan Y. 2000. *Getting @ttention: Leading-Edge Lessons for Publicity and Marketing*. Boston: Butterworth Heinemann.

Kotler, Philip, and Alan R. Andreasen. 1996. *Strategic Marketing for Nonprofit Organizations*. 5th ed. Upper Saddle River, NJ: Prentice Hall.

Kotler, Philip, and Gary Armstrong. 1999. *Principles of Marketing*. 8th ed. Upper Saddle River, NJ: Prentice-Hall.

Kreig-Sigman, Kelly. 1995. "Kissing in the Dark: Promoting and Communicating in a Public Library Setting." *Library Trends* 43, no. 3 (Winter): 418–30.

"Lane Library Reference: Email Updates." 2001a. [Homepage of the Lane Memorial Library], [Online]. (Updated September 28). Available: http://www.hampton.lib.nh .us/scripts/links/subscribe.pl [Accessed September 28, 2001].

"Lane Library Reference: Homework: Specific Assignments." 2001b. [Homepage of the Lane Memorial Library], [Online]. (Updated September 18). Available: http://www.hampton.lib.nh.us/referenc/Homework/Specific_Assignments/ [Accessed September 28, 2001].

Leerberger, Benedict A. 1989. *Promoting and Marketing the Library*. Rev. ed. Boston: G. K. Hall.

Leland, Karen, and Keith Bailey. 1999. *Customer Service for Dummies*. 2d ed. Foster City, CA: IDG Books Worldwide.

Levins, Ilyssa. 1998. "One-on-One Relationship Marketing Comes of Age." *Medical Marketing and Media* 33, no. 6 (June): 44–52.

"Library Cards Online Registration Form." 2000. [Homepage of the King County Library System], [Online]. (Updated November 27). Available: https://www.kcls.org/cgi-bin /registration.cgi?branch=ap [Accessed September 28, 2001].

Library Focus. 2001. [Online]. (March 4). Available: http://hobbspublib.leaco.net/focuma4 .htm [Accessed September 28, 2001].

Library PR News. Bi-monthly. For subscription information, write: L.E.I., Inc. R.D. 1, Box 219, New Albany, PA 18833.

"Los Angeles County PL Conducts $600,000 PR Drive." 1991. *Library Journal* 116, no. 6 (April 1): 19.

Marconi, Joe. 1999. *The Complete Guide to Publicity: Maximize Visibility for Your Product, Service, or Organization*. Lincolnwood, IL: NTC Business Books.

Marketing Library Services. 8 times/year. For subscription information, write: Information Today, Inc. 143 Old Marlton Pike, Medford, NJ 08055-8750. For more information see http://www.infotoday.com.

Marketing Treasures. Bi-monthly. For subscription information, write: Chris Olson and Associates, 857 Twin Harbor Drive, Arnold, MD 21012.

McDonald, Malcolm H. B., and Warren J. Keegan. 1997. *Marketing Plans That Work.* Boston: Butterworth-Heinemann.

Milner, Eileen. 1996. "Complaints: Who Needs Them?" *Public Library Journal* 11, no. 1 (January/February): 1–4.

Mueller, Elizabeth. 1965. "Are New Books Read More Than Old Ones?" *Library Quarterly* 35, no. 3 (July): 166–72.

Mueller-Alexander, Jeanette M. 1991. "Alternate Sources for Marketing Research for Libraries." *Special Libraries* 82, no. 3 (Summer): 159–64.

Murphy, Beverly, Julie VanDyke, and Derrick Vines. 1998. "When It's Not Free Anymore: Promoting the Unpopular." [Homepage of Duke University Medical Center Library], [Online]. (Updated May 15) Available: http://www2.mc.duke.edu/misc/MLA/webposter/index.html [Accessed September 28, 2001].

Nataloni, Rochelle. 1994. "A Solid 'Foundation' Helps FLP 'Rebuild the Future.' " *Marketing Library Services* 8, nos. 3 and 4 (April/May and June): 1–3.

Nielsen, G. S. 1998. "Les personnes dyslexiques, des etrangers dans nos bibliotheques. [People with dyslexia, strangers in our libraries.]" *Bulletin d'Informations de l'Association des Bibliothecaires* 181, no. 4: 57–61.

"1998 ALA PR/Communications Survey Results." 1999. [Homepage of American Library Association], [Online]. Available: http://www.ala.org/pio/archives/pr%20survey/totalresults.html [Accessed September 28, 2001].

"Oprahlikes." 1999. [Homepage of Lucius Beebe Memorial Library/Wakefield Public Library], [Online]. (Updated June 21). Available: http://www.noblenet.org/wakefield/zraoprah.htm [Accessed September 28, 2001].

Payne, Adrian, et al. 1998. *Relationship Marketing for Competitive Advantage: Winning and Keeping Customers.* Woburn, MA: Butterworth-Heinemann.

Peppers, Don, and Martha Rogers. 1999. *The One to One Manager: Real-World Lessons in Customer Relationship Management.* New York: Doubleday.

Pluse, John. 1991. "Customer Focus: The Salvation of Service Organizations." *Public Library Journal* 6, no. 1 (January/February): 1–5.

Reading, R. Christine Gibson. 1997. " 'E-Marketing' Your Library." *Public Libraries* 36, no. 2 (March/April): 122–23.

Robinson, William C. 1984. "Complaint Handling in the Library." *Occasional Paper* no. 166 of the University of Illinois Graduate School of Library Science.

Rock, Felicity. 1998. "To Raise Your Profile, Raise the Roof." *The Library Association Record* 100, no. 4 (April): 188–89.

Roukens, Joanne P. 1999. "On the Radio." *The Unabashed Librarian* no. 112: 21.

Rubin, Rhea Joyce. 2000. "Defusing the Angry Patron." *Library Mosaics* 11, no. 3 (May/June): 14–15.

Rydquist, Lars. 1992. "Travellers' Tales: Reading for Commuters." *Scandinavian Public Library Quarterly* 25, no. 3: 29–31.

Sabin, Jonathan. 1998. " 'Library Card' Newspaper Column." *The Unabashed Librarian* no. 106: 11–12.

Salzman, Jason, and Jack Salzman. 1998. *Making the News: A Guide for Nonprofits and Activists*. Boulder, CO: Westview Press.

"San Diego PL's Ad Campaign Effective, Research Concludes." 2000. *Library Hotline* 29, no. 27 (July 10): 6.

Sherman, Steve. 1980. *ABC's of Library Promotion*. 2d ed. Metuchen, NJ: Scarecrow Press.

———. 1994. "Service, the Bookseller's Prelude to Promotion." *Publishers Weekly* 241, no. 19 (May 9): 24-25.

The Shy Librarian: Marketing and Public Relations for Libraries. Quarterly. For more information see http://www.shylibrarian.com.

Smith, Duncan. 1992. Telephone interview with Shay Baker, February 12.

St. Lifer, Evan. 2001. "Tapping into the Zen of Marketing." *Library Journal* 126, no. 8 (May 1): 44–46.

Sweeney, Richard T. 1997. "Creating Library Services with Wow! Staying Slightly ahead of the Curve." *Library Trends* 46, no. 1 (Summer): 129–52.

Tax, Stephen, Stephen W. Brown, and Murali Chandrashekaran. 1998. "Customer Evaluations of Service Complaint Experiences: Implications for Relationship Marketing." *Journal of Marketing* 62, no. 2 (April): 60–76.

Thompson, William. 1996. *Targeting the Message: A Receiver-Centered Process for Public Relations Writing*. White Plains, NY: Longman.

Timm, Paul R. 1995. *50 Powerful Ideas You Can Use to Keep Your Customers*. 2d ed. Hawthorne, NJ: Career Press.

Todaro, Julie Beth. 1995. "Make 'Em Smile." *School Library Journal* 41, no. 1 (January): 24–27.

Tuggle, Ann Montgomery, and Dawn Hansen Heller. 1987. *Grand Schemes and Nitty-Gritty Details: Library PR That Works*. Littleton, CO: Libraries Unlimited.

"Under Ben Bulben." [2001]. [Homepage of Online Book Initiative], [Online]. Available: http://ftp.std.com/obi/William.Butler.Yeats/Yeats/UnderBenBulben [Accessed September 28, 2001].

Vavra, Terry G. 1995. *Aftermarketing: How to Keep Customers for Life Through Relationship Marketing*. Chicago: Irwin Professional Publications.

Volpe, Nancy. 1996. "An Information Playground: Kansas City Public's New Marketing Campaign." *Missouri Library World* 1, no. 2 (Summer): 20–21.

Walder, Toni. 1999. "Public Relations: A Good Investment for Small Libraries." *Ohio Libraries* (Spring/Summer): 22–24.

Winter, Ken. 1999. " 'MyLibrary' Can Help Your Library." *American Libraries* 30, no. 7 (August): 65–67.

Wolfe, Lisa A. 1997. *Library Public Relations, Promotions, and Communications: A How-to-Do-It Manual.* New York: Neal-Schuman.

Wood, Elizabeth J. 1988. *Strategic Marketing for Libraries: A Handbook.* Westport, CT: Greenwood Press.

Wright, Peter, and Barton Weitz. 1977. "Time Horizon Effects on Product Evaluation Strategies." *Journal of Marketing Research* 14 (November): 429–33.

Yamamoto, N. 1998. "Suggestion Box to Catch Users' Views." *Toshokan Zasshi* 92, no. 4: 283–85.

"Youthreach: 'Seussamania' in Geisel's Hometown." 1986. *American Libraries* 17, no. 6 (June): 485.

Zemke, Ron. 1995. *Service Recovery: Fixing Broken Customers.* Portland, OR: Productivity Press.

COLLECTION EVALUATION
A PRODUCT ANALYSIS APPROACH[1]

> "Everything should be made as simple as possible but not simpler"— Albert Einstein (Simpson 1997, 218).

Building responsive collections consumes many hours and dollars. To ascertain the effectiveness of these expenditures librarians need to routinely evaluate the collection, a topic that received substantial coverage in the library literature of the 1990s (Evans and Zarnovsky 2000). Intner and Futas (1994) suggest three reasons for this renewed interest:

Accountability—proving that public funds have been beneficially spent

Cooperation—demonstrating the collection's value to attract resource-sharing partners

The economy—optimizing resources in a time of rising costs and limited budgets.

To these we add a fourth: the increased ability of automated circulation systems to provide quick and accurate evaluation data that may, especially when the initial automated vendor is carefully chosen, be configured to meet a given library's special needs.

A number of authors have described a variety of possible collection evaluation techniques (e.g., Nelson, Altman, and Mayo 2000; Strohl 1999; Baker and Lancaster 1991; Powell 1990; American Library Association 1989). Generally, methods fall into two broad classes:

Materials-centered techniques, which focus on the collection in abstract, addressing such issues as collection size, quality, and diversity

Client-centered techniques, which focus on the quality and quantity of collection use and other measures of the match between the items and those who use it

Balanced, comprehensive collections are the result of using professional judgment informed by both materials- and client-centered approaches to evaluation For example, librarians at the Skokie (Illinois) Public Library measure collection quality, size, and diversity by checking collection holdings against a number of lists of "recommended works." They examine various measures of use and availability such as turnover rate, fill rate, and document delivery studies. They also seek patron suggestions about how the collection might be improved (Kozlowski 1998).

This chapter recommends that public libraries consider implementing a four-prong product analysis approach to collection evaluation:

Identifying heavily used currently owned items

Identifying lightly used or nonused currently owned items

Identifying items not currently in the collection but that would likely receive use

Identifying barriers that inhibit collection use

In addition to explaining the benefits of this process, the text and accompanying figures also describe specific evaluation techniques and procedures to help accomplish these tasks.

With evaluation, quality matters more than quantity when resources are limited; adopting a few basic approaches in the short term and carrying them out on a regular and consistent basis often will be more effective than performing many different tasks sporadically, when time permits. To obtain the strongest possible base of information to facilitate collection management decisions, libraries will want to consider phasing in as many evaluation approaches as possible over time.

ASSUMPTIONS AND LIMITATIONS
OF THIS APPROACH

In this combined approach to product analysis, we assume that strong collections, matched to community needs, will receive heavy use and contain diverse items. We also assume that evaluators will keep in mind the inherent limitations of the profession's current use measures. For example, circulation statistics will not correlate perfectly with use. Nevertheless, the few studies that have examined this issue (e.g., Baker 1983) have found that patrons both use and enjoy a high percentage of materials they check out from the public library (reflecting the fact that many patrons briefly examine the works at the library and leave on the shelves those that they find irrelevant or uninteresting). As we have mentioned elsewhere, past use (of specific authors, titles, genres, or subject areas) will correlate strongly (but still imperfectly) with future use, an assumption supported by research. For example, Eggers (1976) found that 93 percent of the books returned to the Iowa City (Iowa) Public Library had also circulated in the previous year, and Brooks (1984a, 1984b) and Slote (1997) both conclude that past circulation records could be used to roughly forecast overall circulation trends.

The approach described in this chapter requires a means of identifying the use of specific titles, such as the number of times users accessed a computerized product remotely or on-site. For circulating items, libraries with automated systems capable of generating circulation histories for each copy of an owned work will find this information relatively easy to collect. (In fact, as shown throughout this chapter, flexible automated systems with extensive reporting capabilities facilitate collection evaluation so greatly that librarians failing to consider these features when choosing a system would err grievously.) Optimally, circulation systems will provide the number of times an item has circulated since it was added to the collection, as well as quarterly circulation records for the past two or three years, which will allow librarians to capture seasonal use patterns. In libraries without flexible automated systems, recording due dates on cards or labels affixed in or on the materials is the easiest way to gather the necessary data. This method works particularly well when the library does not discard old date-due cards or paste new date-due labels over old, filled ones without at least noting the number of circulations and the relevant period of time on top of the new slip. This can be best done when checking items in, rather than when checking them out to a waiting patron. Given that the use of many works varies seasonally, we recommend collecting at least a full year's worth of use data to provide a reliable base of information on which to make weeding decisions.

IDENTIFYING HEAVILY USED CURRENTLY OWNED ITEMS

Because ready availability of desired items significantly contributes to patron satisfaction, libraries will want to routinely identify formats, genres, and subject areas that receive consistent, heavy use—often so heavy patrons have difficulty obtaining them. Once the mechanical task of collecting the data has been completed, the selector can examine these records and note the extent to which heavily used materials share other characteristics corresponding with high use. Knowing these elements (e.g., intended audience, award winning status, or positive user feedback—whether received at service desks or being designated a 4- or 5-star title by amazon.com users) allows evaluators to emphasize purchase of these, as relevant, in the future.

Identifying those authors whose works receive heavy use is also valuable. For example, Spiller (1980) has shown that most public library patrons have mental lists of 10 or 20 fiction writers whose works they want to read, a pattern we still see today. Once a patron has found one of these authors, he or she often seeks out all the books that author has written within a particular series, literally reading Sue Grafton, for example, from A to (someday) Z. The author pattern applies to nonfiction as well. Consider, for example, the number of patrons who come in seeking works written by Joseph Campbell or Ann Rule.

Finally, the evaluator will identify specific titles in such high demand that patrons have difficulty obtaining them, so that the immediate problem can be corrected. As has been noted throughout this book, the average public library cannot immediately fill at least 25 to 30 percent of patron requests. Although most public libraries will want to set higher goals for title availability, each must consider a variety of factors in determining the percentage of requests it will try to meet immediately. (Chapter 9 discusses these in some detail.)

Librarians can employ a number of different methods to identify heavily used titles, authors, and types of works. We recommend using the three approaches that have been used in public libraries for decades, in their automated versions, wherever applicable:

Scrutinizing reserve lists

Examining circulation records of individual works

Examining circulation totals

Scrutinizing Reserve Lists

Examining the lists of titles for which patrons have filed (in automated or non-automated form) reserves, will underestimate demand to some extent, because, as noted in Chapter 5, not every person who wants to borrow an item will make the effort to reserve it. Nevertheless, scrutinizing reserve lists can quickly identify many works patrons want but cannot immediately obtain. We further recommend that someone on staff take the time to examine these lists and categorize them finely, as illustrated in figure 8.1.

Regularly Examining Circulation Records of Individual Works

On a regular basis (no less frequently than every three months), we recommend that printouts of all items that have circulated heavily (more than X times in Y months, with X related to the subject, genre, and format of the work) be routed to selection staff for their scrutiny. Libraries with manual circulation systems or less flexible automated systems will need to identify heavily used titles in another manner, by asking staff checking in returned materials to scan the date due stamps and record heavily used items. Because this process is time consuming, non-automated libraries with limited staff resources may limit such screening to particularly popular collections, such as DVDs or videos.

1. Publicize the fact that patrons can file reserves to alert the many patrons who still don't know about the service. The promotion should be continuous, so that new patrons as well as old will know about the service, but can be simple. For example, the library can post notices at the catalog, on the ends of the stack sections, and elsewhere, that read:

   > If a library item you want is not on the shelf, you may either file a reserve yourself through our automated catalog or stop at the reference desk so we can file one for you.

   Also, ask staff at public service desks to routinely remind patrons that they can file reserve requests.

2. Whenever possible, do not charge a fee for patrons to reserve items. Although charging a minimal reserve fee may deter "excessive" requests, it also deters legitimate requests and discourages patron feedback about what titles are and are not immediately available for use.

3. Review reserve requests frequently, preferably weekly. The demand for the average title often grows rapidly during a short, intense period of time when the publisher, or media, are promoting it. There may be only two reserve requests for an item when it is first published but 20 by the end of a four-week period.

4. Examine reserve lists for specific titles that patrons have requested. Try to fill these within a short period, preferably no longer than one to two months.
   Remember that even a two-month waiting period is less than ideal. By the time a reserve request is placed, processed, and filled, the patron may have forgotten that he or she wanted the item, borrowed a friend's copy, obtained the item at another library, or purchased it.
   As Chapter 9 notes, a library can fill reserve requests in a variety of ways: purchasing popular items in multiple copies, obtaining these works on a lend-lease plan like those offered by Baker and Taylor Books, and/or shortening the length of the loan period.

5. Remember that providing only enough copies to meet the demand for those patrons interested enough in a particular title to place a reserve on it won't guarantee that the library has enough copies to meet current browsing demand. Consider ordering one or more extra copies for those who bypass the catalog.

6. Note specific authors, genres, and subject areas for which reserves are consistently filed. Such trends may be most apparent when past reserve data are analyzed monthly or quarterly. Modify future selection practices to guarantee higher availability rates for these works.

FIGURE 8.1. Directions for Using Reserve Lists to Identify Heavily Used Works.

In any case, once an evaluator identifies items with heavy past circulation, he or she then more thoroughly investigates use patterns of these titles and other works by the same authors by pulling circulation histories either from the automated system or information recorded in the items. The evaluator can then make decisions about whether these titles need duplication or this class needs expansion. (Both actions are explained in more detail in Chapter 9.) Figure 8.2 and Table 8.1 provide directions for the manual screening of returned works.

1. Determine the availability rate that the library wants to achieve. Although studies have found that many public libraries meet approximately 60 to 75 percent of patron requests for specific items, libraries that want to provide superior service will want to better this percentage.

2. Consult table 8.1 to determine the peak circulation rate for achieving the desired availability rate. The peak circulation rate refers to the point at which the availability rate will drop below a certain level. For example, a library with a 21-day loan period for books that wants to achieve a 70 percent availability rate can identify all books that circulated six or more times per year, which will be off the shelf for an estimated 30 percent of the time or more.

   The peak circulation rate will change when the loan period does. Suppose the same library wants to achieve a 70 percent availability rate for compact discs, which have a two-week loan period. The peak circulation rate for these items would be nine.

3. Create a simple form that lists classes to be checked and their peak circulation rates at the top, followed by lines to record item information (author, title, and call number).

4. Have circulation staff routinely scan the date-due stamps in each item as they check in returned materials, recording works that fall at or above the peak circulation rate on the form created in step 3.

   Note that staff will more quickly be able to identify recent date-due stamps if the library changes the color of the ink that it uses to stamp due dates in January of each year. For example, it could use blue ink one year, red the next, and black the third.

5. As each form is completed, check the shelves, noting circulation patterns of other copies of these titles and of other works by these authors. Modify future selection practices to increase the availability of heavily used items.

FIGURE 8.2. Directions for Screening Returned Works.

TABLE 8.1. Peak Circulation Rates for Achieving Selected Availability Rates.

Desired Availability Rate*	Loan Period in Days	Peak Circulation Rate	Loan Period in Days	Peak Circulation Rate	Loan Period in Days	Peak Circulation Rate	Loan Period in Days	Peak Circulation Rate
91–95%	7	4	14	2	21	1	28	1
86–90%	7	7	14	3	21	2	28	2
81–85%	7	10	14	5	21	3	28	2
76–80%	7	12	14	6	21	4	28	3
71–75%	7	15	14	7	21	5	28	3
66–70%	7	17	14	9	21	6	28	4
61–65%	7	20	14	10	21	6	28	5
56–60%	7	23	14	11	21	7	28	6
51–55%	7	25	14	12	21	8	28	6
46–50%	7	28	14	14	21	9	28	7
41–45%	7	31	14	15	21	10	28	8
36–40%	7	33	14	16	21	11	28	8

*These availability rates were calculated by

– multiplying the annual circulation of each item by the length of the loan period to obtain a rough estimate of the number of days that an item will be absent from the shelves;

– subtracting this figure from 365 to estimate the number of days the item will be on the shelf and ready for patron use; then

– dividing the resulting figure by 365 to estimate the percentage of time that the item is on the shelf and available for patron checkout.

Examining Circulation Totals by Class

Traditionally, public libraries have kept statistics on the number of items that have circulated in various

- user groupings (e.g., children, young adult, and adults);
- formats (e.g., CDs and board books);
- genres (such as science fiction and westerns); and
- subjects (from reader interest categories such as car repair, to broad or narrow groupings within the Dewey Decimal Classification System, such as the 100s or the 590s).

Such totals can reveal heavily or poorly used classes of materials and allow selectors to modify their purchases accordingly. For example, the Metropolitan (Oklahoma City) Library System used the knowledge that 84 percent of nonfiction circulation fell into only 33 Dewey Decimal categories to guide bookmobile selections (Little 1990). And the Skokie (Illinois) Public Library (SPL) has developed a spreadsheet that lists circulation statistics with other collection-related data, such as the number of shelves occupied, volume count, and budget allocation for each area. The spreadsheet breaks down information for each Dewey 10 area (i.e., the 640s) and each subject or format, which allows staff members to quickly ascertain which areas of the collection need immediate attention (Jacob 1990). Prior to the advent of both sophisticated automated circulation systems and powerful spreadsheet software, such analysis was tedious and time-consuming. Today, if your automated system does not routinely provide such capabilities (and we strongly encourage you to lobby for these), staff members could develop spreadsheets to make up for this deficit. Librarians who have experimented with these, for example, the centralized selection staff at the Chicago Public Library, will often willingly share copies to use as a model (Jacob 2000).

Among the many methods that libraries can use to analyze circulation records, we recommend beginning with three simple ones that provide a reasonable overview of use patterns:

Examining circulation totals to see if the use of a class is rising or falling

Calculating the stock turnover rate for each class of items

Calculating the relative use of each class

Examining Circulation Totals to Identify Trends

Libraries of all sizes and resource levels can easily determine whether the use of a class of items is rising, remaining constant, or falling, assuming they keep somewhat detailed circulation records, by examining the percentage of circulation accounted for by that class over several years. Assume that a certain library breaks down circulation by format. It might find that although circulation for the entire collection increased by only 5 percent during the three-year period from 1997 to 2000, the circulation of nonfiction CD-ROMs grew 20 percent during that time, music CDs by 50 percent, and computer books by 400 percent. In the same time period, demand for older media (e.g., filmstrips and LPs) fell sharply, as did demand for car fix-it manuals and western novels. The selector can then explore any subtleties inherent in these figures (e.g., computerization of automobile ignition and other systems has decreased the number of home mechanics) when deciding how the data will be used to guide selection decisions (discussed in more detail in Chapter 9). Figure 8.3 provides directions for exploring trends in the use of a particular class.

---

1. Create a simple, four-column, multi-row table. Label column 1 "Class" and columns 2 through 4 "Total _____ Circulation," where the blank for each column lists the year two years ago, last year, and this year, respectively.

2. Determine for which classes of materials the library has separately recorded annual circulation figures. Record these in column 1.[2]

3. Record the total annual circulation of items in these classes for the last three years in columns 2, 3, and 4 of the table.

4. Examine these circulation figures to determine whether the use of each class is rising or falling over time.

5. Circle with a black pen those classes whose use has risen significantly during the last three years. Consider allocating more of the materials budget to purchasing works in these classes.

6. Circle with a red pen those classes whose use has fallen significantly during the last three years. Examine these to determine if there is anything wrong (e.g., circulation may be decreasing because no new books in this area have been purchased) or if lack of use seems to reflect a decline in popularity of this type of work (e.g., LPs). Once the reasons for declining use have been identified, consider changing selection patterns for these classes of works.

FIGURE 8.3. Directions for Determining Circulation Trends by Class.

Calculating the Stock Turnover Rate for Each Class

Calculating stock turnover rate (the average annual circulation per item) requires that the evaluator divide the total annual circulation of a class (preferably finely subdivided) by total volumes held in that class. We recommend that all libraries calculate turnover rate for as many classes of items as feasible, to allow fine examination of the use of related classes of items. A librarian who knows that the average fiction turnover rate is 1.5 can quickly see that patrons more heavily demand mystery fiction, with a turnover rate of 6.0, than fantasy, which has a rate of 1.5, although current materials budgets for each area may be disproportionate to their use. Although many automated systems allow these data to be easily extracted, librarians can also gather this information manually. Figure 8.4 provides directions for calculating the stock turnover rate for different classes.

Calculating the Relative Use of Each Class

Circulation totals can be even more revealing when expressed in terms of relative use, a measure that compares the amount of use that a portion of the collection actually receives with the amount of use that simple mathematical calculations predict. Suppose that works on economics constitute 3 percent of the total adult nonfiction collection and chemistry 4 percent. If the collection matches user needs, we would logically expect economics to receive 3 percent of the total circulation and chemistry 4 percent. If economics actually accounts for 6 percent of the nonfiction circulation and chemistry for only 1 percent, economics is an over-used class and chemistry under-used.

Relative use figures can help libraries of all sizes identify major collection strengths and weaknesses; they are most effective when calculated by fine class. For example, a brief examination might reveal that the 640s are over-used, but a comprehensive analysis could show that 641.5, cookbooks, receives disproportionately high use whereas the other subclasses are either under-used or used at the level expected.

Librarians can calculate relative use figures by subject area, genre area, reading level, format, or author as long as their circulation system allows for the collection of such statistics. For example, staff at the Metropolitan (Oklahoma City) Library System found that uncataloged paperbacks (representing 16 percent of the collection) accounted for 26 percent of its use. Further analysis showed that the cost per circulation for paperbacks was less than one-third the cost for hardbacks, leading that library to greatly expand its softcover collection (Little 1979).

1. Create a simple four-column, multi-row table. Label column 1 "Class," column 2 "Total Yearly Circulation," column 3 "Total Volumes Held," and column 4 "Stock Turnover Rate."

2. Determine for which classes of items the library has information on both the total number of volumes held and the total annual circulation. Record these in column 1 of the table. Group related classes (e.g., all types of adult fiction) together on the form for ease of interpreting the findings.[3]

3. Record in column 2 the total annual circulation of each class.

4. Record in column 3 the total number of volumes held in each class.

5. Divide the figure in column 2 by that in column 3 to get the stock turn-over rate. Record this figure in column 4.

6. Add together all the annual circulation figures from column 2 and record here. _____

7. Add together all the total volume figures from column 3 and record here. _____

8. Divide the figure in line 6 by the figure in line 7 and record the average stock turnover rate for the collection as a whole here. _____

9. Compare the average stock turnover rate for one class with those of the collection as a whole and of related classes. This will help identify areas in which there is particularly heavy demand.

10. Circle with a black pen those classes with turnover rates significantly higher than average. These are classes for which there is currently heavy demand. Ask the selector to strengthen these classes to better meet demand.

11. Circle with a red pen those classes with turnover rates significantly lower than average. Examine these underused classes to determine if anything is wrong. For example, a low use of westerns might be caused by a lack of interest in this genre among library patrons, but it could also be the result of a dingy, outdated, unappealing collection. Ask the selector to change purchasing patterns to resolve the problems identified.

FIGURE 8.4. Directions for Determining Turnover Rate by Class.

How much must use of a class vary from what would be expected before it can be considered over-used or under-used? Mills (1982) correctly notes that simply examining the raw differences between the percentage of holdings and the percentage of circulation of each class can mislead. Using these calculations, a subject occupying 0.6 percent of the collection and receiving 0.8 percent of the use would be equivalent to one occupying 3.5 percent of the collection and receiving 3.7 percent of the use. But the discrepancy between holdings and use is 33 percent for the smaller class and only 6 percent for the larger.

Mills recommends that librarians instead multiply the relative use factor (the percentage of use divided by the percentage of holdings) by 100 to create the percentage of expected use (PEU). Thus, the PEU concept suggests that the expected use of a subject will be 100 percent. The librarian then ranks the PEUs of various classes in a continuum from high to low and designates cutoff points to represent over-used and under-used classes. For example, classes with PEUs below 80 percent may be labeled under-used and those with PEUs above 120 percent over-used, a simple yet viable calculation. An alternative option is to calculate the mean PEU, determine the standard deviation, then label classes with PEUs that are one or more standard deviations above or below the mean as over-used or under-used. This practice, described in some detail by Dowlin and Magrath (1983), will classify about one-third of the classes of materials as under-used or over-used and therefore in need of attention. Given the complexity of the formulas involved, we recommend that this approach be done with a sophisticated spreadsheet package such as Excel.

To interpret relative use data, keep in mind that they indicate a deviation from expected behavior without explaining why. For example, a class could be under-used because it contains dated materials, materials too specialized or technical to meet user needs, or subject matter not popular with patrons, matters the selector will keep in mind when ordering new materials.

Relative use figures will be easiest to calculate for libraries with automated circulation systems that can be programmed to generate information on the number of titles and holdings in a particular class. Indeed, some automated systems even allow relative use to be calculated by subject and location simultaneously (e.g., Nimmer 1980). This is quite useful because branches within the same system might receive different amounts of use in the same subject area due to the different interests of the clients they serve.

Other libraries will have to spend more time manually calculating relative use figures and may wish to phase in relative use calculations, concentrating first on those areas that staff believe are over- or under-used. Figure 8.5 provides directions for calculating relative use rates.

1. Create a form that lists, at the top, the total number of volumes in the circulating collection and the total annual circulation for the collection as a whole. Below that create a six-column, multi-row table. Label column 1 "Class," column 2 "Total Volumes in Class," column 3 "Percentage of Collection Class Occupies," column 4 "Annual Circulation of Class," column 5 "Percentage of Circulation Class Accounts For," and column 6 "Percentage of Expected Use."

2. Determine for which classes of items the library has information on both the total volumes held and the total annual circulation. Record these in column 1, locating related classes (e.g., all adult fiction) next to each other on the form for ease of interpretation.[4]

3. Record in column 2 the total number of volumes held in each class.

4. Divide each figure in column 2 by the total number of volumes held in the circulating collection to obtain the percentage of the total collection occupied by that class. Record these percentages in column 3.

5. Record in column 4 the number of items that circulated in each class during the past year.

6. Divide each figure in column 4 by the total annual circulation for the collection as a whole to obtain the percentage of circulation accounted for by that class. Record these figures in column 5.

7. Divide the figures in column 5 (percentage of circulation) by those in column 3 (percentage of holdings) and multiply by 100 to obtain the percentage of expected use (PEU). Record these figures in column 6.

8. On a separate sheet of paper, list the PEUs of all classes in rank order, with the highest PEU at the top and the lowest at the bottom.

9. Define the thresholds that represent over-used and under-used classes. For example, a library may designate classes with PEUs of 120 or above as over-used and ones with a PEU of 80 or below as under-used.

10. Purchase more materials, following market-based selection practices, to strengthen over-used classes.

11. Examine under-used classes to determine what is wrong (e.g., dated collection of overly technical works, lack of patron interest). Change selection practices and budgets to resolve the problems identified.

FIGURE 8.5. Directions for Calculating Relative Use by Class.

IDENTIFYING CURRENTLY OWNED
ITEMS THAT ARE NOT USED

Identifying poorly used items is part of the weeding process. Regular weeding helps maintain an attractive, appealing collection and ensures that nonfiction works contain relevant, reliable information. Weeding can also stretch existing shelf space. As public libraries continue to collect newly published items and diversify by purchasing materials in new formats, their space needs grow. Yet the governmental bodies that fund libraries cannot always afford to replace crowded facilities. Even when the library's funding agency supports a building project, voters can fail to approve one, especially in times of public skepticism about the economy or government.

By examining poorly used items, evaluators can also determine patterns of nonuse indicating a poor fit between a target market and the items in the relevant collection. Recording nonuse provides objective data that can help selectors make informed decisions about future purchases. It also alerts the library to "good" but little-used works already in the collection that might merit promotion.

In addition to the processes we describe below, works on weeding suggest other practical approaches to identify poorly used titles. In particular, we recommend that librarians examine Slote (1997) and Segal (1995).

Screening Items in
the Circulating Collection

Librarians will need to consider three questions related to this matter. First, how often does the collection require screening? For a small collection, an evaluator will want to try to identify unused works each year, time permitting (Slote 1989). Larger libraries and libraries with limited staff resources will want to try to identify unused titles in each section of the collection at least every other year.

Second, when will screening occur? An evaluator can more clearly identify trends in use if he or she examines an entire section of similar works in a fairly short period of time. For example, the evaluator might screen all westerns during the third week of March, all nonfiction videos during the second week of May, and all online databases during the fourth week of August. This will help ensure a "fair" comparison of works.

Finally, what is a poorly used title? This answer will correspond to the library's overall level of use and the section being examined. A library may consider an audiobook that circulates only three times per year poorly used and a philosophical treatise that circulates the same amount very popular. Librarians can perhaps best answer the question "What constitutes little or no use?" by comparing item circulation to the stock turnover rate (i.e., the annual circulation per volumes held, discussed in "Calculating the Stock Turnover Rate for Each Class," see page 206) for that section of the collection.

Multiplying the turnover rate by the percentage of the section that the library wants to weed will present a minimum circulation standard. Titles that fall below this figure—the least used section of the collection—can be considered for weeding. Libraries with severely overcrowded shelves (and no plans to move into a new building) may want to weed as much as 20 percent of the collection. Libraries that want to increase the size of their collection over time can certainly weed less stringently, although we recommend weeding at least 5 to 10 percent of the collection per year to maintain vitality over time, focusing on nonused works and those that contain dated, erroneous, or non-unique information.

Screening Items in
the Non-Circulating Collection

Studies showing in-house use of materials to be as high or higher than circulation demonstrate the value of regularly examining non-circulating collections. Indeed, in a review of in-house use studies in all types of libraries, Baker and Lancaster (1991) found that ratios of in-house use to circulation ranged from 0.1:1 to 11.2:1.

Where do we obtain in-house use statistics? We recommend asking online vendors to supply the use statistics for their resources (most collect at least some routinely). For other non-circulating materials, we recommend placing signs near the locations of these items asking patrons to put materials they use in-house on tables or in specially marked areas, rather than reshelving them. Volunteers or staff members should collect these items at least once a day, stamp the date used on a label affixed to the inside front or back covers, and reshelve them. These stamped labels then serve the same purpose as the date-due labels in circulating titles, providing a permanent record of use in each work. When ready to screen certain sections of the collection, evaluators can rather quickly scan the labels to identify heavily or poorly used items.[5]

Although this method will underestimate use to some extent—some patrons will ignore the signs and reshelve items anyway (Rubin 1986)—an underestimate of use helps more than no data whatsoever. Figure 8.6, pages 212–14, provides directions for screening the collection to identify under-used items.

1. Determine which sections of the collection will be screened, how often, and when.

2. For each section of the collection, answer the question "What constitutes little or no use?" To determine this for *circulating or computerized* materials:

    • Divide the total annual circulation or use (number of times accessed) of works in this section by the number of holdings in this section to obtain the average usage rate.

    • Determine the percentage of the collection that will be weeded. This figure will likely be in the 5 to 20 percent range for print materials.

    • Multiply this percentage by the average usage rate of a particular section of works. Works whose average yearly circulation or use falls below this represent the least consulted portion of the collection. For example, if a library wants to weed 10 percent of its mystery collection (which has a stock turnover rate of 11.0), it would consider weeding any title whose average yearly circulation fell below 10 percent x 11.0—below 1.1.

    • Computerized resources may also be analyzed by cost per use, dividing the total subscription or licensing costs by the average usage rate for individual products and online resources as a whole.

    To determine this for *noncirculating, noncomputerized* materials:

    • Draw a random sample of items from the section.

    • Add the total number of uses recorded during the last year on the date-used label affixed to each work (that is, add together the total annual use figures for each of the works in the sample).

    • Divide this figure by 100 to give the average annual use per item.

    • Determine the percentage of the collection to be weeded (from 5 to 20 percent).

    • Multiply this percentage by the average annual use per item to obtain a cut-off point for weeding.

3. Identify all works whose annual use falls at or below this cutoff point for this section. For circulating or computerized resources, libraries may be able to request a printout of all works that meet this criterion from their automated system or online product vendor. For libraries without this option and for other kinds of resources, ask a clerical staff member to physically examine the date-due (or date used) slip in each work. Once identified, turn all low-use items spine up.

FIGURE 8.6. Directions for Screening Under-Used Items.

Studies have shown that libraries can predict, with less than a 10 percent error rate, future use of individual items from a single year's use data. This error rate will be an acceptable one for most libraries; however, a library can reduce it even further by calculating the average annual use rate for each item with data from the past two or three years.

5. Examine spine-up works at the shelves to allow use of each item to be placed in context with other materials in that collection.

6. Examine each item, noting the title, author, genre, and format. Based on standard weeding criteria, determine whether the item should be removed from the collection. The most common criteria, other than use, are physical condition, currency of information, and quality or value of contents (Slote 1989). In the latter instance, ask whether the work has enough value to keep it in the collection in spite of low use. For example, is the work

   • listed in *Fiction Catalog*, *Public Library Catalog*, or on one of ALA's "Notable Books" lists?

   • written by an author who lives in this city, state, or region?

   • the recipient of a prize or award for its high quality?

   • part of a series that is not being discarded in its entirety?

   • one of only a few works of its type, genre, or subject area?

   • one that has a larger social or historical significance?

7. Place on a book cart titles to be weeded: those that are not well used, contain inaccurate or obsolete information, are in poor condition, or are no longer of value to the library.

8. List the author, title, and call number of works that would normally be discarded because of low use but are deemed valuable enough to be kept, on a form titled "Under-Used Items to Consider for Promotion." Note the section and date screened at the top. Give completed forms to the person responsible for promoting this section of the collection.

9. Record the names of authors whose works have received little or no use on another sheet titled "Under-Used Authors." Note the section and date screened at the top. These authors are likely to remain under-used over time, although the reasons for this may vary. Forward this information to the relevant selector(s) to de-emphasize future purchases of these authors, when relevant.

(Fig. 8.6 continues on page 214.)

FIG. 8.6—*Continued*

10. Note other consistent trends of nonuse on a third sheet titled "Other Under-Used Items." Note the section and date screened at the top, list each type of work with low use, and suggest possible reasons for this. Some of these trends are consistent across many public libraries, such as low levels of use of older works in the hard sciences or of subject areas that many people would consider technical or esoteric. Other trends, peculiar to a specific library and clientele, are discovered only with careful scrutiny. For example, a public library located in a conservative community may discover that "lust-full" novels (westerns like the Longarm series and spicy romances) are not generally popular with its patrons but that gentle reads (like Jan Karon's Mitford books) are. When identifying possible reasons for low or falling use, take care not to make erroneous assumptions, such as that interest in "high technology" science fiction is dying out if that collection is really just too outdated to be of interest. Forward this information to the relevant selector(s) to de-emphasize future purchases in these areas, as appropriate.

11. Take the cart of items to be weeded to the technical processing area. Follow the library's standard procedures for removing these works from the collection.

IDENTIFYING ITEMS NOT IN
THE COLLECTION
BUT LIKELY TO RECEIVE USE

In addition to focusing on over- or under-used items currently in the collection, evaluators work to identify items currently not in the collection that might meet residents' needs. In the past, librarians have often done this as the opportunity arose, for example, examining the collection after hearing a patron complain that it has no current price guide for antique furniture. We recommend an active approach in which evaluators regularly seek information about specific authors, titles, and types of works that might be added to the collection.

Evaluators can collect this information in several ways: by examining interlibrary loan records, analyzing unanswered reference and readers' advisory questions, soliciting patron suggestions for new purchases, soliciting recommendations from community interest groups and experts, surveying patrons and potential patrons using questionnaires or focus group interviews, and checking recommended lists.

Examining Interlibrary Loan Records

Many librarians automatically consider purchasing requested materials in line with the library's mission and service responses. Optimally, selectors will review interlibrary loan requests at the time they are made to quickly obtain desired titles. Studies have shown that most interlibrary loan requests are for current, in-print titles and that works purchased as a result of interlibrary loan requests circulate at equivalent or higher rates than titles selected by library staff (e.g., Perdue and Van Fleet 1999; Roberts and Cameron 1984).

Librarians will also want to examine past interlibrary loan requests on a regular basis (we suggest monthly) to determine whether patrons consistently request specific types of materials that they need to purchase in greater quantity. For example, a public library may note a number of loan requests for magazines it does not own and then subscribe to the most requested titles in print or via a full-text online service. We recommend analyzing interlibrary loan requests by author, format, genre, and subject area, at least.

Analyzing Unanswered Reference and Readers' Advisory Questions

Many libraries record the subject matter of all reference questions they cannot answer so that they can determine whether they need to augment specific sections of the nonfiction collection. To improve fiction and other popular material collections, staff can record similar information about unanswered readers' advisory questions in a notebook, word processing file, or database designed for this purpose, sharing these questions with the relevant selector(s) on a weekly basis. Both practices require little staff time and can be adopted by libraries of all sizes and resource levels.

Soliciting Patron Suggestions for New Purchases

Libraries of all sizes and resource levels can cheaply, easily, and routinely gather purchase suggestions by widely distributing purchase suggestion forms (e.g., posting them on the Web site as well as placing them in all departments). They can also request that each staff member who works at a public service desk ask each patron whether he or she found what he or she was looking for. In addition to identifying items to consider for purchase, actively soliciting comments reinforces that staff members care about patron needs. Figures 8.7 and 8.8, pages 216 and 217, provide directions for, and the form associated with, soliciting patron suggestions.

Ideally, staff members who work at each public service desk (circulation, reference, audiovisual, etc.) will

- ask each patron who visits the desk, "Were you looking for a specific item or type of work today? (If so) did you find what you wanted?"

  Asking these questions alerts staff to patrons whose needs are not fully satisfied. Staff can then tactfully determine whether patrons checked the catalog or asked the reference librarian for help. If not, patrons can be given further assistance.

- ask patrons who are still unable to find what they wanted if they would complete a purchase suggestion form of the type shown in figure 8.8.

  Note that some libraries will want to save time by requesting that the patron complete one of the order cards that staff routinely use rather than a purchase request form. This works best when the order card

  ✓ is short and easy to complete;

  ✓ requests information about desired authors, titles, subject areas, genres, and formats; and

  ✓ asks the patron if he or she wishes to discuss his collection needs further with a librarian.

- give each completed form to the person responsible for selecting materials in that section of the collection.

FIGURE 8.7. Directions for Soliciting Patron Suggestions.

The library welcomes your suggestions for purchase. Please list below works that you would like to see added to the collection. We will consider every purchase suggestion seriously, although, due to budget considerations, we may not be able to order every item requested. Thank you.

Subject area, genre area, or format of work desired:

Title desired:

Full name of author, composer, or producer of this work:

Publisher and publication date (if known):

If you would like someone on our staff to call you to discuss your request or to notify you when it can be checked out, please list your name and telephone number below.

FIGURE 8.8. Form for Soliciting Patron Suggestions.

Soliciting Recommendations from
Community Interest Groups and Experts

Community interest groups or experts can also provide valuable suggestions about materials to consider adding. Librarians can fairly easily send a customized form letter, seeking purchase suggestions on a relevant area of the collection (e.g., asking the computer club for software recommendations), along with an addressed, stamped envelope in which to return the form. Staff can then check suggestions against current holdings, upgrade the collection as necessary, and promote the improved collection to the group that helped make it better as well as other potential users. Figure 8.9, page 219, and figure 8.10, pages 220 and 221, provide directions for creating such a mailing as well as sample letters.

Speaking directly to local experts or hobbyists who have a vested interest in keeping the library's collection in a particular area strong may result in a higher response rate and perhaps more thoughtful or extensive input. This will be most helpful when the individuals providing assistance are already familiar with the library's current holdings or are willing to review them, because they can then also suggest titles that the librarian may want to consider weeding. For example, the librarian at the Dakota County (Minnesota) Law Library provided the Dakota County (Minnesota) Library with a list of reliable self-help legal guides to replace current titles unsuited to Minnesota court requirements (Archer 2000).

Given the extensive time commitment required, librarians will likely be unable to speak with all clubs, organizations, and experts that could help. Therefore, librarians will need to be mindful of the collections that most need improvement as they decide how many market segments they can feasibly serve, which groups they will target, and which collections will best meet patron needs, before approaching people who can help strengthen these.

1. Select one or more collections librarians want to improve, in keeping with selected service responses and goals—both derived from an assessment of community needs.

2. Identify clubs, agencies, organizations, churches, businesses, and other groups whose members may have insights into the chosen collection(s). These may be found using phone books, Web sites, and other community directories or agency listings, as well as by talking to staff and patrons, personnel of local government, schools for all ages, umbrella social service agencies like the United Way, the Chamber of Commerce, and other institutions aware of community resources, like the senior center, a volunteer placement center, or a welcome program for new residents.

3. Determine the number of groups the library can feasibly contact, remembering that it will take time to consider the information the group provides, address issues they raise or purchase materials they suggest (as relevant), and then re-contact them to let them know the outcome of their assistance. In cases where a large number of groups may be contacted, consider staggering the times at which letters are sent.

4. Determine the name, address, and phone number of the president, community liaison, outreach specialist, or other relevant contact for each selected group.

5. Draft a letter that can be tailored to fit each group, inviting their input on the collection in question. This can be done fairly simply by using the merge function of a word processing program, then massaging the wording of each letter as needed. In the letter, clearly ask what you would like the group to do. Figure 8.10, page 220, contains sample letters.

6. Send the letters, including a postage-paid, self-addressed response card or form and an envelope, with each. Volunteers may assist with the mailing preparation.

7. Record responses received and begin to follow up on suggestions made, passing on tangential collection concerns to the relevant library department. For groups that do not reply within a month, consider calling the contact to make sure the group received the letter and know how much the library would like their input.

8. Contact each group that provided information to thank them and let them know the outcome of their assistance and the name(s) of staff members who can help with any tangential issues previously identified.

FIGURE 8.9. Directions for Soliciting Expert or Interest Group Suggestions.

Complete Sample Letter

January 1, 2002

<u>Ann Philips</u>
<u>Smiley City Senior Center</u>
<u>555 Forest Ave.</u>
<u>Smiley City, NE 68111</u>

Dear <u>Ms. Philips:</u>

As the <u>Director</u> of the <u>Senior Center,</u> you know that the Smiley City Public Library offers a large print collection to help alleviate eye strain and serve the reading needs of those with low-vision. Because <u>a number of your members may enjoy these materials,</u> we hope you can help us in our continuing efforts to build a superior collection.

Please take a few moments to consult with members of your organization and complete the enclosed suggestion form. We have also enclosed an addressed, postage-paid envelope for your use.

Thank you very much for your time and insights.

Sincerely,

Cynthia Jones
Director, Smiley City Library

P.S. Remember, the library offers a community bulletin board where we can post flyers for your organization (mail them to Postings, 123 Main St., Smiley City, NE 68111) and rooms that you can reserve for meetings or programs (call the Information Desk at 123-1234). If there are other services we can provide, please let us know.

First Paragraph of Second Sample Letter

As the <u>President </u>of the <u>Lions Club,</u> you know that the Smiley City Public Library offers a large print collection to help alleviate eye-strain and serve the reading needs of those with low-vision. Because <u>you share this goal,</u> we hope you can help us in our continuing efforts to build a superior collection....

FIGURE 8.10. Sample Letters and Suggestion Form for Library That Has Opted to Improve Its Large Print Collection.

Suggestion Form

Thank you for helping the Smiley City Public Library improve its large print collection.

Please consider the following works for purchase in large print:

Title _____ Author _____

Title _____ Author _____

Title _____ Author _____

Title _____ Author _____

Title _____ Author _____

Title _____ Author _____

Title _____ Author _____

Please purchase more large print works (list specific subjects, authors, or other features desired):

_____

_____

_____

Other ways to improve our collections and services for those your organization serves include:

_____

_____

_____

Please give names and phone numbers of those who contributed to this form, in case we need to get more information.

Name _____ Phone _____

Name _____ Phone _____

Name _____ Phone _____

Name _____ Phone _____

Notes

- Given the topic, librarians would want to consider printing these materials, particularly the response form, in large type. For example, the Director of the Senior Center may ask members with low vision to help her complete the form.

- Items underscored in the letters indicate merge fields.

Surveying Patrons and Potential Patrons
Using Questionnaires or Focus Group Interviews

By talking formally or informally with current and potential patrons—those who do not currently use the library but have an interest in the kind of materials it offers—librarians can learn what collection improvements might better serve or attract them. Such input will be most valuable if the library does one of the following:

- Ask for in-depth comments about one section of the collection at a time. Optimally, this will be a section either given priority in the library's strategic plan or identified as greatly in need of improvement.

- Focus on one target market at a time. For example, the Chicago Public Library used a survey to determine the collection-related needs of one group of public housing residents before planning library service for public housing communities in general (Spiller 1989). In some instances, the choice of target market will be guided by the roles the library will play. In others, it will be influenced by the resources under examination. For example, a library interested in updating its career development materials could solicit suggestions for improvement from high school and college students, guidance counselors, and area career development specialists.

Questionnaires

Questionnaires are often used when a library wants to survey a target market comprising some subset of patrons, such as people with children in tow or CD browsers. Staff can simply ask these users to complete and return questionnaires during a regular library visit.

Questionnaires can also effectively solicit input from a target market outside the library with an easily reached set of members. For example, the Atwood-Hammond (Illinois) Public Library had students in local junior high and high school classes complete questionnaires to determine their general levels of interest in reading, the places where they obtained reading material, and the types of books they most liked to read (Obert 1988). It will, of course, cost the library more to survey target markets outside the library, because of travel and distribution costs. Figures 8.11 and 8.12, pages 223 and 224, provide directions for using materials preference questionnaires and a sample questionnaire.

1. Determine whether the library will pass out questionnaires to all persons in the target market or a sample of the same. The former can be done if the number of persons in the target market is relatively small. If the target market is large, the library can obtain reliable information about how the collection may be improved if it draws a representative sample. Read Hernon and McClure (1990) and other standard research guides in the field for information on choosing a representative sample.

2. (If the library is surveying a group other than its own users) ask for cooperation from group leaders and/or members of the target market.

3. Design a survey form that asks members of the target market about

   - their knowledge of the collection under study;

   - their existing use of this collection;

   - their general suggestions for improving this collection; and

   - their specific suggestions for authors, titles, and types of works that the library might buy.

   An example of this type of survey, designed for distribution to all those who browsed among or who checked out a work from the videotape collection during a two-week period, is shown in figure 8.12.

   The questionnaire should be short, easy to complete, and worded in a clear and unbiased fashion. Read Powell (1997) or other standard research guides in the field for information on designing effective questionnaires.

4. Pretest the questionnaire by asking five to six members of the target group to complete it. Review each question asked with each person surveyed to ensure that its meaning is clear and unambiguous.

5. Revise the questionnaire in light of pretest comments.

6. Make as many copies of the revised questionnaire as are needed.

7. Distribute the questionnaire.

8. Tally and summarize the results.

9. Consider changing selection practices, when relevant, as a result of these findings.

FIGURE 8.11. Directions for Using Materials Preference Questionnaires.

Thank you for agreeing to take five minutes to give us your suggestions for improving our collection of videotapes.

The library has a number of different collections of videotapes. For each kind listed, please check whether you were aware of this collection, whether you have used it during the last year, and (if so) how many times.

	Were you aware of this collection?		Have you used this collection during the last year?		If yes, approximately how many times?
Videotape Collection	Yes	No	Yes	No	
Horror films					
Science fiction films					
Comedy films					
Action/adventure films					
Drama					
Television shows					
Music videos					
Exercise videos					
How-to-do-it videos					
Travel videos					
Walt Disney movies					
Other children's videos					

Are there any specific films that you would like the library to purchase for its collection?

Do you have any other suggestions on how the collection might be improved?

If you would like to talk further about this matter with the librarian responsible for this collection, indicate your name, address, and telephone number below.

Please return completed forms to the circulation desk. Thank you.

FIGURE 8.12. Sample Video Preference Questionnaire.

Focus Group Studies

Because a number of markets, such as women who work outside the home, have no identifiable membership list and are therefore time-consuming to survey, librarians can conduct focus group interviews instead. In brief, focus groups comprise 10 to 15 users or potential users interested in the section of the collection being evaluated and willing to donate one to two hours of their time to sharing their knowledge. Under the direction of a moderator to provide focus, as relevant, group members discuss specific actions the library can take to meet their collection-related needs. Optimally, the interviews are taped to give the library a tangible record of all suggestions made.

Focus groups can provide several other benefits. First, the interaction that occurs during discussions often reveals why patrons feel the way they do, insights crucial to increasing levels of use or satisfaction with the collection. For example, staff at the Iowa City (Iowa) Public Library (ICPL) found that few business people used library resources to help them in their work because of a lack of knowledge about what the library had to offer (Baker 1991a).

As a second added benefit, focus group participants often provide useful suggestions about how a library can effectively promote its collection to those whom participants represent. For example, the Iowa City focus group participants suggested that ICPL publicize its business collection and services in the Chamber of Commerce newsletter and through small tours designed to meet the needs of specific target markets, such as realtors and government employees.

A third advantage of focus groups is that participants may learn more about resources in the existing collection simply by listening to their colleagues talk. At the end of each session, the librarian can also distribute information detailing the kinds of resources in the existing collection and give short tours to interested parties. Those who attended the business focus groups at ICPL, in fact, said that these discussions had made them more aware of and more likely to use existing collections (Baker 1991a).

We recommend scheduling more than one focus group for each collection under discussion to enhance the reliability of results by increasing the number of suggestions and helping the library determine which issues (those repeatedly mentioned in different groups) matter most to participants. The Orange (New Jersey) Public Library followed this practice in 1990 when it scheduled a series of ten focus groups. Five focused on determining the collection-related needs of parents who wanted to expose their children to library services and five on adults who checked out popular materials for their own use (Baker 1991c).

Hutton and Walters (1988) describe how other public libraries have used the process to identify problems and make changes, and Ledingham and Bruning (1998) offer tips for improving focus groups. Figure 8.13, pages 226–27, provides directions for conducting focus group discussions. These assume that the library has already determined the collection and the target markets on which they will focus. For more detailed information about the focus group method, see Krueger and Casey (2000), Johnson (1996), Wagner and Mahmoodi (1994), and Connaway (1996).

As part of the initial planning for the interview,

1. Develop a list of questions that focus specifically on this collection. Ideally, the questions will be open-ended to encourage discussion and placed in a logical order. We recommend concentrating on the participants' current impressions of this collection, their levels of use or nonuse, and their suggestions for how the collection might be improved. Sample questions follow:

   • What do you know about the library's collection of materials on _____?

   • Do you, or does anyone you know, use the collection now?

   • If so, how?

   • If not, why not?

   • What do you currently like about this collection?

   • How might the library improve this collection?

   • Could the library do anything to promote use of this collection more effectively?

2. Type the list of questions for later distribution to focus group participants.

3. Decide how many focus groups will be planned. Scheduling more than one will allow the library to obtain a broader base of suggestions and to identify themes common to all groups.

4. Choose the dates and times of the focus group interviews. Many patrons will find it convenient to attend on weekday evenings or weekend afternoons. Allow one and one-half hours for each session. This time period is long enough to allow in-depth discussion to develop but short enough to recruit willing participants.

5. Choose the location(s) where the focus group interviews will be held. Ideally, interviews will take place within the library to permit participants to review the library's existing collection, if they choose. Choose meeting rooms capable of seating 10 to 20 people around a table.

6. Determine whether interviews will be limited to current patrons or will include potential patrons as well. Although it may be harder to persuade potential patrons to participate, they may have real insight into why an existing collection is unused.

FIGURE 8.13. Directions for Conducting a Focus Group Interview.

7. Solicit from library staff, Friends, trustees, and patrons the names, addresses, and telephone numbers of people who might be willing to donate one to two hours of time to answer the library's questions. The librarian should ask about three times as many people to come as will be needed, because many of the persons invited will not actually attend.

8. Write to possible participants, explaining what the library is trying to accomplish and giving the dates and times of the interviews. Include the list of questions that will be asked so that participants can think about the issues in advance. Include self-addressed, stamped postcards so those invited can inform the library which, if any, session they will attend.

9. Choose someone to serve as moderator of the focus group interviews. The moderator should be friendly and possess good social and communication skills so that group members will feel comfortable talking freely in a group of strangers. Ideally, he or she will also have some training in soliciting comments in a way that will not bias results. Note that, whenever possible, the moderator should not be a library staff member, because this may inhibit critical comments from group participants.

10. Call and remind focus group participants about the interviews two to three days before they are scheduled to come.

11. On the day of each focus group study, the librarian will:

    • have a volunteer make coffee for participants, run the tape recorder during the actual session, and record the names of all persons who attended; and

    • make sure that the moderator understands what needs to be done. This person must greet participants, explain the library's purpose in conducting this sort of study, ask the questions that have been decided on, encourage discussion among participants, obtain clarification when necessary, and tactfully move the discussion forward if any one person tries to dominate the discussion.

12. After the focus group interview is finished, the librarian will:

    • write thank-you notes to all those who attended;

    • have the tape recording transcribed;

    • class the suggestions made into broad categories for easy review;

    • determine which of the suggestions are both suitable and affordable; and

    • change selection practices, when relevant.

Checking Recommended Lists

Finally, librarians may wish to check their holdings against various lists aligned with library goals. For example, a library emphasizing the formal learning support service response may wish to gather school-created booklists, both curriculum-related ones and suggested summer reading, and purchase relevant titles it does not already own. In a similar vein, a library adopting the basic literacy service response may wish to check the annual Public Library Association's Adult Lifelong Learning Section list of recommended adult new readers.

Most libraries will also want to purchase at least some materials found in lists of high-quality items, such as "notable" lists, like those issued by the American Library Association, the National Science Teachers Association, and other professional or educational groups. Other sources include annual compilations of editor's choices of best resources, like those listed in *School Library Journal*, and lists of materials that have won various private awards, like the Hugo or Nebula awards for science fiction and fantasy. Here again, service responses will influence the target percentage of each that a library wants to hold. For example, a library emphasizing consumer information may be satisfied with owning many fewer titles on the RITA romance award winners' list than would a current-topics-and-titles library. Typically, a library may purchase more titles on high profile lists, whether Coretta Scott King or Caldecott winners, the YALSA Best Books for Young Adults annual compilation, or a local newspaper feature identifying the titles that most influenced high-profile area residents as children. Staff members of the White Plains (New York) Public Library buy all titles on the *New York Times* bestseller list for the Express Book Collection, which offers three-day loans (Dow 1998).

IDENTIFYING OTHER BARRIERS THAT INHIBIT USE OF THE COLLECTION

Librarians can also thoroughly explore barriers that inhibit collection use. As Kantor (1976) notes in a classic work on the subject, these may be related to factors associated with

- acquisitions (e.g., the library may not own the needed item);
- circulation (e.g., another patron may be using the title);
- library errors (e.g., mis-shelving may prevent the item from being located); or
- patron errors (e.g., a patron may look for Ellis Peters's latest novel in the general fiction collection rather than in the mystery section).

Some of the evaluation methods already presented attempt to address the first two concerns, identifying desired titles the library does not own at all or in insufficient number. A patron-based materials availability study can also indicate the impact of all four factors by determining the percentage of materials immediately available when patrons seek them and noting the extent to which each of the above barriers hinders availability.

The popularity of patron-based availability studies has risen during the last few years, in part because *Output Measures for Public Libraries* (Van House et al. 1987) promotes this type of measurement. In such a study, staff members distribute questionnaires that ask patrons entering the library on selected days to record the specific items or types of items they were seeking and whether they found them.

Issues Involved in Planning Availability Studies

Public librarians may beneficially follow several guidelines when planning such studies.[6] First, librarians may conduct separate availability studies at each of the institution's major outlets because availability rates from one location may not represent all libraries within the system.

Second, given that availability rates will differ significantly by format, the library may wish to gather separate statistics for print and nonprint material availability. Although higher levels of demand (as for popular videos and audiobooks) account for some of this difference, another large portion may result from a library's practice of using different methods and procedures for acquiring, cataloging, and storing audiovisual materials than it does for print.

Third, to ensure that the library collects data representative of all users, it needs to collect information on a fairly large number of items. Collecting a sample of 500 requests will ensure that the library obtains reliable data on the total percentage of patron needs it fills (Kantor 1984). Small libraries that cannot collect this much information in a reasonable period will want to gather as many questionnaires as possible. Collecting a sufficient number of samples will also allow librarians to analyze information by class to compare availability rates. Optimally, a library would work first on correcting the lowest rates, likely to be for highly popular formats, genre areas, or subjects. The evaluator will need to take care to avoid dividing the sample into too many small subdivisions because availability rates calculated on a handful of items may not be representative of the total group. All but the smallest libraries will want to ensure that these smaller classes contain at least 25 items to accurately calculate availability figures.

The library also needs to take steps to encourage as many patrons as possible to participate in the study to increase the likelihood that the data collected will be representative. We recommend assigning someone to distribute blank questionnaires as patrons enter the library, briefly explain the importance of the study, and collect completed forms as patrons leave. We also suggest posting signs throughout the library to inform patrons of the study in progress and conducting the study in diverse time periods, including morning, afternoon, and evening hours and weekdays as well as weekends.

Finally, the library will need to use a fairly sophisticated questionnaire, such as the one shown in figure 8.14, pages 231–34, to measure availability rates. For example, using a Likert scale rather than simple "yes" or "no" responses for questions that may have shades of gray can discriminate between patrons fully satisfied with the items they checked out and those only partially pleased. A bicyclist may have wanted a book describing cycling tours through the Cotswolds in England but settled for a book listing the names of organizations that offer English biking tours, and a fiction reader may have checked out one of Robert Ludlum's earlier novels when he or she initially sought the latest. To effectively determine subject and author fill rate, an evaluator must determine whether the patrons' needs were fully satisfied, partly satisfied, or not satisfied at all.

Analyzing Availability Data

Regardless of the type of availability study performed, the evaluator primarily must

- note how often patrons successfully located items; and
- if they did not find items, determine why.

A library will want to note the percentage of fully or partially successful title, author, subject, and genre searches for two reasons. First, these figures can document the difficulties that patrons have locating what they want and convince library staff of the need for improvements (Mansbridge 1986). Second, these figures can serve as baseline availability rates. After a library has established programs to help correct any problems uncovered, it can remeasure availability rates and compare them to these baseline figures to gauge program effectiveness.

Library staff can determine the exact reasons why patrons did not find desired items by checking the catalog, shelves, circulation area, and other possibilities for missing "on shelf" items, such as a display or staff member's desk, *on the same day patrons complete their searches*. The evaluator examines the results in some detail, determines the extent to which each of the four barriers to availability is causing problems, then recommends corrective action to eliminate, or at least decrease, these. Most librarians can proceed (again, keeping in mind mission and service roles) by trying to improve first those factors causing the most problems or expected to give the most improvement for the least cost. If the problem is not a collection development issue, the evaluator passes on the information to the relevant supervisor.

Figures 8.15 to 8.18, pages 235–41, provide directions for, and the forms associated with, completing and analyzing the materials availability survey.

(Text continues on page 242.)

We are interested in improving the quality of our collection.

Please complete this survey and return it to any staff member as you leave. Thank you.

Date _____

If you were looking for a specific *title*, please complete Section 1. Otherwise, skip to Section 2.

SECTION 1

Please list each title that you sought today, then tell whether you found it.

Format and Title	Did you find this work in our collection?	
	Yes	No
Examples: book—Hamlet or video—Gone with the Wind		
1.		
2.		
3.		
4.		
5.		
6.		

If you were looking for a work by a specific *author*, please complete Section Two. Otherwise, skip to Section Three.

FIGURE 8.14. Form for Materials Availability Study.

(Fig. 8.14 continues on page 232.)

FIG. 8.14—*Continued*

SECTION 2

Please list the name(s) of each author you sought today, then tell whether you found a work by this author that met your needs.

Format and Author	To what extent did you find a work by this author that met your needs?		
	Fully	Partly	Not at All
Examples: audiobook—John Grisham or CD—Beatles			
1.			
2.			
3.			
4.			
5.			
6.			

If you were looking for a *fictional (that is, imaginary) work* of a particular genre or type, please complete Section 3. Otherwise, skip to Section 4.

SECTION 3

Some people enjoy materials of a certain type or genre, such as:

Mystery	Fantasy	Romance	Historical Fiction
Classics	Horror	Large Print	Science Fiction
Westerns	Adventure	Short Stories	General Fiction

Please indicate the type or genre of fiction you sought and tell whether you found something in our collection to meet your needs.

Format and Genre	To what extent did you find something in our collection that met your needs?		
	Fully	**Partly**	**Not at All**
Examples: paperback—horror or CD book—mystery			
1.			
2.			
3.			
4.			
5.			

If you were looking for a factual work on a particular *subject*, please complete Section 4.

(Fig. 8.14 continues on page 234.)

FIG. 8.14—*Continued*

SECTION 4

Many people enjoy works about a particular subject, such as materials that discuss World War I, home decoration, or a famous person. Please list the specific subject of each factual work you sought today, then tell whether you found something in our collection that met your needs.

Format and Subject	To what extent did you find something in our collection that met your needs?		
	Fully	Partly	Not at All
Examples: video on how to draw cars or book on low fat cooking			
1.			
2.			
3.			
4.			
5.			

Given that fill rates differ significantly from one library to another, we suggest that each branch conduct its own availability study.

At a minimum, the study should be completed during two different weeks of the year (ideally one week each during the Spring, Summer, Fall, and Winter quarters to help capture seasonal patterns of use. In general, the longer the survey period and the more questionnaires collected, the more likely that the data collected will be representative). At least one week should be during the months of March or October, when public library circulation is high. In preparation for each week of the survey, the evaluator should take the following steps:

1. Photocopy a week's supply of the survey form shown in figure 8.14. To obtain reliable data, we recommend collecting information on 300 to 500 requests. If the total number of desired requests has not been collected by the end of the week, extend the survey time for one week or until the requests have all been gathered.

2. Sharpen a supply of pencils patrons can use to complete survey forms.

3. Recruit volunteers who can distribute the forms to every patron who enters the library that week and who can gather completed forms before the patrons leave the library. Volunteers and staff members must also be able to answer questions about how to complete the form and why the library is conducting the study.

4. Arrange for a staff member to check the library's catalog, shelves, and circulation records at the end of each day of the survey to see why certain titles were not found.

5. Tell all staff members when the survey will be distributed.

6. Place a box in which completed surveys may be dropped near the door of the library.

During each survey week, the volunteer should

- realize that it is important to get as many patrons as possible to complete the form to ensure the data are as reliable as they are feasible;

- ask each patron entering the library if he or she is seeking materials and is willing to complete a brief survey to help improve the collection; and

- give a blank questionnaire to patrons who say "yes." People who visit the library more than once during the week should be given a separate form to complete each time they are seeking materials.

FIGURE 8.15. Directions for Completing the Materials Availability Survey.

(Fig. 8.15 continues on page 236.)

FIG. 8.15—*Continued*

At the end of each survey day during the designated week(s), the librarian should

- check the catalog and circulation records, for each title in section 1 that was not found, to see why items were unavailable when the patron wanted them.

- determine the reason for non-availability, using the codes shown in instruction 1 of figure 8.17.

- mark this code in the right margin of the Materials Availability Survey, next to the corresponding title.

At the end of the survey week(s), the librarian should complete the chart shown in figures 8.16 through 8.18 to determine the title, author, genre, and subject fill rates and identify ways that these might be increased.

---

1. Count the total number of titles sought by all patrons (from section 1 of the Materials Availability Survey) and list this figure here: _____

2. Count the total number of titles found by all patrons (from section 1 of the Materials Availability Survey) and list this figure here: _____

3. Divide line 2 by line 1 to obtain the library's title fill rate:

   _____

4. Review the results. A library will want to obtain as high a title fill rate as it possibly can, given its existing financial resources.

FIGURE 8.16. Directions for Determining the Title Fill Rate.

1. Count the total number of titles from the Materials Availability Survey that were marked with each of the two-character codes listed below. List these figures in the spaces provided. Add the figures within each section to obtain the total number of titles that were unavailable because of a particular group of factors.

Acquisitions Barriers Affecting Availability

Code Reason for Nonavailability

A1.   The library does not own the title: _____

A2.   The library has ordered the title, but it has not yet been received: _____

A3.   The library has received the title, but it has not yet been cataloged and processed: _____

Total number of titles that were unavailable because of barriers related to acquisitions: _____

Circulation Barriers Affecting Availability

Code Reason for Nonavailability

C1.   The item is checked out to another borrower: _____

C2.   The item is long overdue from another patron. No replacement decision has been made: _____

Total number of titles that were unavailable because of barriers related to circulation: _____

Library Errors Affecting Availability

Code Reason for Nonavailability

L1.   The item is unavailable because it is being rebound, repaired, recataloged, or relabeled: _____

L2.   The item is "missing": _____

L3.   The item is checked in but is not reshelved: _____

L4.   The item is mis-shelved: _____

FIGURE 8.17. Directions for Determining How to Increase the Library's Title Fill Rate.

(Fig. 8.17 continues on page 238.)

FIG. 8.17—Continued

    L5.   The call numbers on the item and in the catalog do not agree (e.g., book is marked FIC GREEN; catalog is marked MYST FIC GREEN; patron cannot find the title): _____

    L6.   A staff member is currently using the item but has failed to check it out: _____

Total number of titles that were unavailable because of library errors: _____

Patron Errors Affecting Availability

Code Reason for Nonavailability

    U1.   Even though the title is in the correct place on the shelf, the patron does not locate it: _____

Total number of titles that were unavailable because of patron errors: _____

  2.   Read the information given below to determine causes of relatively low availability rates and possible solutions for increasing them. The best way to proceed is to improve first the factor or factors that are causing the most problems or that are expected to give the greatest improvement for the least cost.

Acquisitions Factors That Affect Availability Rates

    If many titles sought by users have not been ordered, the library's collection development policies may be at fault. Sometimes, the reason for an acquisitions problem is easy to identify. For example, the fill rate for books may have decreased when a portion of the book fund was reallocated to purchase magazines.

    At other times, it may be necessary to get a better idea of where the acquisitions problem lies by breaking down the availability figures by the type of work requested. For example, through scanning, a librarian may determine that most of the unavailable titles are mysteries and could allocate a higher percentage of the collection budget to that genre in the future.

    In other cases, the availability problem may be related to difficulties with receiving or processing items. This is particularly likely in larger libraries with a big cataloging backlog. This problem is related less to the library's selection practices than to the priority placed on the quick processing of new materials.

Circulation Factors That Affect
Availability Rates

Often a print item that a patron is seeking will be checked out to another user. Although occasional circulation "interference" is normal, most libraries own a number of titles that are so popular that all owned copies are regularly checked out. That is, the number of copies of a single work present on the shelves also influences availability. The most common methods for increasing the likelihood that popular works will be available when patrons want to use them are to purchase more copies of popular titles or shorten the length of loan periods. These strategies for increasing availability are discussed in some detail in Chapter 9.

Library Errors That Affect Availability Rates

A library error occurs when the catalog indicates ownership but the title is not in circulation or on its allotted shelf. The book may be missing or it may be in some area not identified in the catalog.

The library can correct the problems of mis-shelving and slow reshelving by maintaining full strength in the reshelving unit. It can reduce the missing titles problem by installing an electronic security system; inventorying the collection and eliminating the catalog records for those items not found; or dealing, on a case-by-case basis, with titles thought to be missing. If a book is found to be missing, the selector for that area must determine, as quickly as possible, whether or not the item will be replaced. If so, the order should be placed immediately, and the replacement copy processed as soon as it arrives. If not, the catalog must be corrected.

A more difficult problem is created by books temporarily located somewhere other than their regular places on the shelves. These may be sitting on a staff member's desk or awaiting binding or repair. This problem can be solved, at least partially, in those libraries with automated catalogs that list such temporary locations. Both automated and non-automated libraries can also reduce this type of error by installing signs at the catalog and at various entrances to (and strategic locations within) the stacks that direct patrons to check with staff members when they cannot find specific items.

Occasionally, a different problem arises: The actual location of an item is changed but the catalog is not. This may happen, for example, if the library marks a book with a genre label and shifts its location but fails to mark the catalog entry. The catalog record for any item that has permanently changed its location must be updated to reflect this.

(Fig. 8.17 continues on page 240.)

FIG. 8.17—*Continued*

Patron Errors That Affect Availability Rates

The term "patron error" is somewhat misleading, because it implies that the error is entirely the patron's fault. This is not always true. For example, patrons may be unable to locate the picture book section simply because it was not marked with an appropriate sign. In fact, "patron errors" decrease as patron familiarity with the idiosyncrasies of a particular library increases (Rinkel and McCandless 1983). Librarians, therefore, will want to try to anticipate simple and frequently occurring patron errors and plan for ways to avoid them.

Many patrons err when searching the catalog for specific titles because they lack basic catalog use skills. Providing bibliographic instruction, librarian help, or clear directions on how to use the catalog may reduce this problem.

A related error occurs when the patron correctly locates a title in the catalog, then (1) incorrectly records the call number or (2) relies on short-term memory of the number when trying to retrieve the item. Providing pencils and paper slips on which patrons can record the number or installing printers at online catalog terminals may reduce these types of errors.

Even when they have the correct call number, some patrons may look in the wrong location for an item. Librarians can help correct this problem by designing better guiding and orientation systems. They can also post signs, at the catalog and in the stacks, encouraging patrons to ask for help, because fill rates often increase when the librarian helps the patron search for materials.

1. Examine sections 2 through 4 of the Materials Availability Survey. Count the total number of authors, genres, and subjects sought and record this information in the chart below. (Note: If an author, genre, or subject is listed by more than one patron, count each listing separately.)

2. Count the total number of times patrons indicated they found something that fully met their needs and record this in the chart below.

3. Count the total number of times patrons indicated they found something that partially met their needs and record this in the chart below.

4. Divide the total authors sought by the corresponding fully satisfied number. Do the same for genres and subjects. List the complete fill rates in the chart below.

5. Divide the total authors sought by the corresponding partially satisfied number. Do the same for genres and subjects. List the partial fill rates in the chart below.

	Total Sought	Fully Satisfied	Partially Satisfied	Complete Fill Rate	Partial Fill Rate
Authors					
Genres					
Subject					

6. To improve these rates, examine the barriers that prevented patrons from finding needed items when that occurred. Lower fill rates generally result from acquisitions or circulation factors. The librarian can review the discussion of acquisitions and circulation barriers in figure 8.17, pages 237–40, to see what steps may be taken to improve fill rates.

FIGURE 8.18. Directions for Determining the Author, Genre, and Subject Fill Rates.

CONCLUSION

We recommend that libraries devote resources to systematically and comprehensively collecting and reviewing data about how the library's current collection is used or not used, as well as what it does not contain. Although a program of this sort is not inexpensive, the data it provides can be used to make consistent collection management decisions to increase availability of desired materials. The growing use of automated circulation systems, particularly those provided by vendors that work with user groups to determine and make necessary modifications to current programs, will ease this data collection, although libraries with manual systems can also use any or all of the techniques presented here. Training a staff member to coordinate collection evaluation efforts can also facilitate data gathering, prevent duplication of effort, and ensure that evaluative tasks occur as part of an integrated plan.

We end this section, not with our familiar plea for more research, but with a plea to librarians to lobby for better statistics from two sources. The first is vendors. We will be unable to keep collection evaluation costs down, particularly over the long term, unless we purchase automated systems that have sophisticated reporting capabilities. Libraries can readily lobby their existing vendors for sophisticated and flexible statistical breakdowns, begin publishing consumer reports that compare vendor products, and switch vendors when necessary (assuming that lobbying efforts have failed).

State library agencies could also provide additional useful data. Currently, much of the information gathered on annual reports concerns matters other than collections.[7] However, with the increased availability of online reporting (which reduces the once horrendous costs of publishing and distributing data for all libraries within a state), these agencies would be able to use an online form to gather significant collection data for comparison purposes. In the United States, at a minimum, states could collect data on the use and size of collections subdivided, for example, by the Dewey 100s for nonfiction, the recommended list of genre fiction subdivisions we provide in Chapter 10, all major formats, and three age groups (children, young adults, and adults). Failing state collection of such data, national groups such as the Public Library Association might supplement their existing statistical reports (e.g., Public Library Association 2000) with relevant data. Even collecting data on subsets of the collection (e.g., the 600s and 700s) at five- or ten-year intervals could help fill in knowledge gaps.

NOTES

1. The ideas expressed in this chapter expand on those developed in Baker (1991b).

2. Common classes for which the library may keep separate circulation figures include subject areas (e.g., broad classifications such as 700–799 of the Dewey Decimal Classification System—the arts), narrower classifications (e.g., 740–749 of the Dewey Decimal Classification System—drawing and the decorative arts), and topic-specific classifications (e.g., 747 of the Dewey Decimal Classification System—interior decoration), genres (e.g., horror, romance, or short stories); reading or age level (e.g., adult, young adult, easy reader, picture book), format (e.g., large print, e-book, CD-ROM, CD, or art print), and location (e.g., main library, branch library, bookmobile).

3. Common classes for which the library may keep separate circulation figures include subject areas (e.g., broad classifications such as 700–799 of the Dewey Decimal Classification System—the arts), narrower classifications (e.g., 740–749 of the Dewey Decimal Classification System—drawing and the decorative arts), and topic-specific classifications (e.g., 747 of the Dewey Decimal Classification System—interior decoration), genres (e.g., horror, romance, or short stories); reading or age level (e.g., adult, young adult, easy reader, picture book), format (e.g., large print, e-book, CD-ROM, CD, or art print), and location (e.g., main library, branch library, bookmobile).

4. Common classes for which the library may keep separate circulation figures include: subject areas (e.g., broad classifications such as 700–799 of the Dewey Decimal Classification System—the arts), narrower classifications (e.g., 740–749 of the Dewey Decimal Classification System—drawing and the decorative arts), and topic-specific classifications (e.g., 747 of the Dewey Decimal Classification System—interior decoration), genres (e.g., horror, romance, or short stories); reading or age level (e.g., adult, young adult, easy reader, picture book), format (e.g., large print, e-book, CD-ROM, CD, or art print), and location (e.g., main library, branch library, bookmobile).

5. See Rubin (1986) for an excellent review of other techniques.

6. For a discussion of the mechanics of conducting reliable materials availability studies, see Van House (1988) and D'Elia (1988a, 1988b).

7. For a discussion of public library use of statistics in general, see Liu and Zweizig (2000).

REFERENCES

American Library Association. 1989. *Guide to the Evaluation of Library Collections*. Chicago: American Library Association.

Archer, Mary Ann E. 2000. "Widening the Gateway to Legal Information: Building Partnerships with Public Libraries." In *Gateways to Leadership: American Association of Law Libraries Educational Program Handout Materials*, 93rd Annual Meeting, July 15–20, 2000, 223–27. Chicago: American Association of Law Libraries.

Baker, Sharon L. 1983. "An Adult User Survey." *Illinois State Library Statistical Report* 7 (May): 1–33.

———. 1991a. "Improving Business Services Through the Use of Focus Groups." *RQ* 30, no. 3 (Spring): 377–85.

——— . 1991b. "Public Libraries." In *Collection Management: A New Treatise*, ed. Charles B. Osburn and Ross Atkinson, 395–416. Greenwich, CT.: JAI Press.

——— . 1991c. "Results of Focus Group Interviews, December 1990, for the Orange Public Library." Unpublished consultant's report, University of Iowa, School of Library and Information Science.

Baker, Sharon L., and F. W. Lancaster. 1991. *Measurement and Evaluation of Library Services*. 2d ed. Arlington, VA: Information Resources Press.

Brooks, Terrence A. 1984a. "Naive Vs. Sophisticated Methods of Forecasting Public Library Circulations." *Library and Information Science Research* 6, no. 2 (April): 205–14.

——— . 1984b. "Using Time-Series Regression to Predict Academic Library Circulations." *College and Research Libraries* 45, no. 5 (November): 501–5.

Connaway, Lynn Silipigni. 1996. "Focus Group Interviews: A Data Collection Methodology for Decision Making." *Library Administration and Management* 10, no. 4 (Fall): 231–39.

D'Elia, George. 1988a. "Materials Availability Fill Rates: Additional Data Addressing the Question of the Usefulness of the Measures." *Public Libraries* 27, no. 1 (Spring): 15–23.

——— . 1988b. "The Usefulness of Fill Rates: Research and Debate—A Response to Van House." *Public Libraries* 27, no. 1 (Spring): 28–31.

Dow, Orrin B. 1998. "The Cover: Express Book Service Reduces Reserves, Pleases Patrons." *The Unabashed Librarian* no. 107: 31.

Dowlin, Ken, and Lynn Magrath. 1983. "Beyond the Numbers: A Decision Support System" In *Proceedings of the 1982 Clinic on Library Applications of Data Processing*, ed. F. W. Lancaster, 27–58. Urbana: University of Illinois, Graduate School of Library and Information Science.

Eggers, Lolly. 1976. "More Effective Management of the Public Library's Book Collection." *Minnesota Libraries* 25, no. 2 (Summer): 56–58.

Evans, G. Edward, with the assistance of Margaret R. Zarnosky. 2000. *Developing Library and Information Center Collections*. 4th ed. Englewood, CO: Libraries Unlimited.

Hernon, Peter, and Charles R. McClure. 1990. *Evaluation and Decision Making*. Norwood, NJ: Ablex.

Hutton, Bruce, and Suzanne Walters. 1988. "Focus Groups: Linkages to the Community." *Public Libraries* 27, no. 3 (Fall): 149–52.

Intner, Sheila S., and Elizabeth Futas. 1994. "Evaluating Public Library Collections: Why to Do It and How to Use the Results." *American Libraries* 25, no. 5 (May): 410–13.

Jacob, Merle. 1990. "Get It in Writing: A Collection Development Plan for the Skokie Public Library." *Library Journal* 115, no. 14 (September 1): 166–69.

——— . 2000. (Head of Materials Selection, Chicago Public Library). Telephone interview with Sharon Baker, Spring.

Johnson, Debra Wilcox. 1996. "Focus Groups." In *The Tell It! Manual: The Complete Program for Evaluating Library Performance*, ed., Douglas Zweizig et al., 176–87. Chicago: American Library Association.

Kantor, Paul B. 1976. "Availability Analysis." *Journal of the American Society for Information Science* 27, nos. 5–6 (September): 311–19.

———. 1984. *Objective Performance Measures for Academic and Research Libraries.* Washington, DC: Association of Research Libraries.

Kozlowski, Barbara A., rev. 1998. *Collection Development and Resource Action Plan for the Skokie Public Library.* 2d ed. Skokie, IL: Skokie Public Library.

Krueger, Richard, and Mary Anne Casey. 2000. *Focus Groups: A Practical Guide for Applied Research.* 3d ed. Thousand Oaks, CA: Sage Publications.

Ledingham, John A., and Stephen D. Bruning. 1998. "Ten Tips for Better Focus Groups." *Public Relations Quarterly* 43, no. 4 (Winter): 25–28.

Little, Paul. 1979. "The Effectiveness of Paperbacks." *Library Journal* 104, no. 2 (15 November): 1411–16.

———. 1990. "Collection Development for Bookmobiles." In *The Book Stops Here: New Directions in Bookmobile Service,* ed. Catherine Suyak Alloway, 59–73. Metuchen, NJ: Scarecrow Press.

Liu, Yan Quan, and Douglas Zweizig. 2000. "Public Library Use of Statistics." *Public Libraries* 39, no. 2 (March/April): 98–105.

Mansbridge, John. 1986. "Availability Studies in Libraries." *Library and Information Science Research* 8, no. 4 (October-December): 299–314.

Mills, Terry R. 1982. "The University of Illinois Film Center Collection Use Study." Unpublished report, University of Illinois at Urbana, Graduate School of Library and Information Science. ERIC ED227821.

Nelson, Sandra, Ellen Altman, and Diane Mayo. 2000. *Managing for Results: Effective Resource Allocation for Public Libraries.* Chicago: American Library Association.

Nimmer, Ronald J. 1980. "Circulation and Collection Patterns at the Ohio State University Libraries, 1973–1977." *Library Acquisitions: Practice and Theory* 4, no. 1: 61–70.

Obert, Beverly. 1988. "Collection Development through Student Surveys and Collection Analysis." *Illinois Libraries* 70, no. 1 (January): 46–53.

Perdue, Jennifer, and James A. Van Fleet. 1999. "Borrow or Buy? Cost-Effective Delivery of Monographs." *Journal of Interlibrary Loan, Document Delivery & Information Supply* 9, no. 4: 19–28.

Powell, Nancy, ed. 1990. *Pacific Northwest Collection Assessment Manual.* 3d ed. Salem: Oregon State Library Foundation, Pacific Northwest Conspectus Database.

Powell, Ronald R. 1997. *Basic Research Methods for Librarians.* 3d ed. Greenwich, CT: Ablex.

Public Library Association. 2000. *Public Library Data Service: Statistical Report 2000.* Chicago: American Library Association.

Rinkel, Gene K., and Patricia McCandless. 1983. "Application of a Methodology Analyzing User Frustration." *College and Research Libraries* 44, no. 1 (January): 29–37.

Roberts, Michael, and Kenneth J. Cameron. 1984. "A Barometer of 'Unmet Demand'." *Library Acquisitions: Practice and Theory* 8, no. 1: 31–42.

Rubin, Richard.1986. *In-House Use of Materials in Public Libraries*. Urbana: University of Illinois, Graduate School of Library and Information Science.

Segal, Joseph P. 1995. *The CREW Manual: A Unified System of Weeding, Inventory, and Collection-Building for Small and Medium-Sized Public Libraries* revised and updated by Belinda Boon and Library Development Staff. Austin: Texas State Library.

Simpson, James B., ed. 1997. *Simpson's Contemporary Quotations*. New York: Harper Collins.

Slote, Stanley J. 1989. *Weeding Library Collections*. 3d ed. Englewood, CO: Libraries Unlimited.

———. 1997. *Weeding Library Collections: Library Weeding Methods*. 4th ed. Englewood, CO: Libraries Unlimited.

Spiller, David. 1980. "The Provision of Fiction for Public Libraries." *Journal of Librarianship* 12, no. 4 (October): 238–65.

Spiller, Deborah J. 1989. "Library Service to Residents of Public Housing Developments: A Study and Commentary." *Public Libraries* 28, no. 6 (November-December): 358–61.

Strohl, Bonnie, comp. and ed. 1999. *Collection Evaluation Techniques: A Short, Selective, Practical, Current, Annotated Bibliography, 1990–1998*. Chicago: Reference and User Services Association, American Library Association.

Van House, Nancy A. 1988. "The Usefulness of Fill Rates: Research and Debate—In Defense of Fill Rates." *Public Libraries* 27, no. 1 (Spring): 25–27.

Van House, Nancy A., et al. 1987. *Output Measures for Public Libraries*. 2d ed. Chicago: American Library Association.

Wagner, Mary M., and Suzanne H. Mahmoodi. 1994. *A Focus Group Interview Manual*. Chicago: American Library Association.

MARKETING-BASED SELECTION POLICIES AND PRACTICES

"You can't have it all"—Maxim.

Armed with knowledge of community needs, collection content, and how well the two currently meet, a librarian can forge ahead to consider selection practices, remaining mindful of two common practices that may actually impede the development of integrated and responsive collections. First, extensively subdividing and parceling out selection responsibilities, when done without thoughtful leadership, can result in inconsistent collection development—for example, disproportionate growth in subsets of the collection or building highly disparate collections, each area reflecting its selector's personal biases.

Over-reliance on either objective data or subjective impressions poses a second barrier to rigorous collection development. For example, guided strictly by circulation and sales figures, libraries may develop highly traditional CD collections that make it difficult for patrons to sample new artists or musical styles. On the other hand, subjective impressions of what patrons need can be skewed toward those who are most vocal, as the Indianapolis-Marion County (Indiana) Public Library example in "Key into the Community" in Chapter 2 showed. Research indicates the necessity of both in superior decision making (Bridges and Hirsh 2000).

This chapter presents a five-point approach to addressing these issues while building strong collections well suited to patrons' varying needs and desires:

Writing a detailed, synthesized collection development policy

Reviewing materials budget allocations to ensure consistency with library goals

Establishing a centralized selection unit to cost-effectively purchase routine items

Carefully assigning selection responsibilities and thoroughly training selectors

Asking professional selectors to augment their impressions by reviewing the objective data collected about collection use, then following three marketing principles

WRITING A DETAILED, SYNTHESIZED COLLECTION DEVELOPMENT POLICY

A collection development policy, a living document that requires regular review and revision, communicates collection purpose and priorities to the public as well as the staff. The processes of crafting and following such policies prompt staff thought and discussion on what collections will beneficially include and how resources can be focused to create these (Inter 1996; Futas 1995). Clearly, such policies may guide decisions to purchase or keep items and reduce the influence of extraneous variables (e.g., personal bias) that may otherwise influence selectors.

Although a majority of U.S. public libraries (78 percent in 1993) have written collection development policies approved by a board or other authority (Futas 1995), a review of those policies posted on the Internet shows that their content differs widely, presumably in keeping with differences among the communities served. Abundant articles and books, including Evans and Zarnosky (2000), Clayton (1998), Futas (1995), Cassell and Futas (1991), and the American Library Association (1989), discuss elements to include in a collection development policy and how to write one. We recommend creating a policy sufficiently general to be manageable yet thorough enough to clearly communicate collection purpose to the public and provide useful guidelines for selectors. Such a policy could easily serve as the basis for a newspaper article, answering the "Five-Ws-and-an-H" questions known to every journalism student:

- Who is the library serving with its collection? Effective collection development policies emanate from the informed comprehension of the characteristics and needs of the library's service community. The policy also indicates who selects materials.

- What materials are selected? The policy outlines which product lines the library collects and in what depth and notes resources available to patrons through interlibrary loan, reciprocal borrowing, and similar cooperative arrangements. To clarify collection boundaries and discourage unwanted gifts, the policy may also specify certain classes of materials beyond the library's scope. For example, the Latah County (Idaho) Library District selection policy lists 13 reasons materials may not be purchased ("Materials" 2001).

- When do staff members make selection decisions? Although most purchasing decisions will be made on an ongoing basis, significant events, such as the announcement of prize winners or major news stories, may trigger additional purchases. Collection maintenance and de-selection decisions will optimally be made on a scheduled basis, according to a weeding plan. As studies and experience show, a well-weeded collection increases both material usage and patron satisfaction, saves staff time as well as shelf space, and allows room for new technologies (Slote 1997). The policy may also address methods of acquiring materials in a timely manner, such as using standing order plans, leasing certain materials, or automatically purchasing another copy when the holds-to-copies ratio exceeds a certain level.

- Where will materials come from? The policy may note any vendors (online, local, with approval plans, or otherwise) a library routinely uses, how the library treats gifts, and the major review journals, catalogs, materials lists, and other awareness sources in which staff discover items for purchase consideration. It may also note any expert counsel it receives on its collections, such as if the local art guild advises selectors on purchases for the framed art collection.

- Why are materials selected? The policy furnishes the rationale connecting the who and the what, possibly noting the target markets for different classes of materials and explaining why staff deem certain items suitable for community needs and the library mission. This information often appears as a list of selection criteria, differing significantly from one product line to another. Thus, the considerations for electronic resources (noted in Kovacs 2000; Chadwell and Brownmiller 1999; Strong 1999; Johnson 1997) may vary from those for paper resources. The why of collection development also finds expression in philosophical statements woven into or appended to the policy, such as the statements of intellectual freedom noted in ALA's Library Bill of Rights.

- How can patrons become involved in the collection development process? The policy explains how patrons can make purchase or reconsideration requests and notes any roles that local subject experts or avid users of a particular collection play in evaluation. For example, once a year, a librarian may attend a meeting of a science fiction club to solicit purchase suggestions and commentary on the existing collection. "How" questions related to the process of ordering, acquiring, processing, maintaining, evaluating, and weeding materials and collections belong in a separate procedure manual.

The in-depth collection development policy does not address these questions in isolation. Rather, when written to reflect the library's long-range strategic and marketing plan, it encourages accountability and reinforces library goals and mission, including roles or service responses determined through a planning process. For example, the collection development policy of the Kenosha (Wisconsin) Public Library notes that the video collection at the Simmons branch, which serves as the centralized reference center, features "business, investment, job hunting and self improvement" titles. In contrast, the bulk of the video collection at the Uptown branch, which has adopted an elementary and junior high school educational support role, consists of "general and informational titles primarily for children" ("Collection" 2001a).

An integrated collection development policy will also include specific commitments to promotion. Assume, for example, that a library collects local authors' works comprehensively even though past experience has shown that patrons do not actively seek out these items in the stacks. Including a pledge in the collection development policy to both purchase and promote these items (e.g., through "local author" stickers affixed to their spines) helps justify the expenditure and encourages staff to carry out their good intentions. A detailed promotional plan, which may be developed later, can be recorded elsewhere.

MONITORING AND STRETCHING THE MATERIALS BUDGET TO FURTHER LIBRARY GOALS

Library Journal's annual survey of expenditures of 100 public libraries—diverse by size, geographic area, and population served (rural, urban, or suburban)—reports that in recent years public libraries have spent, on average, about 16 percent of their operating budgets on books and other materials (Hoffert 2000). We consider this figure a minimum one to build on existing strengths, fortify collections that do not fully meet patron demand, and enhance the library's ability to meet long-term community interests. To ensure that the collection budget reflects the strategic plan, staff and board members can check the correlation between stated goals and objectives and materials allocations for different user groups, formats, genres, or subject areas and then make any necessary corrections. Martin (1995) also provides suggestions for monitoring expenditures over the fiscal year to guarantee achievement of desired effects.

In its review, each library will need to address four major questions. The first two demand fairly concrete answers about how allocations will be made among different classes of materials: Are materials budget allocations in line with library service responses or roles? Does information collected during the product analysis stage suggest a need to change budget allocations? The third question requires that the library make a major philosophical decision about how the library's duplication policy will influence money spent within a particular budget category. The fourth calls for creativity and assertiveness: In what ways can the library stretch or increase the pool to be divided?

Are Materials Budget Allocations in Line with Library Service Responses or Roles?

Given that budget allocations communicate priorities (directly or indirectly, consciously or unconsciously, theoretically and in practice), the library must commit sufficient resources to meeting primary goals before deciding where to spend remaining funds. How much is enough for each of these broad endeavors? The latest PLA planning process, found in *The New Planning for Results: A Streamlined Approach* (Nelson 2001) does not prescribe percentages to be directed toward primary and secondary goals. Rather it proposes that staff consider current allocations to identify any that must be reconsidered. For example, the library may have dedicated either a disproportionately large amount of money to collections tangential to established service responses or roles or a disproportionately small amount to collections central to the same. Staff can then determine resources necessary to excel at selected service responses (based in part on the current state of the collection) and develop a plan for closing gaps and reallocating surpluses.

Publication costs also affect the definition of "sufficient" funding. Consider the amount of money required to build an outstanding collection of paperbacks for teen leisure reading as opposed to the greater expense required to acquire an outstanding selection of art books. *The Bowker Annual Library and Trade Book Almanac* (Bogart 2000) and other resources that list current average prices by subject and format can help here. This information is particularly useful in completing the budget allocation forms given in Nelson, Altman, and Mayo (1999).

Does Information Collected During the Product Analysis Stage Suggest a Need to Change Budget Allocations?

To determine whether they will shift money from one budget category to another, librarians also will wish to examine three major forms of information gathered during the product analysis stage: on the circulation trends, turnover rate, and relative use of major classes. This information can help librarians make decisions about increasing or decreasing allocations. For example, after identifying under-used classes, librarians may reduce allocations for music on audiotape, maintain current spending on multicultural works in the 800s (making a simultaneous commitment to promoting them), and both weed and rebuild the collection on sculpture. In large part, the decision will depend on the relationship between the particular collection and the long-term goals of the library and its community.

How Will the Library's Duplication Policy Influence How Much Money Will Be Spent Within a Particular Budget Category?

As noted throughout this book, public librarians can enhance patron satisfaction by increasing title availability rates. Reported rates indicate that on any given day at least 25 to 30 percent of public library patrons nationwide cannot find specific titles they want on the shelves and ready for checkout (Public Library Association 1998). This most commonly occurs because other users already have these titles checked out, a somewhat unsurprising fact given that a significant majority of the circulation in the average library comes from a significant minority of its works (Blecic 2000; Britten 1990; Ettelt 1988; Trueswell 1969).

The question then becomes: what can libraries do to improve their availability rates? An observation made more than 25 years ago by Buckland (1975) contains the germ of the answer. He noted that three major factors influence the availability rate of a specific title:

The level of patron demand for it

The number of copies the library provides

The length of its loan period

Changes in any of these directly affect the likelihood of an item already being checked out.

In most cases, factors outside the librarian's control affect the level of patron demand for a title. For example, demand may rise suddenly when a local teacher assigns 100 students to read Nathaniel Hawthorne's *The Scarlet Letter* or when a particular book adaptation appears on the silver screen. Because library staff members have little direct influence over promotion efforts that they do not institute, they will primarily rely on two methods of increasing item availability:

Duplicating titles that are, or are predicted to be, heavily-used

Shortening the length of the loan period for popular works

Duplicating Titles That Are, Or Are Predicted to Be, Heavily Used

Prior to the 1970s, a number of factors contributed to the reluctance of public librarians (at least in the United States) to purchase multiple copies of popular works. First, broad-scale evaluation efforts used to be the exception rather than the rule. As a result, few librarians realized how often popular works were off the shelf and, therefore, unavailable for patron use. Moreland (1968) describes one of the earliest studies, conducted at the Montgomery County (Maryland) Public Libraries, to explore this issue. Librarians at 11 branches identified 122 popular titles that they felt were in continuous demand, mostly contemporary classics, like *Fahrenheit 451*, *To Sir, With Love*, and *Black Like Me*. Each librarian chose 60 titles from this list, ordered at least 10 (uncataloged) paperback copies of each, then placed the books in their collections. The librarians checked the shelves at regular intervals to ensure that patrons could always find a copy of each work, reordering books in multiples of five whenever the supply of a title on hand fell to three copies. During the 11-month study period, the branches bought a total of 21,821 copies of the 122 titles, yet still had not reached the satisfaction point—at least one copy always available—for all titles. Originally designed to raise user satisfaction, this experiment in duplicate buying demonstrated to staff the inadequacy of their former purchasing patterns, which provided only one or two copies of each work for each branch.

Public librarians have also been reluctant to duplicate works for fear that best-selling titles would consume the bulk of their budgets. In actuality, items in short supply in many libraries vary greatly. These include contemporary and older classics; recent materials on health, arts and crafts, home improvement, and other popular subjects; items that have received a Grammy, Pulitzer Prize, or other award for their quality; materials by authors with long-standing reputations, such as Kurt Vonnegut; and CDs, audiobooks, DVDs, and other popular formats. Particularly when promoted, high-quality items can be in great demand. Consider the experience of the Greenville (South Carolina) Middle School Library, which offered a before-school read-aloud of the Newbery-winning title *The Giver* by Lois Lowry and over a six-month period had 85 students on the waiting list for it, despite the fact that the library had 38 copies available for loan ("Developing" 1997).

Librarians have also been hesitant to purchase multiple copies because of reluctance to "waste" duplicates by discarding them once demand has faded. We suggest that it will often be no more wasteful to discard a duplicate copy that circulated 20 times during a two-year period than a title that circulated a total of 20 times over 10 years. Moreover, libraries can sell duplicates in periodic book sales, online auctions, or prominently placed displays housed in each branch, then use the receipts to buy more popular works. They can place older duplicates in read-and-return collections (described more fully in Chapter 6) that invite the public to browse collections of works in public places, take home titles that interest them, and return the works to the library when finished. As another possibility, they can donate them to local charities and nonprofit organizations, such as senior centers and battered women's shelters.

Other libraries have resolved the "wastefulness" issue by using lend-lease plans for popular items, which allow a library to select a certain number of titles from an annotated list on a regular basis (most commonly monthly for books). Titles arrive shelf-ready and can be returned for credit when demand wanes. Commonly used lease plans include Baker and Taylor's Book Leasing System, which offers separate plans for fiction and computer books; McNaughton's (Brodart) plans for adults, children, and young adults that include both fiction and nonfiction as well as the AudioBound plan for audiobooks; Landmark Audiobook Leasing Program; and Taped Editions Library Leasing Programs for audiobooks.[1]

Budgetary constraints provide the fourth, and often most significant, reason that librarians have been hesitant to systematically duplicate popular works. Buying multiple copies of some titles forces the selector to purchase fewer different titles overall, an action that can significantly affect collection diversity. For this reason, some libraries duplicate only a small number of works, for example, checking the availability of a "core" collection of titles on a regular basis and ordering one or more extras as necessary (e.g., Eggers 1976). Other libraries duplicate titles consistently used for school assignments, with many reserves on them, or with very high circulation rates, as identified using procedures like those described in Chapter 8. Duplicating only a small percentage of materials in the collection or funding duplicate titles by selling them when demand wanes reduces the budgetary impact of providing multiple copies and encourages collection diversity.

Some public libraries have chosen to duplicate much more heavily. For example, the Baltimore County (Maryland) Public Library (BCPL) once created a stir throughout the library world with its policy of heavy duplication (e.g., Yamamoto 1999a, 1999b, 1999c). Although the library has adopted a more balanced selection strategy in recent years, selectors still examine various factors related to demand. These include the use of earlier creations by the same author or of other similar (e.g., by genre, subject area or format) works, the amount of money the publisher commits to advertising the work, and the extent of planned promotion on major radio and television talk shows (Wisotzki 1989, 2000). BCPL still purchases best-selling fiction titles in large quantities, generally from 190 to 450 copies for more than 20 branches. It buys nonfiction in significantly smaller numbers (e.g., 30 copies for the system), and most literary fiction in still smaller numbers (e.g., 8 copies).

Heavy duplication can work for small libraries as well as large ones. The Wiggin (Stratham, New Hampshire) Memorial Library, which serves a population of 7,000, emulated the best aspects of the BCPL approach and in so doing doubled annual circulation and increased tax support by 70 percent over a five-year period (Sullivan 2000).

Varying the Length of the Loan Period

Although libraries can increase availability rates by shortening the loan periods for popular works, borrowers often want to use materials at their leisure, creating a potential conflict of interest that must be resolved thoughtfully.

A library could increase title availability fairly simply by shortening the loan periods for its entire collection. It may determine, for example, that patrons could find approximately 50 percent of desired works on the shelves if the library had a four-week loan period, 65 percent with a three-week loan and 75 percent with a two-week loan. However, cutting loan periods for the total collection will not always make the most sense. Although it would increase the availability for already heavily used titles, shortening the loan period for the large percentage of titles already sitting on the shelves when patrons want them is both unnecessary and potentially detrimental to patron satisfaction.

A few libraries have taken the opposite tack and instituted demand-dependent loan policies that apply to each individual item in the collection. For example, when a university library in England learned that its users could find what they wanted less than two-thirds of the time, it reprogrammed its own privately designed, automated circulation system to match the demand level of a particular item with a suitable loan period. For a title that had very recently circulated, the computer automatically assigned a loan period as short as three days. If the title had circulated less recently, the system gave it a longer loan period, from two weeks to two years, depending on how long it had been since the last checkout. Results were dramatic. Title availability immediately rose from 60 to 90 percent. Circulation rose also, by 200 percent in a two-year period, as patrons found that they could consistently locate needed items on the shelves. Although such an increase in use would have caused title availability rates to plunge rapidly under a standard circulation system, the adaptive properties of this system—loan periods fully dependent on demand—helped ensure high title availability levels (Buckland 1983, 1975).

Even though automated circulation systems are becoming increasingly adaptive, thanks largely to client-server architecture, many automated circulation systems still in use today are not flexible enough to compute different loan periods for each title based on past demand. Nor do staff members have time to compute loan periods manually for each title being checked out. Furthermore, patrons checking out 20 children's books, for example, may be dismayed (at best) to learn that they have 15 different due dates. A solution is to use preset loan periods of different lengths for various classes of materials.

Under this approach, libraries establish shorter loan periods for overused categories of materials. These will include

- *works in popular formats.* Thus, a library might lend DVDs and videos for one week, audiobooks for two weeks, and books for four weeks.

- *works in over-used classes.* For example, a library could set a two-week rather than a four-week loan period for the four most over-used sections of its print collection (e.g., new books, mysteries, diet books, and computer manuals).

- *works with prolific circulation only during the on-season.* For example, a library could establish one-week loan periods for holiday books during the month before that holiday and for state and federal income tax guides between January 15 and April 15 each year. It could place on reserve or set very short loan periods for works that relate to a class assignment given to numerous area students.

- *works written by a particular author.* For example, a library could fix a four-week loan period for most authors, a two-week loan period for those authors who have a relatively strong following, and a one-week loan period for blockbuster authors.

- *particular titles.* For example, a library could set a one-week loan period for works that appear on various bestseller lists, like those that appear in the Sunday *New York Times* or *Rolling Stone* magazine, or for those with more than X number of reserves. These practices will be made easier if libraries using automated circulation systems clearly communicate their desire for sophisticated program capabilities to the vendors developing these.

The library can then help offset patron costs for shortened loan periods in a number of ways, including

- allowing renewals (and publicizing this service) for as many classes of materials as possible (e.g., for all but those items with holds on them) to keep overdue numbers low.

- permitting renewals of materials over the telephone and Internet as well as in person (and publicizing this service).

- setting its daily overdue fines at the lowest effective level.

- establishing an after-hours materials return (and publicizing this service), so that patrons can keep items as late as possible on the day they are due.

- granting exceptions to the shortened loan period in certain cases, such as for new books of over 500 pages or audiobooks containing more than 15 tapes.

Finding the Correct Balance Between Duplication and Loan Periods

Each of the solutions discussed here has drawbacks. Shortening loan periods can inconvenience patrons, possibly raising the cost of using the library to the point that patrons become irritated and, in the worst-case scenario, decide that costs exceed benefits. But the significant expense of purchasing or leasing duplicate copies of items devours money that could fund the purchase of a greater variety of titles, thus reducing collection diversity. Deciding which techniques to emphasize will be easier if a library considers three principles.

First, actions taken to reduce availability rates beneficially reflect selected service responses or roles. For example, a library emphasizing lifelong learning and committed to building a wide-ranging collection of instructional, self-help, and other personal enrichment materials relevant to the needs of all ages can increase title availability while maintaining collection diversity by primarily reducing loan periods. In contrast, the library that has chosen a service response of current topics and titles may deem it reasonable to heavily duplicate current and popular works in a variety of formats.

Second, we reinforce here the need to recognize that duplication and reduction of loan periods afford interrelated means of increasing availability. That is, these tactics must be judiciously combined to achieve the desired effect.

Third, as with all comprehensive decisions, we recommend that librarians design their selection practices for the best interests of the entire library, not just an individual branch. For example, the BCPL crafted a plan to address a major selection difficulty at two of its branches, which served many heavy readers of adult fiction and often had reserve lists of 50 to 100 patrons for many new but not best-selling fiction titles. To avoid either greatly limiting the number of different fiction titles each branch could provide or taking many months to fill these reserves, BCPL developed a computer program to match reserves with the number of copies ordered at a particular branch. When either branch had one and one-half times more holds than copies ordered, the program subtracted 25 percent of the available copies due to each of the other branches in the BCPL system and earmarked these copies, for one circulation only, to the branch with the outstanding reserves (Wisotzki 1989).

In What Ways Can the Library Increase the Pool to Be Divided?

We urge libraries to make every reasonable effort to stretch traditional collection funds, spending money wisely, guided by the kind of product analysis data Chapter 8 describes, and seeking partnerships. For example, the Broward County (Florida) Public Library conducted a serials usage study that documented that it could reasonably drop its subscriptions to about 50 rarely used titles, saving over $5,000 in the process (French and Pollard 1997). Libraries may also form consortia to negotiate the best prices with vendors or make cooperative purchasing agreements with each other, such as when neighboring libraries alternate purchasing expensive annual reference materials and offer each other priority faxing from the newest edition when necessary. Some libraries have found outsourcing some of their technical services work a way to save money and decrease the amount of time it takes to get popular items to the public; however, others have experienced significant problems with outsourcing (e.g., Strickland 1999; Mackenzie 2000; Wilson and Colver 1997).

Yet even when librarians make every effort to spend funds wisely, the long-term health and viability of the collection also require efforts to increase monies allotted to it: reallocating funds within the overall budget, enlarging it, or supplementing it.

Reallocated funds will preferably be removed from expenditures superfluous to library goals and channeled to support selected service responses directly. Even in a relatively painless situation—for example eliminating an expensive program, tangential to the library mission, that has a very limited audience—there may be a few staff and patrons alike who regret its passing. Such a change can be eased by explaining where saved funds will be redirected and showing any positives that will come of this measure. In addition, decision makers must take care to avoid a quick fix that backfires in the long run. Consider the probable effects of laying off a full-time cataloger to increase the acquisitions budget. Before long, additional materials purchased would likely linger in Technical Services for an excessive amount of time, as the remaining staff combat both a backlog and a morale problem.

Alternate approaches involve attempts to increase the bottom line. Libraries may create some self-supporting collections, such as the San Diego County Library's video collection, completely funded by a 50 cent per video rental fee, which raises about $38,000 annually (Waznis 1998).[2] They may also appeal to the funding authority for a larger budget. Although "ask and you shall receive" may be overly optimistic, "don't ask and you won't get" rings with truth. Cultivating political allies can help secure increased funding at budget time. For example, when the Russell (Middletown, Connecticut) Library recognized it would require added revenue to accomplish its goals, it sponsored orientation visits for the mayor, city department heads, and city council members. Staff consciously continued to contact these decision makers to explain library needs and plans for the future, which contributed to the 8 percent increase in the operation budget the library procured for the following year (Meyers 1998). For guidance on preparing and delivering an effective budget presentation, see Lynch (1999), Smith (1996), Johnson (1995), Swan (1990), and Cargill (1987). ALA also offers a training program, Library Advocacy Now!, to help recruit library supporters and keep them active (Schuman 1999), and Turner's (1997) book *Getting Political*, offers strategies for cultivating public and political support for libraries.

Of course, public libraries seek to serve their entire communities, not just those who can afford to pay for access to materials. Moreover, city councils, county boards, and voters faced with finite resources may not grant a library's request for additional funds, no matter how persuasively presented. This helps explain why libraries, either independently or through a foundation, are hosting fundraising events or drives, seeking grants, creating endowments, and using a slew of innovative techniques to supplement their budgets. St. Lifer (1999) found that library fundraising activities rose 228 percent between 1993 and 1998, with average fundraising levels increasing almost 10 percent from FY97 to FY98. Some libraries even have professional fundraisers working for them on a regular basis; the San Antonio (Texas) Public Library has its own foundation with a full-time staff of five (Goldberg 1993).

Clearly, fundraising methods require different amounts of staff time, skills, and other assets and can be scaled up or down based on these and on available community resources. The following examples give an idea of the range of current practices:

- In a profitable variation on the traditional book sale, the Anoka County (Minnesota) Library earned over $130 selling four discarded, somewhat rare books on the Internet auction site eBay. That success has prompted continued eBay business and added hundreds of dollars to library coffers (Baxter 2000).[3]

- For its hundredth birthday, the Waco-McClennan (Texas) Library System raised $100,000 for its children's book collection through a fundraiser featuring Ray Charles and the Waco Symphony Orchestra ("News" 1998).

- The Evanston (Illinois) Public Library collected $65,000 in community donations to support a variety of collections, including art, poetry, science, and reference books; first novels; picture books; descriptive videos; audiobooks; and business videos ("Funds" 1997).

- The Kansas City (Missouri) Public Library raised $23,500 using its Web site to solicit donations to the NovelBall—not a function to attend but a designated evening on which donors were encouraged to read (King 2000).

- The Rock Island (Illinois) Public Library joined with Stern Beverage Recycling to initiate a program that allows residents who take aluminum cans and clear plastic bottles to the recycling company to ask that earned money be given to the library to purchase new books (Martin 1992). Similarly, the Oakton (Illinois) District Public Libraries Literacy Coalition, which includes nine public library members plus the Oakton Community College, routinely participates in the Jewel-Osco food and drug store "Shop & Share" program, wherein the store gives the literacy coalition 5 percent of the total sales from all shoppers who submitted a coupon on specially designated days.[4]

- The Providence (Rhode Island) Pubic Library raised $25,000 for its book budget with a literary luncheon, attended by more than 800 people, featuring author Frank McCourt ("Author" 1997).

- The East Brunswick (New Jersey) Public Library's budget got a charge from a township MasterCard card, for which the library earns 5 percent of gross revenues, estimated to be between $25,000 to $30,000 the first year and $40,000 to $50,000 in subsequent years ("Mastering" 1996).

- In Wisconsin, 165 public libraries formed a consortium, which helped them receive a $189,000 grant to buy a test collection of eBook resources ("PLs" 2000).

- The Portland (Connecticut) Library began a bestseller donation club, wherein readers contribute the library's discounted cost of a title, then the library buys it, processes it within one week of the donation, and loans it first to the donor, who also can claim a tax deduction ("Best" 1995).

Libraries can also directly solicit materials donations, rather than the funding for them. For example, the Richmond (British Columbia) Public Library's "Chinese Language Book Donation Campaign" brought in 1,800 books to improve the browsing collection of Chinese-language books ("PLA's" 1995). Such programs work best when library selectors let patrons know ahead of time which titles they want or at least inform patrons that only those donations meeting selection criteria will be added to the collection. For example, staff at the Northeast Branch of the New Hanover County (North Carolina) Public Library place "Buy Me for the Library" bookmarks in desired titles in three cooperating bookstores, which give shoppers a 20 percent discount when they purchase the book and leave it at the store for library staff to collect. Donors can also ask that the item contain a book-plate noting that it has been given in honor or in memory of someone ("Buy" 2000).

For other success stories and recommended strategies, we recommend Craft (1999), Payne (1997), Steele and Elder (2000), Camarena (2000), Hannah (1997), Brazin (1999), and Burlingame (1995). We also suggest reading "The Librarian's Bookshelf" bibliography in the *Bowker Annual Library and Trade Book Almanac*, which includes a section on fundraising (Bogart 2000), or the ALA's "Library Fund Raising" bibliography, available at their Web site ("LARC" 2000).

Some librarians worry that actively seeking funding from private sources will undercut public support. However, this is not often the case (Carrigan 1994). In fact, fundraising efforts can provide leverage to help a library obtain additional public funds, encouraging its funding body to "contribute its fair share" (Clay and Bangs 2000, 614). For example, when the Seattle Public Library Foundation set out to raise $5 million for its collections over five years, the substantial donations it received demonstrated to the mayor and council the extent of support for the library and helped secure a 25 percent increase for its operating budget (Jacobs 1998). For the 1997–1998 fiscal year, the San Diego County (California) Board of Supervisors challenged the library to raise more money for its materials budget, pledging to match up to $250,000 in donations (Goldberg 1997).

ESTABLISHING A CENTRALIZED SELECTION UNIT TO DO FORMULA-BASED PURCHASING

A number of public libraries have tried to make the time-consuming and costly task of selection more efficient by establishing a centralized selection unit in which a small group of people make at least a few selection decisions for the entire system. In a survey of the Public Library Association's Metropolitan Libraries Section (PLA-MLS) members, 67 percent of respondents described a portion of their collection development efforts as centralized, with centralization becoming more likely as materials budgets increased (Irvine 1995).

The composition of centralized selection units varies significantly. Some employ only professional librarians, others only paraprofessionals, still others a mixture of the two. Some units choose all materials for the system as a whole; others perform specific selection tasks. The PLA-MLS study found bestsellers the category most frequently selected centrally, with 62 percent of those surveyed doing so, followed by video (43 percent) and audio (42 percent).

We recommend that whenever possible public libraries establish a centralized selection unit, staffed by paraprofessionals and supervised by a professional librarian, to do formula-based purchasing. These individuals can buy the materials that appear on various lists for which clear-cut purchasing rules can be devised: bestsellers, award-winning titles, and reserved items. Large libraries or regional cooperatives especially will want to compile a series of lists (like those distributed in the Chicago Public Library) to alert professional selectors to items receiving significant promotion in the news media or otherwise worthy of purchase.

Establishing such a central selection unit greatly reduces the number of different people engaged in the never-ending chore of list checking. This frees professional librarians from a routine activity, allowing them to spend time on selection tasks that require professional judgment and action, from reviewing results of collection evaluation efforts to reading reviews and identifying titles to fill collection gaps. The centralized unit also encourages the quick purchase and processing of new materials in high demand, helping to ensure availability at the peak of popularity.

Although little research has quantified possible savings, centralized selection can clearly conserve resources (e.g., van Vaerenbergh 1997). Three libraries responding to the PLA-MLS survey analyzed their finances after moving to centralized selection and reported saving 750 hours of librarians' work time and $250,000 in labor costs, as well as reducing full-time equivalents from 14 to between 5 and 7 (Irvine 1995). In addition to saving staff time, which has been redirected into training activities and serving a growing number of users, centralized selection has allowed the Indianapolis-Marion (Indiana) County Public Library to get new materials to the public more quickly (Gibson 1998).

Staff members in the central selection unit perform four major tasks. First, they purchase materials in all formats, genres, and subject classes that appear on best-selling lists targeted for library acquisitions. Sources for these lists include various trade and non-trade magazines and newspapers or their online equivalents, such as *The New York Times*, *Publishers Weekly*, and *Rolling Stone*; information updates from jobbers like the Ingram Book Company and Baker and Taylor Books; and locally specific lists, such as the amazon.com bestsellers for a particular city.[5]

The unit supervisor draws on circulation data, staff contributions, and other information and knowledge about patron needs and publishing trends to devise formulas that specify how many copies of materials in various classes will be bought for the system as well as their initial loan periods. Any given formula may take into account a number of factors, including

- service responses or roles;
- policies regarding duplication and loan periods;
- the popularity of the author, composer, or other creator;
- the popularity of the genre or subject area;
- the cost of the item; and
- the format.

Staff members then determine how many copies will be distributed to each branch, based on a formula devised by the unit supervisor with input from branch selectors. For example, a branch whose circulation represents 21 percent of the total systemwide circulation may get 21 percent of the copies of an ordered title. The unit supervisor may also develop more complex formulas that look at circulation data for specific areas of the collection and consider other branch characteristics, such as particular service responses.

As a second task the central selection unit focuses on lists of "best" items and award-winning titles identified as relevant to the library's needs. The central selection unit will verify that the library owns these items (presumably professional selectors will have already ordered most of them), duplicate them in relevant quantities, and develop formulas for distributing these copies to branches (drawing, for example on demand and additional branch characteristics, such as current collection strengths and deficits).

The central selection unit also purchases extra copies of reserve titles, using the procedures presented in figure 8.1 (see page 201) to identify reserved titles in heavy demand. Extra copies may be purchased according to an established titles-to-holds ratio. For example, in keeping with its selected service response of current topics and titles, the Westlake Porter (Ohio) Public Library purchases one added copy of a title for every two reserves placed on it (Nelson 2001). Reserve purchasing formulas may also take into account characteristics of the item itself, for example, raising the ratio for materials that cost more than $50. Again, library policies will provide guidance about how many copies of high-demand titles to order and which loan period to assign.

Some centralized selection units have set up programs designed to process their reserve orders quickly and efficiently. For example, the Cuyahoga County (Ohio) Public Library allows patrons to file reserves several months before it receives an anticipated bestseller, recording both the date of the request and the patron's "home" branch. When the title arrives, the central selection unit sends the item directly to the home branch of the first patron to file the reserve. Upon check-in of an item with holds placed on it, the automated circulation system informs the clerk which patron is next in line for the work and where the patron will collect it. If the item must go to a different branch, it travels there quickly via the intra-library delivery system. When all reserves on a particular title have been filled, the item is placed on the browsing shelves of the branch that originally ordered it (Berlin 1989).

The central selection staff's final task is to compile lists of works that are not yet bestsellers but are receiving or scheduled to receive lots of news media attention, for use by professional selectors in each area. The "Awareness of the Author and/or Title" section of Chapter 4 details specific sources useful in identifying heavily publicized titles. The centralized selection unit updates these lists frequently, preferably every week; sorts them by class; and distributes them to the selector(s) in each area for quick action.

Some libraries have established centralized selection units to handle all purchases, including the Davis County (Utah) Library (Irvine 1995) and the Metropolitan (Oklahoma City) Library System, which had found it difficult to foster a systemwide selection philosophy when a large number of professional staff were choosing materials. But other libraries, such as the Cuyahoga County (Ohio) Public Library (CCPL), have limited the tasks of their central selection unit to formula-based purchasing. After closely examining its service area—600,000 people of diverse socioeconomic, cultural, and ethnic backgrounds—CCPL decided to give each of its more than two dozen branches a materials budget and the autonomy to select materials to meet the special needs of its patrons.

Little published research has compared the effectiveness of centralized selection units that do formula-based purchasing only to units that purchase all materials for the system. Anecdotally, staff reactions to the latter have often been mixed, especially during the initial days of the change to centralized selection. In part, this has been due to the reluctance of professional librarians to relinquish the "fun" task of selection. But it has also been caused by a feeling that centralized selection staff, who often have no direct patron contact, lack requisite knowledge to make effective decisions.

How necessary is routine patron contact to the ability to select suitable materials? Evans (1969), working in an academic library, found that public service librarians routinely selected a higher percentage of titles in demand among patrons than their non-public service counterparts. However, other studies have verified that materials selected by librarians who have gathered extensive data on past patterns of use and clients' current needs also receive higher levels of use—levels indicative of a good match between patrons and the collection (Diodato and Diodato 1983; Evans and Argyres 1974). Taken as a whole these data (in the continued absence of comprehensive studies) suggest that a centralized selection staff that has access to product analysis information, such as the data recommended in Chapter 8, will also be able to make effective selection decisions.

In situations where staff fears about centralized selection prove unfounded—when the collection continues to meet patron needs, perhaps to an even higher degree than in the past—and when communication between the central and other selectors remains strong, resistance will fade over time. When libraries in the province of North Holland (The Netherlands) tried centralized selection and acquisitions, many staff affected expressed skepticism at first but supported the change after it had been in place for about a year (Eggink 1999).

Further research on these issues would be welcomed.

THOUGHTFULLY ASSIGNING SELECTION RESPONSIBILITIES AND CREATING A THOROUGH CONTINUING EDUCATION PROGRAM FOR ALL SELECTORS

Surprisingly little research has focused on the selector's relative knowledge of assigned subject areas. Yet we in the field can anecdotally document many cases in which a library entrusts a new selector with a materials budget of thousands or tens of thousands of dollars (or even more) in an area largely outside his or her expertise.

Obviously, when selectors lack knowledge about their area(s) of responsibility, collection strength can suffer. For example, two highly accurate titles on clothing design principles are those by Mathis and Connor (1993), which refers to the works of master artists to discuss common body structures of women, and Kibbe (1987), which clearly identifies 13 major categories of body type. Yet many public library collections lack these works, including instead simplistic fare that refers to only five or six of those body types and leaving a majority of patrons scrambling for advice.

Those with preexisting expertise will likely either have formal education in a subject area, such as a second master's degree or an undergraduate major or minor, or seriously pursue a related hobby or interest in some depth, whether it be vegetarian cuisine, horror movies, or economic theory. To gain a quick overview of the situation, a library may route a summary of the classification scheme used to all selectors, asking them to indicate areas of significant subject knowledge and/or a willingness to develop it.

When Shay gathered these data among selectors at three Midwestern public libraries, she found a dearth of subject experts in the 500s of the Dewey Decimal Classification system and large, significant gaps in each of the other Dewey 100s. Moreover, she found high levels of frustration among staff members who recognize the impossibility of achieving a strong collection when asked, for example, to select "all nonfiction book titles for adult readers."

Addressing this issue will be an ongoing process involving numerous strategies. These should include, at a minimum,

- reassigning collection responsibilities as relevant (a task that would have offended only one of 30 selectors at those Midwestern public libraries noted above);

- identifying, again by routing a detailed summary of the library's classification scheme, others on the staff and in the volunteer pool (this includes board members) who have strong subject expertise they would willingly share;

- as selector positions become vacant, hiring new staff members with expertise in "gap" collections;

- asking all selectors to continue to develop their subject expertise by reading articles, trade magazines, and texts; visiting related Web sites; attending seminars or taking classes; and talking to experts and avid users of the collection; and

- making a concerted effort to identify subject experts who would willingly give their time to help the library obtain and maintain a high-quality, usable collection in a given area.

The last point in particular merits expansion. Few libraries will have enough selectors to read voluminously in each area of assignment without help. Indeed, consider all the small libraries out there with one selector choosing literally everything for the collection. Thus, we strongly recommend that selectors take time each month to seek out associations and individuals who will willingly provide advice to supplement the selector's knowledge. Qualified advice is often freely available on the Web sites of associations, whether these be formal and national in nature or founded by knowledgeable hobbyists. Local experts can also be identified via area newspapers, directories of clubs and other organizations, and even by watching to see which patrons consistently check out materials in a given subject area. Effective collections cannot be built, by any but the knowledgeable genius, without such cooperative approaches.

In addition to carefully considering subject knowledge when assigning collection responsibilities, libraries can provide thorough collection development training for new selectors. Although graduates of a library and information science program will (we trust) have considered the philosophical underpinnings of collection development and acquired some key application abilities, they may well not have experienced, and almost certainly will not have mastered, the full range of requirements to proficiently select materials (Johnson 1999). For this reason, we recommend that an experienced selector spend time each week with a novice for at least the first month.

Further education can also benefit veteran selectors, especially those new to a particular library or specific collection responsibility. Continuing education can reinvigorate well-trained, long-time selectors, helping them keep current with relevant developments and acquire higher level skills, such as creating Web pages to organize Internet collection development tools.[6] A recent Spanish study exemplifies the need for such ongoing instruction; it found that the horror, science fiction, and fantasy collections of 17 local libraries contained many more classic than contemporary works, in large part because individual selectors lacked in-depth knowledge of these genres (Pulido and Parejo 1999).

Collection development training will integrate the big picture (i.e., the characteristics of the population served and library mission, service responses, and goals and objectives) with discussions of collection goals and all relevant policies. At a minimum, the basic training program will also cover

- materials budgeting issues;
- the current state of the collection(s) and evaluation techniques;
- an introduction to the relevant subject, genre, or format and the audience for these;
- selection sources and criteria;
- vendor, publisher, and distributor information, including relative strengths and trends;
- acquisition channels and procedures; and
- weeding, replacement, and preservation options and criteria.

Both Johnson (1999) and Fales (1996) present detailed lists of collection development competencies, with the latter suggesting three levels of activities to help selectors achieve these. The Arizona Department of Library, Archives, and Public Records sponsors a Web-based collection development training program that may be of particular interest to new selectors at smaller libraries ("Collection" 2001b).

We also recommend that librarians contact staff at other libraries in their vicinity to determine what joint collection development activities may be pursued.

ASKING SELECTORS TO REVIEW OBJECTIVE DATA ON COLLECTION USE AND FOLLOW THREE MARKETING PRINCIPLES WHEN MAKING SELECTIONS

Although the percentage of formula-based selections has risen, most selectors will continue to order the bulk of materials title by title.[7] In addition to specific selection criteria and other guidelines outlined in the collection development policy, we recommend that selectors follow three broad marketing principles, applying them in a manner consistent with chosen service responses or roles.

Marketing-Based Selection Principle 1

When an item or type of item hasn't been used, don't buy it again without an overriding reason to do so.

Profit-making organizations regularly review the vitality of their products, withdrawing them when demand dissipates, a practice that Chapter 8 encourages libraries to follow in a modified fashion. Because past use of materials correlates more than loosely with future use, librarians may also wish to avoid purchasing products highly similar to those that have been withdrawn for lack of use.

The no-use, no-purchase principle applies to the following four kinds of materials:

- *individual items considered for replacement due to poor physical condition.* It generally will not be cost-effective to replace or even rebind these when they have not been consistently used in the past. However, in an age when gently used books with intact dust jackets can be located quickly and purchased inexpensively over the Internet, it may be possible to replace (rather than rebind in subdued covers) an out-of-print, ruined item whose use indicates continued demand.

- *works by authors who have generated very little interest among patrons over time* (as explained in detail in Chapter 8).

- *classes of materials that receive little use,* determined by examining circulation trends, turnover rate, and relative use by class (as explained in Chapter 8).

- *other categories of materials bypassed by patrons* (as identified using the techniques presented in Chapter 8).

At times, a selector may choose to violate the no-use, no-purchase principle. For example, a library emphasizing cultural awareness may purchase works by certain foreign authors and award winners even if past circulation for these writers has been less than impressive as long as it simultaneously commits to promoting these works frequently, upon receipt and throughout their lives.

Marketing-Based Selection Principle 2

If an item or type of item has been or is likely to be used heavily, duplicate it or assign a shortened loan period to keep a patron's chance of finding it on the shelf high.

Regardless of the service responses the library has chosen, to meet the short- and long-term demands of patrons, selectors must pay particular attention to the purchase of materials likely to be used heavily. Although the central selection unit can readily use standardized formulas to order best-selling titles and individual titles with many reserve requests, professional selectors will also be ordering other materials expected to be used heavily, again keeping in mind use records of similar titles. We recommend that this decision consider both the extent of duplication and the loan period that will be assigned to each work. The goal is to meet the needs of those who have filed reserves as well as browsers, without leaving a large number of unused copies on the shelves. Checking use records of other titles by a particular author or in a subject or genre areas or format can help the selector estimate the extent of demand, as can reviewing the factors that affect use of a particular item, detailed extensively in Chapter 4.

Marketing-Based Selection Principle 3

If an item or type of item not now in the collection may be useful to patrons and levels of potential use justify its expense, buy it. Place primary emphasis on purchasing works that support the library's selected service responses or roles.

If a library has followed the product analysis procedures described in Chapter 8, it will have used a variety of mechanisms to identify non-owned works patrons desire. By inspecting standard selection sources, individual selectors will note other new and retrospective items relevant to the collection and can order titles that support the library's service responses or roles, will likely be used by patrons, and have reasonable anticipated cost-to-use ratios.

To prevent significant overspending in areas unrelated to the library's service responses or roles, selectors will need to more cautiously treat costly items or those that fall outside the scope of the collection or appear to represent the highly specialized interests of a single patron. This will reduce the possibility that the library will be unable to buy needed works because it has already spent all monies allocated for a particular class of materials, a problem that Kovacs (1990) found common to all libraries. In many cases, librarians will obtain specialized, technical, or extremely expensive items on interlibrary loan, rather than purchasing them. Again, a key here will be service response and patron interest. For example, it is possible for even a medium-sized public library to have significant interest in a relatively expensive title such as Helen Armstrong's *Patternmaking for Fashion Design* (2000). This textbook received a five-star amazon.com rating, and the number of home sewers wanting to make their own patterns has increased in response to the reduction in the number of significantly different styles offered by major pattern companies.

CONCLUSION

The five-part plan spelled out in this chapter requires staff time and energy and a firm commitment to incorporating marketing principles throughout the selection process. Yet it also helps libraries precisely sow and carefully tend their materials dollars, allowing them to blossom into a vibrant collection. As Martin writes, "The collection is at once an investment in the past and in the future, a salutary reminder to those who concentrate solely on the present that that present will soon be the past. Fads in learning, trends in management, crises in finance come and go, but the library's collections are a reminder that human wisdom is permanent, cumulative, and all-encompassing. What has been spent is not lost. It is still there, represented by the collections, and still earns its keep" (1995, 4). Building and maintaining such a collection—one that meets both the short-term demands of library patrons and the long-term needs of the community—merits the effort and funds expended.

NOTES

1. For more information about these plans, see Baker (2001) for Baker and Taylor plans, McNaughton (2001) for McNaughton plans, "Just for Librarians" (2001) for the Landmark Audiobook plan, and "Library Programs" (2001) for the Taped Editions plan.

2. For an in-depth look at the possible fees and fines a library can charge, see Martin and Park (1998).

3. The Milwaukee Public Library has also had success selling books on eBay ("eBay" 2000).

4. For more information about the Shop & Share program, see "In Your Community" (2000).

5. To see amazon.com's city-specific bestseller lists, choose the Purchase Circles link under special features and browse through the Geography choices until you reach the appropriate area.

6. For information on this last topic, see Rabine and Brown (2000).

7. For example, in 1992 the Duluth (Minnesota) Public Library centrally ordered just 13 percent of its materials budget and the Tacoma (Washington) Public Library, only 33 percent (Irvine 1995).

REFERENCES

American Library Association. 1989. *Guide for Written Collection Policy Statements*. 2d ed. Chicago: American Library Association.

Armstrong, Helen Joseph. 2000. *Patternmaking for Fashion Design*. 3d ed. New York: Prentice Hall.

"Author Luncheon Draws SRO Crowd." 1997. *Public Libraries* 34, no. 6 (November/December): 336.

"Baker & Taylor Library/Book Leasing." [2001]. [Homepage of Baker & Taylor, Inc.], [Online]. Available: http://www.btol.com/librarydtl.cfm?mode=3&cat=2&sc=8&sv =7&sca=7,8,9,10,11,12,5,13 [Accessed September 28, 2001].

Baxter, Kathleen. 2000. "Your Discards May be Somebody's Treasure." *Library Journal* 125, no. 8 (April 1): 62–63.

Berlin, Susan. 1989. "Best Sellers and Public Service: Can Public Libraries Provide Both?" *Reference Librarian*, nos. 27–28: 451–57.

"Best Seller Book Club Builds Library Collection." 1995. *The Unabashed Librarian* no. 96: 11.

Blecic, D. D. 2000. "Monograph Use at an Academic Health Science Library: The First Three Years of Shelf Life." *Bulletin of the Medical Library Association* 88, no. 2 (April): 145–51.

Bogart, D., ed. 2000. *The Bowker Annual Library and Trade Book Almanac*. 45th ed. New Providence, NJ: R. R. Bowker.

Brazin, L. R. 1999. "A Grant Writer's Application of the Internet." *Bottom Line* 12, no. 3: 120–22.

Bridges, William, and Sandra Krebs Hirsh. 2000. *The Character of Organization: Using Personality Type in Organization Development*. Palo Alto, CA: Davies-Black.

Britten, William A. 1990. "A Use Statistic for Collection Management: The 80/20 Rule Revisited." *Library Acquisitions: Practice and Theory* 14, no. 2: 183–89.

Buckland, Michael K. 1975. *Book Availability and the Library User*. New York: Pergamon Press.

———. 1983. *Library Services in Theory and Context*. New York: Pergamon Press.

Burlingame, Dwight F. 1995. *Library Fundraising: Models for Success*. Chicago: American Library Association.

" 'Buy Me' Program Stocks New Library Shelves." 2000. [Homepage of the New Hanover County Public Library], [Online]. (Updated July 18). Formerly available: http://www.co .new-hanover.nc.us/lib/pages/cal_fundraising.htm [Accessed April 16, 2001].

Camarena, Janet. 2000. "A Wealth of Information on Foundations and the Grant Seeking Process." *Computers in Libraries* 20, no. 5 (May): 26–31.

Cargill, Jennifer. 1987. "Bottom Line Blues: Preparing Library Budgets." *Wilson Library Bulletin* 61, no. 10 (June): 31–33.

Carrigan, Dennis P. 1994. "Public Library Private Fund-Raising: A Report Based on a Survey." *Public Libraries* 33, no. 1 (January/February): 31–36.

Cassell, Kay Ann, and Elizabeth Futas. 1991. *Developing Public Library Collections, Policies, and Procedures: A How-to-Do-It Manual for Small and Medium Sized Public Libraries.* New York: Neal-Schuman.

Chadwell, F. A., and S. Brownmiller. 1999. "Heads Up: Confronting the Selection and Access Issues of Electronic Journals." *Acquisitions Librarian* no. 21: 21–35.

Clay, Edwin S., III, and Patricia C. Bangs. 2000. "Entrepreneurs in the Public Library: Reinventing an Institution." *Library Trends* 48, no. 3 (Winter): 606–18.

Clayton, Peter. 1998. "Guidelines for the Preparation of a Collection Development Policy." [Homepage of the National Library of Australia], [Online]. Available: http://www.nla.gov.au/libraries/resource/acliscdp.html (Updated December 3). [Accessed September 28, 2001].

"Collection Development and Materials Selection Policy." 2001a. [Homepage of Kenosha Public Library], [Online]. (Approved May 9). Available: http://www.kenosha.lib.wi.us/policies/cllndev.html [Accessed September 28, 2001].

"Collection Development Training for Arizona Libraries." [2001b]. [Homepage of Arizona Department of Library, Archives and Public Records], [Online]. Available: http://www.dlapr.lib.az.us/cdt/intro.htm [Accessed September 28, 2001].

Craft, Mary Anne. 1999. *The Funding Game: Rules for Public Library Advocacy.* Lanham, MD: Scarecrow Press.

"Developing Children Into Avid Readers." 1997. *American Libraries* 28, no. 8 (September): 72.

Diodato, Louise W., and Virgil P. Diodato. 1983. "The Use of Gifts in a Medium-Sized Academic Library." *Collection Management* 5, nos. 1–2 (Spring-Summer): 53–71.

"eBay Auction of Old Books Opens New Option for Public Library." 2000. *Library Hotline* 29, no. 29 (July 24): 3.

Eggers, Lolly. 1976. "More Effective Management of the Public Library's Book Collection." *Minnesota Libraries* 25, no. 2 (Summer): 56-58.

Eggink, G. 1999. "Breder aanbod en tijdwinst door centraal collectioneren: ervaringen in Noord-Hollands experiment. [A wider choice and time-saving through centralised acquisition: experiences from the North-Holland experiment.]" *BibliotheekBlad* 3 no. 18 (September 3): 8–10.

Ettelt, Harold. 1988. "Does the 80/20 Rule Apply to Books?" Hudson, NY: Columbia-Greene Community College. ERIC ED298963.

Evans, G. Edward. 1969. "The Influence of Book Selection Agents Upon Book Collection Usage in Academic Libraries." Ph.D. diss., University of Illinois.

Evans, G. Edward, and Claudia White Argyres. 1974. "Approval Plans and Collection Development in Academic Libraries." *Library Resources & Technical Services* 18, no. 1 (Winter): 35–50.

Evans, G. Edward, with the assistance of Margaret R. Zarnosky. 2000. *Developing Library and Information Center Collections.* 4th ed. Englewood, CO: Libraries Unlimited.

Fales, Susan L., ed. 1996. *Guide for Training Collection Development Librarians.* Chicago: American Library Association.

French, Carol, and Eleanor Pollard. 1997. "Serials Usage Study in a Public Library." *Public Library Quarterly* 16, no. 4: 45–53.

"Funds Are Excellent in Evanston." 1997. *Public Libraries* 34, no. 5 (September/October): 276.

Futas, Elizabeth, ed. 1995. *Collection Development Policies and Procedures*. 3d ed. Phoenix: Oryx Press.

Gibson, Catherine. 1998. " 'But We've Always Done it This Way!' Centralized Selection Five Years Later." In *Public Library Collection Development in the Information Age*, ed. Annabel K. Stephens, 33–40. New York: Haworth Press.

Goldberg, Beverley. 1997. "Money Matters: Municipal Match Game." *American Libraries* 28, no. 8 (September): 33.

Goldberg, Susan. 1993. "Fund Raising, Friend Raising: The San Antonio Public Library Foundation." *Bottom Line* 7, no. 1 (Summer): 37–39.

Hannah, Kathryn Covier. 1997. "Alternative Funding for Libraries: A Plan for Success." *Bottom Line* 10, no. 4: 169–75.

Hoffert, Barbara. 2000. "Book Report 2000: Circulation Dips, But Buying Still Up." *Library Journal* 125, no. 3 (February 15): 130–32.

"In Your Community." 2000. [Homepage of Jewel-Osco], [Online]. Available: http://www.jewelosco.com/jewel/pr/pr_shopnshare.asp?cat=9&subcat=5 [Accessed September 28, 2001].

Intner, Sheila S. 1996. "The Ostrich Syndrome: Why Written Collection Development Policies Are Important." *Technicalities* 16, no. 6 (July/August): 1.

Irvine, Ann. 1995. "Is Centralized Collection Development Better? The Results of a Survey." *Public Libraries* 34, no. 4 (July/August): 216–19.

Jacobs, Deborah. 1998. "Private Funding Ensures Public Support." *American Libraries* 29, no. 8 (September): 42.

Johnson, Peggy. 1995. "Preparing Materials Budget Requests." *Technicalities* 15, no. 4 (April): 8–9.

———. 1997. "Collection Development Policies and Electronic Information Resources." In *Collection Management for the 21st Century*, ed. G. E. Gorman, and Ruth H. Miller, 83–104. Westport, CT: Greenwood Press.

———. 1999. "Dollars and Sense in Collection Development: Skills and Competencies for Collection Development and Management." *Technicalities* 19, no. 5 (May): 1, 7–9.

"Just for Librarians." [2001]. [Homepage of Landmark Audiobooks], [Online]. Available: http://www.landmarkaudio.com/library.php?PHPSESSID=0cb698c7467c9dde 36f1afab816f09e1 [Accessed September 28, 2001].

Kibbe, David. 1987. *Metamorphosis*. New York: Atheneum.

King, David. 2000. "Soliciting Virtual Money." *NetConnect* supplement to *Library Journal* and *School Library Journal* (Fall): 39–41.

Kovacs, Beatrice. 1990. *The Decision-Making Process for Library Collections: Case Studies in Four Types of Libraries*. Westport, CT: Greenwood Press.

Kovacs, Diane. 2000. *Building Electronic Library Collections: The Essential Guide to Selection Criteria and Core Subject Collections*. New York: Neal-Schuman.

"LARC (Library and Research Center) Fact Sheet Number 24: Library Fund Raising." 2000. [Homepage of the American Library Association], [Online]. (Updated February 1). Available: http://www.ala.org/library/fact24.html [Accessed September 28, 2001].

"Library Programs." [2001]. [Homepage of Taped Editions], [Online]. Available: http://www.tapededitions.com/library1.htm [Accessed April 16, 2001].

Lynch, Mary Jo. 1999. "Compared to What? Or, Where to Find the Stats." *American Libraries* 30, no. 8 (September): 48–50.

Mackenzie, Christine. 2000. "Outsourcing: the Brisbane Experience." *Australasian Public Libraries and Information Services* 13, no. 2 (June): 59–62.

Martin, Murray S. 1992. "Unique Relationships." *Bottom Line* 6, no. 1 (Spring): 8.

———. 1995. *Collection Development and Finance: A Guide to Strategic Library Materials Budgeting*. Chicago: American Library Association.

Martin, Murray S., and Betsy Park. 1998. *Charging and Collecting Library Fees and Fines: A Handbook for Libraries*. New York: Neal Schuman.

"Mastering the Possibilities." 1996. *Library PR News* (July/August): 11.

"Materials Selection." [2001]. [Homepage of Latah County Library District], [Online]. Available: http://norby.latah.lib.id.us/about/policy.html [Accessed September 28, 2001].

Mathis, Carla Mason, and Helen Villa Connor. 1993. *The Triumph of Individual Style*. Menlo Park, CA: Timeless Editions.

"McNaughton Catalogs." [2001]. [Homepage of Brodart], [Online]. Available: http://www.brodart.com/books/mcn/mcnhome.htm [Accessed September 28, 2001].

Meyers, Arthur S. 1998. "Money Matters: Baiting the Gateway to Full Funding—With Food." *American Libraries* 29, no. 8 (September): 30–31.

Moreland, George B. 1968. "Operation Saturation." *Library Journal* 93, no. 10 (15 May 15): 1975–79.

Nelson, Sandra, for the Public Library Association. 2001. *The New Planning for Results: A Streamlined Approach*. Chicago: American Library Association.

Nelson, Sandra, Ellen Altman, and Diane Mayo. 1999. *Managing for Results: Effective Resource Allocation for Public Libraries*. Chicago: Public Library Association.

"News Fronts USA—It Wasn't Crying Time Again . . . ." 1998. *American Libraries* 29, no. 11 (December): 16.

Payne, Bonnie R. 1997. "Straw into Gold: Could Private Fundraising be the Answer." *Public Libraries* 36, no. 3 (May/June): 174–77.

"PLA's 1994 National Achievement Citations Awarded." 1995. *Public Libraries* 34, no. 3 (May/June): 172.

"PLs Form Consortium for E-Book Resources." 2000. *Library Hotline* 29, no. 26 (July 3): 4–5.

Public Library Association. 1998. *Public Library Data Service Statistical Report 1998*. Chicago: Public Library Association.

Pulido, M. A., and A. M. Parejo. 1999. "Valoracion y estudio de generos de la literatura de imaginacion en bibliotecas publicas de la Comunidad Autonoma de Extremadura. [Assessment and analysis of genres of imaginative literature in public libraries of the Extremadura Autonomous Community.]" *Boletin de la Asociacion Andaluza de Bibliotecarios* 14, no. 54 (March): 9–31.

Rabine, Julie L., and Linda A. Brown. 2000. "The Selection Connection: Creating an Internal Web Page for Collection Development." *Library Resources and Technical Services* 44, no. 1 (January): 44–49.

Schuman, Patricia Glass. 1999. "Speaking Up and Speaking Out: Ensuring Equity through Advocacy." *American Libraries* 30, no. 9 (October): 50–53.

Slote, Stanley. 1997. *Weeding Library Collections: Library Weeding Methods*. 4th ed. Englewood, CO: Libraries Unlimited.

Smith, Mark L. 1996. "Using Statistics to Increase Public Library Budgets." *Bottom Line* 9 no. 3: 4–13.

St. Lifer, Evan. 1999. "Libraries Succeed at Funding Books and Bytes." *Library Journal* 124, no. 1 (January): 50–52.

Steele, Victoria, and Stephen D. Elder. 2000. *Becoming a Fundraiser: The Principles and Practice of Library Development*. Chicago: American Library Association.

Strickland, Stephanie A. 1999. "Outsourcing: the Hawaiian Experience." *Journal of Library Administration* 29, no. 2: 63–72.

Strong, Rob. 1999. "A Collection Development Policy Incorporating Electronic Formats." *Journal of Interlibrary Loan, Document Delivery and Information* 9, no. 4: 53–64.

Sullivan, Michael. 2000. "Giving Them What They Want in Small Public Libraries." *Public Libraries* 39, no. 3 (May/June): 148–55.

Swan, James. 1990. *Fundraising for the Small Public Library: A How-to-Do-It Manual for Librarians*. New York: Neal-Schuman.

Trueswell, Richard W. 1969. "Some Behavioral Patterns of Library Users: The 80/20 Rule." *Wilson Library Bulletin* 43, no. 5 (January): 458–61.

Turner, Anne M. 1997. *Getting Political: An Action Guide for Librarians and Library Supporters*. New York: Neal Schuman.

van Vaerenbergh, J. 1997. "Openbare bibliotheek sleutelt aan openingsuren te Leuven: gedifferentieerde dienstverlening: om u beter te kunnen dienen. [Leuven's public library tackles opening hours: a rearrangement of services provides a better service]." *Bibliotheek- en Archiefgids* 73 no. 6: 214–19.

Waznis, Betty. 1998. "Materials Budget Allocation Methods at San Diego County Library." In *Public Library Collection Development in the Information Age*, ed. Annabel K. Stephens, 25-32. New York: Haworth Press

Wilson, Karen A., and Marylou Colver, eds. 1997. *Outsourcing Library Technical Services Operations: Practices in Academic, Public, and Special Libraries*. Chicago: American Library Association.

Wisotzki, Lila. 1989. "Duplicate, Circulate: Demand Buying." Paper presented at the Collection Development Conference, Public Library Association, Chicago, Illinois, March 19.

———. 2000. (Head of Materials Selection at the Baltimore County[Maryland] Public Library). Telephone conversation with Sharon Baker, October.

Yamamoto, A. 1999a. "Collection Development at Baltimore County Public Library: Its Impact on the Theory of Collection Development, Part One." *Toshokan-Kai (The Library World)* 50, no. 5 (January): 204–23.

———. 1999b. "Collection Development at Baltimore County Public Library: Its Impact on the Theory of Collection Development, Part Two." *Toshokan-Kai (The Library World)* 50, no. 6 (March): 278–99.

———. 1999c. "Collection Development at Baltimore County Public Library: Its Impact on the Theory of Collection Development, Part Three." *Toshokan-Kai (The Library World)* 51, no. 1 (May): 18–25.

10

MARKETING-BASED PROMOTIONAL POLICIES AND PRACTICES

"Of course I'm a publicity hound. . . . How can you accomplish anything unless people know what you're trying to do?"—Vivien Kellems (Partnow 1977, 253).

Chapter 7 introduces a range of strategies to help ensure that the public knows about collection development efforts and offerings. This chapter further explores techniques to accompany these approaches, considering both internal and external promotional practices that may effectively increase use and user awareness of the collection.

WHAT INTERNAL PROMOTIONAL PRACTICES CORRELATE WITH HIGH USE OR USER AWARENESS OF THE COLLECTION?

The percentage of fiction browsers in public libraries, who by definition bypass bibliographic control devices in their quest to find fulfilling materials, consistently equals or surpasses the percentage searching for specific items or information. In addition, the percentage of nonfiction readers who browse totals 30 percent or more in most libraries (Shearer 1998; Hage 1997; Towey 1997; Baker 1996). Yet browsing can both be frustrating and yield less than optimal results, as figure 10.1, page 276, culled from the work of Jennings and Sear (1986; Sear and Jennings 1986) illustrates.

Samples from a Major Browsing Study

- Four out of five of the users surveyed in several British public libraries accepted shelf arrangements as they were.

- Fifty-two percent of those looking for fiction had looked for certain authors unsuccessfully; 92 percent of these took home substitutions.

- Readers who came browsing for specific authors already known to them were most likely to enjoy the titles they borrowed. Those using the most common method of selection (browsing for something that looked interesting) were least likely to have enjoyed the books they returned. In all, 18 percent of browsers did not enjoy the titles they read (so much so that they did not finish them); another 22 percent were lukewarm, and 60 percent liked the titles they chose.

- Those who had not fully enjoyed a work expressed disappointment with the match between the work's content and style and their own reading tastes. They often noted that the work was not what they expected; in the brief time spent on selection, they inaccurately assessed the work's content, series, or other characteristics.

- Four prevalent reasons for patron dissatisfaction were that
  1. the desired books were not on the shelves (i.e., missing, checked out to other readers, etc.);
  2. the libraries had fewer current materials than patrons desired;
  3. patrons had run out of authors they enjoyed; and
  4. patrons found the act of browsing difficult in and of itself, because they didn't know what they were looking for.

- Only 34 percent of the browsers felt it was "easy" to choose fiction from the library's shelves. Forty-five percent found it "so-so," and 21 percent found it "difficult."

FIGURE 10.1. Samples from a Major Browsing Study. Culled from *How Readers Select Fiction* (Jennings and Sear 1986; Sear and Jennings 1986).

We believe that these difficulties result partly from information overload, a decreased efficiency in handling information that comes from sifting excessive data; moreover, time constraints potentially increase the likelihood of frustration and errors in searching and retrieval (e.g., Bawden, Holtham, and Courtney 1999; Baker, 1986b). Certainly, as professionals we have the job of teaching patrons to comprehend and use the potentially confusing, complex bibliographic control devices already in place (e.g., the catalog). But we can also reduce both overload and frustration for casual users by focusing browser attention on a small subset of items via any of the following techniques:

Display shelving

Displays

Booklists

Fiction categorization

Reader interest categorization

Personalized reference and readers' advisory services

Display Shelving

Currently, a majority of public libraries still pack standard shelving units with materials housed spine out. Yet when Long (1986) took a group of 300 titles with equivalent circulation in a branch of the Durham (North Carolina) County Library and subdivided them into two groups, one shelved face front and the other spine out, the former immediately and significantly began to out-circulate the latter. Presumably the visual appeal of the covers captured patrons' attention and provided graphic and written information that helped in their selection. Although few libraries scientifically test the effects of display shelving, a number note that its use increased circulation and patron satisfaction with their collections (e.g., "Face-Out" 1988). Even when space concerns prohibit the extensive use of face-front display, librarians can selectively use this technique.

Materials on shelves from eye to knee level will be most visible and accessible (Underhill 1999) and thus most used by browsers, as a number of studies confirm (e.g., Forbes 1971; Shaw 1938). When Spiller extensively questioned browsers, he discovered that shelf position rarely mattered when respondents sought a specific book. However, 29 percent of the respondents browsing at random "felt they were influenced to some extent by the height of the shelf, in the way that supermarket shoppers are more prone to impulse buying of goods at eye-level. There were 27 specific complaints against top shelves, 17 of these because of the difficulties caused by wearing bifocals. Forty-eight respondents singled out bottom shelves for criticism, a gamut of medical complaints (blood pressure, bad back, arthritis, dizziness, etc.) being held responsible for their inaccessibility" (Spiller 1980, 249).

Our shelving recommendations include the following:

- Avoid shelving works on the top and bottom tiers of standard eight-shelf units, assuming the library either already has adequate shelf space or can create it through selective weeding. If space remains a problem, try to ensure that no work spends its entire circulating life on either the bottom or top shelf, shifting the shelves at regular intervals. For example, keep a three-shelf buffer at the beginning and end of a collection, then shift materials so that works formerly on shelves two to four move to shelves five to seven and vice versa. Obviously, infrequent shifts (preferably done with the help of volunteers) will be the most feasible.

- Use chevroning (placing books on specially designed lower shelves that kick out and tilt upward slightly so that patrons can read titles housed there without stooping) whenever possible. Alternatively, tilt existing bottom shelves, lowering the rear shelf supports only by one or two notches, for a chevron effect. As Shaw (1938) demonstrated in a classic study conducted more than 60 years ago this practice helps distribute use more evenly among all but the topmost (i.e., eighth) shelf.

- Purchase shelving that allows face-front or combined face- and spine-front display for particular locations (e.g., shelves that cap range ends) or formats. For example, one pyramid-style rack shelves CDs face-out, while keeping items on lower tiers visible. Another displays seven hundred CDs in just three square feet of floor space, allowing users to browse by flipping through front covers. News articles and advertisements in the general library literature feature such shelving. *Publishers Weekly* regularly publishes articles that discuss new kinds of shelving and list the names of firms that can help design shelving systems for maximum effect.

- Train pages to shelve books face out whenever feasible, using bookstands if necessary, to help reduce the spine-effect.

Displays

Many libraries entice their patrons to try something different by designing attractive displays of materials, often focusing on a particular product line, such as spy stories or government publications, possibly linking fiction and nonfiction works as well as multiple formats by a common theme.[1] Displays can

- expose patrons to unknown yet intriguing items;
- remind patrons of authors or titles they have heard about and would like to borrow; or
- trigger patron recognition of latent needs that they have not previously acted upon.

For example, as noted in Chapter 4, patrons may express a willingness to try new authors but lack knowledge of specific appealing works, a difficulty display can ease. When libraries in several British counties mounted multiple topical displays of high-quality literature, 74 percent of patrons borrowing materials took a book by an author they had never before read (McKearney 1990).

Using only a few topical displays does not increase overall library use; it concentrates use among these featured works, as Roy (1993) and Baker (1986a) have shown. However, the widespread use of numerous displays may reduce patron costs of finding intriguing works and ultimately cause them both to return to the library more frequently and tell family, friends, and colleagues about the positive browsing experience. In the first five months of using displays, the Tukwila branch of the King County (Washington) Library System experienced a 21 percent increase in circulation over the same period during the previous year (Riquelme 1998).

Research and experience suggest several guidelines for effective displays. First, displays will significantly increase use and user awareness of the materials they contain only when placed in well-traveled, highly visible and accessible locations (Baker 1986a, 1986b; Goldhor 1981, 1972). Particularly effective locations for displays are

- inside the library's entrance, past the transitional zone discussed in Chapter 6;

- at the end of cross aisles located in heavily traveled areas; and

- at or near the circulation desk, or any other public service desk where patrons queue, optimally positioned to be accessible to the second or third patron in line (Underhill 1999).

As noted in Chapter 6, positioning displays at an angle so that approaching patrons can easily see them and designing multi-sided displays will increase their visibility and use.

Other guidelines for creating effective displays follow:

- Locate materials on flat or tilted surfaces positioned at eye level (between 36 and 60 inches from the floor) for easy visibility. Libraries can buy special display units or construct pyramid-like structures to house materials at this height.[2]

- Stock displays with materials patrons can pick up, then immediately check out if they choose (i.e., avoid display of single-copy titles in the windows of the building or in locked cases, potentially frustrating patrons by drawing their attention to materials they cannot immediately access).

- Stock displays with visually pleasing materials. In spite of their internal content, materials with plain, dull, or rebound covers will appeal less to most patrons than works with bright, colorful covers. Rebinding may be less cost-effective today than buying a used copy of the same work, complete with dust jacket, on the Internet.

- Restock displays as patrons take materials and avoid overly orderly, elaborate displays that discourage browsing. For example, Underhill (1999) tells of one store that mounted a bagel-chip display so artfully constructed that it inhibited people from touching it, a problem solved when staff members purposely messed it up a bit.

- Change displays frequently. The optimal length of a display corresponds to the length of time between visits for a "typical" patron (Underhill 1999) which, for many libraries, may coincide with the length of a checkout period.

- Add simple, colorful headers or signs to attract patrons to the display. Well-designed, durable signs indicating broad subject or generically labeled (e.g., "Staff Favorites," "Academy Award Winners," or "Old-Fashioned Love Songs") can be re-used for cost-effectiveness.

- Recognize that patrons and staff may have difficulty finding specific items taken from their regular shelf location and placed in a display. This problem can be mitigated by changing the shelf status of displayed items to "display," if the online catalog allows; alerting staff, particularly pages and those who work at public service desks, of the topics of current displays; and/or placing shelf dummies where the displayed items would normally be. Because purchased shelf dummies can be expensive, libraries may want to create their own. Library volunteers could neatly wrap discarded or donated books in plain, heavy paper and write "On Display" on the spine. A card bearing the title could be placed in a pocket on the front of the dummy under a label telling the patron where to find the display.

Book, CD, Video, and (Fill-in-the-Blank) Lists

Materials lists also help alleviate overload by focusing patron attention on a smaller group of specific titles. Such lists may significantly increase selection of the materials listed only when distributed widely and in a manner that requires little patron effort to obtain them (Baker 1986b). Effective distribution techniques for materials lists include the following:

- Give them directly to patrons. For example, when Golden (1983) and the Prince George's County (Maryland) Memorial Library System ("Service" 1989) put a book list into each set of items an adult patron borrowed, use of featured works increased significantly.

- Place the lists (with a large accompanying sign) just inside the entrance for patron pick up. Parrish (1986) found patrons picked up 63 percent of booklists this way; they took only 28 percent from a brochure stand by the reference desk.

- Ask staff to distribute these lists to patrons who ask related reference or readers' advisory questions. When one academic library did this to ease the plight of patrons trying to browse for genre fiction materials classed within the Library of Congress schedule, use of promoted titles significantly increased (Wood 1985).

Many libraries are also experimenting with electronic distribution of such lists. The Iowa City (Iowa) Public Library catalog menu offers "featured lists" in different categories, such as Oprah's Book Club selections, allowing patrons to immediately check on the shelf status of desired materials ("Other" 2000). Numerous other libraries post materials lists on their Web sites, including

- the East Providence (Rhode Island) Public Library's new videos list ("New" 2001);

- the Salt Lake City (Utah) Public Library's monthly annotated bibliography of "good reads" ("Good" 2001);

- the Gwinnett County (Georgia) Public Library's selection of topical research guides listing print, computer, and audiovisual resources ("Topical" 2001); and

- the Chicago Public Library's list of teen favorites, gathered by asking teens who attended their 1998 summer reading program party to vote "on books they would or would not like to invite to a 125th birthday party for the Library" and why ("Teen" 1998).

Materials lists can even encourage patrons to check out materials that have not circulated for a substantial time. Parrish (1986) divided 70 titles that had not been checked out for at least four years into two groups with similar average numbers of circulations, copyright dates, acquisition years, and months since the last circulation. Over an eight-week period, 63 percent of the titles from group one, featured on booklists throughout the library, circulated for a total of 33 checkouts; 11 percent of the titles in the control group (i.e., not so featured) circulated for a total of four checkouts only.

Note that materials lists (which require a search of the stacks) will be somewhat less effective than displays in increasing use. For example, Goldhor (1981) found that placing titles on a booklist increased their circulation fourfold but placing titles on display increased their circulation sevenfold.

Librarians may take the time to compile their own materials lists or adapt lists that someone else has created to suit their collections. Such lists can be located in journals such as *The Unabashed Librarian*, the *Library Literature* index, or "Swap-and-Shop" sessions at library conferences. In addition, the Internet, including individual library Web sites, various genre sites, and relevant archived electronic mailing lists, like Fiction_L, provides a handy source of (mostly noncopyrighted) lists.[3] Unannotated lists containing works focusing on a single theme (e.g., cleric detective novels) have been shown to be as effective as annotated ones (see, e.g., Golden 1983). However, when a single list has multiple themes, we recommend short annotations worded to capture the flavor of the titles featured.[4]

To avoid sending patrons to the shelves for works already checked out, librarians emphasizing a popular materials service response may feature titles for which they have multiple copies, names of prolific authors and musicians, and subject headings and call numbers of popular nonfiction areas.

Fiction Categorization

Since the early part of the twentieth century, practitioners in the United States have experimented with genre subdivisions. Those publishing the results, including Bordon (1909), Haig (1933), Briggs (1973), Baker (1988), Cannell and McCluskey (1996), and Brown (1997), have clearly demonstrated that such grouping increased both circulation of the genre titles and patron (and often staff!) ability to select desired works quickly and easily. Although it takes time to adjust to a new fiction scheme (as long as two years for infrequent users, as one Finnish study showed [Saarti 1997]), an overwhelming majority of patrons desire this categorization (e.g., Sappiie 1995, Lasko and Puukko 1992, Spiller 1980). For example, when Reader (1982) surveyed patrons at a public library in Hertfordshire England, he found that 70 percent were very satisfied with the library's practice of categorizing fiction into seven different classes, 13 percent did not mind it, and only 8 percent disliked it. Related studies show that 79 percent of the readers in a British public library and 88 percent of students using a junior high school library said they liked their fiction separately categorized into genre areas (Ainley and Totterdell 1982; Briggs 1973).

One major reason for this overwhelming support is that fiction categorization helps patrons quickly identify previously unknown authors who write the kind of book they like, valuable because most fiction readers try to expand their list of favorite authors by browsing for preferred genres (Spiller 1980). Indeed, as Baker (1988) documented, fiction categorization can successfully alert browsers in various sizes of libraries to lesser-known desirable works in a particular genre, reducing their reliance on a small number of popular authors and titles.

Certainly, most public librarians recognize the value of fiction categorization. Indeed, Harrell (1985, 1996) found that more than 94 percent of U.S. library systems serving populations of 50,000 or more people have categorized at least part of their adult fiction collection.

Our principles for selecting categories follow:[5]

- Include categories popular with many patrons (of all ages), such as new fiction, mysteries, "novels with a (regional) connection," classics and award-winners (which will circulate when patrons know what they are), and multicultural fiction. Mueller (1965) showed that new titles circulated at notably higher rates in area libraries that displayed them separately; in contrast, they were "lost" in libraries that interfiled them with older fiction on the regular shelves.

- Include formats, such as large print, audiobook, and adult new reader titles that can help those with disabilities as well as those just learning the language(s) of the area.

- Create genre collections in all media formats, as relevant.

- Use genre headings easily understood by a wide span of patrons, avoiding highly specialized terms, such as "bildungsroman" and "picaresque," used in the scholarly classification of fiction.

- Use genre headings in fairly common usage from facility to facility to ease possible confusion of patrons hopping between multiple branches or libraries.

- Avoid merging two or more categories with significantly different readership, such as science fiction and fantasy.

- As the size and complexity of the fiction collection grows, increase the number of sub-genres. A collection of 10,000 mysteries, for example, could include sub-genres of police procedurals, private investigators, and amateur sleuths.

- Incorporate affinity patterns (noted in Chapter 6) into shelf arrangement, locating categories with overlapping audiences, such as adventure and mystery, next to each other.

- Choose categories that allow quick yet effective subdivisions, realizing that there will be no perfectly "clean" distinctions between genres.

Although we recommend Schabel's (1997) *classification* scheme, with its hierarchical structure and extensive definitions of 14 genre and 122 sub-genre areas, for creating booklists and bibliographies that focus on U.S. fiction, we have not found a published *categorization* scheme that met all our criteria. Therefore, figure 10.2, pages 284–86, offers our own, which includes recommendations for adult fiction collections (in all formats) in particular, with suggested modifications for young adult and children's collections. We encourage libraries to test this, perhaps at one location, making judicious adaptations as relevant for the entire system.

Library Literature and *Bibliographic Index* can help staff locate bibliographies useful in subdividing a fiction collection by genre and sub-genre. We find the following full-length bibliographies particularly relevant for fiction published in North America: *Fiction Catalog* (Yaakov and Greenfieldt 2001) and *Good Reading* (Waldhorn, Weber, and Zeiger 1990); the genre-specific series titles *Genreflecting* (Herald 2000), *Teen Genreflecting* (Herald 1997), and *Junior Genreflecting* (Volz, Scheer, and Welborn 2000); and the genre-specific series titles *What Do I Read Next?* (Barron et al. annual), *What Do Young Adults Read Next?* (Spencer 1999), and *What Do Children Read Next?* (Spencer and Ansell 1999). The first two titles particularly help with serious and classic literature, the latter ones with popular materials.

FICTION CATEGORIZATION SCHEME

Suggested Format Subdivisions for All Fiction Collections (as owned):

Novels and Short Stories

Large print

Audiobooks

CD books

Videos

Digital Video Discs (DVDs)

CD-ROMs

e-Books

Adult Fiction Collections

We recommend that libraries of all sizes consider establishing the categories marked with asterisks and that libraries with large general fiction collections subdivide them by adding non-asterisked categories and sub-genres.

General Instructions for Subdivisions:

- Classify short stories within major genre areas. Put cross-genre collections in general fiction.

- Classify award-winning titles within the major genre areas, labeling the spine of each with an award-winner sticker.

Categories

- * Adult New Readers—include high-interest, low vocabulary titles and works on Laubach and other adult new reader lists.

- * New Fiction—to ensure that both infrequent patrons and "regulars" have a chance to review new titles, place new fiction here for three months to a year, as space allows.

- * General Fiction—include serious modern fiction and other fiction that cannot be categorized within a single genre.

- * Classics—include older (at least a decade), non-genre titles that have retained their readership or appear on credible lists of "best" works and recommendations for the college-bound.

   Psychological Fiction—include works that focus heavily on psychological aspects of the main characters.

FIGURE 10.2. Recommended Fiction Categorization Scheme for Public Libraries.

* Multicultural Fiction—include here titles with perspectives from other ethnic cultures, countries, and continents; place many titles that would otherwise end up unread in the 800s of the Dewey Decimal classification here.

   Humorous Fiction

* Fantasy

* Science Fiction

* Horror

* Historical Fiction—given the strongly overlapping readership, examine the layout of the building to determine whether "Historical Fiction" could be placed near "Biography" and nonfiction historical works without confusing patrons.

* Mystery

* Westerns

* Romance

* Adventure, War Stories, and Espionage

* Inspirational Fiction—include Christian and other religious fiction here

   Gentle Reads—include here titles with little or no sex or violence

* Fiction with a Regional Interest—include titles by regional authors or focusing on settings in the library's region.

* Add any additional locally relevant categories for groups of highly popular titles identified with a particular individual or group (e.g., Oprah's recommendations, PBS features)

Young Adult Fiction Collections

We recommend the same categories as for adults, with the following modifications.

Add:	Delete:
*Newbery Award Winners	Adult Easy Readers
*Sports Stories	Psychological Fiction
*Series Fiction—shelve by series	
*Contemporary Life—place "problem novels" here	

(Fig. 10.2 continues on page 286.)

FIG. 10.2—*Continued*

Children's Fiction Collections

We recommend the same categories as for adults with the following modifications:

Add:
*Alphabet and Counting Books
*Colors and Shapes
*Caldecott Winners
*Fairy Tales and Folklore
*Holiday Fiction—subdivide by holiday
*Sports Stories

*Series Fiction—shelve by series
*Board Books
*Kits—book and tape sets
*Picture Books
*Easy Readers
*Chapter Books

Change
Horror to Spooky Stories

Delete:
Adult Easy Readers
Psychological Fiction
Adventure, War, and
    Espionage
Romance
Humorous Fiction

Finally, we note that although libraries can use spine labels to designate genre and leave items interfiled in a single scheme, patrons will find it quicker to browse separate collections than to pick out genre-labeled books from among all fiction titles. Indeed, in a tightly controlled experiment Baker (1988) found that physically separating books increases use substantially more than the simple labeling of genre titles.

Many libraries may also classify fiction to assist those readers who use the catalog to identify relevant works. We applaud this action, particularly when libraries work closely with two sets of recommendations: *Guidelines on Subject Access to Individual Works of Fiction, Drama, Etc.* (American Library Association 2000) and the extensive fiction subject heading lists developed at the Hennepin County (Minnesota) Library by Sanford Berman and his colleagues (Hennepin County Library 1992).

READER (OR VIEWER OR LISTENER) INTEREST CATEGORIZATION

We also recommend considering, as local needs dictate (e.g., for bookmobiles and other small collections), the grouping of nonfiction by reader interest categories—natural language categories that correspond to user needs and interests—rather than by Dewey Decimal, Library of Congress, or another alphanumeric classification scheme. Common categories are cooking, relationships, psychology, music, religion, computers, travel, and sports.

In the early 1940s the Detroit (Michigan) Public Library (DPL) tried reader interest categorization on a widespread basis (Rutzen 1952). When some patrons were overwhelmed by the large main library collection, DPL arranged a smaller collection of items by reader interest categories in an alcove near the circulation desk. Patron response proved so positive that DPL organized six new branch collections and 13 old ones entirely by reader interest categories between 1948 and the late 1950s. It also used such categories to organize subsets of the collections at other large branches in its system.

Today such categorization is widely used in U.S. bookstores and in many public libraries in Europe. We encourage other libraries to consider its use, at least on a limited scale, because it can make the arrangement of the library's collection both understandable and attractive to patrons of all ages (see, for example, Langhorne 1987; Webb 1985). One researcher has even documented that reorganizing fiction books using reader interest categories marked with symbols instead of words facilitated collection use among children who could not yet readily understand an author arrangement of fiction, while helping foster a sense of independence and self-worth (Williams 1973).

This reduction in the cost of using the collection may increase use; indeed, libraries that have tried reader interest categorization have experienced increases in the circulation of both nonfiction materials and of the collection in general. Consider the following examples:

- Reported increases in overall circulation range from an 18 percent increase at one branch of the Multnomah County (Oregon) Library to a 84 percent increase (over a four-year period) in a 6,500-book architecture collection ("New" 1989; "Face-Out" 1988; Hubbard 1967).

- The circulation of nonfiction materials rose by 30 percent after they were displayed in reader interest categories in a British public library branch and by an average of 70 percent in six libraries of a South African library system (Venter 1984; Sawbridge and Favret 1982).

- When Cropper (1986) arranged paperbacks in six reader interest divisions (biography, home, history and travel, social affairs, sports and hobbies, and science and medicine), he found fewer patrons asked for help in finding materials and more were introduced to materials formerly unknown to them. Circulation increases were so significant that within 10 days of introducing the arrangement patrons had checked out all of the books in four categories, prompting the library to purchase additional copies.

A reader interest categorization system collection can readily handle a collection of up to 30,000 nonfiction volumes, making this arrangement practical for smaller collections, such as those housed on bookmobiles, in branch libraries, in deposit collections at jails, and in small towns and villages. In the United States, bookstores with inventories of up to 150,000 volumes use such schemes.

Libraries with larger collections of nonfiction may wish to catalog all new works received within the Dewey Decimal System, then add an additional reader interest label above the regular call number on current and popular works only. Labeled titles can then be shelved by reader interest category in an area specially designed for use by browsers, preferably one near the library's entrance. As use of selected works declines over time, staff can quickly remove the reader interest labels and shelve the works among the nonfiction in the regular stacks.

To avoid placing works on the same subjects in two different locations, some libraries have arranged entire sections of the classification system—particularly those likely to appeal to browsers—by reader interest categories. Materials on all other subject areas are either placed in subject departments or in the regular stacks. For example, the Willesden Green Library in England organized a collection of 140,000 volumes in this type of two-tier classification system (Morson and Perry 1982). Although libraries that have tried these two-tier categorizing approaches have reported varying degrees of user satisfaction and circulation, as Ainley and Totterdell (1982) note, most have felt that the benefits outweigh the costs.

Libraries can also establish readily understandable interest categories for other formats. For example, staff can group CDs by musical genres such as folk, rock, jazz, and classical and then shelve works within them by the name of the performers or composers, either in strict alphabetical order or grouped by the first letter of the name. Most patrons (and staff) will find such an arrangement more intuitive than the Alpha-Numeric System for Classification of Recordings (ANSCR) that many public libraries use today.

Libraries that choose to use RIC groupings will need to consider a number of operational details. First, librarians must determine categories, which they can do by

- designing interest categories that reflect the most used subject categories within the existing classification scheme;

- using categorization schemes other libraries and organizations have developed, such as the 26-category scheme, shown in figure 10.3, that the American Booksellers Association and National Association of College Stores (ABA/NAS) developed for categorizing paperbacks; or

- combining the first two methods, modifying an existing scheme to reflect local interests and requirements. A library using the ABA/NAS scheme could, for example, add a category called "Spanish Books" to meet the needs of the large Latino population it serves.

However librarians determine reader interest categories, these do not replace standard subject headings and tracings, still assigned to enhance catalog access to titles.

Art	Literature
Biography	Medicine
Business	Music
Cooking	Nature
Crafts	Philosophy
Drama	Poetry
Education	Political Science
Fiction	Psychology
Games	Reference
History	Religion
Humor	Science
Juvenile	Sociology
Language	Travel

FIGURE 10.3. Reader Interest Categories Used by the American Booksellers Association and the National Association of College Stores. List of recommended subject headings given in *Paperbound Books in Print* (1992). Reprinted with permission.

Library staff should also mark RIC materials with relevant spine labels. Custom-designed stickers that reflect the library's scheme can be purchased fairly inexpensively from most library suppliers, then added to new materials and, as relevant, already owned items. As Milton (1986) notes, any major reclassification will be easiest to accomplish if the library prepares a table like the one shown in table 10.1, pages 290–91, to convert the existing classification scheme into each of the reader interest categories.

Finally, after assigning these category labels to the collection, staff must estimate the amount of shelf space required for each category and plan the new shelf layout.[6] The library can choose to house all interest categories separately from the fiction categories it has already set up or to group together (or even integrate) fiction and nonfiction categories that may have common readers (e.g., Humor, 827, and Cartoons, 741.5). Tables 6.3 and 6.4, pages 147 and 148, list some of these affinities.

TABLE 10.1. The Relationship Between the Reader Interest Categories Used by One Library and the Dewey Decimal Classification Scheme.*

Category Name	Symbol (for marking book and catalog)	Main Dewey Allocations
Animal life & pets	ANI	156**, 500.9, 590**, 636, 638, 639
Archaeology & ancient history	ARC	560**, 573**, 930
Art, architecture & photography	ART	069**, 700-779*
Astronomy & space	AST	500.5, 520, 629.4, 999
Biography	BIO	920 (preferred unless better placed with subject)
Cars & cycles	MOT	338.7**, 629.2**, 796.6-7
Collecting & antiques	COL	069**, 090, 391**, 681.1, 684**, 688**, 700-769**, 790.1
Crafts	CRA	646**, 680**, 700-769*
Crime & police work	CRI	327.1**, 345, 363.2, 363.4, 364-365, 614.1**, 652.4**, 658.47*
Economics, business & management	ECO	003**, 330, 343-344**, 346**, 368, 380-384**, 650-653, 657-659
Electronics	ELE	001.5-6**, 621.37**, 621.38
Entertainments & performing	ENT	394.3**, 790-792**, 793.3, 808.5
Food & drink	FOO	394.1**, 637, 640-642**, 647**, 663-664
Government, law & politics	GOV	320, 335, 340-349**, 350-352.1
Great Britain, travel, geography & history	GRE	327**, 367.9**, 391**, 394**, 526**, 912**, 941-942*
Health, welfare & public services	HEA	178, 312**, 344**, 352.4-7, 360-363**, 610-619, 628**, 646.7**, 649.8
House maintenance & decorating	HOU	333.3**, 621.3**, 643-645, 648, 684**, 690**, 714**, 717**, 747

Indoor games	GAM	394.3**, 398.6**, 790-795*
Literature & languages	LIT	010-029, 070-080, 098, 398.5-.9**, 400, 800
Living and learning	LIV	131-131.3, 137.7, 150-155.9, 158, 170**, 300-307.7, 312**, 323**, 326, 362.6-8, 366**, 367**, 369**, 370**, 391.6, 395, 646.7**, 649
Local history	LOC	Any with Surrey interest
Music	MUS	780
Philosophy	PHI	003**, 100-129**, 140-199*
Plant life & gardening	PLA	156**, 580**, 630-635**, 712**, 714-719*
Popular beliefs & the supernatural	BEL	001.9, 128.5-129.4, 133-135, 137.7**, 138-139, 147**, 149.3**, 292-299**, 366**, 390*
Quick reference	REF	As appropriate
Religion	REL	200-291, 292-299**, 377
Science & the earth	SCI	156**, 372**, 389, 500-519**, 526**, 530-550, 560-599*
Sport & outdoor activity	SPO	394.3**, 796-799*
Technology	TEC	001.5**, 601-609, 620-622**, 624, 627, 628**, 629.8, 630-631, 660-662, 665-699**, 710-711, 713, 714**, 717*
Transport	TRA	380.5, 385-388, 526**, 527-527.5, 621.33**, 623.8**, 625-625.7, 629-629.3**, 688.6*
Wars & warfare	WAR	343.1, 355-359, 363.3, 369**, 623-623.7, 623.8**, 794**, 904.7**, 940-999* (accounts of wars)
World travel, geography & history	WOR	324-325**, 327**, 367-9**, 391**, 526**, 647.9**,901-912**, 929.8, 940-999*

*Reprinted with permission from Milton (1986, 16-17).

**Indicates either that only part of the sequence is applicable or that books should be allocated to the most appropriate category. N.B. Occasionally these headings are amended if they do not fit on shelf guiding or are combined with other categories.

Personalized Readers' Advisory and Reference Services

The internal promotional techniques presented so far, which cost-effectively help multiple patrons identify and locate needed materials with minimal direct staff interaction, cannot completely substitute for providing individual patron guidance. Thus, most public librarians also promote the collection, one work at a time, through personalized reference and readers' advisory (RA) services that link individual patrons with items that they might find fulfilling. Librarians performing a reference function generally connect users with products that meet a specific information need: a circulating work that discusses Elizabethan fashion, a Web site with job search strategies, the average humidity in Tahiti, or other specific facts from a source that the patron may not even examine. That is, reference librarians try to satisfy information needs using the catalog, online resources, indexes, their knowledge of the collection, and so forth.

In contrast, readers' advisers help patrons find fiction and other leisure reading, viewing, and listening materials.[7] A patron might ask for an interesting biography of an "ordinary" person, an action-packed story with female protagonists, or a series of online stories by an author who writes like Stephen King. Ideally, patrons will leave with items they believe they will enjoy or the names of authors, titles, or Web sites to seek out in the future.

Given that few public libraries provide in-depth access to fiction in their catalogs (i.e., access by some means beyond author or title, such as character or setting), a readers' adviser often uses other sources to locate suitable works. For example, when Burgin (1996) surveyed 162 readers' advisers, he found that when suggesting materials they relied primarily on personal reading, followed by (unspecified) RA sources, then patron comments. This result, combined with May et al.'s (2000) finding that librarians frequently let their personal preferences guide their suggestions, potentially implies that readers' advisers may stress some genres and slight others. Burgin's survey suggests what favored genres may be, documenting that 96 percent of readers' advisers read at least one title per year in general fiction, 85 percent in mystery, and 59 percent in romance. Only 35 percent had read science fiction; 32 percent, fantasy; 28 percent, horror; and 18 percent, westerns.

Public libraries have not always stressed RA services. For example, a 1972 survey of 150 public libraries in the United States showed that less than one-fifth had a fully designated position of readers' adviser (Reagan 1973). This situation has improved since the 1980s in the United States, as librarians have realized the extent of the confusion that patrons, especially browsers, feel when faced with numerous choices and have undertaken efforts to promote such services. At the grassroots level, RA advocates have helped organize conference programs on this topic; formed RA roundtables at the local, regional, and national levels; and written an increasing number of works—both how-to and research related—on the subject.

Of continuing concern is the need for widespread promotion of the existence and value of RA services. Tracz (1997) found that a majority (69 percent) of Ohio public libraries surveyed do not promote their RA services, and May et al. (2000)

found no signage advertising RA services in any of the 54 libraries in Nassau County, New York. In a survey of subscribers to the Fiction_L (2001) electronic discussion list—an excellent resource for readers' advisers—three of the top four barriers to service that respondents identified concern promotion. About 40 percent indicated a need for both more signage and increased visibility of readers' advisory (desks, bibliographies, etc.) in their libraries, and a quarter noted that librarians need to train the public to ask for help (Saricks 1998).[8]

We urge librarians to follow the lead of those who are trying such promotion. The Downers Grove (Illinois) Public Library's Web site, for example, explains:

> Staff members are trained in Readers' Advisory, which involves putting people and books together. We actively work to match readers with books they will enjoy. . . . If you love good spy thrillers and constantly search for new titles, we can help. . . . If you have read all the works of Mary Higgins Clark or Tom Clancy, our staff can suggest similar books by other authors that you may enjoy. ("Literature" 2001)

Similarly, the Bettendorf (Iowa) Public Library Information Center's homepage invites people with RA questions to stop by the information desk, call, send questions via an online form, or e-mail the library (Bettendorf 2001). A number of libraries also highlight RA services in their newsletters. The Schaumburg Township (Illinois) District Library even publishes a quarterly newsletter devoted solely to RA services that includes book annotations, listings of upcoming displays, current movies based on books, new readers' advisory reference works, and similar items ("Reader" 2001). Coupling readers' advisory with other, better-known programs or services can also expose patrons to it, as when the Skokie (Illinois) Public Library incorporated readers' advisory service into their 1999 summer reading program, "Go Fish! for a Good Book." Program publicity explained that participants would draw from a fish bowl "to catch a fish with a literary genre printed on it—mystery, biography, sports, historical fiction, etc. Library staff at the Readers' Services Desk will happily suggest titles within the genres" ("Adult" 1999).

Gracious, Effective Service

Both reference and RA services involve personal promotion of materials that will meet patron needs. The most effective public service librarians exhibit certain characteristics. First, they possess a strong service orientation—a personal desire to provide the best service possible, which helps them devote their full energy and passion to assisting patrons. Service improves when librarians show they care by volunteering help (e.g., when a patron looks lost), checking to ensure that materials to which they refer patrons actually help them, and encouraging patrons to ask follow-up questions as necessary (Ross and Dewdney 1994).

Second, strong public service librarians must be both friendly and approachable to encourage users to overcome their reluctance to "bother" librarians, whom patrons often believe are too busy or even unwilling to assist them (e.g., Westbrook 1984). Although most librarians wait for patrons to initiate reference and RA queries (e.g., Wilkinson 1972; May et al., 2000), they can quietly and tactfully approach customers (who might otherwise be embarrassed to ask) to see if they require assistance. When Joe (1999), over a five-day, 20-hour study period, approached 189 patrons using the online catalog to see if they needed assistance, 44 percent immediately accepted the offer. Even those who declined seemed pleased to be asked. Moreover, the number of questions asked at the reference desk did not decline during the study period, suggesting that the users Joe helped would not otherwise have sought assistance.

Staff can also minimize the number of "never asked questions" by demonstrating approachability when at a service desk. Such actions include immediately acknowledging the presence of a patron moving toward the desk (if not verbally, then through establishing eye contact or eyebrow-flashing), smiling, speaking in a friendly tone, and indicating active listening through nodding and other evaluative gestures (Crouch 1981; Gothberg 1976; Kazlauskas 1976). One controlled experiment indicated that library users feel more satisfied after being helped by librarians who display such behaviors, even when the librarians who don't act in these ways have competently answered their questions (Gothberg 1976). Similarly, Dewdney and Ross found patrons more willing to return to librarians who "use welcoming body language" and "signal encouragement to users to ask reference questions" (1994, 229). When given a choice between two similarly receptive librarians, an overwhelming majority of patrons choose to ask standing ones for help, perceiving a seated librarian as busy and averse to being interrupted (Kazlauskas 1976).

Third, highly effective reference and RA librarians communicate with patrons in a helpful, professional fashion, conducting comprehensive interviews to determine each patron's requirements, because stated questions may not initially convey the real information need (Taylor 1968; White 1992). Further, given that the appeal of an item may vary for different people, to truly match patrons with items that will satisfy, librarians must ask insightful questions and listen thoughtfully to the answers (Chelton 1999). Continuing education efforts along these lines have been successful. For example, Stephan et al. (1988) gave a three-day workshop for reference librarians in Maryland's public libraries that increased participants' awareness of how they were handling reference questions; gave them intensive training in more appropriate behavior, particularly in conducting a comprehensive and clear reference interview; and provided them with ample opportunity to practice new techniques. Reference accuracy rates immediately rose from 55 to 77 percent; participants who obtained additional feedback and coaching increased their accuracy rates to 95 percent.

Those interested in exploring tested methods of conducting successful reference or readers' advisory interviews may wish to refer to Jennerich and Jennerich (1997), Katz (1997), Saricks and Brown (1997), and Straw (2000) for electronic interviews, and Gross (2000) for those working with children. In addition, Berinstein's (1994) book *Communicating with Library Users* offers strong advice on assessing and improving all forms of interpersonal communication, including reference and readers' advisory interviews, by understanding nonverbal elements of communication, reducing "noise" (in the sense of the model presented in Chapter 7), and so forth.

The value of strong communication skills in successful reference or RA transactions becomes still clearer upon reading Durrance's (1995) study of patrons' willingness to return to the same librarian. Ninety-six percent of patrons indicated they would return to a librarian who used open questions very effectively, 94 percent to librarians who determined the need behind the question, 92 percent to librarians with very good listening skills, and 91 percent to librarians who appeared very interested in the question.[9] In a related study, Baker and Field (2000) found that patron satisfaction most often hinged on the librarian's interpersonal skills, demonstrated interest in the question, and knowledge of reference sources. And Shearer's (1996) study of RA service suggests that a patron may leave with satisfactory materials and still feel discontented with the interaction if the librarian lacked a pleasant manner and good communication skills.

Fourth, librarians who serve a special target market (e.g., people who are hearing impaired) may benefit from additional specialized training. For example, youth services librarians knowledgeable about children's developmental needs should have, on average, a higher probability of matching a child's stated requirements with suitable titles.[10]

Finally, librarians need a comprehensive knowledge both of the collection and ways to access it. Research indicates that librarians do not always use efficient search strategies or exploit the catalog and other access tools as well as they might.[11] Libraries may offer continuing education to improve librarians' searching skills and encourage staff to increase their knowledge of the collection through informal methods, such as examining new materials as they arrive, browsing the shelves, selecting materials for displays and materials lists, and helping weed.

Libraries hiring staff will want to select individuals who have the aforementioned traits. They can also encourage the further development of staff members by providing continuing education and training programs, including those that use the RUSA *Guidelines for Behavioral Performance of Reference and Information Services Professionals* as a training tool. Developed by the American Library Association's Reference and Adult Services Division, the document describes observable behaviors "correlated with positive patron perceptions of reference librarian performance" (RASD 1996, 200).

For the Solo Artist

Even if knowledgeable, service-oriented librarians encourage patrons to ask for help, a few individuals will prefer to find materials on their own. Libraries can subtly assist by using the merchandising techniques discussed previously in this chapter. For example, they may display *Genreflecting* (Herald 2000), *Fiction Catalog* (Yaakov and Greenfieldt 2001), *What Do I Read Next?* (Barron et al. annual), and other readers' advisory tools on special shelves in the fiction stacks; *Leonard Maltin's Movie and Video Guide* (Maltin annual), *Halliwell's Film and Video Guide* (Walker 2000), and other movie guides next to the video and DVD collections; and assorted bibliographies and pathfinders near the nonfiction. To help patrons waiting for hot new releases, the Rolling Meadows (Illinois) Public Library has preprinted colorful bookmarks that say, "Looking for the newest _____ ? In the meantime try . . ." In the blank spot—a yellow polygon—staff write an author's name, then insert the bookmark in a readalike housed in a bookstand on the readers' services desk—a simple, yet very visible and effective technique.

Staff suggestion files can also help. The Schaumburg Township (Illinois) District Library maintains a "Bibliofile" box with brief annotations for books staff members enjoyed. Staff color-code Bibliofile entries to identify their genre and post the most recent submissions on a bulletin board near the readers' services desk ("Reader" 2001). Other libraries solicit and disseminate patron recommendations. The Phoenix Public Library sponsored a contest that asked children to "tell us why we should read your favorite book . . . in twenty-five words or less" (Meyers, Kist, and Sugden 1999, 32). To reach as many children as possible, the library made English- and Spanish-language ballots available in the Kids Page of the city's major newspaper, at Border's Books and Music, and on its homepage as well as in the libraries. Staff also sent faxes to teachers explaining the contest. The library received more than 1,600 entries. When staff incorporated the 100 entries judged most enticing into a book list distributed to schools and libraries during Children's Book Week and honored the writers at a special reception, the list generated much media coverage as well as attracting readers.

Librarians can also make electronic readers' advisory resources available, such as NoveList (EBSCO) or What Do I Read Next? (Gale), which each provide access to close to 100,000 fiction titles by subject, character, setting, genre, award, and other dimensions ("New" 2001; "What" 2001). In 1999, six statewide networks—in Georgia, Illinois, North Carolina, Ohio, Tennessee, and Wyoming—offered NoveList access to all public libraries in the state ("NoveList" 1999).

The Book Forager, developed through the Society of Chief Librarians' Branching Out project in Britain, takes the more complex approach of recommending items according to their appeal. Patrons set 12 sliding scales to indicate the degree to which they want certain features in a book: happy to sad, funny to serious, safe to frightening, expected to unpredictable, romantic to realistic, beautiful to repulsive, gentle to violent, easy to demanding; no sex to sex, conventional to weird, optimistic to bleak, and short to long. From the 20 million possible permutations, the software creates suggested booklists (van Riel 1999; "Welcome" 2001). Similarly, based on patron input about preferred length, tone, style, characterization, and more, the Reader's Robot, a free Web site created by the Thompson Nicola Regional District Library System (British Columbia), lists titles the reader may enjoy. And the RatingZone Web site, free to libraries that will allow on-site advertising and available via paid subscription to others, asks users to rate 25 or more titles, then recommends other books, music, or movies those individuals may enjoy ("Reader's" 2001; Oder 2000).

Librarians may also choose to create readers' advisory Web sites or provide links to others' sites. Johnson (2000a, 2000b) provides an overview of ways that libraries can use the Internet for readers' advisory as well as an array of links to useful sites. Schultz (2000) and Stevens (2000) also evaluate selected readers' advisory sites.

Finally, libraries may offer additional specialized readers' advisory services, with or without the use of technology. For example, patrons of the Morton Grove

(Illinois) Public Library who register for the MatchBook service complete an interest profile, then receive a monthly, automatically generated list of new materials customized for their tastes ("MatchBook" 2001). At the Cumberland County (North Carolina) Public Library and Information Center, staff will create a personalized reading list for patrons who complete a profile indicating their reading preferences (Casto 1999).

We wish to reemphasize here the need to provide readers' advisory for materials other than books. For example, the Canterbury (New Zealand) Public Library Web site lists 14 well-known classical pieces. A patron who has enjoyed listening to one of these can click on it to see a list of other works he or she may also like ("If" 1999). Given the popularity of audiovisual materials with many patrons, we strongly recommend that all librarians consider the breadth of their readers' advisory lists, incorporating software, magazine, DVD, video, and Web site suggestion lists (broken down by subject or genre), among others.

Programming

A public library may offer a range of programs designed to educate, entertain, and encourage discussion, which may also either directly or indirectly promote the collection.

For example,

- the Perins Community School (Alresford, England) library sponsored a reading club wherein students read 12 books, two each from five genres of their choice (of a possible nine) and two classics (Wilkins 1997);[12]

- more than 10,000 teens joined Spider-Man at the third annual Teen Comic Art and Animation festival held at the Los Angeles Public Library ("Webmaster" 1998);

- the Washington-Centerville (Ohio) Public Library organized an Arthur (the aardvark featured in Marc Brown's popular children's series) Library Card Sign-Up Event, with a live Arthur character, Arthur stories and crafts, and a contest; circulation was 144 percent above normal for the day ("ALA" 2000); and

- the Seattle Public Library celebrated National Poetry Month 1997 with 18 related events, including open mikes, poetry readings, and writing workshops as well as a poem-a-day bulletin board and other displays (Higashi 1998);

- the Kansas City (Missouri) Public Library held a weeklong online scavenger hunt in which participants answered questions about library services based on information found on the library Web site that changed every day. Entries submitted via an online form were entered into a raffle for soccer and theater tickets and other prizes (King 2000).

In fact, numerous programs can promote library materials. Youth storytimes expose the children and caretakers who attend to the wonders and joys of books and reading aloud as well as to the specific titles shared. Storytimes can also promote a product line, as the Fullerton (California) Public Library did when it presented "Millions of Cats," a weekly preschool storytime featuring books with cats introduced by the puppet "Black Kitty" ("Millions" 1996). Libraries can host or sponsor Great Books, "Let's Talk About It," and other groups that discuss a specific book, subject, or issue (e.g., Gendler 1997; "Not" 1996). Assisted by the Milwaukee (Wisconsin) Public Schools and the Milwaukee Art Museum, the Milwaukee Public Library featured a family discussion series on the art of children's picture books ("Why" 1993). The Chicago Public Library hosts the "Mystery Beat Book Club" for children, who read in the genre and hear police detectives explain how they solve real crimes. And the El Segundo (California) Public Library sponsors a children's science fiction, fantasy, and horror group wherein members talk about favorite genre books, enjoy author visits, and put on plays and puppet shows (Machado et al. 2000). Libraries may also facilitate the formation of other community discussion groups. For example, staff at the Pasco County (Florida) Library System created a resource kit that matched people with similar reading interests and then offered guidance in starting a discussion group ("Program" 1997).

A number of libraries also use their Web sites to promote the OnLine Book Club, an initiative that e-mails (under their library's name) registered patrons a short (approximately five-minute) excerpt from that week's featured title Monday through Friday (Fialkoff 2000). Five clubs exist: the original, audio, business, teen, and good news ("Books" 2001). Patrons whose appetites have been whetted for the books may be able to check library copy availability or place a reserve with a few clicks of a mouse, such as on the Minneapolis Public Library site ("Online" 2001). The Logan (Utah) Library provides the same service for a list of upcoming selections ("Logan" 2001).

Even non-materials-based programs can encourage collection use by piggybacking on other promotional efforts. For example, the Ocean County (New Jersey) Library System and its Friends group co-hosted a "Mini-International Food Tasting Festival." Along with food samples, entertainment, and an exhibit of memorabilia from around the world, the program included displays of travel books and videos ("Library" 1997). The Orange County (Florida) Library and the Florida Theatrical Association cosponsored a series of question-and-answer sessions with members of the casts and crews of the Orlando Broadway Series' 1995–1996 season. Librarians prepared a display of theater- and play-oriented materials for the sessions, many of which attracted more than 100 patrons ("Discovering" 1996).

Carpenter (1998) also advocates offering computer training as a means of promoting CD-ROM, online, and Internet resources; once patrons become comfortable accessing these, they will be able to use them more, and more successfully. In this vein, the Lubbock (Texas) City-County Library features a technology center in which it offers a variety of computer classes from "Basic PC: 'How Do You Turn This Thing On?' " to "Catching the Genealogy Bug on the Web" (Bridwell 2001). Libraries are increasingly providing patrons with such instructional opportunities.

Bertot and McClure (2000) found that 55.1 percent of public libraries offer Internet training to adult patrons and 43.7 percent to children.

Programs may entice people into the library who do not regularly frequent it, affording the library an opportunity to promote itself and its collections through its inviting atmosphere; eye-catching displays and materials lists; appealing, well-organized collections; and friendly staff. The Midland County (Texas) Public Library brought nonusers into the library with its 1995 summer reading club kick-off party. Club registration increased 55 percent over the previous year, and the completion rate stayed the same (20 percent), suggesting that at least some of the new patrons the party attracted continued using the library (Agosto 1996). We encourage data collection of this kind; the extent to which programs either bring in potential new patrons or increase circulation through direct or indirect means has not been established.

WHAT EXTERNAL PROMOTIONAL PRACTICES CORRELATE WITH HIGH USE OR USER AWARENESS OF THE COLLECTION?

To encourage potential patrons to come to the facility and use library materials or to promote library use outside the building (e.g., through deposit collections), librarians employ a host of external promotional techniques. Among these are creating and disseminating promotional messages through direct mail (paper or electronic), posters, flyers, automated phone systems, Web sites, and public service announcements; arranging media interviews; or placing radio, television, newspaper, magazine, and other media advertisements. One institution used a $38,000 LSCA grant to send eight direct mailings, urging residents of low-income neighborhoods to "Come to Know the Bloomington [Illinois] Public Library." The mailings included such incentives as coupons for free photocopies or free entries into a drawing for a gift certificate. Based on the number of coupons redeemed, the library estimated a 4.85 percent response rate (2 percent is considered "acceptable" for direct mailings) (Tepper 1989). The Miami-Dade (Florida) Public Library System's 11 delivery vans and trucks, which travel throughout the county, each bear a message encouraging people to get a library card ("Miami-Dade" 2000). The North Greenwood Branch of the Clearwater (Florida) Public Library System got its message out through bipedal power when staff and volunteers stuffed book bags with magnets, bookmarks, and information about library services and delivered them door-to-door to 100 homes ("Streetwalker" 1994). The Moore County (North Carolina) Public Library advertised its bookmobile service by placing doorhangers on residences near stops and increased usage by as much as 26 percent in some areas (Causey 1989). In an arguably too successful promotion, the Loveland (Colorado) Public Library filled its Internet training classes almost six months in advance after advertising them in city utility bills (Carpenter 1998). The Schaumburg Township (Illinois) District Library took another innovative approach to promotion when it worked with two area McDonald's restaurants to distribute information about the library on tray placemats handed to thousands of customers during National Library Week ("Fast" 1993).

External Programming

Librarians may also present programs outside the library, such as materials talks, storytelling, or slide-tape presentations (e.g., using a BiFolkal kit[13] at a nursing home or senior center). For example, Warsaw (New York) Public Library staff members spent an afternoon at the local Women, Infants, and Children Office, presenting brief programs on library services and the importance of reading to children to 500 women and children at half-hour intervals. They also passed out flyers, brochures, bookmarks, and coupons for free books redeemable at the library. Almost 20 women had redeemed these coupons by the end of the following day ("Outreach" 1997).

Libraries may also offer regularly scheduled programming. Multnomah (Oregon) County Public Library's LIBROS (Library Outreach in Spanish) program routinely presents Spanish storytimes and talks with parents at 15 community locations ("Library" 1999); librarians at the Arapahoe (Littleton, Colorado) Library District have given monthly booktalks at the local jail (Clark and Patrick 1999); and Bethel Park (Pennsylvania) Public Library volunteers regularly read aloud and reminisce with nursing home residents ("Outreach" 2001).

A library might choose to provide external programming "upon request." For example, the Evanston (Illinois) Public Library's Speaker's Bureau offers local organizations a range of free programs from 20 to 45 minutes long. Topics include "Raising Readers," "Business Information Resources at the Evanston Public Library," and "Home, Health, and Travel Information at the Library" ("Evanston" 1997).

Open houses and community festivals are other reasonable promotion venues. The Indianapolis-Marion County (Indiana) Public Library entered an award-winning float in the 125th Anniversary Indianapolis 500 Festival parade, attended by 250,000 people ("Librarian" 1998). The Brooklyn (New York) Public Library offered a workshop on its multimedia math and science resources at the citywide fair "Parents + Math + Science = A Formula for Our Children's Success" attended by more than 1,100 people ("Fair" 1996).

Staff at the Lucy Robbins Welles (Newington, Connecticut) Library pursued an extremely successful, less formal kind of "programming" when they spent a six-month period visiting 50 area businesses and talking to employees about services the library could offer them. The program was so well-received by the corporate community that city administrators, the Chamber of Commerce, and the Economic Development Commission contributed $5,000 for it to continue (St. Lifer 1993).

Partnerships

Partnerships with other organizations can both directly provide materials and/or services and get the word out about the library's collection and services. Consider the various ways in which public librarians work with schools. In a survey of public libraries in Ohio, Turano (1997) identified common kinds of school-public library cooperation: class visits to the library (95 percent), written or oral promotion of library services to school employees (88.1 percent), promoting summer reading programs (84.7 percent), assignment alerts (67.8 percent), and resource sharing (55.9 percent). Such efforts can reap significant rewards. For example, the Sno-Isle (Marysville, Washington) Regional Library System recently began visiting kindergarten classes at the beginning of the school year. By distributing specially colored applications, librarians learned that the visits have increased the number of kindergartener cards given out by 19 percent (Kelly 1999). Similarly, in their first year visiting all the third grade classrooms in 76 county public schools, librarians at Anne Arundel County (Maryland) Public Library spoke to 4,500 students, ultimately issuing 1,500 *new* cards ("Library" 1994).

Public library-school collaborations can also assume many other forms. The Arlington Heights (Illinois) Memorial Library offers student teachers an orientation to library resources (Barsun 1996), and the Eisenhower (Harwood Heights, Illinois) Public Library District has hosted breakfasts introducing teachers to library resources relevant to their discipline (Blubaugh 1995). Some libraries even hire staff solely to provide school service. For example, the Multnomah (Oregon) County Public Library employs five "School Corp" librarians who try to strengthen its relationship with county public and private schools by encouraging students and teachers to obtain library cards, training them to use library technology, presenting booktalks, and creating lists of helpful Web sites. In one 16-month period, the School Corp served almost 34,000 teachers and students (Minkel 1999).

Libraries can also form partnerships with a wide-variety of other groups. Some examples follow:

- The Fullerton (California) Public Library's bookmobile follows a local hospital's healthmobile on its rounds through the Latino community, attracting customers waiting for medical services. Hospital staff members also provide expert advice on the development of the library's health-related collections (Alire and Archibeque 1998).

- Working with the local police department, transit authority, and public art group, Chicago Public Library staff recruited talented high school students to paint a public transportation bus that runs between two branches. Called the "Knowledge Express," the vehicle bears the words, "Two Libraries Under Blue Skies. Albany Park and Douglass Branch Libraries" over the students' original artwork. The project gave the students an alternative to painting illegal graffiti, a.k.a. "tagging," as well as an opportunity to work with established artists, and the library gained a unique and highly visible advertisement on wheels (Burnette 1998; Chelton 1997).

- The Minnesota Library Association hit a promotional grand slam when it worked with the Minnesota Twins to create posters, picturing professional baseball players with books, that urge, "READ every chance you get." Libraries, health clinics, child-care centers, and correctional facilities have all displayed the posters; the images also helped create 20 billboards in the Twin Cities (Watkins 1997).

- In Decatur, Illinois, the library, hospitals, and schools worked together to form Baby TALK (Teaching Activities for Learning and Knowledge), a nonprofit organization that encourages early childhood development and parenting skills. Baby TALK offers a wide variety of services, including an after-delivery hospital visit introducing new parents to the program and offering a free children's book,[14] library lap-sit programs for children aged one to three, and a first birthday party at which parents can share thoughts on life with a 12-month-old and the children choose a free book as a gift. The program has been replicated in 28 states and Canada ("Notice" 1998; "Baby" 2001).

- The Kalamazoo (Michigan) Public Library and Bronson Methodist Hospital lead a coalition of 20 community organizations to sponsor "Ready to Read," which strives to ensure that Kalamazoo County children arrive at school prepared to learn and read. Program activities include volunteers reading and modeling book-sharing techniques at health agencies and child-care centers; pediatricians and other health care personnel giving free books, prescriptions for parental reading, and invitations to visit the local library; librarian-sponsored "Parents as Partners in Reading" workshops; and book collections at child-care centers (Kars and Doud 1999).[15]

- The Houston (Texas) Public Library worked with other city departments, the mayor, city council, Houston Independent School District, Reliant Energy, the Children's Museum, and a host of other organizations and businesses to sponsor its "Power Card Challenge," an effort to increase library usage among Houston school-aged children. The first year of the effort garnered much publicity (including radio and television coverage, prominent newspaper stories and editorials, 200 donated billboards, and a cable public service announcement that aired more than 200 times), registered more than 90,000 new juvenile cardholders, and increased children's circulation by 21 percent (Jones 2000).

Librarians may also represent the library in business organizations like the Chamber of Commerce, service clubs like Rotary or Kiwanis, or social service alliances such as literacy coalitions. Joining such groups helps build relationships with other organizations and individuals and provides a means of learning more about the community as well as informing others about the library and it collection.

Libraries can form effective partnerships with each other, as well. For example, the Dorset, Hampshire, and West Sussex County Library Authorities in England joined forces to form Well Worth Reading, a group dedicated to promoting contemporary fiction. Among other ventures, Well Worth Reading has published several editions of BOOX, a magazine written by teenagers and designed to promote reading to them, which has been used as the basis of many successful programs. For example, fiction circulation increased by 253 percent in one school library when the librarian talked to every English class about BOOX and sponsored writing workshops, music and readings, and a Readathon (Ashby 1998). A public librarian spoke about BOOX at the local school and used it to begin surveying teens about their reading habits and preferences. As a result, teenagers became involved in collection development, and the number of materials they were borrowing increased 50 percent (Ashby 1998).

External Distribution

Distribution options (discussed in detail in Chapter 6) can publicize the library in addition to making materials more accessible. For example, each book in the Westport (Connecticut) Public Library doctors' offices deposit collections contains a letter inviting the reader to the library for "more good books just like this one" (Fader 1991). And a bookmobile, which offers a flexible means of making materials available to patrons, also serves as a traveling billboard for the library. After heavy flooding forced hundreds from their homes, the Monterey County (California) Free Libraries brought their bookmobile to an emergency shelter, providing a valuable service as well as obtaining favorable exposure for the library and its collection ("Library" 1995).

History of Outreach

Some libraries make extensive use of external promotion. For example, the St. Louis (Missouri) Public Library calculated that in fiscal year 1997, one-third of its staff-patron contacts occurred outside a library building (Holt and Elliott 1998). External promotion can also be called "outreach," efforts to make library services more widely known by, relevant for, and accessible to members of various target markets, especially by going out into the community. The term did not become widely used in U.S. library literature until the 1960s, but libraries began practicing outreach activities long before then (Shubert 1991). For example, in 1898 the Carnegie Library of Pittsburgh (Pennsylvania) conducted summer story hours at selected neighborhood playgrounds (Locke 1992), and in 1910 the New York Public Library circulated books to 802 stations outside the library, including "public schools, fire stations, factories, asylums, department stores, long-shoremen's reading rooms, prisons, mental hospitals, and even one United States battleship" (Likosky 1985, 64).

Although libraries have used external promotional techniques for years, few rigorous studies have measured the extent to which they increase awareness or use of the collection. The next section presents research on the most-studied of these, the booktalk.

Booktalks (and Talks Promoting
Other Types of Materials)

Many public libraries present, to a range of clubs and organizations, talks about specific products or product lines that the group might find useful. For example, a library could promote its collection of materials on recycling at a meeting of a local environmental club and materials on time management to a group of business and professional women.

Many writers thoughtfully advise on the tactical aspects of presenting book (and other materials) talks (e.g., Littlejohn 2000, 1999; Baxter 1998; Jones 1998; Chelton 1976), but only a few document, in detail, the exact effects of such talks. Although primarily conducted in school libraries, the existing (older, yet still applicable) research reveals several pertinent points.

First, booktalks given to students can significantly increase use of promoted titles. For example, Nollen (1992) found that 80 percent of students checking out featured titles were primarily motivated to do so because of the booktalk. Bodart (1986a, 1986b) discovered that circulation of 14 titles to high school freshmen increased 1,773 percent—from 15 during the prior school year when they received no publicity to 266 during the first five months of the school year in which they were featured in booktalks presented to half of the freshman class.

Second, people who hear booktalks often share information about promoted titles with friends. For example, in the Bodart study cited above, this "grapevine effect" was associated with a 500 percent increase in circulation of featured titles among sophomores, juniors, and seniors, from a total of 18 circulations during the 1983–1984 school year to 90 during the first four months of 1984–1985.

Third, public librarians should not expect rises in use to be as dramatic as those experienced in school libraries. It requires greater effort for public library patrons who hear booktalks outside the library to travel there to borrow featured titles than it does for students who hear booktalks at school to walk down the hall to check out the books. Moreover, Nollen (1992) noted that the effects of a booktalk were short-lived, with almost all the circulations they prompted occurring soon after the presentation. Nevertheless, anecdotal evidence suggests that public libraries can increase user awareness of their overall services, at least temporarily, by presenting booktalks outside the library. For example, parents visiting the Girard (Ohio) Free Public Library said their children " 'bugged' them to come to the library" after hearing a booktalk at the local school (Sauline and Ague 1998, 35). Similarly, Ristau (1982) reports that after she presented booktalks in area school libraries, teens' use of the New Ulm (Minnesota) Public Library collection increased and the relationship between the teens and the library staff improved.

Fourth, although single-presentation booktalks given at school do not appear to affect student attitudes toward reading in general (Bodart 1986a, 1986b)—consistent with the low probability of people's values and attitudes changing after a single exposure to a stimulus—it may be possible to encourage changes in individual use of libraries or attitudes toward reading by exposing people to library materials via a series of booktalks over a period of time. This may explain, at least in part, why Level (1982) managed to increase the library use of students with low reading abilities to 75 percent of the use of students with high reading abilities by giving a series of twelve 15-minute booktalks to the former group.

Further Research on External Promotion

A review of the statistics and anecdotal evidence reported by libraries that have tried external promotion reveal some consistent (although not conclusive) patterns. First, public libraries, which compete with numerous profit-making and nonprofit organizations to capture consumer attention, seem to have the best chance of arousing a great deal of public interest when they

- get well-known personalities to promote library materials. For example in 1990, the American Library Association and the American Association of School Librarians jointly promoted the "Night of 1,000 Stars," a program that encouraged celebrities to read aloud at the library. Thousands of people at hundreds of libraries around the country turned out to hear participants, who ranged from the world-famous, like Charlton Heston and Aretha Franklin, to local celebrities like mayors and ministers, read from their favorite titles ("Night" 1990).

- use promotional materials creative or funny enough to capture consumer attention. For example, one public librarian interested 5,000 schoolchildren in the library's summer reading program by rapping about specific titles and popular literary characters (Reid 1988).

Second, the more publicity that occurs, the more likely use and awareness will increase. For example, the publicity blitz used by the Springfield (Massachusetts) Library to promote its "Seussamania" festival (described in detail in Chapter 7) resulted in a 50 percent increase in circulation of children's materials during the festival ("Youthreach" 1986).

Third, even if large-scale promotions cost more to produce initially, they may be the most cost-effective because of the number of households reached. For example, the Beverly Hills (California) Public Library has aired a 30-minute cable television show (reaching 140,000 households) twice a week to promote its collection indirectly, via interviews with famous authors as well as others involved in the book business (e.g., editors, illustrators, and publishers). A similar program produced by the Denver (Colorado) Public Library reached an estimated 81,000 people in and around the city (Dower 1990).

Fourth, the increases in awareness and use that external promotional efforts generate may fall off rapidly unless the library can convince patrons who try collection resources that the benefits of this use will outweigh the costs over the long term. In particular, efforts directed toward existing and potential patrons have strong chances of long-term success.

However, libraries can also convince patrons of the value of library services by carefully designing promotional efforts to meet the needs of a target market. Consider, for example, some outreach to the home-schooling community. The Oregon City (Oregon) Public Library sponsors a reception for homeschoolers at which it presents information about helpful resources and provides lists of relevant Internet sites and books ("Introducing" 1998). The Joliet (Illinois) Public Library recognizes the special requirements of parent-educators by issuing them teachers' cards that allow a six-week checkout period and by presenting special storytimes just for homeschooled children (Brostrum 1997). The Minneapolis (Minnesota) Public Library tries to learn about homeschoolers' needs by having staff attend the annual Minnesota Homeschooler's Alliance Conference and read the *Grapevine*, a homeschooling newsletter. This knowledge helps staff build a quality collection of home-education books (Brostrum 1997).

Finally, "standard" promotional methods may not work for every situation. As noted in Chapter 7, librarians need to consider the characteristics and needs of their target members when designing techniques to reach them. The Woodson Regional Library of the Chicago Public Library found this out when it tried to recruit teen mothers and fathers for a parenting course "through traditional channels (flyers, radio, etc.) [and] discovered that many at-risk parents do not read the newspaper, visit the library, or think they need the help if they hear an ad on the radio. What proved to be successful was collaboration with groups who deal routinely with teen parents: hospitals and the Department of Public Aid" (Chelton 1997, 19-20). Similarly, the San Antonio (Texas) Public Library worked with a variety of community entities—including its Friends organization and foundation; a group that serves mothers with limited education and income; a homeless shelter; Headstart; the Women, Infants, and Children (WIC) program; and AT&T—to publicize its 1998 summer reading program, Shake, Rattle & Read/Muevete Y Ponte a Leer, and credits these efforts with increasing registration by 71.4 percent (Machado et al. 2000). The liaison with the Hispanic community at the Public Library of Charlotte and Mecklenburg County (North Carolina) recognized that she needed to do more than tell the target audience about the library's "Early Intervention Reading Program"; she also needed to explain the importance of storytelling and reading to children. To accomplish this, she took flyers to health fairs, festivals, schools, churches, and other organizations that serve Hispanics; went on radio programs; and wrote articles that appeared in a local Hispanic newspaper. Most successfully, she developed relationships with Hispanic mothers living in areas with concentrated Hispanic populations. These "Mom Leaders" let the staff member present programs in their homes and helped spread the word about the service (Patterson 1998).

This example illustrates the power of identifying and developing relationships with confederates, members of the target audience who help the library reach the rest of the target group. The Tuckahoe (New York) Public Library has also successfully employed this strategy. When attendance at its monthly "Stories in

Japanese" program dwindled, librarians talked with a group of Japanese residents to find out why. Their input allowed the library to design programs of greater interest to the Japanese community and also opened up an effective avenue—word-of-mouth—to promote these programs. Consequently, the library's programs now attract more Japanese residents, who have increased their other use of the library as well (Sachs 1995).

Such cooperation may have additional benefits. For example, when the Queens Borough (New York) Public Library worked with Turkish community leaders to provide a workshop in Turkish on coping skills for new Americans, the success of this venture spawned other collaborations, including a donation by the Turkish-American Women's Alliance of 60 Turkish-language books (for which no U.S. source exists) compatible with library collection development guidelines (Gitner 1999).

CONCLUSION

Guided by research findings and the experiences of others,[16] librarians have concocted ingenious ways to increase patrons' awareness of the collection or specific products within it. Librarians can increase customers' incentives to use the library by pointing out the benefits of such use, arming patrons with the data necessary to make an informed decision about how to best meet their information, education, and entertainment needs. When done in conjunction with the other aspects of marketing—those concerning product, price, and place—promotion lets a community know what the library can do for it.

However, promotion alone will not likely cause awareness or use to increase on a permanent basis. As noted previously, some internal promotions can shift awareness or use from non-promoted to promoted titles, rather than increasing overall circulation. Further, although external promotions may increase library awareness or use, the increase will be temporary unless new users believe that the benefits of collection use outweigh the costs.

These findings suggest that libraries will want to avoid overemphasizing promotional efforts at the expense of other tasks. Instead, as has been suggested throughout this book, they will want to develop integrated marketing schemes that involve analyzing the products in their collections, redesigning these collections to meet the needs of both existing patrons and the community in general, and promoting them to potential patrons. Moreover, promotion, the third step in a marketing-based collection management program, cannot be the last. Libraries must continually repeat the cycle of evaluation, selection, and promotion to obtain current information on materials community residents require and will use to reap the rewards of a satisfied, faithful community.

NOTES

1.   Everhart, Hartz, and Kreiger (1989) give more than 50 examples of thematic displays that can be used to promote books and other library materials and provide practical guidelines for constructing displays.

2.   Construction of these works is explained in some detail in Bronson (1982).

3.   See "Fiction_L" (2001) for more information about this discussion list, including access to its archives and instructions for subscribing.

4.   For a thorough discussion of writing annotations, see Haines (1950).

5.   These principles of categorization significantly expand those identified in Baker and Shepard (1987) and refined in the first edition of this book.

6.   Milton (1986) provides instructions for performing this task.

7.   For a comprehensive look at readers' advisory services in public libraries, see Saricks and Brown (1997).

8.   The other challenge listed in the top four was the need for more (staff) training. See "Fiction_L" (2001) for subscription information.

9.   In a similar study, Ross and Dewdney (1994) also found use of open-ended questions an important element of a successful transaction.

10.   See Gross (2000) for more on this topic.

11.   For a more comprehensive review of this subject, see Baker and Lancaster (1991).

12.   Although most of the hard research on reading clubs has focused on their effect on children's reading levels, anecdotal evidence suggests that reading clubs increase circulation (e.g., Howes 1986; Carter 1988).

13.   For more information or a catalog, contact BiFolkal Production, Inc. at 1-800-568-5357.

14.   Many libraries provide welcome letters, library cards, books, and/or informational materials to new parents; FOLUSA (Friends of Libraries USA) offers one popular program of this nature. See Sager (1998).

15.   The ALA Born to Read Project also encourages library and health care provider partnerships. For more information, see "Born to Read" (2001) or Judge (1995).

16.   In addition to general interest library and public library periodicals, *Library Media and PR*, *Library PR News*, *Marketing Library Services*, *Marketing Treasures*, and *PR-Talk* are good sources of learning about promotions that have (and have not) worked for others.

REFERENCES

"Adult Summer Reading Club." 1999. *NEWSKOKIE* [Online] (June). Formerly available: http://www.skokie.com/manager/Newskokie/Archive/1999/June/page10.html [Accessed September 15, 2000].

Agosto, Denise. 1996. "Party Hearty!" *School Library Journal* 42, no. 2 (February): 46.

Ainley, Patricia, and Barry Totterdell. 1982. *Alternative Arrangement: New Approaches to Public Library Stock*. London: Association of Assistant Librarians.

"ALA announces Library Card Sign-up Month Sweepstakes Winners; Five Libraries Receive Arthurâ Book Sets." 2000. [Homepage of the American Library Association], [Online]. (Updated November 22). Available: http://www.ala.org/news/v6n7/Arthur_winners.html [Accessed September 28, 2001].

Alire, Camila, and Orlando Archibeque. 1998. *Serving Latino Communities: A How-to-Do-It Manual for Librarians.* New York: Neal-Schuman.

American Library Association. 2000. *Guidelines on Subject Access to Individual Works of Fiction, Drama, Etc.* Chicago: American Library Association.

Ashby, Sue. 1998. "BOOX: Getting Good Reads to Teenagers." *School Librarian* 46, no. 4 (Winter): 181, 185.

"Baby TALK." [2001]. [Homepage of Baby TALK], [Online]. Available: http://www.babytalk.org/ (and linked pages) [Accessed September 28, 2001].

Baker, Lynda M., and Judith J. Field. 2000. "Reference Success: What Has Changed over the Past Ten Years?" *Public Libraries* 39, no. 1 (January/February): 23–30.

Baker, Sharon L. 1986a. "The Display Phenomenon: An Exploration into Factors Causing the Increased Circulation of Displayed Books." *Library Quarterly* 56, no. 3 (July): 237–57.

———. 1986b. "Overload, Browsers, and Selections." *Library and Information Science Research* 8, no. 4 (October-December): 315–29.

———. 1988. "Will Fiction Classification Schemes Increase Use?" *RQ* 27, no. 3 (Spring): 366–76.

———. 1996. "A Decade's Worth of Research on Browsing Fiction Collections." In *Guiding the Reader to the Next Book*, ed. Kenneth Shearer, 127–47. New York: Neal-Schuman.

Baker, Sharon L., and F. Wilfrid Lancaster. 1991. *Measurement and Evaluation of Library Services.* 2d ed. Arlington, VA: Information Resources Press.

Baker, Sharon L., and Gay W. Shepherd. 1987. "Fiction Classification Schemes: The Principles Behind Them, and Their Success." *RQ* 27, no. 2 (Winter): 245–51.

Barron, Neil, et al. annual. *What Do I Read Next?* Detroit: Gale.

Barsun, Rita. 1996. "Communication and Cooperation Between Public Librarians and Public School Teachers: A Review of the Literature." *Indiana Libraries* 15, no. 2: 4–14.

Baxter, Kathleen. 1998. "Booktalking Basics." *School Library Journal* 44, no. 6 (June): 70. (Readers may also wish to look at other issues of *School Library Journal* for more of Baxter's "Nonfiction Booktalker" columns.)

Bawden, David, Clive Holtham, and Nigel Courtney. 1999. "Perspectives on Information Overload." *Aslib Proceedings* 51, no. 8 (September): 249–55.

Benezra, Barbara. 1978. "A New Arrangement." *Ohio Media Spectrum* 30, no. 1 (January): 69.

Berinstein, Paula. 1994. *Communicating with Library Users: A Self-Study Program.* Washington, DC: Special Libraries Association.

Bertot, John Carlo, and Charles R. McClure. 2000. "Public Libraries and the Internet 2000: Summary Findings and Data Tables." [Homepage of the National Commission on Libraries and Information Science], [Online]. (September 7). Available: http://www.nclis.gov/statsurv/2000plo.pdf [Accessed September 28, 2001].

"Bettendorf Public Library—Reader's Advisory Services." [2001]. [Homepage of Bettendorf Public Library], [Online]. Available: http://www.rbls.lib.il.us/bpl/services /readera.htm [Accessed September 28, 2001].

Blubaugh, Penny. 1995. "Guess Who's Coming to Breakfast." *School Library Journal* 41, no. 1 (January): 42.

Bodart, Joni. 1986a. "Book You!" *Voice of Youth Advocates* 9, no. 1 (April): 22–23.

———. 1986b. "Booktalks Do Work! The Effects of Booktalking on Attitude and Circulation." *Illinois Libraries* 68, no. 6 (June): 378–81.

"Books We're Reading Week of October 1–5." [2001] [Homepage of Chapter-a-Day], [Online]. Available: http://www.chapter-a-day.com/html/main.html [Accessed September 28, 2001].

Bordon, William Alanson. 1909. "On Classifying Fiction." *Library Journal* 34, no. 6 (June): 264–65.

"Born to Read: A Project Fact Sheet." 2001. [Homepage of American Library Association, Association for Library Service to Children section], [Online]. (Updated April 20). Available: http://www.ala.org/alsc/born.html [Accessed September 28, 2001].

"The Bridwell Technology Center." [2001]. [Homepage of Lubbock City-County Library], [Online]. Available: http://library.ci.lubbock.tx.us/bridwell/index.htm [Accessed September 28, 2001].

Briggs, Betty S. 1973. "A Case for Classified Fiction." *Library Journal* 98, no. 22 (15 December): 3694.

Bronson, Que. 1982. *Books on Display*. Washington, DC: Metropolitan Washington Library Council.

Brostrum, David. 1997. "No Place Like the Library." *School Library Journal* 43, no. 3 (March): 106–9.

Brown, Vandella. 1997. "African-American Fiction: A Slamming Genre." *American Libraries* 28, no. 10 (November): 48–50.

Burgin, Robert. 1996. "Readers' Advisory in Public Libraries: An Overview of Current Practice." In *Guiding the Reader to the Next Book*, ed. Kenneth Shearer, 71–85. New York: Neal-Schuman.

Burnette, Sheila. 1998. "Book 'Em! Cops and Librarians Working Together." *American Libraries* 29, no. 2 (February): 48–50.

Cannell, Jeffrey, and Eileen McCluskey. 1996. "Genrefication: Fiction Classification and Increased Circulation." In *Guiding the Reader to the Next Book*, ed. Kenneth D. Shearer, 159–65. New York: Neal-Schuman.

Carpenter, Beth. 1998. "Your Attention, Please! Marketing Today's Libraries." *Computers in Libraries* 18, no. 8 (September): 62–66.

Carter, Vivian. 1988. "Challenging Programs: The Effect of Summer Reading Program Participation on the Retention of Reading Skills." *Illinois Libraries* 70, no. 1 (January): 56–60.

Casto, Jane. 1999. (Headquarters Services Manager, Cumberland County [North Carolina] Public Library and Information Center). "Tell Us About Books (fwd)." E-mail to Karen Wallace, May 18.

Causey, Helen. 1989. "Bookmobile Promotion Proves to be SELA Winner." *The Southeastern Librarian* 39, no. 3 (Fall): 123–24.

Chelton, Mary K. 1976. "Booktalking: You Can Do It." *School Library Journal* 22, no. 4 (April): 39–44.

———. 1999. "What We Know and Don't Know about Reading, Readers, and Readers Advisory Services" *Public Libraries* 38, no. 1 (January/February): 42–47.

Chelton, Mary K., ed. 1997. *Excellence in Library Services to Young Adults: The Nation's Top Programs*. 2d ed. Chicago: American Library Association.

Clark, Sheila, and Bobbie Patrick. 1999. "Choose Freedom Read: Book Talks behind Bars." *American Libraries* 30, no. 7 (August): 63–64.

Cropper, Barry. 1986. *Going Soft: Some Uses of Paperbacks in Libraries*. London: Branch and Mobile Libraries Group of the Library Association.

Crouch, Richard K. C. 1981. "Interpersonal Communication in the Reference Interview." Ph.D. diss., University of Toronto.

Dewdney, Patricia, and Catherine Sheldrick Ross. 1994. "Flying a Light Aircraft: Reference Service Evaluation from a User's Viewpoint." *RQ* 34, no. 2 (Winter): 217–30.

"Discovering Broadway at the Library." 1996. *Public Libraries* 35, no. 3 (May/June): 160.

Dower, Kim Freilich. 1990. "Tune in to Reading: Pushing Books Via Cable." *Library Journal* 115, no. 14 (September 1): 171–72.

Durrance, Joan C. 1995. "Factors That Influence Reference Success: What Makes Questioners Willing to Return?" *The Reference Librarian*, nos. 49/50: 243–65.

"Evanston Public Library Speaker's Bureau." 1997. [Homepage of Evanston Public Library], [Online]. (Updated September 12). Available: http://www.evanston.lib.il.us/library /speakers-bureau.html [Accessed September 28, 2001].

Everhart, Nancy, Claire Hartz, and William Kreiger. 1989. *Library Displays*. Metuchen, NJ: Scarecrow Press.

"Face-Out Book Shelving in Multnomah County." 1988. *Southeastern Library Services Regional Rag* 15, no. 5 (March-April): 7.

Fader, Ellen G. 1991. "The Doctors' Office Collection." *School Library Journal* 37, no. 6 (June): 48.

"Fair Formula for Success." 1996. *Public Libraries* 35, no. 2 (March/April): 109.

"Fast Food for Thought." 1993. *Public Libraries* 32, no. 5 (September/October): 244.

Fialkoff, Francine. 2000. "Move Over Oprah." *Library Journal* 125, no. 17 (October 15): 52.

"Fiction_L: An Electronic Mailing List on Reader's Advisory Topics." 2001. [Homepage of Morton Grove Public Library], [Online]. (Updated January 18). Available: http://www.webrary.org/rs/FLmenu.html [Accessed September 28, 2001].

Forbes, Eric. 1971. "Stagnant Pools." *School Librarian* 19 (September): 210–12.

Gendler, Ann. 1997. "Let Them Read Greats!" *American Libraries* 28, no. 8 (September): 46–48.

Gitner, Fred J. 1999. "New Americans Program: Part 2." *Reference and User Services Quarterly* 38, no. 3 (Spring): 243–44.

Golden, Gary A. 1983. "Motivation to Select Books: A Study of Annotated and Unannotated Booklists in Public Libraries." Ph.D. diss., University of Illinois at Urbana-Champaign.

Goldhor, Herbert. 1972. "The Effect of Prime Display Location on Public Library Circulation of Selected Adult Titles." *Library Quarterly* 42, no. 4 (October): 371–89.

———. 1981. "Experimental Effects on the Choice of Books Borrowed by Public Library Adult Patrons." *Library Quarterly* 51, no. 3 (July): 253–68.

"Good Reads!" [2001]. [Homepage of Salt Lake City Public Library], [Online]. Available: http://www.slcpl.lib.ut.us/reading/goodreads.html [Accessed September 28, 2001].

Gothberg, Helen. 1976. "Immediacy: A Study of Communication Effect on the Reference Process." *Journal of Academic Librarianship* 2, no. 3 (July): 126–29.

Gross, Melissa. 2000. "The Imposed Query and Information Services for Children." *Journal of Youth Services in Libraries* 13, no. 2 (Winter): 10–17.

Hage, Christine Lind. 1997. "The Fact Is That Fiction Dominates." *Public Libraries* 36, no. 3 (May/June): 153–54.

Haig, Frank. 1933. "The Subject Classification of Fiction: An Actual Experiment." *Library World* 36: 78–82

Haines, Helen E. 1950. *Living with Books: The Art of Book Selection.* 2d ed. New York: Columbia University Press.

Harrell, Gail. 1985. "The Classification and Organization of Adult Fiction in Large American Public Libraries." *Public Libraries* 24, no. 1 (Spring): 13–14.

———. 1996. "Use of Fiction Categories in Major American Public Libraries." In *Guiding the Reader to the Next Book,* ed. Kenneth D. Shearer, 149–57. New York: Neal-Schuman.

Hennepin County Library. 1992. *Unreal! Hennepin County Library Subject Headings for Fictional Characters and Places.* 2d ed. Jefferson, NC: McFarland.

Herald, Diana Tixier. 1997. *Teen Genreflecting.* Englewood, CO: Libraries Unlimited.

———. 2000. *Genreflecting: A Guide to Reading Interests in Genre Fiction.* 5th ed. Englewood, CO: Libraries Unlimited.

Higashi, Chris. 1998. "How to Plan a Movable Feast of Poetry." *American Libraries* 29, no. 2 (February): 52–54.

Holt, Glen E., and Donald Elliott. 1998. "Proving Your Library's Worth: A Test Case." *Library Journal* 123, no. 18 (November 1): 42–44.

Howes, Mary. 1986. "Evaluation of the Effects of a Public Library Summer Reading Program on Children's Reading Scores Between First and Second Grade." *Illinois Libraries* 68, no. 7 (September): 444–50.

Hubbard, Lee. 1967. "A Boost for Browsing." *Library Journal* 92, no. 7 (April 1): 1392.

"If You Like. . . ." [2001]. [Homepage of Canterbury Public Library], [Online]. Available: http://library.christchurch.org.nz/Guides/IfYouLike/ [Accessed September 28, 2001].

"Introducing the Library to Homeschoolers." 1998. *Public Libraries* 37, no. 1 (January/February): 26.

Jennerich, Elaine Z., and Edward J. Jennerich., eds. 1997. *The Reference Interview as a Creative Art.* 2d ed. Englewood, CO: Libraries Unlimited.

Jennings, Barbara, and Lyn Sear. 1986. "How Readers Select Fiction—A Survey in Kent." *Public Library Journal* 1, no. 4: 43–47.

Joe, Ronald K. 1999. "Offering Assistance at the OPACs." *The Reference Librarian* no. 65: 137–59.

Johnson, Roberta S. 2000a. "The Global Conversation: Reader's Advisory on the Internet." [Homepage of fictional.org], [Online]. (Updated April). Available: http://www.fictional.org/ranetfull.html [Accessed September 28, 2001].

———. 2000b. "Internet Sites for Fiction Lovers." [Homepage of fictional.org], [Online]. (Updated May). Available: http://www.fictional.org/ralinks.html [Accessed September 28, 2001].

Jones, Patrick. 1998. *Connecting Young Adults and Libraries.* 2d ed. New York: Neal-Schuman.

———. 2000. "Packing the Power: The Houston Public Library's Library Card Campaign." *Public Libraries* 39, no 3 (May/June): 156–60.

Judge, April. 1995. "Nurturing a Baby's Love of Learning." *American Libraries* 26, no. 11 (December): 1134–36.

Kars, Marge, and Mary Doud. 1999. "Ready to Read: A Collaborative, Community-Wide Emergent Literacy Program." *The Reference Librarian* no. 67/68: 85–97.

Katz, William A. 1997. *Introduction to Reference Work.* Vol. 2, *Reference Services and Reference Processes.* 7th ed. New York: McGraw-Hill.

Kazlauskas, Edward. 1976. "An Exploratory Study: A Kinesic Analysis of Academic Library Public Service Points." *Journal of Academic Librarianship* 2, no. 3 (July): 130–34.

Kelly, Mary. 1999. "Re: What REALLY Has an Impact on Circ. and Other Library Use Stats?" [Online posting to prtalk@ala.org], (July 27).

King, David. 2000. "Soliciting Virtual Money." *NetConnect* supplement to *Library Journal* and *School Library Journal* (Fall): 39–41.

Langhorne, Mary Jo. 1987. "Marketing Books in the School Library." *School Library Journal* 33, no. 5 (January): 31–33.

Lasko, J., and O. Puukko. 1992. "Classification of Fiction by Topic in the Light of Experiments Carried out in Two Public Libraries." *Kirjastotiede ja Informatika* 11, no. 2: 61–65.

Level, June Saine. 1982. "Booktalk Power—A Locally Based Research Study." *School Library Media Quarterly* 10, no. 2 (Winter): 154–55.

"Librarian Floats to Sweepstakes." 1998. *Public Libraries* 37, no. 5 (September/October): 289.

"Library for Spanish Speakers." 1999. *The Bookmark: News from Your Multnomah County Library, Electronic Edition* [Online] 7, no. 1 (Spring). Available: http://www.multnomah.lib.or.us/lib/bkmark/99spring/bkmk2.html [Accessed September 28, 2001].

"Library Goes on the Road to Promote Reading." 1994. *The Unabashed Librarian*, no. 92: 13.

Library Media and PR [Online]. Available: http://www.ssdesign.com/librarypr/index.html [Accessed September 28, 2001].

"Library Promotes Good Taste(s)." 1997. *Public Libraries* 36, no. 6 (November/December): 337.

Library PR News. Newsletter issued bi-monthly. For subscription information, write to L. E. I., Inc. R. D. 1, Box 219, New Albany, PA 18833.

"Library Responds to Flood." 1995. *Public Libraries* 34, no. 4 (July/August): 198.

Likosky, Stephen. 1985. "Reexamining Public Library Outreach" *The Bookmark* 43, no. 1 (Winter): 64–68.

"Literature and Audio Services Department." [2001]. [Homepage of Downers Grove Public Library], [Online]. Available: http://www.sls.lib.il.us/DGS/litaudio.html [Accessed September 28, 2001].

Little, Paul. 1979. "The Effectiveness of Paperbacks." *Library Journal* 104, no. 20 (15 November): 2411–16.

Littlejohn, Carol. 1999. *Talk That Book: Booktalks to Promote Reading.* Worthington, Ohio: Linworth.

———. 2000. *Keep Talking That Book!: Booktalks to Promote Reading Volume II.* Worthington, OH: Linworth.

Locke, Jill L. 1992. "Summer Reading Activities—Way Back When" *Journal of Youth Services in Libraries* 6, no. 1 (Fall): 72–78.

"Logan Library Online Book Club." [2001]. [Homepage of the Logan Public Library], [Online]. Available: http://www.logan.lib.ut.us/linfo/linfo2/friends/bookclub.html [Accessed September 28, 2001].

Long, Sarah P. 1986. "The Effect of Face-Front Display on the Circulation of Books in a Public Library." Master's Research Project, University of North Carolina at Greensboro, Department of Library Science/Educational Technology. ERIC ED278415.

Machado, Julie, et al. 2000. "A Survey of Best Practices in Youth Services around the Country." *Journal of Youth Services* 13, no. 2 (Winter): 30–35.

Maltin, Leonard, ed. annual. *Leonard Maltin's [Year] Movie and Video Guide.* New York: New American Library.

Marketing Library Services. Newsletter issued 8 times/year. For subscription information, write to Information Today, Inc. 143 Old Marlton Pike, Medford, NJ 08055-8750.

Marketing Treasures. Newsletter issued bi-monthly. For subscription information, write to Chris Olson and Associates, 857 Twin Harbor Dr., Arnold, MD 21012.

"MatchBook: How, When, and Why: A Service of the Morton Grove Public Library." 2001. [Homepage of Morton Grove Public Library], [Online]. (Updated September 5). Available: http://www.webrary.org/rs/matchbookhist.html (and linked pages) [Accessed September 28, 2001].

May, Anne K., et al. 2000. "A Look at Reader's Advisory Services." *Library Journal* 125, no. 15 (September 15): 40–43.

McKearney, Miranda. 1990. "Well Worth Reading: Fiction Promotion Scheme Comes of Age." *Public Library Journal* 5, no. 3: 61–70.

Meyers, Elaine, Marijo Kist, and Sarah Sugden. 1999. "Top One Hundred Kids' Books: Readers Talking to Readers." *Journal of Youth Services* 13, no. 1 (Fall): 32–34.

"Miami-Dade Public Library Trucks and Vans Encourage Drivers to Obtain Library Cards." 2000. *Public Libraries* 39, no. 2 (March/April): 70.

"Millions of Cats." 1996. *Public Libraries* 35, no. 1 (January/February): 19.

Milton, Ian S. 1986. *Changing Faces: A Practical Guide to Reader Interest Categorisation and Library Facelifts*. Wheathampstead, St. Albans, England: Branch and Mobile Libraries Group.

Minkel, Walter. 1999. "Five Librarians, One 50-Foot Phone Cord, and a Whole Lot of Chutzpah." *School Library Journal* 45, no. 3 (March): 108–11.

Morson, Ian, and Mike Perry. 1982. "Two-Tier and Total: Stock Arrangement in Brent." In *Alternative Arrangement: New Approaches to Public Library Stock*, eds. Patricia Ainley and Barry Totterdell, 101–18. London: Association of Assistant Librarians.

Mueller, Elizabeth. 1965. "Are New Books Read More than Old Ones?" *Library Quarterly* 35, no. 3 (July): 166–72.

"New and Replacement Videos—East Providence Libraries." 2001. [Homepage of the East Providence Public Library], [Online]. (Updated September 26). Available: http://www.clan.lib.ri.us/epl/newvideos.html [Accessed September 28, 2001].

"New Stock Layouts." 1989. *Library Association Record* 91, no. 3 (March): 133.

"A New Year with NoveList!" 2001. *NoveList News* 7, no. 1 [Online] (January). Available: http://novelist.epnet.com/nlwebp/NoveListNews/NLNewsJan01.PDF [Accessed September 28, 2001].

"Night of 1000 Stars: A Wellspring of Love." 1990. *American Libraries* 21, no. 6 (June): 494.

Nollen, Terrence David. 1992. "The Effect of Booktalks on the Development of Reading Attitudes and the Promotion of Individual Reading Choices." Ph.D. diss., University of Nebraska-Lincoln.

"Not for Children Only." 1996. *Public Libraries* 35, no. 3 (May/June): 161.

"Notice." 1998. *Library PR News* 19, nos. 1 and 2 (January/February): 7–8.

"NoveList State-wide Contracts: Georgia, Illinois, and Wyoming." 1999. *NoveList News*, [Online] (January). Available: http://novelist.epnet.com/nlwebp/NoveListNews/nlnews9901.htm [Accessed September 28, 2001].

Oder, Norman. 2000. "An Automated Reader's Advisory?" *Library Journal* 125, no. 13 (August): 13–14.

"Online Book Club." 2001. [Homepage of Minneapolis Public Library], [Online]. (Updated September 4). Available: http://www.mpls.lib.mn.us/bookclub.asp [Accessed September 28, 2001].

"Other Options." 2000. *The Unabashed Librarian* no. 114: 18.

"Outreach Success Story." 1997. *The Unabashed Librarian*, no. 103: 4.

"Outreach to Older Adults." [2001], [Homepage of Bethel Park Public Library], [Online]. Available: http://www.einpgh.org/ein/bethpark/Outreach.htm [Accessed September 28, 2001].

Paperbound Books in Print: Spring 1992. 1992. New Providence, NJ: R. R. Bowker.

Parrish, Nancy B. 1986. "The Effect of a Booklist on the Circulation of Fiction Books Which Have Not Been Borrowed from a Public Library in Four Years or Longer." Master's research project, University of North Carolina at Greensboro. ERIC ED282564.

Partnow, Elaine, ed. 1977. *The Quotable Woman.* Los Angeles: Corwin Books.

Patterson, Irania Macías. 1998. "Charlotte Public Library Speaks Español: Approaching the Hispanic Community Through Storytelling." *North Carolina Libraries* 56, no. 4 (Winter): 145–47.

"Program Gets Reading Groups Off the Ground." 1997. *Public Libraries* 36, no. 3 (May/June): 147.

PR-Talk. American Library Association discussion list. To subscribe, send a message to listproc@ala.org. Leave the subject line blank, and in the body of the message type: subscribe PRTalk yourfirstname yourlastname.

RASD Ad Hoc Committee on Behavioral Guidelines for Reference and Information Services. 1996. "RUSA Guidelines for Behavioral Performance of Reference and Information Services Professionals." *RQ* 36, no. 2 (Winter): 200–203.

Reader, Den. 1982. "User Orientation in a Hertfordshire Branch." In *Alternative Arrangement: New Approaches to Public Library Stock*, eds. Patricia Ainley and Barry Totterdell, 34–46. London: Association of Assistant Librarians.

"Reader Services." 2001. [Homepage of Schaumburg Township District Library], [Online]. (Updated July 13). Available: http://www.stdl.org/dptserv/rs/rs.htm [Accessed September 28, 2001].

"Reader's Robot." 2001. [Homepage of The Reader's Robot], [Online]. (Updated September 27). Available: http://www.tnrdlib.bc.ca/rr.html (and linked pages) [Accessed September 28, 2001].

Reagan, Lee. 1973. "Status of Reader's Advisory Service." *RQ* 12, no. 3 (Spring): 227–33.

Reid, Rob. 1988. "Practically Speaking: Rappin' Them into the Library." *School Library Journal* 34, no. 7 (March): 134.

Riquelme, Marcia. 1998. "Read a Winner." *Library Mosaics* 9, no. 6 (November/December): 12–13.

Ristau, Holly. 1982. "Defining the Young Adult and Describing the Effect of Book Talking on That Population." *Minnesota Libraries* 29, nos. 2 and 3 (Summer/Autumn): 48–49.

Ross, Catherine Sheldrick, and Patricia Dewdney. 1994. "Best Practices: An Analysis of the Best (and Worst) in Fifty-Two Public Library Reference Transactions." *Public Libraries* 33, no. 5 (September/October): 261–66.

Roy, Loriene. 1993. "Displays and Displacement of Circulation." *Collection Management* 17, no. 4: 57–77.

Rutzen, Ruth. 1952. "Shelving for Readers." *Library Journal* 77, no. 6 (March 15): 478–82.

Saarti, Jarmo. 1997. "Feeding with the Spoon, or the Effects of Shelf Classification of Fiction on the Loaning of Fiction." *Information Services & Use* 17: 159–69.

Sachs, Elizabeth-Ann. 1995. "A Door to the West." *School Library Journal* 41, no. 9 (September): 136.

Sager, Don. 1998. "Welcome Kits for Newborn." [Homepage of Publib and Publib-Net], [Online]. (February 4). Available: http://sunsite.berkeley.edu/PubLib/archive.html. [Accessed September 28, 2001].

Sapiie, Jacquelyn. 1995. "Reader-Interest Classification: The User-Friendly Schemes." *Cataloging & Classification Quarterly* 19, no. 3–4: 143–55.

Saricks, Joyce. 1998. "Survey Results." [Homepage of Fiction_L], [Online]. (April 28). Available: http://www.webrary.org/rs/Flarchive.html [Accessed September 28, 2001].

Saricks, Joyce G., and Nancy Brown. 1997. *Readers' Advisory Service in the Public Library*. 2d ed. Chicago: American Library Association.

Sauline, Kathleen, and Elma Ague. 1998. "Public Library Outreach to Schools: Enhancing the Tradition at Girard Free Library." *Ohio Libraries* (Summer): 34–36.

Sawbridge, Lynn, and Leo Favret. 1982. "The Mechanics and the Magic of Declassification." *Library Association Record* 84, no. 11 (November): 383-84.

Schabel, Charles R. 1997. "Concerning the Use of a Decimal System to Classify Fiction According to Its Genre: Brand-Named Fiction Finder." Master's research paper, North Carolina Central University, School of Library and Information Sciences.

Schultz, Kristine. 2000. "An Overview of Readers' Advisory Service with Evaluations of Related Websites." *The Acquisitions Librarian* no. 23: 21–33.

Sear, Lyn, and Barbara Jennings. 1986. *How Readers Select Fiction. Kent County Library Research and Development Report*, No. 9. Kent County, England: Kent County Council, Education Committee.

" 'Service of the Month' in Prince George's County." 1989. *Library Journal* 114, no. 8 (May 1): 25.

Shaw, Ralph R. 1938. "The Influence of Sloping Shelves on Book Circulation." *Library Quarterly* 8, no. 4 (October): 480–90.

Shearer, Kenneth. 1996. "The Nature of the Readers' Advisory Transaction in Adult Reading." In *Guiding the Reader to the Next Book*, ed. Kenneth Shearer, 1-20. New York: Neal-Schuman.

———. 1998. "Readers' Advisory Services: New Attention to a Core Business of the Public Library." *North Carolina Libraries* 56, no. 3 (Fall): 114–16.

Shubert, Joseph F. 1991. "Public Library Outreach Services." *The Bookmark* 49, no. 4 (Summer): 271–78.

Sivulich, Kenneth G. 1989. "How We Run the Queens Library Good (and Doubled Circulation in Seven Years!)" *Library Journal* 114, no. 3 (February 15): 123–27.

Smith, Duncan. 1997. "The Readers' Advisory Renaissance and Electronic Resources." *Ohio Libraries* 10, no. 3 (Winter): 20–23.

Spencer, Pam. 1999. *What Do Young Adults Read Next?* 3d ed. Detroit: Gale.

Spencer, Pam, and Janis Ansell. 1999. *What Do Children Read Next?* 3d ed. Detroit: Gale.

Spiller, David. 1980. "The Provision of Fiction by Public Libraries." *Journal of Librarianship* 12, no. 4 (October): 238–65.

St. Lifer, Evan. 1993. "Libraries Make it with Marketing." *Library Journal* 118, no. 15 (September 15): 34.

Stephan, Sandy, et al. 1988. "Reference Breakthrough in Maryland." *Public Libraries* 27, no. 4 (Winter): 202–33.

Steptowe, C. G. 1987. *A Case Study of Fiction Provision in a Public Library.* Master's diss., Loughborough University.

Stevens, Catherine A. 2000. "Reader's Advisory Web Sites." *The Acquisitions Librarian* no. 23: 5–19.

Straw, Joseph E. 2000. "A Virtual Understanding: The Reference Interview and Question Negotiation in the Digital Age." *Reference and User Services Quarterly* 39, no. 4 (Summer): 376–79.

" 'Streetwalker' Promotion Lures Patrons Back to Library." 1994. *Wilson Library Bulletin* 69, no. 1 (September): 16.

Taylor, Robert S. 1968. "Question-Negotiation and Information Seeking in Libraries." *College and Research Libraries* 29, 3 (May): 178–94.

"Teen Read Week, October 19-25, 1998." 1998. [Homepage of Chicago Public Library], [Online]. (Updated October). Available: http://www.chipublib.org/008subject/003cya/trw.html [Accessed September 28, 2001].

Tepper, Krysta. 1989. "Direct Mail Marketing: A Library Application." *The Unabashed Librarian*, no. 73: 13–17.

"Topical Research Guides." 2001. [Homepage of the Gwinett County Public Library], [Online]. (Updated August 31). Available: http://www.gwinett.public.lib.ga.us/Topical.html [Accessed September 28, 2001].

Towey, Catherine. 1997. "We Need to Recommit to Readers' Advisory Services." *American Libraries* 28, no. 11 (December): 31.

Tracz, Catherine M. 1997. "Status of Readers' Advisory Services in Ohio Public Libraries." Master's research paper, Kent State University. ERIC ED413908.

Turano, Frances M. 1997. "A Survey of Types of Cooperation Between Schools and Public Libraries in Ohio." Master's research paper, Kent State University. ERIC ED401939.

Underhill, Paco. 1999. *Why We Buy: The Science of Shopping.* New York: Simon & Schuster.

van Riel, Rachel. 1999. "A Book to March Your Mood." *The Library Association Record* 101, no. 5 (May): 292–93.

Venter, Trude. 1984. " 'n Rangskikkingsmetode om die gebruik van nie-fiksie in openbare biblioteke te bevorder." *South African Journal for Librarianship and Information Science* 52, no. 4 (December): 109–12.

Volz, Bridget Dealy, Cheryl Perkins Scheer, and Lynda Blackburn Welborn. 2000. *Junior Genreflecting: A Guide to Good Reads and Series Fiction for Children*. Englewood, CO: Libraries Unlimited.

Waldhorn, Arthur, Olga Weber, and Arthur Zeiger. 1990. *Good Reading: A Guide for Serious Readers*. 23d ed. New York: R. R. Bowker.

Walker, John, ed. 2000. *Halliwell's Film and Video Guide*. 16th ed., rev. and updated. New York: HarperResource.

Watkins, Christine. 1997. "Yes, Read Every Chance You Get. . . . But Don't Forget to Catch the Ball!" *American Libraries* 28, no. 6 (June/July): 90–93.

Webb, Terry D. 1985. "Phoenix Public Library: Reorganization Based on a Hierarchy of User Types." In *Reorganization in the Public Library*, ed. Terry D. Webb, 52–66. Phoenix: Oryx Press.

"Webmaster at the Library." 1998. *American Libraries* 29, no. 11 (December): 14.

"Welcome to Book Forager." [2001]. [Homepage of Branching Out], [Online]. Available: http://www.branching-out.net/forager/titlepage.htm [Accessed September 28, 2001].

Westbrook, Lynn. 1984. "Catalog Failure and Reference Service: A Preliminary Study." *RQ* 24, no. 1 (Fall): 82–90.

"What Do I Read Next?" 2001. [Homepage of Gale], [Online]. Available: http://www.gale.com /servlet/ItemDetailServlet?region=9&imprint=000&titleCode=GAL10&type=4&id=111002 [Accessed September 28, 2001].

White, Herbert. 1992. "The Reference Librarian as Information Intermediary." *The Reference Librarian*, no. 37: 34.

"Why Are Picture Books Attractive?" 1993. *Public Libraries* 32, no. 2 (May/April): 76–77.

Wilkins, Felicity. 1997. "Explore the World of Fiction: Reading Promotion in a Secondary School." *School Librarian* 45, no. 1 (February): 9.

Wilkinson, Billy R. 1972. *Reference Services for Undergraduate Students: Four Case Studies*. Metuchen, NJ: Scarecrow Press.

Williams, Dianne T. McAfee. 1973. "A Study to Determine the Effectiveness of an Interest Grouping Classification for Primary Grade Children." Master's research paper, Western Michigan University.

Wood, Richard. 1985. "The Experimental Effects of Fiction Book Lists on Circulation in an Academic Library," *RQ* 24, no. 4 (Summer): 427-32.

Yaakov, Juliette, and John Greenfieldt, eds. 2001. *Fiction Catalog*. 14th ed. New York: H. W. Wilson.

"Youthreach: 'Seussamania' in Geisel's Hometown." 1986. *American Libraries* 17, no. 6 (June): 485.

MAKING MARKETING RESONATE THROUGHOUT THE LIBRARY

"He chose to include the things that in each other are included, the whole, the complicate, the amassing harmony"—Wallace Stevens (Bartlett 1992, 640).

Successful marketing programs inform and affect the library's culture as a whole (Drucker 1974), from climate to philosophy, organization to decision-making structures, demanding that the complete operation continually be viewed with the patron in mind, a practice Scholtes (1998) refers to as customer-in thinking, in contrast to a product-out approach. Achieving such an orchestrated approach requires gaining the support of everyone directly or indirectly providing library service: the board of trustees, top administrators, the staff, and volunteers.

How can we avoid implementing marketing strategies on a piecemeal basis? We can allow automated functions to continue to take part of the burden of library operations—using them to help hone operational practices, master routine, and solve issues of inventory control on a day-to-day basis—so that we have time to spend on other leadership activities. We must devote additional efforts to exploring philosophical questions about why the library exists and what it strives to accomplish, scanning the environment to discover and anticipate issues, developing thoughtful service principles, and identifying innovative solutions to improve effectiveness. Without leadership throughout the organization to comprehend such matters, keep service quality high in both the short and long term, elicit effective contributions from all, and incorporate these throughout the score of library operations, the resulting performance will fall flat.[1] Our goal is a resounding performance by all in which the strengths and perspectives of individuals and sections enrich the library's work and create a commitment to excellence that energizes everyone to move in a unified direction and yields success, encouraging future endeavors.

Such an accomplishment requires time, effort, and patience. As a number of studies have documented, implementing a marketing program without an informed staff and sufficient supporters to achieve critical mass may be counterproductive. For example, in one survey of companies from around the world, Williams found that marketing initiatives introduced without significant employee support waste almost half of their marketing communication budgets (Schultz 1998)! Although it will be impossible to wait for everyone involved to be fully supportive of marketing efforts before proceeding with them, nonbelievers may be converted over time as they see the successes of early, well-considered initiatives.

Leaders also must work to keep the marketing program in sync. Effective control requires a loose-tight combination; loose control prevails except in critical and/or crisis situations where oversight must be tightly exercised (e.g., for legal or ethical reasons).

To accomplish this, leaders (formal and informal, at all library levels) must continuously work to establish climates in which required change can proceed smoothly.[2] We therefore recommend a broad-scaled approach that assumes that libraries will

- introduce and reinforce staff member knowledge of basic marketing and other service concepts, so each individual can fully participate in developing and carrying out the marketing plan discussed in depth previously in this text;

- directly provide or otherwise obtain sufficient resources to implement the plan;

- evaluate relative success or lack of the same and make necessary refinements;

- adopt a broad range of techniques to reinforce staff awareness of and support for marketing and service concepts on a regular basis; and

- be aware of issues relating to resistance to change.

This approach rests on the belief that agencies that devote significant resources to cultivating an underlying, in-depth philosophy that mixes marketing with service will develop strong collections and ultimately earn high customer satisfaction ratings and support (emotional, financial, and otherwise). This assumes that public libraries will introduce marketing efforts on the largest affordable scale, phasing in additions and refinements—whether listed in this book, designed by staff, or noted in other works—over time.

WE CAN'T ALL PLAY BY EAR!

A strong grounding in standard marketing concepts can provide staff members with the added technique required to master their parts. Such understanding forms the basis for shared communication on, goal setting about, and action toward any marketing activities. Related questions on this topic include the following:

- Who will receive such training?
- What concepts might be emphasized?
- What forms of preparation are effective?

Educating the Players

We recommend providing exposure to basic marketing concepts and techniques for all those who work on behalf of the library: those with master's degrees in library and information science, with degrees in other relevant areas, or without degrees at all; technical and public services staff; administrators, trustees, key volunteers, and others who play vital leadership roles in setting library policy and in allocating or directing both human and non-human resources.[3] This In-Search-Of-Excellence [4] approach to continuing education assumes that ineffective performance by anyone can affect service quality, satisfaction ratings, and overall perceptions of the library. It is also in keeping with our need to strengthen the commitment to staff development in general and to otherwise prepare staff for the library of the future, matters addressed in Hayes and Baaske (2000) and Winters (1999).

Choosing Concepts to Emphasize: From Scales to Bach

More than 10 years ago studies documented that knowledge and understanding of marketing concepts within the profession was erratic at best (e.g., Vavrek 1988). Even recent graduates from schools of library and information science had little such knowledge, reflecting, at least in part, the fact that few schools of library and information science taught marketing principles and even fewer integrated these throughout the curriculum (Weingand 1989). This situation has markedly improved, as an examination of the objectives listed on the Web sites of many of these same programs demonstrates today.

Nevertheless, we believe that the marketing expertise of all individuals in any given institution ranges as widely as the octaves on a piano (and does not always correlate highly with formal degrees held). This implies that marketing education programs must address, then build on, basic concepts, introducing more intricate ideas along the way.

Among the questions to consider in such programs, preferably in a comprehensive and engaging fashion, are the following:

- What is marketing? How is the business term *marketing* related to the library term *service*?

- What is a societal-marketing orientation? Why might we consider this for a nonprofit organization?

- What are the library's major products and services? Which are successful? Which bear close scrutiny?

- What do the concepts of product design, pricing, placement, and promotion mean when applied to patron service? How do the concepts of short- and long-term patron satisfaction interrelate with the four Ps and with marketing in general?

- What can each department do to decrease inhibitors and increase incentives to library use?

Advanced work can extend the repertoire of staff members who will assume immediate responsibility for carrying out complex aspects of the library's marketing plan (e.g., providing outreach services to one or more groups of patrons or designing promotional techniques) or who, having mastered the fundamentals, can face new challenges. For example, a library may wish to train several of the most public-relations-minded staff members to specialize in dealing with patrons who have problems. Such training can clearly be informed by the numerous publications that focus on advanced marketing issues in some depth. For example, in recent years the Public Library Association has made available conference taped programs and even full-length books on such topics as bookstore methods of promotion and display that will benefit libraries ("Collaborators" 1998; "Built" 1998; "How to Develop" 2000), marketing to culturally diverse communities ("Marketing" 1998), and promoting the library's Web site to local businesses ("Attracting Business" 2000). Numerous other publications discuss advanced marketing issues in some depth.

Questions relevant to the design of such continuing education efforts include the following:

- How much formal marketing research on the needs of community residents will be conducted? How much will we rely on intuition and/or informal research?

- How will the library collect sophisticated information about community residents' need for and use, or potential use, of library services?

- Whom does the library currently serve well? Whose requirements are being slighted?

- To what degree are competitors meeting these unmet needs? To what extent will the library work with these associations and individuals? To what extent will it develop its own services or coordinate with other agencies to fill any gaps?

- On whom will the library concentrate its efforts?

- How will the library integrate information on targeted groups and individuals with its mission, service responses, goals, and objectives?

- How can the library translate this work into an action-oriented marketing plan?

What Medley of Techniques Will We Use?

To ensure breadth of coverage and cater to multiple learning styles, we recommend pursuing multiple forms of training. These may include videos that teach promotional strategies; crossword puzzles emphasizing famous service concepts (Ranganathan, anyone?); substantive materials published in the library, business, and not-for-profit presses;[5] programs at library conferences; and formal courses, including seminars, in-service programs, and perhaps even college classes, on marketing (for profit or nonprofit organizations). We offer two caveats here:

- Programs of two hours or shorter are less likely to change motivational states unless follow-up activities (e.g., peer coaching) reinforce the concepts learned (Griffore and Griffore 1983).

- Discussion and guided application of concepts can both reinforce and clarify them.[6]

Many larger libraries (or coalitions of smaller ones) may find it cost-effective to contract with consultants who have the expertise (and effective presentation styles) to present in-house workshops or seminars. Grunenwald, Felicetti, and Stewart (1990) documented that well-constructed efforts can significantly

- expand participant understanding of basic marketing concepts;

- reduce the perception of marketing as mere hype and hustle; and

- reduce the belief that marketing is less relevant for nonprofit organizations.

The content of such workshops can be attuned to the needs of a particular library (or a set of libraries for cost-effectiveness) and of the individual participants. Moreover, workshops can be scheduled in a flexible, staggered fashion, so that all interested parties can attend.

OBTAINING THE PROPER INSTRUMENTS

We can intuit that the availability of adequate resources to successfully implement the marketing plan significantly influences both employee productivity and job satisfaction. Such resources may include additional money or time, the latter often made possible through increases in productivity occasioned by the use of automation, operations analyses, or other techniques. Although superior marketing in nonprofit organization requires significant effort and resources, it can also pay for itself in both the short and long terms when it helps generate high use, patron satisfaction, and community support (monetary, emotional, etc.).

Public libraries beginning marketing on a rudimentary scale can help finance such efforts by reapportioning money and staff time in new budgets from existing, less-than-successful programs. Shifting resources can also increase overall efficiency, effectiveness, and patron satisfaction, which can enhance staff morale and, when done thoughtfully and in keeping with the strategic plan, will usually make reallocations less controversial.

Nevertheless, limiting the initial investment in marketing activities to those funds generated through budget reallocation ultimately may not prove the best solution. Although almost no one is rigorously studying this issue, we found one older study (Berger 1979) that demonstrates what we perceive: Libraries that invest more money in marketing activities receive significantly more support from their funding bodies than those that do not. How much libraries are spending on marketing today, no one knows. In the only study we found that examined this issue, libraries devoted an average of only 2 percent of their budgets to marketing ("Marketing" 1992), a figure we encourage you to increase significantly.

We feel so strongly about this that we repeat here our recommendation: that public libraries introduce marketing on the largest scale deemed possible. We encourage large libraries to consider hiring marketing specialists (full- or part-time, preferably with a strong and/or demonstrated interest in libraries) to help staff anticipate and respond to trends. Libraries with small budgets may consider contracting with a marketing consultant or firm to help with projects on an as-needed basis, recognizing that although these firms have expertise in conducting surveys, they will need someone to sit down with them and explain fine details about library operations and possibilities.

Libraries may even recruit skilled volunteers to help with large or one-time projects. The Denver (Colorado) Public Library gathered a research team comprising volunteers from area marketing firms and students from the Business Department at the University of Denver to survey parents and youths about the facilities needed for a children's room (Walters and Sandlian 1991). Skillful volunteer coordinators, who can recruit talented individuals (including those who may not previously have considered working in a library), coordinate their efforts, provide necessary data about the library environment, and oversee activities prove invaluable in such efforts.[7]

In addition to providing personnel resources to carry out the marketing plan, the library will need to set aside cash for collecting data, expanding particular sections of the collection, advertising the library's wares, and so forth. Therefore, we also support using various fundraising techniques, such as those described in Chapter 9.

CRITIQUE

Evaluating the success of marketing plans will allow libraries, in both the short and long terms, to enhance current services and build more successful future campaigns. Masterful evaluation plans strive to answer such questions as, "How well were marketing activities met?," "Did the library's marketing program improve services or collections to the target markets(s)?," and "How much did satisfaction rise?" In the case of a public library endeavoring to increase high school students' knowledge and use of the reference collection by 15 percent, staff members might begin in September by surveying rates of use by teenagers who attend the citywide high school. In October a reference librarian could visit each English class to promote reference tools of likely value. She might show sophomore classes resources that will aid with a range of homework, junior classes resources to help them complete assigned term papers, and senior classes resources to assist with college and career choices. Several months later the library can re-survey each group of students to determine whether and/or how significantly their awareness and use of the reference collection has increased. Should the evaluation reveal, for example, that use of reference sources increased by 22 percent among juniors, 5 percent among sophomores, and 7 percent among seniors, staff might decide to link all future marketing efforts to specific class assignments.

Libraries may give a number of reasons for lacking comprehensive evaluation programs, notably limited staff time. We encourage thinking this rationale through to its logical conclusion, because it is those libraries experiencing severe shortages (of staff, money, patronage, or more) that stand to benefit most from evaluation of marketing and other efforts. Skillfully handled evaluation may increase the efficiency and effectiveness of library operations, saving time in both the short and long run. Hiring outside consultants (full- or part-time) to perform initial evaluations and set in place an evaluation program, or assigning part-time evaluation responsibilities to a member of each department, with library leaders coordinating the overall effort, are two possible solutions.

The scarcity of staff members with sophisticated, specialized knowledge of evaluation techniques raises a related issue. For evaluation results to be both reliable and valid, staff members must be able to accurately collect and skillfully analyze and interpret market research data. Even those with formal coursework in evaluation, statistical analysis, or research methods could supplement this knowledge via continuing education classes or workshops covering evaluation in general (such as the one-week workshop given by Kent State University in 1998 for librarians in Ohio) or collection-related evaluation in particular. Relevant works include monographs by Zweizig et al. (1996) and Bawden (1990), an extensive bibliography

(Gabriel 1995), and Pickton's (1989) overview of evaluation techniques commonly used by marketing and advertising specialists.

Staff fear and anxiety, often associated with assessments that uncover flaws in the library's existing marketing efforts (Neenan 1986; DuMont and DuMont 1979), must be handled well, recognizing that excellent appraisal programs are also developmental activities. Existing strengths can be supported and solutions to problems found, whether this requires modifying marketing strategies, providing or encouraging additional education, adding resources, or making other service refinements. Trepidation can often be lessened when evaluators share information on how data will be collected, interpreted, and used to keep service quality high (Alkin, Stecher, and Geiger 1982). In turn, staff may share their comprehension of patron needs—information that may advance a common understanding of underlying service issues and ultimately result in superior staff performance (Braskamp and Brown 1980).

Failure to make necessary changes based on the results presents another major obstacle to meaningful appraisal. For example, Schlachter and Belli (1976) discovered that in 78 percent of the California public libraries in which evaluations were performed, no changes were made! Although an institution may take no action (e.g., because of lack of resources to solve the problem) in the short run, the fact that, in this study (and, we believe, in other cases) a large majority took no steps and another significant percentage took only a few, indicates pro-forma assessment. This pattern, which has also been documented in settings other than libraries, can be significantly reduced when evaluators take an active (preferably subtle) role in fostering the use of the information, involving other leaders (formal or informal) as relevant (e.g., Braskamp and Brown 1980).

PRACTICE MAKES PERFECT— OR AT LEAST DARN GOOD

Although library patrons naturally reinforce many marketing concepts by sharing their thanks, comments, and complaints with those who work on public service desks, those who work behind the scenes do not always receive such direct patron feedback. Libraries can encourage all staff members to make marketing efforts a driving force in their work by

- providing continued training in marketing concepts, as needed;
- hiring replacement staff with strong marketing and service orientations;
- scheduling regular discussions of customer needs, services, and marketing concepts at meetings of the staff and board of trustees;
- using positive motivators to stimulate marketing efforts; and
- building customer-service components into employee evaluation procedures.

Advanced Technical Training

We recommend that public libraries introduce new staff to basic marketing concepts and provide periodic training to reinforce and expand the marketing knowledge of existing staff. The first can be incorporated into employee orientation sessions—when given. Horror stories abound of librarians thrust onto a service desk the day they arrived, without even knowing such basic information as the location of the restrooms(!), the major collections, or the procedures for something as basic as filing reserve requests. Although little research has been conducted on this issue, the existing studies verify that orientation sessions may be brief and poorly planned. For example, Stabler (1987) found that new reference staff members were often introduced to their colleagues, then given short building tours and small amounts of very general information about the institution as a whole. Orientations such as these can clearly be associated with less-than-optimal performance in the early days on the job.

Thorough, well-planned orientations can keep new employees' apprehension and stress low, positively affect their job progress, and influence both how long they will stay with an organization and their degree of loyalty to it. This suggests that libraries may encourage outstanding service by providing sufficient orientations.[8] At the very least, new employees require information on the history and mission of the library, its organizational structure, the particulars of the jobs they were hired to perform, and the same information on service-oriented marketing that other employees have had (perhaps via videos of former activities). General guidelines, such as those the Fairfax County (Virginia) Public Library (1997) hands out on collection development, merchandising, and basic reference sources, are welcome, as are in-depth discussions about the major collections and services the library offers. Obviously, the complexity of the job to be performed and the employee's previous knowledge will dictate the length of the training program, which may range from several days to several weeks.[9]

Providing continuing education opportunities in more sophisticated marketing concepts once staff members comprehend the basics is also imperative. Such training will help individuals keep abreast of new developments in the field and develop expertise at conducting focus group sessions, writing persuasive promotional materials, and related tasks. The Queens Borough (New York) Public Library, for example, had the regional sales manager of the B. Dalton bookstore chain present a continuing education program on merchandising collections (Sivulich 1989). The abundance of information online may encourage e-learning of all sorts. For example, management could ask each individual to browse other libraries' Web sites to identify one new marketing idea that can be shared during a regular staff meeting. Such trolling can bring in numerous ideas in a short period of time. For example, a staff member may share insights from the UK Library Association research that clearly documents how most of the business use of the library comes from two groups: small businesses (60 percent of users) and the self-employed (19 percent) ("Public" 1997).

Can We Require Auditions
for Service Positions?

Why not? The service provided by individual staff members greatly affects user satisfaction and levels of use and support (whether financial or otherwise) given to the library. Further, staff members who lack a service orientation can, intentionally or not, undermine the efforts that have been taken to attract patrons. As Underhill notes, "Bad service undoes good merchandise, prices, and location almost every time" (1999, 160). Although training can greatly contribute to improved service (see Chapter 10 for a discussion of service-oriented behaviors managers can encourage staff to exhibit), it "can only go so far in inculcating the right attitudes in employees" (Andreasen and Kotler 1996, 333). Because of this, Hernon and Whitman (2001) stress the importance of "hiring right" (83-84). We recommend that libraries actively recruit personnel who exhibit strong service and marketing orientations. This is already being done to some extent; for example, 21 percent of the 261 job ads for public services librarians analyzed by Allen and Allen (1992) named service orientation as a selection criterion. It was mentioned less frequently than many other qualifications, such as computer literacy and library experience, even though one could persuasively debate the point that people without computer skills can more quickly be taught to use various applications than unfriendly persons can be taught to be friendly.

In keeping with this last statement, Coffey (1992) has suggested developing competency models to identify "attitude qualifications" for different positions. The Illinois State Library Association has also explored using competencies for hiring, assessing, and developing staff, presenting a program at its 1999 annual conference entitled, "You Can Teach a Turkey to Climb a Tree, But It's Easier to Hire a Squirrel" (*Bridging* 1999, 19).

Setting the Tempo at Regular Meetings of
the Library Staff and Board of Trustees

Although many libraries devote a majority of the time spent at departmental and librarywide staff meetings to discussing policy and procedural changes, these meetings can also be used to strengthen marketing constructs. An administrator can take the opportunity to praise the employee who designed an especially effective display, took the time to lead a puzzled patron to the relevant stack section, or redesigned his or her work station to process new materials more quickly.

Leaders can also give 10- or 15-minute talks to explain new marketing concepts or discuss application of previously presented ideas. Such talks may be particularly effective when designed by different staff members, who bring their own unique insights to bear on an issue.

Trustees can also discuss policy issues related to marketing at regular board meetings. One classic study that analyzed the contents of 80 different sets of minutes from the meetings of a representative sample of Illinois public library trustees found little consideration of marketing-related issues. Discussions of community analysis and library service were held at only 6 percent of the meetings, of policy issues at 7 percent, of public relations at 4 percent, and of short- or long-term planning at only 1 percent. Although trustees admitted that such complex and substantive issues were important, they primarily focused on matters with immediate and concrete results, including paying routine utility bills and making decisions about insurance coverage (Baker 1984). Shavit (1986) drew a similar conclusion when discussing the politics of public librarianship. As both Baker and Shavit found, head librarians set most board meeting agendas, which makes changing such practices easily within grasp.

Coaching and Recognition

Library directors can use a range of motivational techniques to encourage employees to think in marketing terms. For example, supervisors may lead discussions, early on, of how each individual's job affects the success of the marketing program. This conversation will underscore the more general discussion of how departmental tasks affect patrons' satisfaction and reinforce that the supervisor both recognizes and values the work each employee performs.

Job enrichment—adding challenge to routine tasks in an effort to keep the work interesting over time—can also be used to stimulate marketing activities. For example, a full-time page may eventually lose interest if his or her only responsibility is endless reshelving. However, the page may become more intrigued if the supervisor gives him or her complete responsibility for redesigning shelving procedures both to improve their efficiency and to showcase materials for patron use. Job enrichment practices involving each employee in efforts to increase patron satisfaction and reduce costs also encourage individual responsibility and accountability for work performed, thus increasing productivity.

Coaching activities, wherein either a supervisory or a non-supervisory employee helps another improve skills, solve problems, and build on strengths, also reinforce marketing concepts. A supervisor may ask a technical services worker to list ways to increase productivity so that patrons won't have to wait as long for new materials. The supervisor then monitors the employee's performance, praising him or her for actions that lead to increased productivity and exploring (jointly, as relevant) ways to develop his or her ideas further. The coaching technique can be particularly effective when used immediately after introducing a new concept. When Stephan et al. (1988) directed intensive workshops on conducting a proper reference interview, reference accuracy rates rose from 55 to 77 percent and further increased to 95 percent in two libraries that used follow-up coaching.

Although praise is particularly critical as an employee practices a new task, thoughtful supervisors will ideally continue to commend each employee who applies marketing concepts correctly or reveals a strong service orientation. People have a natural desire for recurring recognition, a desire that praise can meet effectively and inexpensively. What's more, consistent praise can improve both short- and long-term performance significantly. For example, Goddard (1987) describes a series of studies that found that 87 percent of college students who received praise for current work improved both the quality and quantity of future performances.

We cannot overstate the extent to which feeling appreciated affects employees' performance. In one study, originally conducted in 1946 and replicated in 1981 and 1995, 1,000 employees ranked 10 workplace rewards in order of their incentive power. Supervisors ranked the same rewards according to their perceptions of what employees want. In each study, the employee groups rated "full appreciation of work done" much higher than did the supervisors (Glanz 1996). Indeed, "one of the keys to customer satisfaction is employee satisfaction. Studies have shown that service organizations with high levels of employee satisfaction also have high levels of customer satisfaction, and low employee turnover is also closely linked to customer satisfaction. Similarly, employees who feel accountable are more likely to provide better customer [service]" (Morgan 1998, 50). Others have taken the point even further, persuasively noting that a successful customer service program must begin by creating a positive work environment (Lisker 2000, Sherman 1994, Gorchels 1995).

Hernon and Whitman (2001), who also note the link between employee and customer satisfaction, suggest that managers occasionally try to assess job satisfaction levels, using such methods as questionnaires, focus groups, or surveys, and give employees an opportunity to let management know what would make them happier at work. Studies suggest that the vast majority of people find motivation when the workplace meets one or more of seven needs:

Esteem—desiring recognition and praise, as discussed above

Achievement—being able to use personal talent and skill to meet challenges

Power—being in a position to lead or influence others

Affiliation—relishing regular interaction with others

Autonomy—having the freedom to make choices and work independently

Safety and security—enjoying a high level of job security, a low-risk environment, and satisfactory pay and benefits

Equity—feeling treated fairly and comparably to others ("Employee" 1998)

Using this and similar information as background, savvy managers will explore the individual needs of their employees and then seek ways to meet these. Two library-specific studies in the 1990s suggested that many support staff members feel out of the loop, both in terms of knowing what's happening and being able to influence policies and procedures (Payne 1999), and a study of the Wake County (North Carolina) Public Library System indicated that communicating regularly with the supervisor enhances an employee's job satisfaction (Bartlett 2000). Knowing this, a circulation supervisor might identify a few clerks who demonstrate a desire for power and autonomy and ask them to serve on a committee charged with proposing ways to increase two-way communication in the department and the library as a whole. The supervisor would also want to ensure that other employees have an opportunity to provide input throughout the process, including its evaluation.[10]

Evaluating Artistic Excellence and Technical Merit

Libraries can also encourage a marketing orientation by integrating this aspect of performance into the evaluation and merit raise process. Recognizing and rewarding those employees who demonstrate initiative; accuracy and responsiveness; consistent, efficient, and effective service; and tact provides additional incentives for others to exhibit these behaviors (Dragon and Leisner 1983).

Evaluations can both communicate service expectations to employees and ensure that they receive compensation for meeting (or exceeding) them. For example, the Columbus (Ohio) Metropolitan Library performance appraisal document includes measurable behaviors from a staff-developed customer service training program that all employees attend (Ramsey, Spradlin, and Allen 1997). The Rocky River (Ohio) Public Library created an evaluation system that has as its first of three (or, for supervisors, four) parts standards measuring service to patrons and coworkers (Belcastro 1998).[11]

Supervisors can gather factual evidence about an employee's service orientation from personal observation of interactions with patrons; patron letters, suggestions, and comments; or other staff members. The Jones Library in Amherst, Massachusetts, asked staff members to assess their own performance and the performance of coworkers, based on eight criteria that measured an employee's ability to relate to the public (Turner 1978). Supervisors summarized and analyzed this information, then held discussions with employees about possible improvements.

Paying Attention to Mood and Tempo

A library can more easily implement the changes discussed here if all employees, particularly supervisors and other leaders, demonstrate sensitivity to the natural fears and anxieties that people experience when asked to change.[12] Problems can occur when a leader, frustrated by someone resisting change, makes a statement that seems to attack the other person (Riggs 1988). Supervisors can avoid inadvertently contributing to this behavior by asking tactful questions designed to determine whether an employee has a valid reason for the resistance. For example, an employee may resist change if the library fails to provide enough resources to implement it effectively, causing significant stress.

A common reason for resistance is fear, particularly of embarrassment if the employee cannot successfully perform a new task. Adopting a "to err is human" mindset, and promoting this to employees, can help minimize such fears. For example, the welcome gifts new employees of the Des Plaines (Illinois) Public Library receive include an eraser to convey the message that mistakes will naturally occur and that the library would rather see staff stretch and fail than never try at all.

Employees may also resist spurious changes. In one Ohio public library, staff opposed efforts to reintegrate the genre books into the general fiction collection, noting that patrons valued having mysteries and other genres separately shelved and that those who wish to cross-browse collections could certainly do so.

In all cases, questioning the reasons behind employee resistance allows both supervisor and employee to determine and then address the real barriers to change, rather than any surface reluctance that may appear to be inflexibility.

FINALE!

Public libraries from large to small are increasingly using the types of collection marketing schemes discussed here. Librarians are devoting their time to increasing patron satisfaction and keeping patron costs of using the library low; setting up programs to evaluate their collections and the immediate and long-term needs of community residents; redesigning their collections, guided by marketing principles, to meet these needs; and using effective promotional techniques. Finally, they are considering ways to create a marketing mindset that reverberates throughout the library.

We hope that those working in libraries of all sizes use the process described in this final chapter to orchestrate their own symphonies of collection development. Educating staff about marketing concepts and thoughtfully planning and implementing marketing activities reinforce the melody. Library leaders who encourage employee contributions can help ensure that diverse, yet harmonious, voices are heard in a composition that resounds throughout people's lives.

NOTES

1. For an in-depth review of the research on leadership, see Bass (1990).

2. Damanpour et al. (1989) provide an overview of the relationship between organization performance and the adoption of innovation over time.

3. Stiles et al. (1983) present a brief but thoughtful overview of the role the board can play in setting public relations policy. The model policy statement they include could readily be expanded to cover marketing activities in general.

4. *In Search of Excellence* by Thomas J. Peters and Robert H. Waterman, Jr. (1982) presents eight principles of management shared by successful companies.

5. Two older but excellent bibliographies of this literature are provided in Norman (1989) and Tucci (1988).

6. Creth (1989) provides a good overview of general principles that trainers can use to design effective continuing education programs for library staff.

7. Mueller-Alexander (1991) discusses the advantages and disadvantages of using volunteers, consultants, students, and other resources for marketing research.

8. See "Checklist" (2000) for a brief list of elements to include in employee orientation.

9. Information on orientation and other training programs offered by libraries around the nation can be obtained from the American Library Association Headquarters Library. Interested parties can request materials from the Staff Development Clearinghouse organized by the Library Administration and Management Association, Personnel Administration Section, Staff Development Committee.

10. For further discussion of ways (many of them low-cost) to keep employees satisfied and the work environment enjoyable, see McCandless (1999), Weinstein (1996), Glanz (1996), and Jeffries (1996).

11. See also Goodson (1997) for a discussion of elements of effective evaluation systems and common pitfalls to avoid.

12. See Buch (1997) for an interesting perspective on managing the human side of change.

REFERENCES

Alkin, Marvin C., Brian M. Stecher, and Frederica L. Geiger. 1982. *Title I Evaluation: Utility and Factors Affecting Use*. Northridge, CA: Educational Evaluation Associates.

Allen, Gillian, and Bryce L. Allen. 1992. "Service Orientation as a Selection Criterion for Public Services Librarians." *Journal of Library Administration* 16, no. 4: 67–76.

"Attracting Business: Promoting Your Library's Business Website." 2000. Conference Program (audiotape) #PLA044. Chicago: Public Library Association.

Baker, Sharon L. 1984. "A Survey of Illinois Public Library Trustees." *Illinois Library Statistical Report* 14 (August): 1–60.

———. 1989. "Managing Resistance to Change." *Library Trends* 38, no. 1 (Summer): 53–61.

Bartlett, Chrystal. 2000. "Supervisory Communication and Subordinate Job Satisfaction: The Relationship between Superiors' Self-Disclosure, Offers of Help, Offers of Cooperation, Frequency of Contact, Trust, and Subordinates' Job Satisfaction." *Public Library Quarterly* 18, no. 1: 9–30.

Bartlett, John. 1992. *Familiar Quotations: A Collection of Passages, Phrases, and Proverbs Traced to Their Sources in Ancient and Modern Literature*. 16th ed. revised and enlarged, ed. Justin Kaplan. Boston: Little, Brown.

Bass, Bernard M. 1990. *Bass and Stogdill's Handbook of Leadership: Theory, Research, and Managerial Applications*. 3d ed. New York: Free Press.

Bawden, David. 1990. *User-Oriented Evaluation of Information Systems and Services*. Brookfield, VT: Gower Publications.

Belcastro, Patricia. 1998. *Evaluating Library Staff: A Performance Appraisal System*. Chicago: American Library Association.

Berger, Patricia. 1979. "An Investigation of the Relationship Between Public Relations Activities and Budget Allocation in Public Libraries." *Information Processing and Management* 15, no. 4: 179–93.

Braskamp, Larry A., and Robert D. Brown. 1980. *Utilization of Evaluation Information*. San Francisco: Jossey-Bass.

Bridging the Millennia: Libraries for a New Era. Illinois Library Association Annual Conference Preliminary Program. 1999. Chicago: Illinois Library Association.

Buch, Kim. 1997. "Managing the Human Side of Change." *Library Administration and Management* 11, no. 3 (Summer): 147–51.

"The Built Environment as a Marketing Tool." 1998. Conference Program (audiotape) #PLA810. Chicago: Public Library Association.

"Checklist for New Employee Orientation." 2000. *Library Personnel News* 13, no. 1–2 (Spring/Summer): 15–16.

Coffey, James R. 1992. "Competency Modelling for Hiring in Technical Services: Developing a Methodology." *Library Administration and Management* 6, no. 4 (Fall): 168–72.

"Collaborators or Competitors: Chain Bookstores and Public Libraries." 1998. Conference Program (audiotape) #PLA848. Chicago: Public Library Association.

Creth, Sheila D. 1989. "Staff Development and Continuing Education." In *Personnel Administration in Libraries.* 2d ed., ed. Sheila Creth and Frederick Duda, 118–51. New York: Neal-Schuman.

Damanpour, Fariborz, Kathryn A. Szabat, and William M. Evan. 1989. "The Relationship Between Types of Innovation and Organizational Performance." *Journal of Management Studies* 26, no. 6 (November): 587–601.

Dragon, Andrea C., and Tony Leisner. 1983. "The ABC's of Implementing Library Marketing." *Journal of Library Administration* 4, no. 4: 33–47.

Drucker, Peter. 1974. *Management: Tasks, Responsibilities, Practices.* New York: Harper & Row.

DuMont, Rosemary R., and Paul F. DuMont. 1979. "Measuring Library Effectiveness: A Review and an Assessment." In *Advances in Librarianship,* ed. Michael Harris, 9: 103–41. New York: Academic Press.

"Employee Tips: What Motivates Employees?" 1998. *Library Personnel News* 12, no. 1 (October): 4–7.

Fairfax County (Virginia) Public Library. 1997. *Information Services Training Checklist.* 2d ed. Chicago: Public Library Association.

Fine, Sara F. 1986. "Technological Innovation, Diffusion, and Resistance: A Historical Perspective." *Journal of Library Administration* 7, no. 1 (Spring): 83–108.

Gabriel, Michael R. 1995. *Collection Development and Collection Evaluation: A Sourcebook.* New York: Scarecrow Press.

Glanz, Barbara A. 1996. *Care Packages for the Workplace: Little Things You Can Do to Regenerate Spirit at Work.* New York: McGraw-Hill.

Goddard, Robert W. 1987. "Well Done!" *Management World* 16, no. 6 (November/December): 14–16.

Goodson, Carol F. 1997. *The Complete Guide to Performance Standards for Library Personnel.* New York: Neal-Schuman.

Gorchels, Linda M. 1995. "Trends in Marketing Services." *Library Trends* 43, no. 3 (Winter): 494–509.

Griffore, Robert J., and Gaile D. Griffore. 1983. "Some Effects of Study Skills and Adjustment Skills Workshops on College Students." *NASPA Journal* 20, no. 3 (Winter): 34–41.

Grunenwald, Joseph P., Linda A. Felicetti, and Karen L. Stewart. 1990. "The Effects of Marketing Seminars on the Attitudes of Librarians." *Public Library Quarterly* 10, no. 2: 3–10.

Hayes, Jan, and Ian Baaske. 2000. "Preparing Staff for the Library of the Future." *Public Libraries* 39, no. 5 (September/October): 280–85.

Hernon, Peter, and John R. Whitman. 2001. *Delivering Satisfaction and Service Quality*. Chicago: American Library Association.

"How to Develop Professional Displays in Your Library." 2000. Conference Program (audiotape) #PLA010. Chicago: Public Library Association.

Jeffries, Rosalind. 1996. *101 Recognition Secrets: Tools for Motivating and Recognizing Today's Workforce*. Chevy Chase, MD: Performance Enhancement Group.

Kotler, Philip, and Alan R. Andreasen. 1996. *Strategic Marketing for Nonprofit Organizations*. 5th ed. Upper Saddle River, NJ: Simon & Schuster.

Lisker, Peter. 2000. "The Ties that Bind: Creating Great Customer Service." *Public Libraries* 39, no. 4 (July/August): 190–92.

"Marketing the Library." 1992. *Library Administrator's Digest* 27, no. 1 (January): 3.

"Marketing to Culturally Diverse Communities." 1998. Conference Program (audiotape) #PLA831. Chicago: Public Library Association.

McCandless, Patricia A. 1999. "Service-Oriented Personnel." In *People Come First*, ed. Dale S. Montanelli and Patricia F. Stenstrom, 142–56. Chicago: Association of College and Research Libraries.

Morgan, Eric Lease. 1998. "Marketing Future Libraries." *Computers in Libraries* 18, no. 8 (September): 50.

Mueller-Alexander, Jeanette M. 1991. "Alternative Sources for Marketing Research for Libraries." *Special Libraries* 82, no. 3 (Summer): 159–64.

Neenan, Peter A. 1986. "Impact Evaluation: Context and Function." *RQ* 25, no. 3 (Spring): 305–9.

Norman, O. Gene. 1989. "Marketing Library and Information Services: An Annotated Guide to Recent Trends and Developments." *Reference Services Review* 17, no. 1 (Spring): 43–64.

Payne, Patricia C. 1999. "Personnel Matters: Improving the Lot of Support Staff: A Matter of Respect." *Technicalities* 19, no. 1 (January): 1, 11–12.

Peters, Thomas J., and Robert H. Waterman, Jr. 1982. *In Search of Excellence*. New York: Harper & Row.

Pickton, David. 1989. "Evaluating a Campaign Programme: Will It Work, Is It Working, Has It Worked . . . Why?" In *Planned Public Relations for Libraries: A PPRG Handbook*, ed. Margaret Kinnell, 88–109. London: Taylor Graham.

"Public Libraries and The Business Community." 1976. *Management Accounting* 75, no. 11: 50–54.

Ramsey, Wendy, Diane Spradlin, and Larry Allen. 1997. "A Touch of CLASS: The Columbus Metropolitan Library's Customer Service Training Is a Plus for Patrons and Staff." *Ohio Libraries* 10, no. 1: 22–23.

Riggs, Donald E. 1988. "Leadership Versus Management in Technical Services." In *Library Management and Technical Services: The Changing Role of Technical Services in Library Organizations*, ed. Jennifer Cargill, 27–39. New York: Haworth Press.

Schlachter, Gail, and Donna Belli. 1976. "Program Evaluation—An Alternative to Divine Guidance." *California Librarian* 37, no. 4 (October): 26–31.

Scholtes, Peter R. 1998. *The Leader's Handbook: Making Things Happen, Getting Things Done.* New York: McGraw-Hill.

Schultz, Don E. 1998. "It's the Employees, Stupid!" *Marketing News* 32, no. 20 (28 September): 6.

Shavit, David. 1986. *The Politics of Public Librarianship.* Westport, CT: Greenwood Press.

Sherman, Steve. 1994. "Service, the Bookseller's Prelude to Promotion." *Publishers Weekly* 241, no. 19 (May 9): 24–25.

Sivulich, Kenneth G. 1989. "How We Run the Queens Library Good (and Doubled Circulation in Seven Years)." *Library Journal* 114, no. 3 (February 15): 123–27.

Stabler, Karen Y. 1987. "Introductory Training of Academic Reference Librarians: A Survey." *RQ* 26, no. 3 (Spring): 363–69.

Stephan, Sandy, et al. 1988. "Reference Breakthrough in Maryland." *Public Libraries* 27, no. 4 (Winter): 202-3.

Stiles, Florence Frette, Janet R. Bean, and Virginia Beckler. 1983. "Public Relations for the Public Library." In *Persuasive Public Relations for Libraries*, ed. Kathleen Kelly Rummel and Esther Perica, 47–59. Chicago: American Library Association.

Tucci, Valerie K. 1988. "Information Marketing for Libraries." In *Annual Review of Information Science and Technology*, ed. Martha E. Williams, 23: 59–82. New York: Elsevier Science Publishers.

Turner, Anne M. 1978. "Why Do Department Heads Take Longer Coffee Breaks? A Public Library Evaluates Itself." *American Libraries* 9, no. 4 (April): 213–15.

Underhill, Paco. 1999. *Why We Buy: The Science of Shopping.* New York: Simon & Schuster.

Vavrek, Bernard. 1988. "The Public Library at Crisis: Is Marketing the Answer?" *North Carolina Libraries* 46, no. 3 (Fall): 142–47.

Walters Suzanne, and Pamela Sandlian. 1991. "A Room of Their Own: Planning the New Denver Children's Library." *School Library Journal* 37, no. 2 (February): 26–29.

Weingand, Darlene E. 1989. "Educating Staff for Public Relations." In *Planned Public Relations for Libraries: A PPRG Handbook*, ed. Margaret Kinnell, 3–8. London: Taylor Graham.

Weinstein, Matt. 1996. *Managing to Have Fun: How Fun at Work Can Motivate Your Employees, Inspire Your Coworkers, Boost Your Bottom Line*. New York: Simon & Schuster.

Winters, Sharon. 1999. "Strengthening the Commitment to Staff Development." *Public Libraries* 38, no. 4 (July/August): 248–52.

Zweizig, Douglas, et al. 1996. *The TELL IT! Manual: The Complete Program for Evaluating Library Performance*. Chicago: American Library Association.

APPENDIX

LIBRARIES CITED BY NAME

LIBRARIES IN THE UNITED STATES, SUBDIVIDED BY SIZE OF SERVICE POPULATION, THEN REGION

This list does not include libraries cited anonymously or in the aggregate (e.g., "five public library districts in Sweden"). For specific page references, see index.

Regions:

New England (CT, ME, MA, NH, RI, VT)

Mid Atlantic (DE, MD, NJ, NY, PA, D.C.)

South Atlantic (FL, GA, NC, SC, VA, WV)

South Central (AL, AR, KY, LA, MS, OK, TN, TX)

East North Central (IL, IN, MI, OH, WI)

West North Central (IA, KS, MN, MO, NE, ND, SD)

Mountain (AZ, CO, ID, MT, NV, NM, UT, WY)

Pacific (AK, CA, HI, OR, WA)

Up to 9,999

East North Central
Atwood-Hammond Public Library
Grandview Heights Public Library
Wright Memorial Public Library

Mid Atlantic
Lyons Public Library
Tuckahoe Public Library
Warsaw Public Library
Waterford Public Library

New England
Portland Library
Wiggin Memorial Library

South Atlantic
Greenville Middle School Library
Valdosta State Univerity Odum
    Library

10,000 to 24,999

East North Central
Algonquin Area Public Library
    District
Ela Area Public Library District
Hussey-Mayfield Memorial Public
    Library
Morton Grove Public Library
Rocky River Public Library
Rolling Meadows Public Library
Thomas Ford Memorial Library

Mid Atlantic
Cornell University Library
Somerville Free Public Library

Mountain
Colorado State University Libraries
Lewistown Public Library

New England
Lane Memorial Library
Ridgefield Library
Westport Public Library
Wilbraham Public Library

Pacific
California Polytechnic State Univer-
    sity/San Luis Obispo Robert E.
    Kennedy Library
El Segundo Public Library

South Atlantic
Duke University Medical Center
    Library
Virginia Commonwealth University
    Libraries

West North Central
New Ulm Public Library
Ottawa Public Library

25,000 to 49,999

East North Central
Bartlett Public Library District
Downers Grove Public Library
Escanaba Public Library
Girard Free Public Library
Glen Ellyn Public Library
Indian Prairie Public Library District
Oak Creek Public Library
Orion Township Public Library
Park Ridge Public Library
Rock Island Public Library
Southern Illinois University, Carbon-
    dale Morris Library
University of Illinois at Urbana-
    Champaign library system
Urbana Free Library
Vernon Area Public Library District
Warren-Newport Public Library
    District
Westlake Porter Public Library
Wilmette Public Library

Mid Atlantic
Bethel Park Public Library
East Brunswick Public Library
Orange Public Library
White Plains Public Library

Mountain
Latah County Library District
Logan Library

New England
Dover Public Library
Jones Library
Lucius Beebe Memorial Library
Lucy Robbins Welles Library
Russell Library

Pacific
Beverly Hills Public Library
Juneau Public Libraries
Oregon City Public Library
Richland Public Library
San Jose State University Library
University of Washington University
    Libraries

South Atlantic
North Carolina State University
    Libraries

South Central
Beauregard Parish Library
Coppell Public Library
University of Oklahoma Libraries

West North Central
Bettendorf Public Library Information
    Center
Hastings Public Library

50,000 to 99,999

East North Central
Arlington Heights Memorial Library
Bloomington Public Library

Decatur Public Library
Des Plaines Public Library
Emporia Public Library
Evanston Public Library
Hayner Public Library District
Joliet Public Library
Kenosha Public Library
Lakewood Public Library
Mount Prospect Public Library
Muncie Public Library
Poplar Creek Public Library District
Rochester Hills Public Library
Skokie Public Library
Washington-Centerville Public
    Library
Westerville Public Library

Mid Atlantic
Adams Memorial Library

Mountain
Carson City Library
Hobbs Public Library
Loveland Public Library
Missoula Public Library
Santa Fe Public Library

New England
Meriden Public Library
East Providence Public Library

Pacific
Fairbanks North Star Borough Public
    Library
Livermore Public Library
Mountain View Public Library
Newport Beach Public Library

South Atlantic
Delray Beach Public Library
Martinsburg-Berkeley County Public
    Library
Moore County Public Library
Pine Mountain Regional Library
Williamsburg Regional Library

West North Central
Ames Public Library
Davenport Public Library
Duluth Public Library
Iowa City Public Library

100,000 to 499,999

East North Central
Akron-Summit County Public Library
Eisenhower Public Library District
Grand Rapids Public Library
Kalamazoo Public Library
Medina County District Library
Middletown Public Library
Ohio Valley Area Libraries
Schaumburg Township District
    Library

Mid Atlantic
Anne Arundel County Public Library
Morris County Library
Ocean County Library
Onondaga County Public Library

Mountain
Arapahoe Library District
Davis County Library
Salt Lake City Public Library
Washoe County Library System

New England
Cambridge Public Library
Springfield Library

Pacific
Berkeley Public Library
Fort Vancouver Regional Library
Fullerton Public Library
Monterey County Free Libraries
Salem Public Library
Tacoma Public Library

South Atlantic
Charleston County Public Library
Clearwater Public Library System
Cumberland County Public Library
    and Information Center
Davidson County Public Library
    System
Durham County Library
Manatee County Public Library
    System
New Hanover County Public Library
Norfolk Public Library
Pasco County Library System

South Central
Lubbock City-County Library
Midland County Public Library
Mobile Public Library
Plano Public Library System
Waco-McClennan Library System
Williamson County Public Library

West North Central
Anoka County Library
Dakota County Law Library
Dakota County Library System
Kansas City Public Library
Minneapolis Public Library
Springfield-Greene County Library
St. Louis Public Library
Topeka and Shawnee County Public
    Library
Wichita Public Library

500,000 to 999,999

East North Central
Columbus Metropolitan Library
Cuyahoga County Public Library
Indianapolis-Marion County Public
    Library
Milwaukee Public Library
Public Library of Cincinnati and
    Hamilton County

Mid Atlantic
Baltimore County Public Library
District of Columbia Public Library
Enoch Pratt Free Library
Montgomery County Public Libraries
Prince George's County Memorial
    Library System

Mountain
Denver Public Library

New England
Boston Public Library

Pacific
Alameda County Library
Fresno County Library
Multnomah County Public Library
San Diego County Library
San Francisco Public Library
San Jose Public Library
Seattle Public Library
Sno-Isle Regional Library System

South Atlantic
DeKalb County Public Library
Fairfax County Public Library
Gwinnett County Public Library
Orange County Library System
Public Library of Charlotte and
    Mecklenburg County
Wake County Public Library System

South Central
Memphis/Shelby County Public
    Library and Information Center
Metropolitan Library System
Public Library of Nashville and
    Davidson County

West North Central
Hennepin County Library
St. Louis County Library

1,000,000 or more

Library of Congress

East North Central
Chicago Public Library
Detroit Public Library

Mid Atlantic
Brooklyn Public Library
Carnegie Library of Pittsburgh
Free Library of Philadelphia
New Jersey State Library
New York Public Library
Queens Borough Public Library
Suffolk Cooperative Library System

Mountain
Arizona State Library
Phoenix Public Library

New England
Providence Public Library

Pacific
County of Los Angeles Public Library
Hawaii State Public Library System
King County Library System
Los Angeles Public Library
Sacramento Public Library
San Diego Public Library

South Atlantic
Broward County Library
Miami-Dade Public Library System

South Central
Houston Public Library
San Antonio Public Library

West North Central
St. Paul Public Library
State Library of Iowa

LIBRARIES OUTSIDE OF THE UNITED STATES, SUBDIVIDED BY COUNTRY

Australia
East Gippsland Shire Library Service
Mitchell Shire Library
Pine Rivers Shire Library Service
Upper Goulburn Regional Library

Canada
Edmonton Public Library
Montreal Public Library
Richmond Public Library
Thompson Nicola Regional District
    Library System

Colombia
Comenfalco Family Compensation
    Bureau Libraries

England
Birmingham Libraries
Broughton Public Library
Dorset Library Authority
Hampshire Library Authority
Perins Community Schools Library
West Sussex Library Authority
Willesden Green Library

Finland
Espoo City Library

France
Paris Public Library

Italy
Nonantola, Italy Public Library

Japan
Fuji Muncipal Central Library

Kenya
Kenya National Library Service

New Zealand
Canterbury Public Library
Tauranga District Libraries

Scotland
Renfrew Library District
West Lothian Public Library Services

INDEX